Peace, Democracy, and
Human Rights in Colombia

RECENT TITLES FROM THE HELEN KELLOGG INSTITUTE FOR
INTERNATIONAL STUDIES

Scott Mainwaring, *general editor*

The University of Notre Dame Press gratefully thanks the Helen Kellogg Institute for
International Studies for its support in the publication of titles in this series.

Vikram K. Chand
Mexico's Political Awakening (2001)

Glen Biglaiser
Guardians of the Nation? (2002)

Sylvia Borzutzky
Vital Connections (2002)

Alberto Spektorowski
The Origins of Argentina's Revolution of the Right (2003)

Caroline C. Beer
Electoral Competition and Institutional Change in Mexico (2003)

Yemile Mizrahi
From Martyrdom to Power (2003)

Charles D. Kenney
Fujimori's Coup and the Breakdown of Democracy in Latin America (2003)

Alfred P. Montero and David J. Samuels
Decentralization and Democracy in Latin America (2004)

Katherine Hite and Paola Cesarini
Authoritarian Legacies and Democracy in Latin America and Southern Europe (2004)

Robert S. Pelton, C.S.C.
Monsignor Romero: A Bishop for the Third Millennium (2004)

Guillermo O'Donnell, Jorge Vargas Cullell, and Osvaldo M. Iazzetta
The Quality of Democracy (2004)

Arie M. Kacowicz
The Impact of Norms in International Society (2005)

Roberto DaMatta and Elena Soarez
Eagles, Donkeys, and Butterflies (2006)

Kenneth P. Serbin
Needs of the Heart (2006)

For a complete list of titles from the Helen Kellogg Institute for International Studies,
see http://www.undpress.nd.edu

Peace, Democracy, and Human Rights in Colombia

Edited by

Christopher Welna and Gustavo Gallón

University of Notre Dame Press

Notre Dame, Indiana

Library of Congress Cataloging-in-Publication Data

Peace, democracy, and human rights in Colombia / edited by Christopher Welna
and Gustavo Gallón.
  p. cm.
"From the Helen Kellogg Institute for International Studies."
Includes bibliographical references and index.
ISBN-13: 978-0-268-04409-1 (pbk. : alk. paper)
ISBN-10: 0-268-04409-0 (pbk. : alk. paper)
1. Colombia—Politics and government—1974—Congresses. 2. Human rights—
Colombia—Congresses. 3. Guerrilla warfare—Colombia—Congresses.
I. Welna, Christopher. II. Gallón Giraldo, Gustavo. III. Helen Kellogg Institute for
International Studies.
JL2881.P39   2007
986.106'35—dc22
2006032385

Contents

Acknowledgments

The conference that gave rise to this volume was made possible through a generous grant from the Ford Foundation's Santiago, Chile, Office. We are grateful to Alex Wilde and Augusto Varas for their far-sightedness and their commitment to addressing the conflict in Colombia through the grant programs they directed.

Many people beyond the authors of the chapters helped to make this book possible. First and foremost is Fr. Theodore Hesburgh, C.S.C., who encouraged us to think creatively about how a university in the United States might contribute to resolving Colombia's conflict through analysis and scholarly exchange. We are grateful to all of the authors in this volume for their insightful work and their extensive, careful revisions.

Other participants in the conference enriched the discussion and the chapters that now form this volume. They include Ambassador Luiz Alberto Moreno, Michael Shifter, Luis Eduardo Galan, John Dugas, Juan Méndez, Iván Orozco, Francisco Thoumi, Ricardo Vargas, Carlos Nasi, Amparo Cadavid, Robin Kirk, and Clemencia Rodriguez.

Marlene De La Cruz and Jean Olson played crucial roles in organizing the conference that first convened the authors. Elizabeth Rankin and Peg Hartman worked closely with the editors and each chapter author to prepare the manuscript. We appreciate their help tremendously.

Finally, we wish to thank our editors at the University of Notre Dame Press, Barbara Hanrahan, Lowell Francis, Rebecca DeBoer, and Elisabeth Magnus, for their support and careful recommendations, as well as the anonymous readers who provided valuable feedback to the editors and each of the authors.

Tables and Figures

Tables

Figures

Introduction

chapter one

Colombia's Triple Challenge

Peace, Democracy, and Human Rights

CHRISTOPHER WELNA

Veering between deep pessimism and cautious optimism, Colombia's long-standing democracy struggles with widespread violence and killings, as well as with political corruption, fragmented political parties, and a multisided internal war. U.S. military and economic aid to Colombia has risen steadily since the approval of Plan Colombia in 2000, while Colombia's economy has declined and drug trafficking has expanded. The complexity, persistence, and interconnectedness of these problems in Colombia raise profound questions about the viability of democracy under duress. What can stem the violence perpetrated against Colombian citizens, which has made public security a paramount political issue? Why do political parties and many politicians in this long-standing democracy garner only unstable domestic support? Most fundamentally, why has peace been so elusive?

Unfortunately, information and analysis on the domestic political challenges of human rights, democracy, and peace are far less available than are studies on the questions of U.S. policies and drugs. The premise of this book is that, while drug trafficking and U.S. foreign assistance have attracted extensive attention, it is imperative to understand Colombia's underlying political challenges—which have not received adequate analysis—in order to properly understand and address the conflict, as well as the trafficking and

3

U.S. assistance issues. For example, while drug interdiction efforts have sought to stop production by destroying illegal crops, this policy has been undermined by the protection and support growers receive in exchange for "taxes" paid to leftist guerrillas or rightist paramilitaries. Indeed, the war efforts from many sides of this multilateral conflict help to fuel the powerful demand for drug production.

In an analogous fashion, political rules also undermine eradication efforts. Existing electoral rules create incentives for politicians at various levels of government to add further to the demand for drug production by accepting monies generated by trafficking. Politicians do so because electoral rules have produced extremely weak party control over their member politicians, while at the same time they have increased intraparty competition, making electoral campaigns ever more expensive. As long as current electoral rules persist, internal demands from political actors are likely to thwart efforts to reduce drug production.

Meanwhile, although the U.S. government has sought to combat drugs and insurgents through assistance to the Colombian armed forces, widespread concerns about human rights continue to constrain that policy. Indications of persistent links between the military and right-wing paramilitary groups, for example, as well as the presence of military personnel who continue in office despite allegations of human rights abuses, work to undermine the legitimacy of the armed forces. This in turn weakens the legitimacy of government as provider of public goods, especially security. Ongoing concerns about military-paramilitary relations and about impunity for abuses have constrained the positive impact of security improvements and demobilization efforts achieved by the Uribe government, limiting Uribe's scope to use these advances to improve state authority or expand support for his political initiatives. Even as U.S. aid helps the Colombian military improve its protection of citizens from the violence that has helped to make security the top public priority, human rights concerns are likely to persist if they are not addressed. Indeed, as the military succeeds in reducing guerrilla threats, public concern about human rights issues is likely to increase as fears of guerrilla attacks diminish. Better understanding of the domestic politics in Colombia of human rights, democratic governance, and peace could improve both drug interdiction and U.S. foreign assistance policies.

A second theme of this book is that these three fundamental political issues are closely interrelated. Of the three issues, the questions related to war and peace in Colombia are undoubtedly the most prominent. Nonetheless, as this chapter will argue, while it is sensible to start with an analysis of these questions to chart a path to peace, implementing any such plan will require sustained political leadership and will. To generate the political agreement to achieve peace, however, Colombia's democracy is likely to need reforms to alter the existing rules that create perverse constraints on its ability to generate collective action in the legislature to produce public goods. At the same time, broad public support for Colombia's democracy is contingent on its ability to provide public security, which, as the authors argue in this book, is ultimately contingent on its ability to protect human rights and bring peace. Violations of human rights on all sides of the war ultimately undermine the trust that Colombia's government needs in order to negotiate an enduring end to the war, and the violations lower public confidence in elected government. As the chapters in this book show, the links between these issues create constraints on what ultimately can be done on one issue alone without addressing the other two as well. Of course, as this book illustrates, these linkages are not just about constraints: they also generate opportunities to make progress on the two corollary issues when addressing any one of these three core political issues.

An increasing number of scholars and policy makers—as well as a growing number of students and general readers—do want to know more about the internal politics of the Colombian case. Despite that shift, the scholarly literature on Colombia has not kept pace with the growing interest in the politics of this country on South America's northernmost rim. While Colombia has Latin America's fourth largest population and fifth largest economy, most authors preface their studies of the country lamenting the paucity of scholarly books on the subject. Notable exceptions in last five years include Crandall's (2002) critique of U.S. drug policy toward Colombia, Taussig's (2003) ethnography of local rural violence, Richani's (2002) modeling of a stable war system equilibrium to explain the ongoing violence, and Van Cott's (2000) assessment of indigenous rights in Colombia since the 1991 constitutional reform. Interesting studies by journalists during this period include Dudley (2004) on the demobilization and subsequent extermination of guerrillas in the 1980s and early 1990s and Kirk (2003) on the personal courage of Colombians facing violent abuses and their links to consumption and policy choices in Colombia's biggest export market, the United States.

Moreover, while Colombia boasts some of Latin America's leading universities and one of the region's best-educated populations, very little analysis by Colombian scholars themselves has appeared in the United States. Recent exceptions are Thoumi (2003), which examines the illegal drug industry's international and domestic origins, and two coauthored books, Berquist, Peñaranda, and Gonzalo Sánchez (2001) on the conduct of the war and peace efforts in the 1990s and Safford and Palacios (2001) on nineteenth-century and pre-1974 Colombia. In short, few in-depth studies are available to help explain Colombian politics today, guide analysis of the prospects for policy choices, and understand the historical sources of today's interrelated challenges.

This book aims to help fill the gap in the literature on contemporary Colombia by providing in-depth yet diverse analysis of the core political challenges facing Colombian democracy today, authored by leading scholars from both Colombia and the United States. In the chapters that follow, we examine Colombia's attempts at negotiating peace, the weakening of political institutions, patterns of violence, and human rights policies, considering also the influential role played by the United States and the impact of drugs on politics. This book's most distinctive contribution is its nuanced analyses by leading Colombian as well as U.S. scholars of the core political challenges in Colombia that lie behind the issues more commonly discussed in the United States, drugs and foreign aid.

For scholars, this book applies theory to understand the dynamics of human rights violations, corruption, political fragmentation, and reform. Policy makers will find careful analyses and debate about policy outcomes, alternatives, and recommendations for action to protect rights, strengthen democracy, and pursue peace. Students and general readers will find in this book a timely, topical route to understanding the history and dynamics of Colombia's contemporary challenges of human rights, democracy, and peace.

This introduction takes up the core political questions about peace, democracy, and human rights. It outlines several approaches advanced in the book to answer these questions, lays out the organization of the book, and discusses the origin of this volume.

Peace

Colombia is home to the longest-running guerrilla war in this hemisphere, and this war has evolved into a multisided conflict. Today's elder guerrilla leaders launched their campaign to overthrow the government in the wave of Latin American revolutionary movements that followed Fidel Castro's successful overthrow of Cuba's Batista in 1959. While the movements in other countries from that era have all negotiated settlements or suffered defeat, in Colombia two major guerrilla groups soldier on, at times in competition with each other. Moreover, while the initial ideological impulse for these groups—the Colombian Revolutionary Armed Forces (FARC) and the Army of National Liberation (ELN)—has largely faded with time and with changed circumstances, the FARC and ELN have in the years since been joined in the conflict by different antagonists among whom alliances have been sometimes struck, although rivalry generally prevails. Over the decades drug traffickers, right-wing paramilitary squads, other smaller guerrilla organizations, government police units, Colombia's armed forces, occasional technicians from foreign insurgent groups, and, recently, U.S. advisors have all joined the fray. With the conflict metamorphosed into a shifting and multisided war, after so many years of conflict Colombians cycle through periods of deep pessimism and cautious optimism in their assessments of the prospects for achieving an enduring peace in the proximate future.

Why has Colombia's internal war persisted so long? Why have peace efforts failed to produce durable agreements? Are there lessons from past cycles of negotiations and breakdowns that could help break the cycle?

Although various analysts argue that ideology among the guerrillas has waned, long-standing grievances have endured to help sustain the conflict. Colombia has one of the world's most unequal distributions of income, and its concentration of wealth and land has increased since the late 1980s. The gulfs are deep between rich and poor, between rural and urban cultures, and between regions where the government is present or absent. These inequities provide plentiful sources for both opportunism and resentment. They are economic but also cultural and political. They derive not only from the fact that Colombia never achieved a major land reform but also from the urban disdain for rural cultures and the spotty presence of state institutions (let alone government control) in the Andean highlands and lowland agricultural frontiers.

One line of analysis about the conflict emphasizes social structure, culture, and inequality. The historian Herbert Tico Braun has developed this argument, and in this book he addresses the question, "Could it be that it is a cultural chasm, a flippant urban arrogance in the face of ignorant *campesinos* and their ragged teeth, and a bitter rural resentment against the effrontery of urban folk, that has fueled the conflict in the Colombian countryside for over a half century . . . ?" From this vantage point one concludes that the conflict is likely to persist until inequality is reversed, and this is surely an important piece of the puzzle. Achieving a stable peace will require an understanding of the dynamics of persistent grievances.

Yet grievances alone generally are not sufficient to sustain armed conflict. Resources are necessary as well. The configuration of armed parties in the Colombian conflict has evolved over the years, and foreign sources of support became less available as the Cold War ended. Meanwhile, drug trafficking offered new opportunities for funding. For many analysts, particularly in the United States, ending the drug trade is key to ending the war, in order to choke off the resources that sustain mobilization. However important this source has become, and despite the massive attention it has attracted, it is not the only source of revenue. The guerrillas in particular have employed kidnappings and other forms of "taxation" as well.

Nor is drug money as a revenue source a fixed target, as Álvaro Camacho Guizado and Andrés López Restrepo demonstrate in this volume. At different times, drug traffickers have gained influence among opposing parties on different sides of the conflict. Additionally, as these two authors analyze in detail, the organization of the trafficking industry has shifted repeatedly in response to market changes and competition, as well as from official curtailment. These changes have altered the industry's relations with the armed parties, and such alliances are likely to continue to shift over time. From this analysis, which considers both economic and political resources from trafficking, it is evident that market mechanisms could provide levers for hastening an end to the conflict (or, conversely, for prolonging the war) by shifting the availability of resources that can be derived from contraband. Of course, the illegal status of the drug commodities reduces the opportunities to affect their movement as traded goods with market mechanisms alone, especially in comparison to the possibilities for controlling the illegal movement of diamonds or oil that have fueled civil wars elsewhere. Yet market forces still drive the business of drugs, and they do hold potential to help alter the resources this commerce currently provides for the war.

While grievance and resource causes might be addressed through social reforms and market mechanisms, bringing peace still requires negotiating an end to the war. Most analysts recognize that even if the costs of war become untenable (whether through a shrinking of resources or through the dominance of one party over the others), negotiation will be necessary to conclude the violence. A number of analysts, many in the Uribe government, feel that making the costs of war unacceptably high to the guerrillas through escalation may be the only way to force negotiations, although others, such as Richani (2002), argue that U.S. aid to escalate government attacks merely helps to subsidize the cost of war and delays negotiations.

The history of negotiations thus far, however, is dispiriting. At different times various parties have made major concessions, but in repeated instances their opponents have exploited such first steps for narrow advantage. These responses, chronicled most recently in Dudley (2004), have ranged from simple failure to reciprocate good-faith gestures with similar good faith to outright betrayals where, for example, demobilized guerrillas have been killed by government, paramilitary, or other guerrilla forces. Moreover, while negotiations have at times led both guerrillas and paramilitaries to demobilize, repeated efforts have yet to establish an enduring peace.

Thus far, successive governments have each taken different negotiating strategies, breaking sharply with previous efforts. The limited success of negotiations, however, has left a trail of deepening distrust among all the parties. Unfortunately, disappointment and disillusion with past negotiations have meant that lessons from those efforts, which merit greater study, have been largely neglected. As Daniel García-Peña Jaramillo points out in this book, although these experiences have been frustrating they do provide a rich source of material to guide future negotiations. While partial demobilizations have allowed the conflict to endure, the history of negotiations does provide instructive lessons for today's efforts.

External actors have long been important to sustaining the conflict, providing resources to bolster one side or another at different times. The United States is, increasingly since the end of the Cold War, the single most important external actor, and some believe its role will be decisive in Colombia. The U.S. government provides rising levels of military assistance, but, as Cynthia Arnson argues in this book, many U.S. officials still believe that military action is not ultimately the solution to the conflict. She describes, for example, a disjunction during the Clinton administration between official acknowledgment that peace negotiations were necessary to resolve the conflict and official actions geared predominantly toward augmenting the

Colombian military's capacity to step up the war, and she compares the U.S. role in Colombia's protracted peace process to similar efforts elsewhere. Her analysis suggests that while future negotiations will have a military dimension, the most realistic hope for ending the conflict will involve addressing social and political reform as a basis for negotiations.

Grievances, contraband resources, negotiation failures, and military aid have all sustained the conflict to date. While these are large issues to tackle, they have been addressed successfully in other countries. Doing so in Colombia, as elsewhere, depends on political will.

Democracy

Political will, of course, depends in turn on both leadership and institutions. Colombia boasts one of the longest-running electoral democracies in Latin America. Yet discontent with elected officials and the policies they choose runs deep—not only among the armed opposition but among the voting public as well. In 2001 the public voted overwhelmingly to elect the maverick opposition candidate Alvaro Uribe to the presidency and then two years later gave their votes largely to the leftist opposition in midterm elections, at the same time rejecting thirteen of fourteen referenda Uribe had proposed.

In the 1950s, when the Liberal and Conservative parties ended a bloody civil war by agreeing to centralize political control in the presidency and take turns alternating in power, Colombia's political system yielded to elitism and exclusionary institutions. Recognizing the opposition to this arrangement among voters as well as among guerrillas, politicians finally rewrote the constitution in 1991. While the reform did open the political system as hoped by allowing representation of new groups, it also generated unanticipated side effects.

New electoral rules adopted in the 1991 reform brought partial changes with inconsistent incentives for election strategies. These changes heightened competition among politicians but also encouraged personalistic rather than policy-based campaigns, a practice of "sharing" legislative seats through a sequence of colluding substitute legislators, and an atomized internal fragmentation of the two major political parties. The net result has been intense competition within more than between parties, weak or nonexistent party leadership, extreme difficulty achieving collective agreements in Congress, and laws written so poorly that a high proportion are rejected by judicial review. Rather than alleviate discontent with Colombia's democratic institutions, these new problems have frequently worked to amplify it and, when they do, sap the potential for generating sustained political consensus.

Why has Colombia's long-standing democracy had such difficulty garnering stable popular support? What could enhance political will in Colombia? What are the prospects for democratic survival in Colombia?

Various approaches can be taken to address these questions. A historical analysis provides one line of response. Voting decisions are framed by history and informed by observations and analysis of the past, after all, even when voters consider promises about the future as they decide how to vote.

Unfortunately, Colombia's historical record contains enough uncertainties, betrayals, and corruption to daunt even the most idealistic voter. Drug money has fueled even presidential candidates' campaigns. Meantime, M19 guerrillas who laid down their arms to join electoral politics were systematically assassinated in the early 1990s. And the 1991 reforms—which, like any reform, were a product of idealists, realists, and cynics together— thus far seem to have diminished the link between voters and their representatives, even as they have provided a welcome expansion of the scope for participation.

The historical analysis by Eduardo Pizarro and Ana María Bejarano in this volume indicates that politicians may have overreached as they opened Colombia's political system, gutting its capacity to achieve policy consensus to produce public goods. Flaws in their choices of electoral rules hang over elections in Colombia today like the clouds that produced unending rains in Gabriel García Márquez's *One Hundred Years of Solitude,* working in this case to drown out and ultimately fog over both politicians' and voters' views of the future. In this line of analysis, the survival of democracy in Colombia depends on correcting the macro-level balance between responsiveness and governability in the political system.

While such broad rebalancing is a desirable goal, it raises new questions too. How would such rebalancing reforms occur in a political system that is severely weakened, where consensus and public support are difficult to achieve? More specifically, what should the new rules say? After all, electoral reform has been put on the legislative agenda repeatedly by both the presidents Pastrana and Uribe. Yet the politicians empowered to set laws won their positions under the current legislation, so they have strong incentives to stick with the status quo rather than reform election laws.

Nonetheless, politicians are not entirely immune from public frustration or citizens' enthusiasm for reform. As Matthew Shugart, Erika Moreno, and Luis Fajardo point out in this volume, politicians can find it in their interest to reform election laws if the arena for competition shifts or if the opportunity costs of reform come to outweigh the benefits of the status quo. At times public pressure can create incentives that override politicians' attachment to the status quo. Yet, as these three authors argue, for reform to occur politicians would still need additional information. In particular, they would need to feel confident that a given reform would actually work better than the last reform and that the changes it introduced would minimize their potential political losses. Shugart et al. compare Colombia's electoral rules with rules in other countries to highlight where distortions occur and to propose a reform that would build on existing rules. This reform would tailor modifications to address existing distortions and minimize redistribution of political groups' access to power. In contrast to the historical institutional approach, this comparative institutional approach explains citizens' disaffection at the micro level from specific features of rules and provides a more fine-grained blueprint for reform.

While the historical institutional approach taken by Pizarro and Bejarano faults Colombia's freewheeling hypercompetitiveness as one of the causes of politicians' weak accountability to citizens, Shugart et al. are more optimistic about the pluralism and competitiveness achieved since 1991 and the prospects for ongoing reforms to fine-tune the constitution. A third, more narrowly rational-choice approach developed in this book by Francisco Gutiérrez Sanín suggests that this very competitiveness actually may have helped Colombia evade political domination by drug traffickers who sought to take advantage of the system's openness and their own expanded purchasing power to buy their way into political power.

Although Thoumi (2003) argues that Colombian politics is more vulnerable to the effects of illegal drugs than is its economy, Gutiérrez arrives at a more optimistic conclusion in this volume. Gutiérrez uses a behavioral rational-choice framework to model the traffickers' efforts at political control and the system's response. He argues that their relationship with politicians was built on a principal-agent problem that made the relation an "unhappy marriage." While democratic competition left the system permeable to influence and vulnerable to corruption, this competition also weakened traffickers' control over politicians and protected the polity from takeover by the traffickers.

This argument is a tonic to the many analyses of the system's failings. Weak and deficient as Colombia's political system may be, it has successfully survived daunting domestic challenges. By pointing out the system's positive resilience, this approach at the same time lends support to the institutionalists' contention that reform in Colombia should aim at balancing and tailoring rather than wholesale overhaul.

Human Rights

Despite accomplishments such as avoiding political domination by traffickers, Colombia is distinctive among its neighbors because the challenges to its political leaders and citizens are both so profound and so interrelated. Human rights abuses, official corruption, multisided armed conflict, drug trafficking, endemic poverty, public distrust of politics, and weakened government control all interact in a cascading fashion to worsen the harm caused by each of the other problems. Even with recent decreases in homicides and kidnappings, compared to the rest of Latin America this destructive synergy has chalked up record levels of violence, especially against noncombatants. The capacity of these problems to cause harm beyond Colombia's borders together with the scale of the violence has attracted U.S. attention and moved Colombia to a priority spot on the U.S. foreign policy agenda. In the end, political violence is an ongoing obstacle to achieving political reforms that could strengthen democratic government and bring stable peace.

Who should be held accountable for this violence? Has U.S. involvement helped? Is the Colombian government a besieged victim or is it complicit?

The various issues on Colombia's extensive roster of acute policy challenges have attracted attention in the United States from a variety of groups and political leaders. This attention has generated widespread, albeit heterogeneous, foreign policy interest in Colombia. Since Colombia is but one locus of U.S. foreign policy, its policies there are developed within a broader conceptual framework. While the U.S. agenda in Colombia has at different times emphasized drug interdiction, counterinsurgency, antiterrorism, police reform, and human rights, U.S. commitments of foreign aid—personnel as well as equipment and funding—have grown steadily since the late 1990s to rank third among those to the countries receiving U.S. assistance.

Has this deepening involvement achieved its goals thus far? While Colombia's problems persist and it is unlikely that outsiders will solve them, both observers and participants do point to an impressive professionalization of the national police with U.S. assistance—a change that undoubtedly has helped human rights in Colombia. On the other hand, despite congressional efforts in the United States to condition military aid on improving human rights by breaking the military's ties with right-wing paramilitaries, in practice the links and impunity for abuses continue even as some paramilitaries demobilize.

In a broad assessment of U.S. involvement in Colombia, Arlene Tickner concludes in this volume that the net effect of U.S. involvement unfortunately has been to worsen the outcomes on human rights and on the other issues that have prompted U.S. involvement. Tickner combines extensive personal interviews with a review of the history of the involvement to argue that realist policy views in the United States have prioritized drug interdiction and military aid, with counterproductive effects across a range of issues.

Other commentators have laid the blame for Colombia's sustained levels of violence and murder more directly on armed nonstate groups—guerrillas, paramilitaries, and drug traffickers. Indeed, Colombians often have difficulty discovering with certainty which of these three parties is behind specific assassinations. Faced with this wide variety of nonstate perpetrators of violence, some observers view the Colombian government as besieged, a victim, and not itself responsible for the country's dismal human rights record.

In contrast, the legal scholar and human rights defender Gustavo Gallón argues forcefully in this volume that Colombia's government is complicit in the violence. Gallón's argument rests on assumptions that governments are responsible for providing public goods of justice, rule of law, and public safety. Gallón builds on this premise to advance an argument central to this book, that protecting human rights is the key to providing this set of public goods. Moreover, he argues, failing to do so makes the government complicit in the broad pattern of violations as much as it is in the instances where it supports agents who are direct perpetrators.

Human rights issues—already pressing—became especially salient after Álvaro Uribe assumed the presidency of Colombia in August 2002, even as violence statistics showed some improvements. Fulfilling campaign pledges, he sought to combat insurgent groups by adding part-time conscripts to the armed forces, by paying private citizens as freelance informants, and by decreeing laws that gave security forces broad new powers to suspend civil liberties. Human rights groups in Colombia and abroad argued that these measures introduced new potential for abuses. Officers have less oversight and control of the activities by part-time soldiers who sleep at home rather than in the barracks. Meantime, the informants program leaves wide scope for some potential informants to make accusations to settle local scores (or to blackmail). Last, the new laws further reduce the domain of civilian courts, expanding military and police authority to detain any person they themselves determine to be suspect, without judicial warrant. Perhaps of greatest concern, Uribe responded to criticism from human rights organizations of his efforts to give military courts jurisdiction over human rights cases and to allow impunity for demobilized paramilitaries by publicly associating human rights groups with the guerrillas.

The Colombian government's ability to address the core security and justice issues of the war depends on its ability to develop state capacity to protect human rights and thereby enhance democratic practices to ultimately generate a sustainable political consensus for peace. At the core of the prolonged and multisided conflict in Colombia is this book's question of what shall be the fundamental political rules that govern conflict among citizens, as well as between the government and citizens.

Organization of the Book

The basic premise of this book is that the political underpinnings of Colombia's conflicts are insufficiently understood. We have organized the volume to address that need by presenting various perspectives on the underlying political issues in Colombia's conflict. The book clusters these analyses in three interrelated and key issue areas: war and peace; the state of democracy; and human rights protection. Other prominent issues—such as drug trafficking and U.S. foreign policy, which cut across these three areas—are not excluded but rather are addressed within these sections. This introduction sets out the broad questions surrounding each of the three issue areas to frame the discussion developed in each section and the overall themes that relate these issues.

The discussion opens in the first section by focusing on the issue area in Colombia that is, sadly, most familiar among all audiences today—the problem of war and peace. The chapters in this section raise the macro-level questions of why the war has persisted so long in Colombia and whether there is any hope for peace in the foreseeable future. They examine these issues from the perspectives of history, political science, conflict resolution, and foreign policy. They look not only at the violence of war and the record of negotiations but also at the impact of drug trafficking and U.S. involvement with the conflict.

Beyond the conflict itself, Colombia's democracy is seriously frayed, and the second section addresses the state of this democracy once proudly praised as one of Latin America's oldest. The chapters in this section explore the meso-level questions about why policy coherence and political parties have weakened so dramatically in Colombia's democracy and the prospects for reform. The authors in this section are all political scientists, but they use different approaches—historical, institutional, and behavioral methods—to diagnose the ills, highlight the strengths, and recommend both broad and specific courses of action. These chapters analyze institutional rules, politicians' behavior, corruption, and the possibilities for reform.

The last section directly addresses human rights, which provide the foundation of contemporary democracy and stable peace. These concluding chapters focus on micro-level questions of how violence at the individual level adds up and who should be accountable for reversing the abuses. Taking international relations and legal perspectives, the authors here lay out patterns of abuses and assess both Colombian and U.S. policies aimed at human rights.

The book concludes with an overview of human rights challenges confronting the Colombian government as it pursues the war.

Origins of the Book

The origins of this book date at least partly from a conversation several years ago with the University of Notre Dame's former president, the Rev. Theodore Hesburgh, C.S.C. As president from 1952 to 1987, Hesburgh had used his position to play a national role as an educational and moral leader, distinguishing himself on civil rights and international issues. He was especially interested in Latin America and raised the monies to create the Kellogg Institute for International Studies at Notre Dame. As chair of the institute's advisory council in 2000, he met with the institute's director, Scott Mainwaring, and the two editors of this volume. Even an eternal optimist such as Hesburgh expressed frustration as our conversation turned to the conflict in Colombia. "We've got to do something about Colombia, but what can be done?' he mused.

Since that conversation, the institute has taken up the challenge implicit in that frustration. Looking to the institute's history and its research agenda, we sought to define a role for a U.S. university in such a complex conflict and to use our resources to help find paths to restore peace and prosperity to one of Latin America's oldest—but severely threatened—democracies.

Earlier, in the years just following its creation in 1982, the Kellogg Institute awarded residential research fellowships to numerous scholars from Latin America's Southern Cone countries—Argentina, Brazil, Chile, Uruguay—which were all under military rule. The institute not only provided a safe haven for scholars whose lives and careers were threatened in those countries but also generated a critical mass of scholarly talent in which these thinkers could continue to work on the political and economic challenges of their countries. Exchanging ideas with each other and with scholars from outside the region, they gained comparative perspective. Together with the former academic director of the institute, Guillermo O'Donnell, and others, they helped to construct the theoretical blueprint for transitions to democracy in the region.

Today, the theoretical challenge is distinct: scholars must now ask, What are the dynamics driving the internal corrosion of democracies—some of Latin America's oldest—in the Northern Rim, from Venezuela through Colombia, Ecuador, Peru, and Bolivia? And how might these democracies be rebuilt to address the profound social conflicts in each country? In broadest terms—terms that resonate not only among Latin America's democracies but also in Africa and Asia—these questions lead us to ask, Why is the performance of democratic governments often disappointing, and what can foster more successful performance?

The practical challenges of the conflict are sadly familiar, however. Like their colleagues in the Southern Cone two decades ago, Colombian scholars have been targeted for threats and murder. With generous support from the Ford Foundation, the Kellogg Institute joined a partnership with the Colombian Commission of Jurists in Bogotá, the Inter-American Dialogue in Washington, D.C., the Center for Civil and Human Rights at the Notre Dame Law School, and the Kroc Institute for International Peace Studies at Notre Dame to take up both sets of challenges.

Under the auspices of this partnership, a series of prominent Colombian social scientists have found space at Notre Dame to continue analyzing the conflicts in their country, working together and exchanging ideas with U.S. and other Latin American scholars, as well as with policy makers in Washington. At the same time, other Colombians have received graduate training and hands-on internships in international human rights law, conflict resolution, and peace studies. In March 2001, a joint conference at Notre Dame gathered policy makers, diplomats, journalists, students, and scholars to discuss the conflict.

The chapters in this book grew out of that meeting, from which authors' papers were first selected, then extensively revised and updated for this volume. Our hope—and the goal of the project that joined these partners—is that in addition to fostering understanding, this book will stimulate initiatives to protect human rights, strengthen democracy, and achieve peace in Colombia.

Note

I am grateful for the thoughtful comments provided at different stages of this essay from Cindy Arnson and Matt Shugart. Of course, I bear responsibility for the final product.

References

Berquist, Charles, Ricardo Peñaranda, and G. Gonzalo Sánchez, eds. 2001. *Violence in Colombia, 1990–2000: Waging War and Negotiating Peace*. Wilmington, DE: Scholarly Resources.

Crandall, Russell. 2002. *Driven by Drugs: U.S. Policy toward Colombia.* Boulder, CO: Lynne Reiner.

Dudley, Steven. 2004. *Walking Ghosts: Murder and Guerilla Politics in Colombia.* New York: Routledge.

Kirk, Robin. 2003. *More Terrible Than Death: Massacres, Drugs and America's War in Colombia.* New York: Public Affairs.

Richani, Nazih. 2002. *Systems of Violence: The Political Economy of War and Peace in Colombia.* Albany: State University of New York Press.

Safford, Frank, and Marco Palacios. 2001. *Colombia: Fragmented Land, Divided Society.* New York: Oxford University Press.

Taussig, Michael. 2003. *Law in a Lawless Land: Diary of a Limpieza.* New York: New Press.

Thoumi, Francisco. 2003. *Illegal Drugs, Economy, and Society in the Andes.* Baltimore: Woodrow Wilson Center Press.

Van Cott, Donna Lee. 2000. *The Friendly Liquidation of the Past.* Pittsburgh, PA: University of Pittsburgh Press.

PART ONE

Peace

"¡Que haiga paz!"

The Cultural Contexts of Conflict in Colombia

Herbert Tico Braun

Could it be that it is a cultural chasm, a flippant urban arrogance in the face of ignorant campesinos and their ragged teeth, and a bitter rural resentment against the effrontery of urban folk, that has fueled the conflict in the Colombian countryside for over a half-century and kept the guerrilla organizations alive all this time?" To answer this question, Braun uses a variety of historical and contemporary materials illuminating the place of honor, conversation, and personal relationships in Colombian political culture. Against this background, he reexamines the fifty-year history of the relationship between the guerrillas and politicians, from their abandonment by Liberal leaders to the repeated failures of current national leaders to come to terms with campesino needs for respect and recognition. His analysis highlights the vast gulf that separates urban politicians from the rural guerrillas, shedding new light on the reasons for the repeated failure of peace negotiations between the two camps. He locates the reasons for the breakdown of negotiations in the inability of urban leaders to understand the deep historical roots of the guerrilla struggle—a struggle for honor and for an equal place in the Colombian nation. Braun's analysis offers a keen insight into the dynamic of negotiation and breakdown that has characterized the Colombian peace process and is an eye-opening account of overlooked factors that might go far toward advancing understanding between the two parties.

What does *Tirofijo* smell like? . . . And speaking of other disgusting things,
how does he slurp his soup? Or, does he grab the slippery piece of chicken
with his hands? And something that is perhaps even more revealing: the
inherited, acquired and reproduced sensibility of the "superior" classes
who go to the Caguán to negotiate, whose stench is camouflaged with
perfumes. Does this sensibility upset the chances for peace?

> Armando Benedetti Jimeno, "El mal olor, un problema político,"
> *El Tiempo*, July 30, 2001

Taciturn Guerrillas

Bands of armed men gathered in the Colombian countryside in the late
1940s and early 1950s. A few years later, Guatemalan guerrillas began to organize long-suffering, indigenous, Mayan peoples who were doing slave
labor for the military—at first taken to large coffee plantations, mainly at
harvest time, and later also forced to pick cotton and cut sugarcane. These
insurgents won significant battles in the early 1980s, and they suffered huge
losses. They have come and gone all over Latin America. In 1959, a small
band of bold guerrillas quickly brought down the Cuban dictator Fulgencio
Batista. Guerrillas no more, they have been in power ever since.

In El Salvador in the 1970s, various guerrilla organizations grew out of
class and cultural antagonisms on coffee farms and beyond in Salvadoran
society, while next door in Nicaragua the Sandinista movement rose in opposition to the dictatorship of Anastasio Somoza. Early and again late in
the 1980s, the Salvadoran guerrillas appeared on the verge of taking power.
The Sandinistas, of course, did take over Managua, and they ruled for a decade before losing in an election. Now armed conflict in these two countries
belongs to the past. Urban guerrillas fighting military dictatorships had
brief public lives in the 1960s and 1970s in Uruguay, Argentina, Brazil, and
Chile. Guerrilla movements developed in Venezuela and Peru in the 1960s
and 1980s, respectively. Most recently, an indigenous rural uprising that
spread out of the coffee-laden hills of Chiapas, in southern Mexico, in the
1990s, has seemingly come to a standstill.

First to emerge, the rural guerrillas of Colombia are the ones that remain, alone in Latin America. While winning few important battles, they
have suffered only small losses, sporadically, here and there. Except for a few
brief years in the 1950s, just after they emerged, there have been no civilian
or military dictatorships to combat. Throughout these many years, Colom-

bia has had a civilian-run, popularly elected government with different political parties, a political system that cannot be classified as exclusive. Colombia may or may not be a democracy, but it certainly has the trappings of one, and participation in politics is possible for many. The guerrillas have not organized rural workers in the coffee groves or in any other productive rural sector. Indeed, the coffee-growing areas have until very recently been enclaves of relative peace and tranquillity. Instead, the guerrillas have helped displaced rural folk to move away into areas less contested by landowners, narco-traffickers, and paramilitaries. The guerrillas have not pitted one class against another in their long years in the countryside.

In a nation with a preponderantly mestizo population, the guerrillas have not emerged to fight for an indigenous population. There are no deep ethnic or racial divides that can explain the conflict. Religious animosities can hardly motivate the contestants. All are Catholic, while Pentecostal inroads are more a result than a cause of the enduring conflict. Poverty and inequality are widespread in Colombia, but so they are in many other nations that have not experienced such a civil conflict, and especially not one that has lasted so long. For stretches of time, the guerrillas have disappeared from view. At no time have they come close to achieving power. Indeed, there is little to indicate that they have been interested in taking over, at least not until very recently. For many of these years, the inhabitants of the many large cities of the nation have been largely unaware of the rural conflicts. Colombian society has rarely felt threatened in any systematic manner.

Less well known internationally than any of their Latin American counterparts have been, the guerrillas remain mysterious even to most Colombians. They have never had a mass popular following. Initially, the guerrillas focused on defending themselves. Over the past twenty years, becoming a more aggressive fighting force, they still appear little interested in establishing a legitimate rural power base. As an emerging rural elite in a hierarchical social order, they look toward the institutions of power more than they look toward the people of the countryside. They have often engaged in macabre forms of violence designed to humiliate poor people whom they suspect might betray them. Heroic passions are rarely discernible. There is little hate, anger, or love. Were it not for recent actual and alleged connections between the guerrilla movement and the export of cocaine and heroin to the United States and elsewhere, it is unlikely that the Colombian guerrillas would be paid any heed on the international scene.

Indeed, without the revenues they obtain by taxing the cocaine trade in local areas, they might be almost as invisible today as they were in the 1960s and 1970s.

While the guerrillas have consistently held to a set of ideas all these years, they have engaged in few, if any, efforts to engage the imagination of Colombians with them and to win the people over to their cause. Their ideology does not appear to be at the forefront of their struggle. As nowhere else in Latin America, and perhaps anywhere in the world, the armed conflict in Colombia has been a muted, almost voiceless struggle. Nor has verbal communication made the conflict more readily intelligible. While the guerrillas have grown dramatically in number over the past ten years or so and are a public force to contend with, they remain enigmatic. Were they to have expressed themselves more creatively, their struggles might well have become part of the curriculum of undergraduate courses in the United States, where academics are prone to studying revolutions in Latin America.

But the guerrillas have not always been so difficult to decipher. When the bands of men started coming together in the countryside over a half-century ago, looking for funds, for guns, and principally for respect from their rural peers and public recognition from their leaders far away in the cities, they desperately wanted everyone to know what they were about. Theirs was an ideology they understood intrinsically, and it made them proud. It defined them and told them who they were. They could shout it from every mountaintop. During the time that they were still struggling alongside their upper-class leaders, following urban and cultured politicians, they held their heads high, for they were Liberals, members of one of the two long-standing, traditional political parties of Colombia. They stood up proudly to defend themselves and their nation against the Conservatives who were out to kill them and whom they understood to be reactionary lovers of religion and superstition, repressive authoritarians bent on returning Colombia to a mythical, pastoral past rather than advancing into a modern future of liberty and progress.

It was only when those Liberal country folk lost their connection to their party and to their leaders in the early 1950s that they turned inward, becoming the silent men in arms that we have witnessed over the decades. Without the mantle of the Liberal Party, these bands of rural folk were forced to seek out other ideas to explain what they were about, not only to others, but especially to themselves. Their efforts were tentative. During the

Cold War they attached themselves to communist and socialist ideas. These have now receded. But the guerrillas did not regain the passion for ideas that they had had when they knew they were Liberals.

Still, the guerrillas' basic notions of what Colombia ought to be—a more open, egalitarian, and just society with room for all—have remained remarkably consistent over the decades.[1] Much has been made of this continuity in urban circles. The ideas of the guerrillas are seen as so old and traditional that they no longer fit into the modernizing nation. With an ever-growing faith in the capitalist market, many Colombian intellectuals have felt little need to think about agrarian and urban reform policies. Moreover, the ideas of the guerrillas have been expressed over time in a mechanical and pedestrian language, making them seem all the more antiquated and dogmatic. The ideas of the guerrillas have been read and understood among cultured circles in urban Colombia with that "unmistakable reticence of the pedantic intellectual."[2] They have been dismissed. The distance between urban politicians and rural insurgents remains as great as ever, maybe greater.

Nevertheless, it is the exclusion from the Liberal Party and the affairs of the nation, more than the ideas the guerrillas have held, that helps explain their origins and their peculiar trajectory. In the early 1950s the conditions were set for this distinctive, even unique series of guerrilla movements to arise in Colombia. In the oft-quoted words of the historian David Bushnell (1993), "Colombia is today the least studied of the major Latin American countries, and probably the least understood" (vii). This is largely because historical patterns in Colombia, especially in the twentieth century, are at odds with those of the other major nations of the hemisphere. The history of Colombia is often distinctive. So too are its twentieth-century rural guerrillas.

The guerrillas have been kept alive by Manuel Marulanda Vélez, known as Tirofijo, or "Sureshot," the septuagenarian founder and leader of the FARC, the Revolutionary Armed Forces of Colombia, the movement formed in 1964 out of the rural bands of men that had been around in one way or another in the Colombian countryside since the late 1940s. He earned the nom de guerre Tirofijo (with which he has been none too pleased) when he was a boy, not because he had a sharp eye for aiming his rifle at men, but because he was good at shooting birds out of the sky.[3] Manuel Marulanda Vélez was not his real name either. He was born Pedro Antonio Marín, and he hailed from a modest family of small landowners. Together with fourteen cousins, he fled from their home to keep from being murdered by bands of rank-and-file Conservatives who were out to rid the land of Liberals.

Today the FARC is a rural movement composed of more than sixty separate cells, or *frentes,* proudly claiming at least eighteen thousand well-trained and dedicated men and women in arms. It is by far the larger of the two remaining, supposedly left-wing guerrilla organizations in the Colombian countryside. The other is the Ejército de Liberación Nacional (ELN), which boasts some five thousand fighters. Although also deeply rural in its origins,[4] it emerged in the mid-1960s in the context of the Cold War and found its inspiration in the Cuban Revolution and liberation theology. The ELN has been more explicitly ideological and contestatory than the older FARC, and as such it more closely approximates those rural rebel movements that emerged elsewhere in Latin America from the 1960s to the 1980s.

The history of the FARC contrasts more sharply with that of the M19, a nationally and internationally well-known, mainly urban insurgency that had much in common with the Sandinista movement of the 1970s in Nicaragua. The M19 sprang up in protest against the seemingly fraudulent presidential elections of April 19, 1970, when the former president (1953–57) and general Gustavo Rojas Pinilla lost to Misael Pastrana Borrero, father of Andrés Pastrana, a major protagonist of this story, for he too would become president. Composed of young urban intellectuals and politicians, some from well-known families with ties to the nation's political elites, the movement also modeled itself expressly in reaction to the slow-moving and stodgy FARC.

In its 1974 opening gambit, M19 guerrillas stole the sword of the liberator Simón Bolívar from his historic home in Bogotá as a symbol of the ongoing revolution. They stormed the embassy of the Dominican Republic in Bogotá, dug a long tunnel into an army barracks just north of the city, and took away loads of guns and ammunition; then, in November 1985, they attacked the Palace of Justice in Bogotá, with horrendously tragic consequences. With many of its leaders dead, and the movement widely rejected, M19 ended its relatively short history in flames. More aggressive than the rural rebels and far more threatening, the group was systematically pursued by the army, which felt humiliated by M19's successes. Well-connected as its rural counterparts were not, surviving leaders of the M19 managed to reintegrate themselves into the elite life of the city. The conflict between the M19 and Colombia's leaders was political and strategic more than cultural.[5]

We can only wonder whether the rural ELN would have suffered the fate of defeated movements elsewhere in Latin America had it not been for the more solid, entrenched, and elusive FARC, which kept the long rural insurgency alive. When Camilo Torres, the celebrated Colombian sociologist and rebel priest, decided that only a violent revolution in the countryside would bring the change he yearned for Colombia, he turned his back on the city and his upper-class background and chose to join the ranks of the ELN and not the FARC. Shortly afterwards, on February 15, 1966, he was shot dead by a soldier as he scampered back from an army ambush to recover a rifle for the revolution.[6]

Marulanda gave himself up at about that same time to Major Carlos Hernando Gil González because he was about to be hunted down by a rival band. The major took Marulanda under heavy guard to General Ricardo Charry Solano, who in turn made sure that he got a job building roads with the Ministry of Transportation. But Marulanda did not last long there, and he returned to the hills.[7] It is popularly rumored—and rumor is a vital part of all these histories—that in 1974 or 1975 the guerrilla leader offered to come to the capital city of Bogotá and turn himself in but that Alfonso López Michelsen, who was president at the time, let it be known that he would not receive him.

Marulanda has now become the world's oldest living guerrilla. Little is known about him. He hardly ever speaks about himself in public. When the stellar reporter Alma Guillermoprieto went out to see him in August 1986,

> He lived in his own little compound a short walk from the central head-quarters, surrounded by an elite guard. Although we knew that he was in charge of military training and combat operations, he acted as if his main concerns were the chickens and the vegetable patch in his front yard. Stocky, almost irritatingly modest and of few words, he carried on one shoulder the white fringed towel worn by the rural people, the *campesinos*. Sometimes he used it to cover his head against the sun. Sometimes he took it off to swat a fly or two. He gave us a rather sketchier version of a discourse we had already had from [Jacobo] Arenas . . . co-founder and chief ideologue of the FARC . . . (who pointed out a little too often that although Marulanda might be a *campesino*, he liked to read books). (Guillermoprieto 2001: 23)[8]

Perhaps Marulanda has been thinking all this time about his old Liberal Party leaders, urban men all of them, who were proud of their culture and erudition.

Hearts and Minds

"Marulanda is a very primitive man," declared President Andrés Pastrana. In the glossy pages of the *Revista Diners,* the monthly magazine for executives, professionals, and others who carry a Diners International credit card in their wallets and purses, and next to advertising for gourmet food, exclusive hotels, restaurants, and vacation spots, the president reflected on what had gone wrong now that his three-year peace process with the guerrillas had come to a precipitous end on February 20, 2002.[9] With his hair turning prematurely grey, the president, once boyish looking, appeared a man of distinction, even of gravitas. But he was clearly tired and deeply frustrated. His presidency was ending in a resounding failure.

At the beginning of his administration in 1998, Pastrana had handed over to the guerrillas a huge, Switzerland-sized tract of land that has come to be known as el Caguán, as a sign of his goodwill in order to get the peace negotiations started. Thereafter, the president had come to believe that he had developed a close personal relationship with Manuel Marulanda. In the *Revista Diners* interview he stated, "[T]he truth is that he is a politician, he likes politics. We would share histories, about why it was that the FARC were born, and what they were about. He likes to talk about politics."[10] The guerrilla leader was someone with whom the president could talk. It seemed they had much in common. "Above all else, he and I reached a *compromiso de palabra*"—they had offered one another their word of honor. In the president's heart, the two men had come to an understanding among *caballeros,* among gentlemen, one of those time-honored relationships that lie at the core of Colombian politics.[11] Downcast, the president reached for an explanation as to why that relationship failed. His conclusion was devastating. "Nobody can say that Andrés Pastrana did not do everything in his reach to bring peace, but the word [of honor] of a *campesino* failed me."[12]

This was a relationship more personal than political. The negotiations were not a matter of history, strategy, ideology, or power. They were about trust between two men. Pastrana felt betrayed, even humiliated by the guerrilla leader. To more fully understand what had happened to him and his nation, he resorted to ideas and to a language that had not been part of the public discourse in Colombia for the past half-century. "It is very sad that Colombia has lost the confidence that it had in the word of a *campesino,* which we all thought the word of Marulanda was. I had confidence in his word. A process that was based on the word of the president of the republic and the word of a *campesino* was very interesting. It was something sacred."

The president wondered aloud how the guerrilla leader must be feeling. "I think that one of the things that must be affecting him the most, emotionally, is that he did not keep his word, because that is very difficult for a Colombian *campesino* not to do." This timeless, bucolic, and deeply paternalistic view of the Colombian countryside and its humble inhabitants, untouched by modernity, individualism, greed, and secularity, had been a staple in the intellectual diet of leading thinkers of the Conservative Party in the nineteenth century and up until the early 1950s, when the violence among rural people that has come to be known as "la Violencia" (1952–65) broke them asunder. While far less common than the more uniformly disdainful and denigrating views of country people held by urban Colombians throughout the nation's history, the president's words vividly expressed the deep cultural divide between the inhabitants of these two interrelated parts of the nation, a divide that lies at the root of the current conflict in Colombia.

The president had gone into the countryside to seek peace with the guerrillas as a Conservative, as his father, also a president of the republic, had gone before him. In the interview, Pastrana recalled Fidel Castro saying, "If I were now facing Manuel Marulanda, I would tell him to make peace with that *godo,* that Conservative." But in the president's mind, Marulanda had not lived up to his promise. He was not what he appeared to be, not a real *campesino.* He was a man either too primitive or not primitive enough. Although in despair, the president in his own heart remained blameless for the failure of the peace talks. It was rumored that Andrés Pastrana turned ever more toward God for sustenance in these dark times.

In the pages of the same magazine, in the same issue, Manuel Marulanda reflected on the peace process before it had come to an end.[13] Asked about his relationship with the president, Marulanda "let loose one of those contained, brief, and silent half-smiles of the distrustful campesino who does not have good teeth," in the words of Antonio Caballero, the famed journalist who went out into the countryside to interview the guerrilla leader.

"Well," Marulanda responded, "he comes here in his helicopter, tells a few jokes, and leaves." The guerrilla leader had a much different view of the relationship than did the president. He even seemed to mock him. "With [President Ernesto] Samper (1994–98) we struggled to get him to demilitarize La Uribe. . . . When Pastrana was a [presidential] candidate, he asked us if in addition to La Uribe we wanted five more municipalities. Well, what were we going to say? Well, yes."

The ritualized meetings with government leaders and others in Colombian society were most likely intensely meaningful experiences for Marulanda, as we shall see. At the same time, it appears that he did not take them seriously as peace negotiations. In his mind, they could hardly have led to much. Pastrana may well have won the presidency in 1998 because of his personal relationship with the guerrilla leader after the unprecedented meeting of the two men out in the countryside. The hopes for peace, which the apparent chemistry between them aroused in the Colombian people, were intense. However, as president, Pastrana did not have the power to negotiate very much at all. His was a weak, minority government, opposed by members of his own Conservative Party, by many sectors of the Liberals, and often by the military, landowners, and industrialists, and the Congress as well.

Moreover, from Marulanda's perspective, little of substance could be discussed until the paramilitaries were brought under control, and that Pastrana and his government were either unwilling or unable to do. For it was the paramilitaries more than the Colombian army that were carrying out the battle against the guerrillas. Finally, with Plan Colombia, the president was successfully obtaining a historically unprecedented military assistance package of at least $1.3 billion from the United States to fumigate the coca fields and deprive the guerrillas—who taxed the commodity as it left the areas under their control—of a major source of income. Marulanda could well have believed that the president was using the talks as a means of gaining time until Plan Colombia could be more fully implemented.

What these negotiations might have been all about, if they had been more than mere posturing on both sides, or even culturally and politically meaningful personal encounters, is difficult to fathom. "The government does not have power," Marulanda told Antonio Caballero. "It doesn't even control its own military. Those who come out here to talk, they just come to shoot the breeze. The oligarchy wants peace without giving anything up.

That is the way it has always been." Marulanda quickly remembered the past. "Like when Colonel Duarte Blum distributed those pickaxes during the time of [General] Rojas [Pinilla] (1953–56), or those taxicabs that Belisario [Betancur] (1982–86) promised us and did not deliver on." Like virtually every public statement that the guerrilla leader has uttered over the past fifty years, this comment referred to incidents—both large and small—that took place years ago, times when Marulanda felt that he and his men were belittled and mistreated by their urban counterparts. Marulanda's mind was driven by his memories.

The guerrilla leader complained sarcastically about all the high commissioners of the peace that the president sent out to talk to guerrillas. He appeared to not even know who they were. "The previous one, what was his name?" "The current one, what's his name, what?" He saw them all as little more than ineffective figureheads. Marulanda asserted that one of the commissioners was so ignorant that he hadn't any idea that it actually cost more for a poor family of coca growers to feed themselves in the Putumayo than it cost the commissioner's family in the capital city of Bogotá. "They don't know. They don't care. They don't want to know." In contrast, one of the few people of the city that Marulanda appeared to have respected was the ninety-year-old industrialist Hernán Echavarría Olózaga. During one of the many encounters between representatives of civil society and the guerrillas that had been taking place over the years, he gave a *discurso*, a speech, on the violence in the 1930s, when Marulanda was just a boy. Afterwards, Marulanda was overheard to say, "*¡Ese hombre es un berraco!*" (That man is a real man!).[14]

In Marulanda's heart, the causes of the continuing struggle appear to have lain in the "egoism," the "arrogance," and the "ignorance" of the urban people with whom he came into contact. His focus on personal attitudes was striking. The president may have felt that he was just engaging in a pleasant conversation when he talked to Marulanda about the origins of his struggle. But for the guerrilla leader it was his very existence, his reason for living, his every breathing moment that was being so airily discussed. And in truth, the president's peace delegates were all very young men who were almost certainly entirely ignorant of the history of the guerrilla movement and had practically no interest in it or in learning something about it. They understood little, if anything, about rural Colombia, or about country people. For these urban politicians, the guerrillas were certainly vestiges of an age seemingly long gone, dinosaurs, as former President César Gaviria (1990–94) had referred to them ten years earlier. There is little to indicate that the negotiators were intrigued by Manuel Marulanda and his long past.

The reactions of the president and the guerrilla leaders to the failure of the peace talks were strangely similar. The president bemoaned that Marulanda had betrayed him. The guerrilla leader complained that Pastrana and his delegates, like so many other men before them, had not taken him and his men seriously. Neither felt that he could be blamed for the failure of the talks. Could the conflict be as much personal as political? To what extent could the relative lack of a dynamic ideology of the guerrillas, and their strange silence over long periods of time, be attributed to the significantly personal character of these conflicts? Could it be that it is a cultural chasm, a flippant urban arrogance in the face of ignorant *campesinos* and their ragged teeth, and a bitter rural resentment against the effrontery of urban folk, that has fueled the conflict in the Colombian countryside for over a half-century and kept the guerrilla organizations alive all this time?

There can be little doubt that in the mind of the president hardly anything of a programmatic, structural, or ideological nature separated the two sides. It was simply a matter of two men personally trusting one another. The reclusive guerrilla leader seemed to come alive when he recalled the personal humiliations he and his men had suffered over the decades. What we do know for certain is that in the on-again, off-again peace negotiations between the FARC and five different governments since 1983 political reforms have not been seriously discussed.

Conversation Rituals

The rural guerrillas and the urban politicians of Colombia have lived a long half-century filled with intimacies and distances, expectations and fears, understandings and misunderstandings. Their relationship emerges from a broad political culture that the English historian Malcolm Deas (1997) describes as unusually "communicative, fluid, unmanichean." These personal histories have resulted, he states, in a "historiography [that] is rich in memoir, anecdote, incident, sketch; it is intimate, conversational, personal, even . . . in its recent revolutionary versions" (379–80). According to Jorge Orlando Melo, rural and urban leaders have participated in a culture of "continuous negotiations, agreements, amnesties, pardons and other processes of peace since 1901, including the ceaseless efforts from 1981 until now. Since 1954 or 1957, a negotiated peace has been seen as the only possible solution to the conflict."[15]

This discursive universe has been made possible by travels back and forth, with guerrillas coming to the city and, more often, with civilian leaders going out into the countryside, with negotiations, *discursos* (speeches), declarations, proclamations, petitions, calls, letters, committees, commissions, delegations, meetings, interviews, and conversations. Guerrillas and civilians have been engaged in a long ritual of intensely verbal peaceful exchanges that appear to be deeply meaningful and highly valued by all sides, but perhaps especially so, at least until recently, by those who have often proudly understood themselves to be *los de abajo* (those from below). Indeed, when seen from the countryside, these exchanges are vital. And from the very start it seems that one of the guerrilla leaders was particularly focused on them. Isauro Yosa recalls that back in the 1950s and 1960s Marulanda "did not like to drink and he did not like to fight. He dreamed about negotiating" (Molano 1994: 53).

The urban politicians and the rural guerrillas together have conformed to a highly gendered existence in which men encounter one another as males. Gatherings are convivial, tension-filled, and distrustful. They begin and end, whenever the hierarchical distance between these men is not too large, or whenever the suspicions are not overwhelming, with *abrazos,* or embraces. At times, formal *saludos,* greetings, have to do, a ceremonious, collective shaking of hands in some careful order, from the most important men of each side to the least. While these encounters are ritualized and culturally scripted, they are far from formulaic and can often be quite awkward. In March 2000, when a group of the most important capitalists of Colombia went out to meet with the guerrillas, they did not quite know how to greet one another. "They greeted the high commander of the guerrillas with one arm over his shoulder, as men greet one another when they sense that a handshake is not enough, but for whom an *abrazo* might be too much."[16]

Cigarettes are passed around, food is shared, and the men drink, usually whisky and brandy, foreign and elite drinks, rather than locally produced beer, rum, or the anise-flavored *aguardiente.* When Antonio Caballero went to interview Marulanda for the article cited earlier, the two men decided beforehand that they would try to avoid alcohol, for they could recall a meeting they had had fifteen years earlier with Jacobo Arenas, the now deceased second-in-command of the FARC, that had gotten so out of hand that "the next day we couldn't remember anything" that was said. Nevertheless, they did start their conversation on the second day, before sunrise, with "pure vodka in small *aguardiente* glasses."[17] When the American James LeMoyne, the UN envoy, went out in a last-ditch effort to salvage the peace negotiations on January 12, 2002, he demonstrated an uncanny sense of local custom when he took with him as a gift a bottle of eighteen-year-old Scotch whisky. The guerrillas reciprocated with their own offering, a twelve-year-old whisky.[18] LeMoyne and Joaquín Gómez, the main guerrilla negotiator, greeted one another with an "effusive *abrazo*."[19]

Politics in Colombia throughout this long period has never ceased to be an art form in which a few men, and now also a few women, get together in order to converse, to get to know one another, to try to reach deals. Personal and public conversations are still the stuff of which public life is made. There is electricity in the air in Colombia when these encounters take place. They call forth a deep sense of personal protagonism among the negotiators. The belief that each one of them might be the one to strike the deal that will bring peace to the nation is clearly intoxicating. These encounters are minutely described in the press. They even elicit something of a popular audience in a nation in which most people want to know little about politics. They are often intense, existential rituals.

The euphoria that filled the hearts of urban politicians and the leaders of the FARC as they traveled, drank, and sang together through Europe in February 2000, in what was dubbed the "Eurotour," reveals the meaningfulness of these encounters, as well as the deep and strong ties that can still bind the antagonists. When they arrived in Norway, "One of the best parties of the whole trip took place there. We were so happy that we almost got up on top of the tables," said one of the negotiators. "That's the way we Colombians are," exclaimed Victor G. Ricardo, the government's high commissioner for peace, "We talk about peace and also politics." "It was an exercise in *convivencia*," in living together in public life, declared Iván Ríos, the coordinator of the Thematic Committee, "which made us understand that we are all part of the same team." Rafael Reyes, one of the leaders of the FARC, declared, "We Colombians can't keep killing each other."[20]

Rarely far removed from these loquacious accounts is the pervasive sense of urban paternalism that lies at the heart of these conflicts. Even at such a moment of singular solidarity between the two sides, one observer could not help but draw the lines between them: "This has been something like the formal presentation in cultured society of a restless debutante."[21] There were some pretty heavy hangovers all around on the next morning, doubtless making the protagonists feel more equal than they actually were.

Origins: Inclusions

It all began long ago. One moment, one of many, is revealing. On December 20, 1951, the former president and elder statesman Alfonso López Pumarejo, at the time the head of the National Liberal Directorate, went hesitantly into the countryside, to the Llanos, the plains to the south and the west of the capital city of Bogotá, to visit with the rag-tag Liberal guerrilla bands that were seeking to defend themselves from the onslaught of the Conservatives, who were in power in Bogotá. He was sixty-six years old. At first he informed the guerrilla bands that he was coming, and then he demurred. The guerrillas wondered whether they were going to be left "with our hair all done up." What would happen to their "flags raised, our pretty girls all dressed up, the bread and marmalade, the bottles of wishky [sic], the cigarettes, and all those things that everybody contributed? Oh, what a great disappointment and what a waste of all that energy, from many leagues around, if the *jefe*, the chief, does not come!" López's visit and the life of the guerrillas of the Llanos is told in marvelously flavorful detail by Eduardo Franco Isaza (1959), a guerrilla leader (262–67).

During this period, the rural insurgents in various parts of the country felt a great deal of admiration for their urban leaders. Reading the newspapers for guidance and information, they followed their urban careers, knew something about their personalities, their oratory, the strength of their convictions. The liberal guerrillas accepted unquestioningly the leadership of the liberal elites. To them it was self-evident that their *jefes* were superior to them. The insurgents traveled often to Bogotá to talk to their leaders. They stayed in their homes, took money from them, protected them as they traveled around the city. The rebels were constantly looking for direction from the city, for *orientación*. Marulanda tells his lieutenant IsauroYosa, "We have to send one of our own to Bogotá to see what kind of *orientación* they have for us" (Molano 1994: 44–45). In the mid-1940s, Yosa, also known as Mister Lister, and one of the first liberal guerrillas to later join the communists, or the *comunes* as they were more informally known, recalled his encounter in the city with the civilian leaders. With a healthy sense of irony, he proudly remembers the *intervención personal* of one of them, Alberto Lleras Camargo, the leader of the party. "We came back feeling very good because we had a chance to greet a *doctor* who was so high and mighty." Mail from the city was their lifeline. "We were just about to leave [for the city]," recalls Yosa, "when they started to yell at us, to come, to come. A letter had arrived from Bogotá" (Molano 1994: 29, 46). They knew many of the national leaders personally. The guerrillas talked about national politics all the time. Rumors flew. They were constantly awaiting the next coup d'état against the Conservative government.

López Pumarejo did finally show up in the Llanos, but only once he had secured a group of military men to back him up. His arrival created "huge expectations and great uproar" on the part of the men in arms and among the surrounding rural population. Once he had gotten off his horse, the former president of the republic was "surrounded by a people anxiously looking at his every gesture and listening carefully to each of his words," recalls Franco Isaza (1959).

The guerrillas made formal, elaborate plans to receive López, whom they referred to as *el doctor*. This traditional term of respect and admiration for those who could offer a public image of men of culture and knowledge, whether they had professional degrees or not, has hung on longer in Colombia than elsewhere in Latin America. The Liberal statesman was also referred to more intimately as "*el viejo* Alfonso." Once the "old man" had arrived and all the initial salutations had been taken care of, the protagonists engaged in various rounds of conversation over a period of two days. Many of the guerrillas had their opportunity to participate, and jokes were made by all as a sense of confidence and conviviality developed. They drank. Franco Isaza asked a colonel, "Sir, will you drink a whisky?" "Gentleman, I will drink a whisky!" the colonel responded. "To Colombia! Salud, *caballeros!*"

López, however, remained cautious, almost aloof. "El doctor López caressed his glass, hardly touching his drink." Nevertheless, "there was happiness, the knives cut the meat, plates were passed all around. The *tiples* and the *maracas* sounded out a good *joropo*. Guns were passed from one *guerrillero* to another *guerrillero*." They talked and talked. Little of substance was discussed, but that did not much matter. "Groups formed, and many things were discussed, and following that habit that we Colombians have, there were plenty of *discursos*. It was a fraternal party."

The *guerrilleros* understood that López's very presence legitimated them as carriers of a broad tradition of liberalism and connected them to the party, the city, other guerrilla groups, and the nation. "Thus the hours passed, without anything concrete being dealt with. We were taking on airs, feeling good. . . . Many must have thought that important things were being discussed, but the important questions had not been broached. We were sounding things out, and without much having been said, one thing was clear. The *bandoleros,* the bandits, were not *bandoleros,* we were revolutionaries. This is what the presence of el doctor López in the Llanos was singing out, and right here in the guerrilla headquarters. Tomorrow and the day after, the newspapers would publish this, and the pictures would appear." The guerrillas desperately sought the legitimating mantle of the politicians.

López's visit was a victory for *los de abajo* because it meant that they were not *bandoleros.* This was a matter of deep personal pride for all of them. They could now be referred to as *revolucionarios,* "and not that other word that so hurts the spirit, that is hammered away at in the daily papers, that so demoralizes poor humiliated people, and hurts more than a bayonet thrust into the chest: *bandoleros.*"

These words may have a melodramatic and propagandistic ring to them as they are read and understood today, outside the immediate context of the rural combatant's lives. But they are deeply revealing. For many of these *guerrilleros,* the difference between being a bandit and a revolutionary was a matter of honor. If they were bandits, they acted for themselves, selfishly, for loot. As revolutionaries, they were at the service of the Liberal Party, of liberty—their highest ideological aspiration—and of the nation. They could understand themselves as part of the large historical project of Colombian and world liberalism, however vaguely they might understand that ideology. As revolutionaries they acted in a disinterested manner. They were more than themselves, more than each of them to themselves. Even more existentially, perhaps, as bandits they could only be local actors. For if they were *bandoleros,* the liberal leaders could clearly not endorse them, support them, be with them. As *bandoleros,* they were disconnected from the nation. As revolutionaries, they were Colombians, patriots. As *bandoleros,* they were forgotten, isolated, living in silence. The rural combatants could not do without their urban leaders. Without them they could have no honor. Without them, they were alone. The rural guerrillas feared nothing more.

Honor and Humiliation

The protagonists in these conversations and these conflicts are men driven by a desire to be recognized, not only as individuals, but principally as part of something larger than themselves. Theirs is a world defined by honor, and when seen in its long historical trajectory in Colombia during this half-century, especially by the loss of honor, by humiliation.

Much of the literature on honor deals with the worlds of antiquity,[22] with the U.S. South (Wyatt-Brown 1983, 2001; Greenberg 1985), and as a phenomenon that emerges from a Mediterranean ethos (Peristiany 1966). The places of honor in Latin America have been better understood for the colonial period than for the twentieth century, and much of our knowledge there deals with the relationship between men, women, and sexuality. Ann Twinam (1998) offers a fine sense of the meaning of honor when she locates it in the public lives of those in the colonial period in Spanish America: "[H]onor was not an internalized prescription for proper ethical action—it was not primarily synonymous with integrity, or honesty, or virtue—although proper action might be necessary to conserve or to pass on honor. Instead, honor was located in the public sphere, where an individual's reputation was malleable and ultimately defined by other peers" (33). Glen Caudill Dealy (1992) sees honor as one of the essential beliefs and forms of behavior of what he terms "caudillaje civilization."

Honor is seen to be part of traditional social orders in which public relationships are more personal than they are contractual, and in societies that are culturally hierarchical. The explicit ranking of individuals and groups is accepted and encouraged. According to J. A. Pitt-Rivers (1961), "He in whom authority is vested, must possess the necessary manliness in order that he may be submitted to without humiliation" (157). Honor becomes one of the key forms of exchange among individuals of unequal status. It speaks to the individual's public role in society. According to the classic definition of T. V. Smith (1932), "Honor is an open acknowledgement of external demand, but an acknowledgement which through pride has become enthroned in the very citadel of the self" (7:456). For Pitt-Rivers (1966), "Honor is the value of a person in his own eyes, but also in the eyes of society. . . . Honor, therefore, provides a nexus between the ideals of a society and their reproduction in the individual through his aspiration to personify them" (21–22).

The humiliation of human beings who sense the need to live with honor is, of course, a universal phenomenon.[23] But we might venture that it has a particularly conspicuous place in the history of Colombia. Daniel Pécaut (2000), the French historical sociologist, seems to have found it so when he first came to Colombia in the early 1960s:

> I sensed that a sentiment of humiliation of the subaltern classes had been created throughout the history of Colombia, one that is very different from the pure sense of poverty. "Humiliation" is the opposite of what the elites called the *clases humildes,* the humble classes. This sentiment has everything to do with the fact that real social and civil rights have not been consecrated. It is not just a matter of concrete rights, but of the lack of a national symbolism capable of making everyone feel like they are members of one same political community. (120)

This humiliation, in his view, made for a prevalence of narrow "ties of social dependency," of local, clientelistic, and arbitrary networks that worked against a more collective, democratic, and egalitarian social order (121). Humiliation, in other words, either depleted nationhood or was an expression of its sparse existence.

While the widespread sense of humiliation that makes itself deeply felt across time in the lives of many Colombians may well be the result of a dearth of more reciprocal forms of behavior in a hierarchical social order, it is only possible for individuals to feel humiliated when they are keenly aware that something is missing. Humiliation is also an expression, a painful one of course, of the very vitality of personal and nationalistic bonds in Colombia. For human beings can feel humiliated by others when they have deep emotional connections to them, when the relationships that they have established are meaningful and people have invested themselves in them, when these relationship embody expectations of reciprocity. In Colombia, individuals are humiliated precisely because they feel tied to others who are above them in the social order and wish to share with them thoughts, ideas, ideals, heroes, and a belief in a better society. Together they can shout, *"¡Viva el Partido Liberal!"* and *"¡Viva el Partido Conservador!"* and *"¡Abajo el Partido Liberal!"* and *"¡Viva Colombia!"*

Individuals and groups can be humiliated when they feel that have the right to make claims, *clamar* and *reclamar* (to clamor for), to use the felicitous words that Michael Jiménez (forthcoming) employs to describe the underpinning of the social bargaining that he sees as being at the heart of social relations in the Colombian countryside in the first half of the twentieth century. This humiliation appears to be deepest when those claims are rejected from above and the expected connections are broken. For the political parties in both their narrow clientelistic networks and their broad ideological messages had made deep connections throughout the Colombian countryside beginning shortly after independence almost a century ago (Deas 1983). These connections intensified dramatically in the 1940s as Jorge Eliécer Gaitán mobilized thousands upon thousands of Colombians in towns and villages throughout the nation, promising them a new and more intimate integration into the life of Colombia (see Braun 1986). That promise vanished with the actions of a lone assassin one rainy Friday afternoon in Bogotá. These social ties unraveled yet again in 1952, as we will see in the next section. Much of the vitality of the Colombian nation, although by no means all of it, comes from below.

Origins: Exclusions

While the *guerrilleros* sensed that they were being betrayed, the *jefes* in the city saw matters far differently. They were not about to lead their rural clientele in an armed rebellion against the Conservative government. To their minds, this would be the height of irresponsibility. Alfonso López had made this patently clear to the guerrillas of the Llanos when he went to visit them in 1951. On August 25, 1952, López wrote a long letter to the moderate Conservative and former president Mariano Ospina Pérez. He made it clear that he and his Liberal colleagues understood that they would almost certainly have to break their ties to their followers. For the sake of peace, they were willing to do so. "If this is 'the last chance of the Liberal leaders to meet their historical destiny,' as the *jefes* of the armed revolt in the countryside claim it to be, then we are prepared to lose it. What is more, we are prepared for a definite break with the people, rather than fail to lead and serve the people as we feel is best for them, or to deprive public confidence of the seriousness of our convictions and purposes that we represent in our pursuit of a politics of peace and understanding" (Franco Isaza 1959: 291). To fight would be to lose their hard-earned place as civilian politicians who believed in the viability of their institutions. It would be to go against everything they believed in.

Eduardo Santos made the point just as dramatically. On March 3, 1953, he wrote: "It is impossible to fight against an organized army with guns, revolvers, and clubs. I publicly desire that all this come to an end, that these forms of struggle be abandoned, that we decide only on civil actions that require as much valor, perhaps even more. Through the paths of armed violence, guerrillas, and civil war, liberalism has nothing to gain and much to lose" (Franco Isaza 1959: 227). To fight would be to lose on the battlefield and to be left with nothing. To urge their followers to get up and fight would be to demand that many give up their lives in a bloodbath that could have no positive results for anyone. This was something that the Liberals were clearly not prepared to undertake. They would not ask for such a huge human sacrifice when little if anything was to be gained from it.

Many of the *jefes* must also have understood that the guerrillas would not put down their guns. López did. "The revolutionaries consider the politics of peace that we have been pursuing to be dead and consequently consider any collaboration with the opposition, that is, with the government, with the Conservatives, to be impossible. Logically, from their standpoint, they invite us to join them in the movement to which they have dedicated themselves" (Franco Isaza 1959: 290). As López and his colleagues faced this plethora of claims from below, they must have sensed that while there was considerable respect for them from below, the "general picture of Colombian society is not one of deference," as Malcolm Deas (1997) would put it years later (362).

The Liberals were between a rock and a hard place, and they knew it. The very existence of the Liberal bands made it possible for the Conservative government to increase its violence against them, and they could do little to bring those bands back into the civilian institutions of the land. To fight would be to play into the Conservatives' hands. The Liberal leaders removed themselves from their followers and lived in the cities, and many went into exile.

The guerrillas had feared this result from the start. At the very beginning of his short visit to the Llanos, López recounted, strangely enough, an anecdote from his youth. He had been ill for months, had visited doctors in London, and been put under all kinds of treatments and medications, all to no avail. He went to New York, where he found "the best doctor, a very intelligent Yankee," who told him to just forget about all the treatments. "Don't do anything. Stop worrying," the doctor told him, and young López quickly left his illness behind. "You see, Franco, what an easy solution," López concluded (Franco Isaza 1959:264).

Franco's immediate thoughts on hearing López's story are telling. "I reflected for an instant, and thought that maybe the old fox was trying to give us that infallible remedy for that terrible evil that is a rebellion: to forget us." Franco Isaza's testimony is filled with this fear. "The army would come and then we would be overcome, caught, shot or imprisoned, as though we were just a bunch of common delinquents. Who would come to our defense? Who could go with authority to say that were not *bandoleros,* but men, sons of the Nation, who rose up in rebellion because of the official violence against us?" (264). They lived in anguish. It was one thing to be attacked, quite another to be left alone. As the Liberal leaders removed themselves more and more, Franco writes, "our party became speechless," and he refers to the "disastrous muteness," of "deaf Liberal leaders." His mind fills with images of "the people alone," of "infinite solitude" and "sticky silence" (173). Being alone, roaming the countryside, and protecting themselves from the well-armed and organized *chulavitas,* the state-sanctioned murderers who were out to kill them, was a terrible fate.

As it dawned on the *guerrilleros* that they were indeed being left out in the cold, they reacted with visceral disgust for the *notables,* as they also referred to their leaders. Franco Isaza's text drips sarcasm. "'We do not authorize and we do not unauthorize'—said *el doctor* Lleras Restrepo—'tell those boys that our hearts are with them'." (Franco Isaza 1959: 153). "'What great *jefes* we have!' Tulio said in a rage" (63). "'Those crazy old men will have us killed without even knowing what time of day it happens,' Minuto concluded sarcastically" (63). "At the same time, the leaders, the intellectuals and the privileged classes of liberalism hide behind their ivory towers, making that small effort to keep quiet, forgetting all the words they have said in their fancy gatherings and in the newspapers" (64). Marulanda thought the dilemma through in perhaps the simplest manner. He was beginning to think "that what the *doctores* of the liberal directorate said was a bunch of shit" (Molano 1994: 66).

The *guerrilleros* turned on the *jefes.* "They plan and they talk of revolution, conspiracies, systems, and panaceas to solve immediate problems. Brilliant theories, so characteristic of all the meetings of the *notables.* . . . What do the *guerrilleros* care about what the *notables* do or say? The *discursos* are totally worthless" (Franco Isaza 1959: 66–67). The guerrillas rejected the civilian leaders because they did not act like real men. Pusillanimous, cautious, and frightened, they did not stand up for what they thought and believed. The guerillas knew exactly which of the *notables* was where and complained that the leaders were off in Mexico City, London, Paris, and Washington, D.C. The guerrillas found it hard to comprehend that López would not even seek to defend his own home in the city when it was burned by a Conservative mob.

Franco sensed that what they were fighting for was something that had previously been theirs. "We young people of today have to fight for something that was lost and that we didn't really know we had until it was gone, when we lost our possessions and were *humillados,* our houses violated and our families in mourning" (Franco Isaza 1959: 77).

Manuel Marulanda's cry is most plaintive:

What plans do they have? What do the Llerases, the Lopezes say? Nothing. Silenced. What does the departmental Liberal Directorate say? Very little news. Absolutely nothing. They stopped opening their mouths. They stripped themselves of thoughts, they stopped thinking, filled with actual, physical fear. Or they are just not doing anything, lost over there in the legal haze of the cities. . . . This is a very complicated situation. It seems that everything has changed. So we have to find a solution. We said to ourselves, "But with whom, with whom do we find it? To whom do we appeal?" Guns? Where are they? How do we get them? If we just stay like this here, they will kill us all. The body just cannot take any more *humillación.* (Alape 1989: 107–8, 77–78)[24]

The *guerrilleros* saw their predicament in masculine terms. When the violence caught up with them, their honor was stripped away.

We escaped like rats. We felt like weak creatures, our consciences filled with a sense of emptiness and misery. They were the strong ones, the powerful ones, who had a right to everything, even a right to our feelings, for they were the conquerors. That is why they took the woman. Maybe she agreed to be taken by them, the ancestral powers overwhelming an aroused female, the feeling of being a desired prey singing in her veins. I felt the despair of *humillación* and jealousy. I, the fugitive rebel, no longer had the right to the company and the love of women. None of us could walk with our head held high. Our companion could be nothing more than the *soledad,* the solitude, all around us. Time slipped by slowly, and an embarrassed *silencio,* silence, turned us mute. Nobody spoke. We crossed furtive looks, pretending not to know. (Franco Isaza 1959: 163)

Solitude

The fear of being alone, of solitude or *soledad,* appears to be a central, driving force in Colombian history. Little studied by historians, it is one of the major themes in Colombian letters. In an essay titled "Solitude and Sociability," in the daily *El Tiempo* in 1952, Eduardo Caballero Calderón, one of the nation's finest authors, concluded that the worst levels of violence took place in those areas where the *campesino* lived "more alone and absorbed in himself, almost without contact with the social medium . . . where he lives materially and spiritually most isolated, confined to his hut. . . . If we do not defeat this *soledad* of the *campesino,* which is his worst enemy, we will not be able to turn him into a civilized being, or into a social animal."[25]

According to Gene Bell-Villada (1990), Gabriel García Márquez is "among the most powerful writers of human solitude and isolation, of abandonment and loss, of the lonely battle for survival, of desolation and even 'alienation.' Few solitudes in fiction can compare with that of the illegitimate Aureliano Babilonia, friendless and bereaved, with total knowledge being scant consolation as Macondo rushes to its end" (12). The solitude not only of Colombia but of Latin America was also the theme of García Márquez's (1988) acceptance speech when he won the 1982 Nobel Prize for Literature. He lamented the great distance between Latin America and the rest of the world, its "cultural remoteness" and its misapprehension by the major powers.

In his classic novel about the violence of the 1950s, *El Cristo de espaldas,* Eduardo Caballero Calderón (1978) evokes life in a "remote" and "anonymous" "sad town," filled with "desolation," where rank-and-file members of the two political parties conspire against one another for their own economic and political gain by enveloping their private desires in the cloak of public purposes. The novel revolves around a young priest who wishes to go out there and minister to the good people of the town. The bishop warns him: "'If you may be able to find a spiritual paradise in that small town, in that *silencio,* in that *soledad,* in that absence of the world, in the simplicity of its customs, its simple town life, you can also fall flat on your face, without even knowing when, in that small hell of petty things'" (29). It takes only a day or so for the priest to be engulfed in the silence, and he can't deal with it. "It is a dead landscape," he moans. "It is death, and behind the death of these things there is only *el silencio*. . . . That flat and superficial *silencio* terrifies me, as though here the land were always dying, and its cadaver always dissolving into a dense and sticky fog. My God! Why this *soledad*, this desolation, this death?" (141).

These *soledades* are felt when expected social exchanges are found to be lacking. In Colombia, Benjamin Franklin's second virtue, silence ("Speak not but what would benefit others or yourself; avoid trifling conversation"), is difficult to practice.[26] While in the United States the wilderness is seen mythically as the place of purity where the individual, off by himself, can find himself, Colombians are constantly in search of one another, of conversation, of being in society. Happiness is found in the recognition offered by others, not in solitude.[27] Dignity and honor are based on reciprocity. Rarely in Colombian history have groups or individuals gone off into the countryside to build small communities with their backs to society.[28] There are few, if any, separatist movements in the history of Colombia.

The *guerrilleros* strove mightily against this solitude. Their many efforts were directed at being collective organizations, *entidades,* or entities. Being disciplined, cohesive, and organized had much to do with basic human survival. They searched for

> [an] entity that could gather the *guerrillas* and organize them toward unified tasks, in intimate association and contact with the government, but responsive and responsible to our own people. An entity that would be the result of all of our sacrifice and that at every moment would represent our people. An entity that would achieve the great unification of the Llanos and would spread liberalism to the people as a whole, overcoming the distances created by the damned *chulavitas*. An organized force capable of obligating the government and whomever else to comply with what had been agreed to. (Franco Isaza 1959: 324)

It was also an effort to keep from becoming *bandoleros*. The guerrillas were constantly recounting their exploits. Franco Isaza (1959) tells of one *guerrillero:* "'Attention everyone! Please pay attention to me,' he yelled out. 'I am General Eliseo Velásquez López, who comes before you to open up his heart in this land to defend the people. I am the one who . . .'" Then Franco states, "There followed a long *discurso*" (101). The guerrillas were always talking, "conversing." "And we started a very animated conversation in the good old *llanero* style, about horses and cowboys, and about rebellions and conjectures, and about our next adventures" (51). They made sure they remembered who they were and what they had done. They called it *hacer historia*, to do history, to recall it. "After doing history and examining the entire situation we were in from the beginning, we got serious and began to elaborate a program" (324).

Urbanity

The tension between the city and the countryside—between a Peoria and a Manhattan, to put it in U.S. terms—is of course a universal characteristic throughout history. "A contrast between country and city as fundamental ways of life," notes Raymond Williams (1973), "reaches back into classical times" (1). This contrast plays in various ways in different places. The countryside has been shunned by Colombians throughout history. Ever since the Spanish colonial imprint, life has revolved around the city (Rama 1996). The countryside represents desolation. Life in the city is the promise of *convivencia,* the rational and cultured living together among others in society. In 1956, the Conservative thinker and politician Azula Barrera expressed this yearning for an urban ideal. "[To] Bogotá . . . gentle, insular, and Mediterranean city, has fallen the task, since colonial times, of forming a nation around her, guiding it, defining its destiny, maintaining it united and compact . . . and being at all times the ancestral home to which come Colombians from the most remote places of the country in search of culture, great national prestige, the fulfillment of an ambitious dream, or, simply, a comfortable and tranquil existence under the shelter of her hospitality."

Today, the ancestral home of Gabriel García Márquez, the nation's most celebrated citizen, in far-off Aracataca, lies in disrepair. Few Colombians would think of visiting it, whether it were safe to do so or not, even though it is a national monument.[29] The columnist Andrés Hurtado García now bemoans this urban bias. "I definitely get very angry at Colombians for whom Miami is the most beautiful city of Colombia. . . . Definitely, in order to fix this country, we have to change the heart of Colombians. That's it."[30]

The past in Colombia is a rural, whispered country. It is understood to be primitive. Colombians react with understandable fear and disgust when reminded of the violence that racked the countryside in the 1950s and beyond. In the 1960s, the cultured elites and most of those, both rich and poor, who lived in urban centers were able to turn away from the past with the carefully constructed, conciliatory, and rational rules of the bipartisan Frente Nacional governments (1958–74).

All along, the violence of the countryside was paradoxically also understood in these cultured and urban circles as somehow predictable, for it was the expression of a dark underside of the Colombian nation that made itself felt in the intrinsically narrow and enclosed lives of provincial, ignorant, and superstitious rural folk. They were whispered about, often quite loudly.

Perhaps more so than any previous generation of leaders, those who separated themselves from their followers in the early 1950s and built the coalition governments by which they could rule together were urban men. They lived at a far greater distance from the countryside and its rustic ways than did those leaders of the previous century who had led their men into battle. They were lawyers and engineers, poets and writers, journalists and intellectuals, men of civilian politics. Some indeed were landowners, and affluent ones at that, but they no longer saw their rural workers as men whom they could take away from their labor and encourage to rise up for the bellicose aims of their respective political parties. Indeed, there can be little doubt that they would feel downright foolish doing so.

These men were concerned for their followers, to be sure, even though they held them at a distance and generally thought little of the promise of their lives. They looked down on rural folk. There is no question that from the city they had urged them on to defend the ideals of the party just a few years before and that these calls had often led to violence and to death. The newspapers were filled with this partisan verbal warfare. The American ambassador, Willard Beaulac, was disconcerted by it all in 1947. "But violence, I found, was more or less taken for granted. . . . Within a few months of my arrival, open warfare between partisans of the two political parties had broken out in several provinces. . . . I could not find," he states, chillingly, "that these things caused excessive concern in Bogotá." The ambassador, found, much to his shock, that "press reports and editorials, and the no less violent statements of certain political leaders exacerbated feelings and incited further violence." He referred to the leaders of Colombia as "complacent democrats" (Beaulac 1958: 226, 556).

The Liberals' best and perhaps only option was to leave those struggles behind. We are reminded of the anecdote about the gringo doctor that

López recounted for Franco Isaza's benefit. "Don't do anything. Just stop worrying." Letting go of the mysterious forces of the dark countryside may have been an idea widely shared at the time. In *El Cristo de espaldas,* the bishop speaks to his frustrated young priest, who has returned to the city after having failed to minister to his flock: "Wait a minute, dear man of God. There is time for everything. You have to learn that in the small towns there are no problems that can't be left for another day. Since by and large they solve themselves, my experience has taught me that it is best not to solve them at all" (Caballero Calderón 1978: 118).

But matters did not take care of themselves in the countryside. In the 1950s, modernizing, populist, and reformist governments in other Latin American countries were seeking various ways to integrate the countryside more thoroughly into the fabric of the nation and to build stronger and more inclusive state institutions. Nothing like the agrarian reform instituted from above by Lázaro Cárdenas in Mexico in the 1930s or the agrarian revolution spawned from below in 1948 in Bolivia made itself felt in Colombia. Nor did the country experience a populist movement like that of Getulio Vargas in Brazil or Juan Domingo Peron in Argentina. Quite the contrary. In Colombia the political elites found that they were trying to disentangle themselves from the widespread, often intimate, personal connections that had for many decades tied those followers emotionally, even passionately, to them. In that chasm, in that breakdown in the relationships between urban leaders and their rural followers, the current conflicts were born. Colombia's history is distinctive compared to its neighbors in the middle years of the past century. Its guerrilla movement remains alive today, alone in Latin America.

The Controversy of the Towel and Other Discordant Encounters

The meetings between the urban politicians and the rural guerrillas were renewed some thirty years after the break between them took place. "*!Que haiga paz!*" "Let there be peace!" Manuel Marulanda had exclaimed in grammatically incorrect, lower-class, folk Spanish as the La Uribe peace negotiations were getting underway in 1984. Alfredo Molano (1994) recalls that the "doors of Casa Verde [the FARC guerrilla headquarters, destroyed in 1991 by a massive military attack ordered by then president César Gaviria] opened up, and then Colombians learned who the commanders of the FARC were. They heard Marulanda talk, and Jacobo. They heard Cano and Raúl Reyes talk. More than one was surprised that they knew how to speak Spanish, and many took Marulanda's phrase '¡Que haiga paz!' as evidence of the level of backwardness of the guerrillas" (207). Marulanda, who had then already been fighting for some thirty-five years, was still little known. He was out in the countryside. Sensational rumors about his capture and death, more than anything else about him, surfaced time and again in urban circles during the 1960s, 1970s, and 1980s (Molano 1994: 207).

The old guerrilla leaders think about the past. For the urban politicians, the past doesn't matter. When President Pastrana went out to meet with Marulanda in el Caguán on January 7, 1999, the president declared, "Today we have come to keep an appointment with history. We have delayed half a century in doing so" (Zuleta Nieto et al. 1999). The president was right, for while there had been many such encounters before, they had hardly dealt with the fifty-year history of the conflicts. It appeared that at long last the head of state was going to address them. But he did not. Marulanda, who did not show up, sending a representative in his stead, had little other than the past on his mind. Just like the *guerrilleros* of the Llanos that we have seen before, Marulanda had to *hacer historia,* to account for the past and for his actions and those of his opponents during years past. His spokesman, who read the guerrilla leader's *discurso,* made a detailed recounting of what had happened since the early 1960s. He thanked his guest for coming, for this meeting "was the first in thirty-four years of armed confrontations declared by the state in 1964 against forty-eight men, with the military and economic assistance of the United States, which handed over to Guillermo León Valencia, the president at the time, five hundred million pesos to get rid of the so-called 'independent republics,' which existed only in the minds of the Congress and in the head of *el doctor* Alvaro Gómez Hurtado, may he rest in peace, who led a forced debate against them in order to justify the repression." And the guerrilla leader went on to recall the early 1990s, when the army had come in and dislodged them from their headquarters at Casa Verde. "With that new aggression, the official army took from us three hundred mules, seventy horses, forty pigs, two hundred chickens, fifty tons of food" (Zuleta Nieto et al. 1999: 300–305).

The guerrilla's words sounded strange, out of place. These petty details about chickens taken from them years before did not seem to fit such a momentous historical occasion. Some of the urban guests were startled. Others smiled, giving off that smugness that is so much a part of urban condescension. They must have wondered whom they were dealing with, whether this small campesino was really up to the task of engaging in serious political discussions.

But Marulanda's words were precise and meaningful. He thought about the past constantly, for that was what his struggle was all about. He felt the wounds of years gone by, of being betrayed, of being attacked, and once again, in 1990, of being forced from his home, from his belongings, his chickens, cattle, and pigs, for these were the staples of guerrilla life. He felt humiliated once again, and he tried to let his urban counterparts know. But they could not understand. Marulanda had keenly sensed the deep distance between him and the urban politicians, for he complained about how the guerrillas had been forgotten and left behind. He referred to what had happened, tellingly, as a "manipulated, partial amnesia" (Zuleta Nieto et al. 1999: 295).

We may now begin to better understand the words that Arturo Alape took down from Marulanda many years ago and that so surprised me when I first read them in 1989. "It's been many years that we have been in this struggle," he said. "We've had, I think, one enemy, the worst of all enemies. You know what it is? I am talking about the isolation of this struggle, which is worse than going hungry for a whole week. Between you, you of the city and us, we who've been out here, there is a huge mountain. It's not a distance of lands and rivers, of natural obstacles. Your voices and ours don't speak to each other. There's little about us that's known among you, and around here there's little of your history that we know" (Alape 1989: 19).

These are hardly the sentiments of a man who has risen up against a social order. They are more nearly the feelings of a man who has been saddened all these years by having been left on the outside. Here is a man who appears to be struggling to be included, to be part of the nation, to be honored and respected. In the words of José Jairo González Arias, the guerrillas search less for political reforms, no matter how broad and generous they may be, than for a "share of the very heart of power."[31] How much political power the guerrillas can achieve, and at what levels, and how they would be included in the governing institutions of the nation, now depends on their military power and on the willingness of the civilian politicians to broker a deal. But up to this point the question of political power has not been broached.

When President Andrés Pastrana went out into the countryside for his third, historic visit with Marulanda on February 8 and 9, 2001, the urban columnist María Isabel Rueda, writing in *Semana*, seemed to discover the guerrilla leader all over again. She saw in him the "natural cunning of this malicious and distrustful campesino." She understood that many in Colombia looked down on him. "Not even the fact that he is an authentic campesino—which leads some people to think simplistically that he is ignorant and naïve—not even the fact that he carries many years on his shoulders, has kept Manuel Marulanda from being who he is: the one who commands the guerrilla movement."[32]

In February 2000, the *Revista Cambio*, owned by Gabriel García Márquez, reported on a meeting of the guerrillas and urban politicians with typical urban wit:

> One could have the feeling that the same thing happens to the guerrilla commanders as happens to the military generals: that when they take off their olive green uniforms, they lose presence. But when one sees them surrounded by all the high negotiators of the peace, each one carefully attentive to the slightest wink of any of the members of the FARC, you can tell their "specific difference," as the Jesuits used to say. It is then that one can tell who they really are, a movement of campesino stock and manners. They have forgotten their urban origins and their dreams of a high school education. . . . Not a single one of them—except Simón Trinidad, who is the only one who knows how to fix his tie in the English rather than the American style—not a single one of them looks comfortable wearing a suit. They look like they are wearing a costume.[33]

On February 14, 2001, Elvira Cuervo, the director of the National Museum in Bogotá, provoked a national controversy when she suggested that Marulanda's towel—one of those "white fringed towels" that Alma Guillermoprieto had observed flung over the *guerrillero*'s shoulder in 1986—be included in a temporary exhibit, along with other items of the nation's material culture, such as the suit worn by presidential candidate Luis Carlos Galán when he was shot dead, and the hat of the urbane M19 guerrilla leader, Carlos Pizarro Leongómez, who was killed on an airplane in midair as he too was running for the presidency. Arguing for the inclusion of the towel in the museum, she stated: "This is a country without memory. . . . Nations that do not know their history are condemned to repeat it."[34] Some were in favor of including the towel, most were not. Others thought the debate frivolous.

The debate inspired famed *El Tiempo* columnist D'Artagnan to unsheath his pen. In the main, he was against the idea, for a towel was too personal, too private an item to display. But should Cuervo decide to go ahead, he hoped that the towel in question would be one that had been well used and cleaned, but not ironed or starched. For if it were, it would become "stiff and sand-papery, making its use risky when it comes to drying what doctors and bullfighters scientifically call the scrotum, that which covers the testicles, what the rest of us mere mortals know affectionately as balls."[35]

The Future

> All Colombians, in their own ways and according to their possibilities, have to do what they can for the nation. People have to be told or reminded what it means in life to have a nation. And perhaps the best way of doing so is by displaying the loss, the *soledad*, the bewilderment, that digs into the very depth of our being when we don't have a nation, or we can't enjoy it because so many threats cause its absence.
>
> Iván Marulanda, "El que quiere país, que ayude hacerlo,"
> *El Espectador*, February 16, 2001[36]

Marulanda's speech of January 7, 1999, from which we have quoted extensively, ends with a call for *reconciliación* (reconciliation) and for the *reconstrucción* (reconstruction) of the country. These two words appear time and again in the declarations of the *guerrilleros* and in their conversations with the urban leaders. The latter term appears at times in the discourse of the politicians, but as *construcción* (construction), not *reconstrucción*. They speak, as do contemporary scholars of nation building, in terms of *la construcción de nación*. Without a past, or with one that has scant meaning, there is little left to rebuild, *reconstruir*. They talk instead of the future, of one that will be better than the past. But for the guerrillas it is also a matter of restoring the ties broken in the past. It is a matter of history.

The term *reconciliación* is absent from the language of the civilian politicians. This is perhaps understandable. In the eyes of the urban politicians, especially the Liberals but Conservatives as well, their past actions do not constitute aggression against their rural followers, especially not at the beginning. They did not engage in an onslaught against the rural population. Quite the contrary. As we have seen, the politicians sought to remove themselves from the lives of their rural clientele. They can understand their actions as being for the good of rural folk. They have not seen themselves as responsible for the violence that took place, even though they must understand at some level that they cannot extricate themselves from it entirely. Living in the city, surrounded by others, in constant social and political activity, in endless conversations, building civilian coalitions, seeking to restore peace, they can have little idea of the desolation and the *soledad* in which the guerrillas were left in the early 1950s and from which they have been trying to extricate themselves ever since. They do not perceive a historical relationship with the guerrillas. For them, there is nothing to *reconciliar* (reconcile).

It is little wonder then, that Andrés Pastrana thought that not much more than a good personal relationship with Manuel Marulanda was needed to bring the conflict to an end. When it did not turn out to be so easy, the president felt humiliated, his honor challenged. Perhaps now he can begin to understand how Eduardo Franco Isaza, and Manuel Marulanda Vélez—Tirofijo—and the rest of the guerrillas felt in the 1950s when they were left to fend for themselves, alone in the countryside. For the urban politicians and the rural guerrillas share a culture defined by a need to be treated honorably and by an abiding quest for sociability.

Notes

1. For recent expressions of the ideas held by the leaders of the FARC, see Lozano Guillén (2002), Comisión Temática FARC-EP (2001), and Corporación Observatorio para la Paz (2001).

2. José Jairo González Arias, "*Remember* a Tirofijo," *Coyuntura Política,* December 1998, 8–11.

3. Pilar Lozano, "Manuel Marulanda, 'Tirofijo,'" *El País* (Madrid, Spain), November 26, 2000.

4. For an inside account of the deep and violent divisions between the rural rebels of the ELN and the urban students who sought to join the guerrilla organization, see Arenas (1971). For a softer but no less critical view of these relations, see Correa Arboleda (1997).

5. For empathic, almost loving, early accounts of the M19, see Lara (1986), Restrepo (1986), Asencio and Asencio (1983), and Carrigan (1993). Two revealing testimonies are Grabe (2000) and Vázquez Perdomo (2000). No such testimonial accounts exist for the rural insurgencies. The prominence of female writers on and of this self-consciously heroic movement is notable. For the rhythms of these different rebellions, see Braun (2003).

6. The most complete biography of Camilo Torres is still *Camilo Torres: A Biography of the Priest-Guerrillero,* by Walter J. Broderick (1975), who is also recently the author (as Joe Broderick) of *El guerrillero invisible* (2000), which contains, in vol. 1, a splendid biography of Santiago Pérez, the Spanish priest who was one of the founders of the ELN. Manuel Marulanda Vélez, with his deeply local rural political roots, and Manuel Pérez, with his more cosmopolitan and intellectual background, offer a telling contrast.

7. "¿Yo capturé a Marulanda?" *Semana.com,* February 24, 2001, retrieved August 3, 2005, from http://semana2.terra.com.co/archivo/articulosView.jsp?id=17039.

8. Jacobo Arenas died of natural causes in 1990.

9. Germán Santamaría, "Cuatro años después," *Revista Diners,* March 2002, 12–19.

10. Ibid., 12–19.

11. For a fine analysis of this central dimension of Colombian politics, see Wilde (1982).

12. Santamaría, "Cuatro años después," 12–19.

13. Antonio Caballero, "A la sombra del fusil," *Revista Diners,* March 2002, 20–26.

14. Juanita León, "Crónica de un encuentro en el Caguán," *El Tiempo,* March 19, 2000.

15. Jorge Orlando Melo, "La paz: ¿Una realidad utópica?" *Semana.com,* December 2, 1999, retrieved August 3, 2005, from http://semana2.terra.com.co/archivo/articulosView.jsp?id=11947.

16. León, "Crónica."

17. Caballero, "A la sombra," 22, 24.

18. Andrew Selsky, "Envoy's Encounters Helped in Colombia," *Associated Press,* January 16, 2002.

19. *El Tiempo,* January 14, 2002.

20. Juanita León, "Chistes, coplas, y brindis par la paz," *El Tiempo,* February 27, 2000.

21. These words were cited by Larry Rohter, "Battling in Colombia but Touring Together in Europe," *New York Times,* February 28, 2000.

22. For a particularly gifted analysis, see Lendon (1997).

23. Miller (1993). For a humanistic prescription of a society in which humiliation does not occur, see Margalit (1996).

24. Marulanda refers to the Llerases and the Lópezes in the plural: to second cousins Alberto Lleras Camargo and Carlos Lleras Restrepo and to former president Alfonso López Pumarejo and his son, Alfonso López Michelsen. Both Llerases and the younger López would in turn become presidents of Colombia.

25. Eduardo Caballero Calderón, "Soledad y sociabilidad," *El Tiempo,* February 9, 1952, 4.

26. For a marvelous contrast, see the work about personal relationships in Colombia by Fitch (1998).

27. For suggestive contrasts between the political culture of the United States and Latin America, see Pike (1992).

28. For a fine exception, see Weisman (1998).

29. Ibon Villelabeitia, "No One Visits García Márquez's 'Macondo' House," Reuters, March 25, 2002.

30. Andrés Hurtado García, "Historias de la selva," *El Tiempo,* January 15, 2002.

31. González Arias, "*Remember* a Tirofijo," 11.

32. María Isabel Rueda, "El presidente y el guerrillero," *Semana.com,* February 15, 2001, retrieved August 3, 2005, from http://semana2.terra.com.co/archivo/articulosView.jsp?id=16940.

33. "Guerrilleros de Everfit," *Cambio,* February 28, 2000.

34. "Continúa debate sobre toalla de 'Tirofijo,'" *El Tiempo,* March 4, 2001.

35. D'Artagnan, "Alto elogio de la toalla," *El Tiempo,* February 21, 2001.

36. Manuel Marulanda and the urban columnist Iván Marulanda are not related to one another, except by the fact that they are compatriots.

References

Alape, Arturo. 1989. *Las vidas de Pedro Antonio Marín Manuel Marulanda Vélez Tirofijo.* Bogotá: Planeta.

Arenas, Jacobo. 1971. *La guerrilla por dentro.* Bogotá: Ediciones Tercer Mundo.

Asencio, Diego, and Nancy Asencio. 1983. *Our Man Is Inside.* Boston: Little, Brown.

Azula Barrera, Rafael. 1956. *De la revolución al orden nuevo: Proceso y drama de un pueblo.* Bogotá: Editorial Kelly.

Beaulac, Willard L. 1958. *Career Ambassador.* New York: Macmillan.

Bell-Villada, Gene H. 1990. *García Márquez, the Man and His Work.* Chapel Hill: University of North Carolina Press.

Braun, Herbert. 1986. *The Assassination of Gaitán: Public Life and Urban Violence in Colombia.* Madison: University of Wisconsin Press.

————. 2003. *Our Guerrillas, Our Sidewalks: A Journey into the Violence of Colombia.* 2nd ed. Lanham, MD: Rowman and Littlefield.

Broderick, Joe [Walter J.]. 2000. *El guerrillero invisible.* Bogotá: Intermedio.

Broderick, Walter J. 1975. *Camilo Torres: A Biography of the Priest-Guerrillero.* Garden City, NJ: Doubleday.

Bushnell, David. 1993. *The Making of Modern Colombia: A Nation in Spite of Itself.* Berkeley: University of California Press.

Caballero Calderón, Eduardo. 1978. *El Cristo de espaldas.* Medellín: Editorial Bedout.

Carrigan, Ana. 1993. *The Palace of Justice: A Colombian Tragedy.* New York: Four Walls, Eight Windows.

Comisión Temática FARC-EP. 2001. *FARC: El país que proponemos construir.* Bogotá: Editorial Oveja Negra.

Corporación Observatorio para la Paz. 2001. *Las verdaderas intenciones de las FARC.* Bogotá: Intermedio Editores.

Correa Arboleda, Medardo. 1997. *Sueño inconcluso: Mi vivencia en el ELN.* Bogotá: FINDESARROLLO.

Dealy, Glen Caudill. 1992. *The Latin Americans: Spirit and Ethos.* Boulder, CO: Westview Press.

Deas, Malcolm. 1983. "La presencia de la política nacional en la vida provinciana, pueblerina, y rural de Colombia en el primer siglo de la república." In *La unidad nacional en América Latina: Del regionalismo a la nacionalidad,* ed. Marco Palacios, 149–73. México: El Colegio de México.

————. 1997. "Reflections on Political Violence: Colombia." In *The Legitimization of Violence,* ed. David Apter. New York: New York University Press.

Fitch, Kristine L. 1998. *Speaking Relationally: Culture, Communication and Interpersonal Connection.* New York: Guilford Press.

Franco Isaza, Eduardo. 1959. *Las guerrillas del llano.* Bogotá: Librería Mundial Distribuidores.

García Marquez, Gabriel. 1988. "The Solitude of Latin America." In *Lives on the Line: The Testimony of Contemporary Latin American Authors,* ed. Doris Meyer, 230–34. Berkeley: University of California Press.

Grabe, Vera. 2000. *Razones de vida.* Bogotá: Planeta.

Greenberg, Kenneth. 1985. *Masters and Statesmen: The Political Culture of American Slavery.* Baltimore: Johns Hopkins University Press.

Guillermoprieto, Alma. 2001 *Looking for History: Dispatches from Latin America.* New York: Pantheon.

Jiménez, Michael. Forthcoming. *Struggles on an Interior Shore: Wealth, Power and Authority in the Colombian Andes.* Durham, NC: Duke University Press.

Lara, Patricia. 1986. *Siembra vientos y recogerás tempestades.* Bogotá: Planeta.

Lendon, J. E. 1997. *The Empire of Honour: The Art of Government in the Roman World.* Oxford: Oxford University Press.

Lozano Guillén, Carlos A. 2002. *Reportajes desde el Caguán: Proceso de paz con las FARC-EP*. Bogotá: Ediciones Nuestra América.

Margalit, Avishai. 1996. *The Decent Society*. Cambridge, MA: Harvard University Press.

Miller, William Ian. 1993. *Humiliation, and Other Essays on Honor, Social Discomfort, and Violence*. Ithaca: Cornell University Press.

Molano, Alfredo. 1994. *Trochas y fusiles*. Bogotá: Instituto de Estudios Políticos y Relaciones Internacionales/Ancora.

Pécaut, Daniel. 2000. "Un mayor compromiso con este país: Discurso con motivo del Doctorado Honoris Causa, Universidad Nacional de Colombia." *Análisis Político*, no. 41 (September–December).

Peristiany, J. C., ed. 1966. *Honor and Shame: The Values of Mediterranean Society*. Chicago: University of Chicago Press.

Pike, Fredrick B. 1992. *The United States and Latin America: Myths and Stereotypes of Civilization and Nature*. Austin: University of Texas Press.

Pitt-Rivers, J. A. 1961. *The People of the Sierra*. Chicago: University of Chicago Press.

———. 1966. "Honor and Social Status." In *Honor and Shame: The Values of Mediterranean Society*, ed. J. C. Peristiany. Chicago: University of Chicago Press.

Rama, Angel. 1996. *The Lettered City*. Durham, NC: Duke University Press.

Restrepo, Laura. 1986. *Historia de una traición*. Bogotá: Plaza y Janés.

Smith, T. V. 1932. *The Encyclopedia of the Social Sciences*.

Twinam, Ann. 1998. *Public Lives, Private Secrets: Gender, Honor, Sexuality, and Illegitimacy in Colonial Spanish America*. Stanford: Stanford University Press.

Vázquez Perdomo, María Eugenia. 2000. *Escrito para no morir: Bitácora de una militancia*. Bogotá: Ministerio de Educación.

Weisman, Alan. 1998. *Gaviotas: A Village to Reinvent the World*. White River Junction, VT: Chelsea Green.

Wilde, Alexander W. 1982. *Conversaciones de caballeros: La quiebra de la democracia en Colombia*. Bogotá: Ediciones Tercer Mundo.

Williams, Raymond. 1973. *The Country and the City*. New York: Oxford University Press.

Wyatt-Brown, Bertram. 1983. *Southern Honor: Ethics and Behavior in the Old South*. New York: Oxford University Press.

———. 2001. *The Shaping of Southern Culture: Honor, Grace, and War, 1760s–1880s*. Chapel Hill: University of North Carolina Press.

Zuleta Nieto, Jaime, et al., eds. 1999. *Conversaciones de paz: Redefinición del estado*. Bogotá: Agenda Ciudadana para la Paz.

From Smugglers to Drug Lords to *Traquetos*

Changes in the Colombian Illicit Drug Organizations

Álvaro Camacho Guizado
Andrés López Restrepo

López and Camacho explore the history and social and political impact of drug trafficking in Colombia from its roots in the endemic smuggling and political violence of the country's past, to its most violent excesses under Pablo Escobar, to its current fragmented state. Using historical materials as well as secondary sources, they begin by showing how cycles of primarily political violence trained each generation, including the smugglers that have populated Colombia's border areas since colonial times, to resolve conflicts by armed means. Then they look at the evolution of the drug trade in Colombia, beginning with the marijuana trade, which was short and had no lasting social and political effects. The most significant phase of this feature of Colombian life is no doubt the bloody and international reign of the cocaine-exporting cartels, especially the Medellín and Cali cartels. López and Camacho describe how Pablo Escobar and others took control of U.S. drug markets through the use of overwhelming violence, amassed vast sums, and then turned their attention to the Colombian state itself, seeking a political role. This ultimately led to their downfall, as their excessive visibility

and hubris led to a concerted attack on them by domestic and international se-
curity forces, as well as by competitors. The disintegration of the cartels led to the
rise of second-tier leaders, commanding small, subterranean organizations that
continue to dominate the drug trade today. They are weaker and less profitable
than the old cartels but continue to dominate the drug trade to the Americas and
Europe, showing the resilience and adaptability of Colombian drug entrepre-
neurs. In the final analysis, drug lords and others who have turned drug profits
into land are becoming more respectable, participating in the paramilitary fight
against the guerrillas, and earning a place next to right-wing landowners. Co-
caine thus fuels both ends of the armed conflict in Colombia.

The Origins and Dynamics of Drug Trafficking in Colombia

Smuggling, Violence, and Drug Trafficking

Considered from a historical perspective, drug trafficking in Colombia is
the most recent manifestation of two forms of illegality: smuggling and violence. Smuggling can be traced back to colonial times. For many centuries,
goods that the state wanted to tax—but could not—infiltrated through Colombia's porous borders. There is hardly a single Colombian border zone
where smuggling is not a part of local tradition, where stories about clandestine paths are not known and shared by all inhabitants. But two particular zones became privileged conduits through which contraband entered
the country almost without restriction: Urabá and, above all, the Guajira
peninsula, where all the inhabitants—elites and common people, aborigi-
nals and Arab immigrants—based their lifestyles on crime.

Violence—generalized violence, which incites political arguments and
affects large population groups—also has a long history, although a less extensive one than smuggling. The republic regularly mobilized hosts of peasants to assassinate their fellow countrymen in the name of one traditional
party or another. This situation led to the period during the 1940s and the
1950s known as "la Violencia" with a capital V, a decade in which more than
150,000 Colombian peasants were killed in the name of either the Liberal or
the Conservative Party.

In actuality, the violence is not one unique kind but rather of multiple
types and of varied origin. There is no relationship whatsoever between today's violence and the kinds of violence that prevailed during the 1940s.

Nevertheless, the various types of violence have been similar enough to allow an "apprenticeship" in violent techniques, which can be used and improved—that is, made more destructive—in the next violent period. Peace apprenticeship is not possible because just when society is learning to negotiate its conflicts in a peaceful manner new arguments or conditions appear that justify the use of violence and launch another cycle of destruction. This is what happened during the 1960s and the 1970s. In the 1960s, after a confrontation almost a century and a half long, the parties were beginning to settle their conflicts in a civilized way, when the Left, following Guevara's political ideals, started to promote revolution. And in the 1970s, the guerrillas were being forced to give in when drug trafficking created the conditions for a new cycle of violence, in which we are still caught.

In the past, smuggling and violence have closely coexisted. The smuggler has always had recourse to violence in order to settle conflicts that cannot be solved otherwise. Traditional drug traffickers, who would cross the ocean in vessels they hoped would be faster than the government's, would usually be armed. In Guajira, honor feuds, along with extensive illegal activities, have been invoked as justifications for the permanent carrying of arms. But the most notoriously violent men did not devote themselves to smuggling before the 1970s. Their main concern was ideology: ideology, as well as some occasional extortion, sustained them, and they therefore kept away from the trade of illegal products. Only during civil wars did it become necessary to introduce a sporadic contraband arms trade with the complicity of Caribbean sailors or inhabitants of the Venezuelan or Ecuadorian border regions.

This situation started to change at midcentury, and Efraín Gonzáles is the person who best embodies this new world from its inception. A member of a conservative family, he educated himself during the partisan violence that devastated the southern part of Great Caldas at the beginning of the 1950s. He then settled in Vélez province, in the Santander Department, and from this base gained control over the various groups that were fighting to manage the emerald mines in western Boyacá. The majority of these mines were state property, as set forth in the 1886 Constitution, whereby all underground wealth belonged to the state. But the Colombian state was incapable then, as it is now, of achieving effective control over its riches, even though western Boyacá is located in the heart of the country, very near the capital. González put into practice what he had learned during "la Violencia" to build an empire, autonomous from state power, where both smuggling and extreme violence became business as usual (Téllez 1993).

For many years, the place where González died remained a place of pilgrimage, as has occurred more recently with Pablo Escobar's grave. The feat these two men achieved was, through the use of violence, to have organized, controlled, and imposed some order on two markets—emerald and cocaine smuggling—that were inherently unstable due to their illegal character. Both men were able to enter the popular imagination by having outwitted the state and its agents, at least until their deaths: González's in 1965 and Escobar's in 1993. Admiration for González was restricted to certain social sectors of the interior, while respect toward Escobar—certainly tinged with fear, at least in Colombia—was more generalized and even extended past Colombia's borders. During the almost three decades that separate the deaths of the bandit and the drug lord, many changes occurred in Colombian society. One of the most important was the spread of crime as a way of life and as a social ascent mechanism.

Establishment of the First Drug-Trafficking Organizations

National legislation against consuming, trading, and producing certain drugs originated with Law 11 of September 15, 1920. Since then there has been clandestine trafficking in drugs, aimed at establishing a connection between drug consumers and producers. Nevertheless, for the first several decades, this traffic was secondary to border smuggling. Its purpose was to introduce drugs into the country—not to export them, as now—through ports on the Atlantic and Buenaventura, on the Pacific. Opiates and cocaine were the smuggled drugs, since marijuana, besides being found abundantly in its wild form almost all over the country, was very easy to cultivate.

According to official U.S. documents, Colombia during the 1930s was already integrated into the secret drug networks that linked Europe—where the main producers of manufactured drugs were to be found—with consumers from the Caribbean countries. These documents state that Colombian ports on the Caribbean—Barranquilla, Cartagena, and Santa Marta—were centers of intense illegal drug traffic. The following report, sent on August 24, 1933, by the business attaché of the U.S. embassy in Bogotá, explains why Colombian authorities were so ineffective in repressing drug smuggling:

> Captain Gustavo Gómez P., general director of Colombia's National Police . . . and several other reliable Colombian officials have confidentially

spoken to me on several occasions about illicit narcotics traffic in Bogotá. Apparently, there are enormous difficulties in controlling the traffic because of the fact that many drug addicts are socially or politically prominent; their personal influences are such that it is impossible to pursue them. Narcotic use habits seem restricted to a rather small class; the high cost of drugs here places them out of reach for the majority of the inhabitants. It is understood that the habit is more extensive in Caribbean coast cities, such as Barranquilla and Cartagena, where there is certain contraband in ships and thus prices are lower. The main source of (heroic) drugs used in Colombia seems to be European.

Drug trafficking followed a similar pattern during the 1930s, although social reaction and legislation had begun to decrease the popularity of manufactured drugs, especially cocaine. The situation completely changed as a consequence of World War II, since the conflict forced an interruption of trade with Europe, eliminating the flow of opium products. The United States provided the drugs required for medical needs, but illicit markets for morphine and heroin were affected, and the prices of these drugs rose dramatically, beyond the reach of habitual consumers. Some of them opted for laudanum, a compound of opium and other substances, which was easier to get in drugstores but which necessitated forging prescriptions.

Until the 1940s, Andean countries were not important in international drug trafficking, and their production for the illegal market was insignificant. Actually, like almost all Latin American countries, Andean countries imported illegal drugs and, on some occasions, were used as transit points for shipments to neighboring countries. But the war, and then the defeat and subsequent occupation of the Axis powers, finished off the traditional international drug-trafficking centers in Europe. As a result, cocaine produced in Peru, where enormous amounts had been stored during the war, found its way to the United States and Cuba after 1945. The U.S. cocaine market was quite small, but rising demand in Cuba compensated for this. Cuba not only served as transit point for the U.S. market, due to its privileged position, but also emerged as a market in its own right, since cocaine was the favorite drug of Mafia bosses and gamblers (Walker 1989; Gootenberg 1999).

The 1950s brought a big change. Smuggling had long been a tradition in Latin America; now it became time to transform it in a two-way business that would include not only imports, such as liquor, cigarettes, and fabric, but also drug exports. Dispatching the merchandise was not a problem, since trained personnel and means of transportation were already available and the routes were known. The only investment required was the installation of processing laboratories for heroin and cocaine production. These drugs were mainly produced for export, but this process also allowed supplies to be produced for the local market, in a successful case of import substitution. Thus, during the 1950s, illegal cocaine laboratories were reported in all the Andean countries: Peru, Bolivia, Chile, Ecuador, Colombia, and even Argentina.

South American drugs were introduced to the U.S. market by Cuban traffickers who faced little competition, since the long-established U.S. mafias, mostly Italian, had enough on their hands with the heroin trade, which had a much more extended market than cocaine. Thus strong ties between Colombian and Cuban criminals were established. In Colombia, the main laboratories were located in Medellín. One of them was mentioned in a U.S. government report: "On February 20, 1957, Colombian Secret Services agents, with the assistance of an anti-narcotics official from the United States, discovered a clandestine factory of heroin and cocaine at the property of Tomás and Rafael Herrán, in Medellín, Colombia. These brothers had been into drug trafficking since 1948. Heroin produced in this laboratory was sold in Cuba, where the accused were arrested by the police when Tomás Herrán was found in the possession of 800 grams of heroin on December 24, 1956."[1]

Everything seems to indicate that an article published in *El Espectador* in May of 1959 referred to the same Herrán brothers. The news story stated that, a year before, FBI agents in Havana had detained a Colombian citizen who had confessed that in Medellín "there was a clandestine laboratory, and that he was one of the persons responsible for it." It was also stated that in that laboratory "heroin, cocaine and morphine were produced, then transported to Havana and from there distributed to Mexico, the United States and other countries of the continent." The laboratory, which was indeed found by federal agents in El Poblado, a neighborhood in Medellín, was open only two months a year, during which it produced five pounds of heroin that were subsequently sold for US$70,000 each. "That is to say, they obtained US$350,000, which led them 'not to work during the rest of the year, in order to avoid danger.'" The newspaper added that the FBI agents had returned to the country "to help reach the definitive culmination of the investigation." One of the authors of the book in which this article is quoted asserts that he knew one of the owners of the laboratory ("two brothers related to important families from Medellín and Bogotá"), a man who spent almost two years in a Cuban prison until Fidel Castro's government deported him. The trafficker remembers that the laboratory processed "coca from Tierradentro and El Paso, in the department of Cauca, and opium gum imported from Ecuador."[2]

A couple of years later, another U.S. government report stated that in New York in May 1961 U.S. antinarcotics agents had detained two crew members from the ship *Ciudad de Pasto* for possession of 218 grams of cocaine. The report went on to say that "the accused declared that they had obtained the cocaine from Jesús García Primero from Cali, Colombia."[3] We are not in the position to establish whether this was a casual incident, resulting from the attempt of two adventurers to earn a few dollars. Rather, it may have been evidence of the deep changes that Latin American drug trafficking was going through as a consequence of the Cuban Revolution.

With Fidel Castro's arrival in power in January 1959, U.S. Mafia bosses and Cuban ruffians who had prospered in the casino world since the 1930s, as well as supporters of Fulgencio Batista's regime, were forced to abandon the island. After settling in Miami, New York, and Union City, New Jersey, Cubans with a dubious, criminal past devoted themselves to the only profession they knew. The ranks thus established were augmented by a considerable number of exiles who had participated in the failed invasion of Bahia Cochinos in April 1961. From that time on, the state of Florida—and to a much lesser extent Union City—became the center of two very closely related phenomena: drug trafficking and anti-Castro politics. The U.S. government, in its intention to back the latter, was complacent toward the former. At first, the Cubans imported just the amount of drugs needed to satisfy the demand of wealthy members of their community, but by the middle of the 1960s they had become aware that there was a demand for cocaine in every corner of the United States. Consequently, they started bringing in drugs in greater amounts (MacDonald 1988).

Beginnings of Colombian Drug Trafficking

The first suppliers of Cuban dealers during the 1960s were Colombians. They would buy coca base from Andean peasants, transform it into cocaine in laboratories located in Medellín, and then sell it to Cubans for U.S. distribution. A report from the U.S. government stated: "By 1965, Colombians supplied nearly 100 percent of the cocaine moving through the Cuban networks. Colombians refined the drug and Cubans trafficked and distributed it in the United States."[4] Similarly, the Colombian market was open to adventurers from all over the world. Until the beginning of the 1970s, according to firsthand testimony, "all [cocaine] buyers . . . were equally welcome, including many youngsters and small independent traffickers from the United States. For them, to negotiate with coca in Colombia was significantly easier than in the extremely tense and paranoid atmosphere of Bolivia or Peru" (Sabbag 1990; see also Henman 1980).

This situation was not to last too long, and neither was the successful job-sharing alliance between Colombians and Cubans. During the 1960s, the flow of immigrants from Colombia to the United States grew significantly, giving rise to ethnic transnational networks, which criminal organizations were quick to exploit. Thus, toward the end of the decade and during the first years of the 1970s, Colombians expanded their operations from production to traffic. At the same time, starting in 1972, the Colombian Security Administrative Department (DAS, Departamento Administrativo de Seguridad) and the National Police started to act against drug traffickers. Their work, although successful in ending the trips of foreign adventurers who came to Colombia to buy drugs that they later sold in their countries of origin, was not able to weaken the Colombian organizations. In fact, it can be concluded that the DAS and police efforts served only to consolidate the power of local drug lords with their elimination of small foreign traffickers. In any case, and as Henman (1980) and Sabbag (1990) attest to, 1973 signaled the end of foreign independent cocaine traffickers.

By 1976, the Colombians, who were constantly denouncing fraud on the part of the Cubans and were unsatisfied with their share in the profits, decide to rebel against their subordination. To this end, they sent gunmen to the United States to systematically eliminate their Cuban rivals in Miami and New York. By 1978, Cubans who remained in the business were working for Colombian organizations, which would, in the future, directly supervise wholesale distribution for most of the U.S. territory (Abadinsky 1997). The Colombians thus seized control of the cocaine business just when the second cocaine epidemic was starting in the United States. Drug exports (and confiscations), which amounted to a few tenths of kilos at the beginning of the 1970s, became tons toward the end of the same decade. Thus Colombian

traffickers accumulated immense fortunes, which surpassed their most fe-
brile fantasies.

The Cubans had been trained by the Central Intelligence Agency (CIA)
for the Bahía Cochinos invasion in the use of automatic weapons and mor-
tar shells, but they were unable to resist the Colombian *sicarios* (Kleinknecht
1996). The reason, it has been argued again and again, was that criminals of
Cuban or Italian origin, bound by a code of honor, directed their attacks toward the designated victim, whereas Colombians, educated in the school of
political violence, showed no qualms about assassinating their victim's families and friends. For this reason, two North American journalists, refer-
ring to the cocaine wars in southern Florida toward the end of the 1970s,
wrote: "Colombian cocaine traffickers brought to Miami a ferocious violence that U.S. law and order agents had never seen" (Gugliotta and Leen
1990). Of course, violence cannot last long as a comparative advantage; it is
enough to be more brutal in order to displace the person who controls it
from the market.

With this background on the history of the drug trade, it is easier to
identify the conditions that allowed Colombia to become the world center
for drug trafficking. Previous efforts to explain why Colombia is in this position have usually opted for broad explanations involving immutable conditions such as the country's geography or certain characteristics inherent
to the nature of Colombians. No doubt geography has played a certain role,
but the determining factors are social. Likewise, it is impossible to talk
about a nature or a global identity that takes into account the multiple individual differences among the members of one society. Colombians, or
rather, some Colombians, came to control gigantic international enterprises
devoted to exporting drugs and violence as a result of a series of events,
some caused by deliberate actions on their part, some by fortuitous natural
conditions or actions by others.

In the beginning, between 1920 and 1940, drug trafficking consisted of
bringing drugs into Colombia, profiting from traditional smuggling networks, a phenomenon similar to what occurred in the rest of Latin America.
Beginning at the end of the 1940s and during the 1950s, Andean countries
became illegal drug exporters, a transformation in which nature had a role
in at least in two different ways. First, coca leaf was a traditional crop in the
region, and poppies were easy to grow in the western mountains of South
America. Second, Andean countries were sufficiently close to the United
States to have easy and cheap access to its market, but also sufficiently far

away so that the United States did not strongly pressure the region to end the trafficking, as was the case in Mexico. Evidently, the volume of illegal drugs reaching the United States from South America at that time was not very remarkable. The U.S. government neglected the problem, and thus Latin American drug networks were able to grow and strengthen.

In earlier years, Colombians had occupied subaltern positions within the trafficking networks managed by Cubans. This situation reversed in stages. First, the increasing migration to the United States during the 1960s allowed Colombians to create transnational drug-trafficking networks and to start direct exports to the United States. Second, Colombian security forces eliminated independent foreign traffickers, thus favoring national exporters. And third, Colombian criminals implemented unusual levels of violence, which allowed them to subordinate their Cuban counterparts. Chance then intervened: U.S. consumers started to demand enormous amounts of cocaine, and almost the only suppliers were Colombian traffickers, who became immensely rich. Unfortunately, this economic success favored extremely violent criminals and Colombia had to suffer the consequences.

The New Colombian Drug-Trafficking Organizations

Since the 1960s, the trajectory of illegal drug production and exports has presented three clearly identified stages. Each one of these stages has shown a specific type of organization and dynamics and has had an uneven effect on the configuration of society and, especially, on Colombia's political processes and the dynamics of violence.

The First Stage: *Marimba* from the Guajira Department (c. 1960–80)

There has been evidence since 1941 of the existence of *marimba* (Colombian slang for marijuana) cultivation in Magdalena Department, around the city of Santa Marta (Sáenz Rovner 1996). The biggest fields for commercial purposes appeared around 1955. According to an International Criminal Police Organization (INTERPOL) report, in 1968 there were "80,000 marijuana traffickers" in Colombia,[5] although this number is definitely quite exaggerated. The national press reported sporadically on marijuana seizures and clandestine flights in Guajira (in northeast Colombia, bordering

Magdalena) in 1972, but it was not until 1974 that this topic started to receive steady coverage by journalists (Vélez, Tamayo, and Pérez 1980). Since then there has been an exponential growth in marijuana production and exports.

During the boom in the 1960s and 1970s, marijuana was mainly produced in the Sierra Nevada de Santa Marta, toward the south of the Guajira peninsula. Its most notable promoters were former local liquor, cigarette, and fabric smugglers who, pushed by U.S. buyers, encouraged peasants and settlers to grow, dry, and pack the plant. The high quality of the crop, "Santa Marta Golden," caused a rapid rise in demand, and marijuana became an important revenue source for the region.

To different degrees, a good portion of the population of these regions benefited from the marijuana trade, which displaced even traditional crops such as coffee and cotton. The marijuana boom was a social phenomenon, but it responded to the rise and fall in demand of U.S. buyers. Thus, when the big increase in demand that had fostered the trade receded, both the marijuana fields and the boomtowns produced by the trade evaporated. This boom, which allowed Colombia to become, for a short period of time, the main producer of marijuana destined for the U.S. market, was a consequence of two antidrug operations: the Buccaneer Campaign, launched by the U.S. DEA (Drug Enforcement Agency) in Jamaica in 1974, and the Mexican government's Permanent Campaign, which introduced the use of the herbicide Paraquat for fumigating marijuana fields in 1977 (Lupsha 1990). Nevertheless, U.S. traffickers were in control all along of both transportation of the drug to the United States and its sale on U.S. territory.

Marijuana: Social Classes and Conflict

Even though marijuana cultivation did not spread significantly throughout the country and therefore did not involve large numbers of individuals, the haughty attitudes, excesses, and proud behavior—at times bordering on aggression—exhibited by people involved in the trade were revolting to the members of the traditional higher classes. Phrases like the "emerging class," used by some of the more conspicuous representatives of the dominant classes to describe these latecomers to the social scene, describe, at least in part, the reaction provoked by marijuana traffickers (Camacho Guizado 1988). This type of reaction illustrates the attitudes of some sectors of the dominant classes toward the increasing modernization of Colombian society and its concomitant upward social mobility. For many of these sectors, which acquired the label of "submerging class" (a class losing power), these processes threatened the existence of a traditional order in which positions of power and privilege were awarded as a result of lineage and ancestry rather than capacity or personal merit.

The Economy versus the Polity: The Process of Integration

Nevertheless, the responses of the traditional dominant classes to changes in the social and cultural order did not echo those of the state or the economic system. On the contrary, the official policy toward the increasing pressure to nationalize foreign currency expressed itself in the creation of the so-called "sinister teller," a mechanism through which the central bank exchanged dollars for pesos without concern for their origin, "no questions asked." With this practice, the state itself contributed to institutionalizing the laundering of dollars from the export of marijuana—and also money from traditional smuggling and, later on, from the cocaine trade. From another perspective, more than a few Colombian businessmen considered the new fortunes of the traffickers an opportunity to engage in good business.

Consequently, some financial institutions lent themselves to the laundering of the new capital. Others sold properties to the new millionaires, who paid in cash or with dollars deposited in foreign countries, which therefore avoided legal registry and taxes; buying land and real estate became the most salient forms of money laundering. Still other businessmen, as figureheads, provided their prominence and expertise to new endeavors, with the goal of bestowing upon the new rich some kind of respectability. Clearly, there was some ambiguity in the way traditional dominant classes dealt with the emerging class. Nevertheless, only a very few marijuana exporters became truly rational and calculating businessmen. Their conspicuous consumption and squandering of money meant that they saved and reinvested little of their fortunes. Once the marijuana export boom was over, the great majority of them returned to their original status.

The Political Options and the Debate on Legalization

During the 1970s, a heated debate around the possibility of legalizing marijuana developed in Colombia. It was clear, however, that the real focus of the discussion was not the legalization of the drug itself but revenues resulting from marijuana exports and the consequent attack on corrupt practices associated with their laundering (Asociación Nacional de Instituciones Financieras 1979). Although the marijuana boom did not last long, it had lasting effects on Colombian society and its relationship to drug trafficking. In particular, the marijuana boom determined the framework within which the Colombian discussion about drug penalization and legalization has taken place. Given the nature of the problem and the interests at stake, many analysts have argued that this debate fostered a certain Colombian permissiveness around the production and export of illegal drugs. On this occasion, the U.S. government, through its ambassador, expressed its deep-seated opposition to any attempt at legalization and thus buried the possibility.

But the debate focused on marijuana, failing to recognize how important cocaine had already become. And what is worse, the debate was concerned with only one aspect of drug traffickers—their drug smuggling—neglecting their roles as producers and exporters of violence. For this reason, by the time it became clear during the 1980s that national conditions, and especially international conditions, made it impossible to consider the legalization of drugs, and even less possible to consider legalizing trafficking, Colombian society had been feeding the hopes for legalization in the most violent traffickers. Furious, they turned their weapons against those who, in their opinion, had deceived them.

The War on Drugs and the Decline of Colombian Marijuana

Early in the 1970s, the U.S. government launched its "war on drugs." The Mexican marijuana fields were sprayed with Paraquat, a very strong defoliant, and this stimulated Colombian production and exports. But at the same time U.S. police departments increased their efforts at the interdiction of marijuana on both the domestic and the international fronts (Bertram, Sharpe, and Andreas 1996; Baum 1997.[6] Confiscation by the U.S. Coast Guard and the U.S. Customs Service started to diminish in 1981. The price of marijuana in the Colombian market also started to go down; it is not presumptuous to assume that the boom reached its end that year. The decisive factor in the ending was the preference on the part of consumers for stronger marijuana varieties, such as sinsemilla, which they could grow at home using hydroponics. This was the final straw, since marijuana's great volume and characteristic smell made its detection during international transit quite easy. Thus, in spite of the reduction of the price of Colombian marijuana, which became much cheaper than that produced in Mexico or the

United States, its share of the U.S. market receded throughout the 1980s to become almost marginal (Gómez 1988; Reuter 1993).

To summarize, the irrational character of the agents involved, technical difficulties related to marijuana transportation, frequent confiscations by the authorities, growing U.S. production of marijuana, international competition, and the policies of the U.S. government were the factors that caused the Colombian marijuana business to wane. Marijuana became another of the many short-cycle agrarian economies that have characterized Colombian economic history (Tovar 1999). Its main effect was as a stimulus for the takeover of lands poorly fit for agriculture but environmentally very rich in the Sierra Nevada and other regions, and the clearing of huge forest areas for marijuana fields, with the obvious adverse consequences to the region's ecology in terms of soil erosion, reduced food production, and higher food prices. Local peasants who were not producers of marijuana were particularly affected, since their incomes did not grow like those of the producers. Today there is still some marijuana production in Colombia: experts calculate that nowadays around five thousand hectares are planted in *marimba*.

Second Stage: The Cartels and the Drug Lords (1970–95)

Cocaine exports began to develop at the beginning of the 1970s. This was a much more lucrative business, which in the hands of more audacious, rational, and organized businessmen soon mushroomed. These pioneers in the cocaine business were also expert smugglers, mainly from the Antioquia Department (Cañón 1994; Arango Jaramillo and Child 1984); very soon the trade grew with the addition of other criminals from the Valle del Cauca region. Illegal drug consumption shows historical cycles of boom and collapse (Musto 1993), and the activity of Colombian drug traffickers coincided with accelerating demand in the United States. The result was the accumulation of enormous amounts of money in the hands of the few businessmen involved.

Cocaine: Social Class and Conflict
Many drug traffickers invested locally, in the banking system, construction, or industry, and tried to build a respectable cover. Others, conversely, followed patterns similar to their ancestors' and devoted themselves, in extravagant and conspicuous consumption, to investing in land and horses,

thus reinforcing their peasant origins (Arango Jaramillo 1988). The main difference with respect to their predecessors was that the sums of money these new traffickers received were far greater. Many anecdotes and first-person reports show how some of these traffickers kept part of their fortune in gold ingots or in paper money that, unused and permanently exposed to humidity, would rot away. In other words, they took in far more money than they could handle.

Although scholars have identified several organizations of cocaine traffickers, two of them became the focal points around which most of the business revolved. The so-called Medellín and Cali cartels came to control, according to experts, more than 70 percent of the Colombian exports during the 1980s and half way through the 1990s. Other less important organizations gravitated around them, and very few independent ones achieved great commercial success.

The differences between this stage and the previous one are noteworthy: the new traffickers directly inserted themselves into an international market, importing raw materials from Peru and exporting their product to the United States, whether directly or through Mexico or other Central American intermediaries. In addition, the immense revenue overflowed the national capacity for money laundering, so that they were forced to establish businesses in fiscal paradises in the Caribbean, the state of Florida, and Europe. Organizing distribution in U.S. cities also meant great entrepreneurial efforts, many of which involved significant deployment of violence (Gugliotta and Leen 1990; Thoumi 1994).

At the national level there were also big differences from the previous stage. The incomparably greater mass of capital involved led to the creation of more complex organizations and the close support of managers, lawyers, accountants, and other experts in dealing with large sums. And in their conspicuous spending, drug lords also surrounded themselves with architects, decorators, and even cultural counselors. They thus created vast networks, which allowed them to develop the business and gain a certain degree of respectability.

An American author, using DEA data, describes the main organizations as follows:

> In Colombia there are some ten core organizations active at any one time. Each is capable of directing the movement of large amounts of cocaine from source to consuming countries and the reflow of the large

illicit proceeds. Together, they handle more than sixty percent of the cocaine reaching North American and European markets. . . . These core
organizations directly employ a relatively small number of people. They
draw upon more than 100 contractors that specialize in such functions
as obtaining base from source countries, processing base into HCL (hy-
drochloride), transporting HCL to market, laundering money, providing enforcement, etc. These specialized organizations range in size from
less than ten to several hundred. Sometimes they link up among themselves. Both the core and the specialized groups hire from a pool of 1,000
or so skilled free-lancers such as pilots, chemists and assassins, and a
much larger number of part time workers who are employed as guards,
laborers and surveillants.[7]

The Political Options

One of the most prominent features of this stage has to do with the different
dimensions, modalities, and political impact of the new type of drug trafficking, which took shape in different ways. The first and most noteworthy
was the collective reaction of the organizations' bosses when a relative of
one of the Medellín leaders was kidnapped by the guerrilla organization
M19 in November 1981. After a meeting in Medellín, the main cartel leaders
organized a group called MAS (Muerte a Secuestradores, Death to Kidnappers), with the purpose of freeing the kidnapped woman and "teaching a
lesson" to the perpetrators. Very quickly, this organization assumed such a
life of its own that it surpassed its initial aim of fighting kidnapping and
became an ultrarightist armed force whose main task was protecting traffickers' lands, especially in the Magdalena Medio region. It also aimed at
eliminating the FARC front that had established a stronghold in the region
and become a local power. MAS, encouraged by other rural landowners,
became the basis for the creation of the powerful Colombian paramilitary
movement, which was to become a politically important armed force. At
one point, MAS even intended to become a political party, calling itself
MORENA (Movimiento de Renovación Nacional, National Renovation
Movement), in reference to the experience of El Salvador and the ARENA
movement.

A second way of becoming involved in politics was related to the decision on the part of some of the drug lords to participate, directly and personally, in electoral competition with Congress. One of them, Carlos Lehder, organized his own movement, Movimiento Latino Nacional (National

Latino Movement), a blurry mixture of nationalism, populism, and Adolf Hitler affinity, which actually elected some representatives in municipal councils in the department of Quindío. Lehder launched his movement with pomp and circumstance, quickly gaining the attention and suspicion of political leaders and journalists who were curious and fearful about the new competitor. Lehder's identity as a drug trafficker was revealed publicly when he acknowledged this role in a radio interview, thus eliminating any doubt with respect to the origins of his fortune. Some time before, he had already given signals with his philanthropy, openly giving money, publicly supporting civic and social causes, and building a huge hotel that was obviously enormously expensive.

Pablo Escobar also felt the need to project himself in the political arena. After investing in civic and philanthropic activities in Medellín and neighboring Envigado, he sought election to the Chamber of Representatives, with the help of some traditional politicians, whose support he achieved with relative ease. Nevertheless, as was the case with Lehder, Escobar's megalomania doomed him. Indeed, he did not foresee the reaction of some political sectors, which considered his presence in Congress indicative of the invasion of the sphere of representative democracy by so-called hot money. Several congressmen from these sectors attacked Escobar head on and in a very short time succeeded in depriving him of his parliamentary seat.

From Electoralism to Terrorism

Escobar's reaction was quite violent. During the process he attempted to discredit his detractors and associate them with drug money, but shortly afterwards he opted for physically eliminating his strongest accuser, Justice Minister Rodrigo Lara Bonilla. With this action Escobar relinquished any parliamentary pretensions and, in exchange, chose direct confrontation with what he would later label the "Colombian political oligarchy."

A third way of doing politics, closely related to Escobar's trajectory, revolved around the rejection of extradition. The 1980 treaty between Colombia and the United States remained undefined, and there was no apparent political will to revive it. Lara Bonilla's death in 1984 convinced President Betancur of the need to reactivate extradition to the United States of individuals charged in U.S. courts. The first reaction of the traffickers was to seek negotiations with the government: they met in Panama with the attorney general and former president Alfonso López. At the meeting, the traffickers offered to stop the production and export of cocaine in exchange for benign treatment by the government. President Betancur rejected this pro-posal, as might be expected, since public opinion was particularly sensitive and the most important leaders of public opinion opposed any negotiation with the traffickers. The memory of Lara Bonilla's assassination was still fresh. Thus the door was closed to later negotiations, opening the way for the option of violent reaction against extradition by the drug lords.

The confrontational character of this dynamic increased when Escobar and his allies opted for a different strategy and proceeded to group them-selves under the banner of a new organization, the Extraditables (*Los Extra-ditables*). This organization unrolled a wave of violence and terrorism that shattered the country during the second half of the 1980s and the beginning of the 1990s. The period was punctuated with the kidnappings and murders of judges, members of the national security corps, and politicians, as well as dynamite blasts whose victims were civilian bystanders.

Part of the battle against extradition involved the continuous pressure put on the members of the assembly whose mission it was to write a new constitution in 1991. The pressure was so intense that the assembly decided . to include an article in the new constitution whereby extradition of Colom-bian nationals was prohibited. Once this goal was achieved, Escobar turned himself in, but he was able nevertheless to impose his own conditions on his prison time. He demanded confinement to a particular prison, particular guards, and special comforts and degrees of permissiveness that would guarantee not only his personal security but also his ability to keep his busi-ness going. Later, after his death in 1995, the extradition article was cut from the constitution.

This political process had several noteworthy consequences. It rein-forced the "godfather" nature of Escobar's organization (Naylor 1995), in which he assumed a leadership role based on confrontation with the state and his power of intimidation over his associates. This leadership style, be-sides embodying the acknowledgment that Escobar was the greatest cocaine exporter in the region, was based on the fact that he himself had directly joined in the political struggle against extradition, supposedly in the name of all the exporters. Due to his enormous need for cash, Escobar demanded huge contributions from his peers. Some of them, feeling that they were being extorted, reacted by leaving him alone or even starting to build alli-ances to fight him. In other words, contradictions inherent to his leadership style ended up creating new enemies for Escobar, even among his former comrades. Many of them organized themselves around the so-called Pepes

(Perseguidos por Pablo Escobar, "pursued by Pablo Escobar") and launched a total war against the drug lord, who had his range of action reduced, parts of his property destroyed, and his closest partners eliminated. Escobar found himself quickly challenged on several battlefronts that, in spite of his immense power, surpassed his capacity for war. The result was his death in a raid by the National Police backed by the DEA.

Terrorism versus State Penetration

Escobar's style of leadership was not necessarily a response to needs inherent to the cocaine trade. In fact, traffickers who had consolidated their organizations were able to export their goods independently. Unified action and "godfathership" (i.e., the consolidation of a specific type of organized crime) were not necessary for the business. But they were essential for the violent confrontation with the state. The Cali cartel bosses understood this and instead of joining in the confrontation preferred to penetrate the state by financing politicians' campaigns and buying their loyalty. This strategy was so successful that with their contributions they were able to influence the presidential race in 1994, when Ernesto Samper was elected. During the subsequent debate in Congress, nearly one-third of its members, as well as a number of high-ranking state officials, were denounced for having had some kind of relationship with the Cali drug lords. Several congressmen, as well as high officials, lost their seats and went to prison.

This alternative way of doing politics was efficient as long as the Cali traffickers were able to keep politicians on their payroll, which they achieved thanks to two strategies. In the first place, their relationships with politicians, officials, and state security agents were kept at a certain level of discretion, so that it was difficult both to initiate judicial processes and to enforce sanctions. In this way, these relationships were uncovered only through rumors. In the second place, especially with respect to the Rodríguez Orejuela brothers, whose role in Valle was similar to Escobar's in Antioquia, they acted as godfathers, but they were careful to try to build their images as legal businessmen, citizens complying with the law, and local benefactors. Some of the Valle traffickers inserted themselves very nicely into some cities of the region, where they found, if not complicity, at least high degrees of acceptance or tolerance (Camacho Guizado 1993). Furthermore, more than a few businesspeople from this region organized joint activities with the drug lords, looking to obtain extraordinary economic benefits. (As it turned out, the capture of some of the heads of the cartel would lead to big financial losses for some of those businessmen.)

But when the Rodríguez brothers and their main partners aimed at their highest target, the presidency, in 1994, a reversal of fortune occurred. The pressure exerted by the president himself, together with the unyielding demands of the U.S. authorities, led to a declaration of war against the traffickers by the police, an institution traditionally accused of corruption and many of whose members were at the service of the Cali cartel. The result was the capture of the top members of the cartel and the voluntary surrender of some second-rank members.

The costs of this political process were extremely high for the country. As part of the rapidly increasing pressure it exerted on Colombia, the U.S. government took retaliatory measures toward the national government. The Colombian president lost his visa, and for two consecutive years Colombia was decertified, decertification being a tool the United States uses to punish governments that, from its viewpoint, fail to cooperate in the war on drugs. Thus Colombian institutional stability was threatened on two fronts: on the one hand by the corruption shown in the complicity of politicians and officials with drug traffickers and on the other by the dramatic and unprecedented deterioration of Colombia's international image.

Drug Traffic and Society

The effects of the actions of the big traffickers were not only political. Their exertions, especially in Medellín, also resulted in the construction of two social types that would come to epitomize Colombian violence. The first is the *sicario*, a poor youngster, mainly from Medellín, who for a sum of money takes care of killing cartel opponents or enemies. In this way, debtors, traitors, noted politicians, judges, judicial officials, and members of the state intelligence and police corps were eliminated. The generalized presence of *sicarios* in Medellín turned the city into one of the world's most violent and accelerated the stigmatization of its poor youth.

Drug traffickers were not the only ones contributing to this process. At the beginning of the 1980s, as a result of peace negotiations with the Betancur administration, the M19 guerrillas attempted to expand into some cities, creating "freedom camps," organizations of poor youngsters whom the guerrilla organization intended to train. When negotiations failed and the M19 was forced to retreat into rural areas, these youngsters became gangsters for hire by the highest bidder. Thus traffickers found that their way had been paved and that the M19 had provided the labor they required to carry on their efforts.

The second social type to emerge was the paramilitary. Originating from MAS, the paramilitary bands soon expanded to become extreme right-wing armies that acted, in some cases, under the tutelage or complicity of state-armed organisms (Medina 1990). More than a few trafficker-landowners took advantage of this opportunity and organized their own private bands. Nevertheless, the need to combat the guerrilla organizations grew in such a way that thanks to the generous financing of landowners—traffickers or not—they have become, as we will see, one of the main enemies of the insurgency.

One of the most important ways drug trafficking was politicized did not emerge as a result of anything the drug traders did. The U.S. government, through Ambassador Lewis Tambs, decidedly contributed in conferring political status on the drug trade and thus fueling confrontation with the state by both guerrilla groups and traffickers. Indeed, in April 1984, a police squad found an enormous cocaine laboratory in the southwestern jungle region of the country. The ambassador seized the opportunity to publicly announce that FARC guerrillas protected this laboratory, which in his opinion was final proof that this organization had ties to the traffickers. He then coined the term *narco-guerrilla*, with the intention of slandering the guerrilla group, ignoring its character as an insurgent political force, and stimulating confrontational politics as an alternative to negotiation, a political strategy that President Betancur seemed to favor. Thus the ambassador, followed by the media and the state armed forces, and with definite support from some U.S. congressmen, constructed "truth" from little more than rumors. His construction was based on the fact that the guerrilla group had received large amounts of money from "taxes" imposed on both direct producers and intermediaries. This contribution *(gramaje)* became the supposed evidence of organic and political ties between FARC and the peasants on the one hand and the drug traffickers on the other. Neither Pablo Escobar's declaration that he was a zealous foe of the guerrillas nor the fact that, along with other traffickers, he was organizing and financing paramilitary groups precisely to fight against the guerrillas was enough to counter this offensive (Camacho Guizado 1988).

Years later, during the Samper administration, and after the news had come out about the Cali cartel's contributions to Samper's campaign, the retiring director of the U.S. DEA in Colombia fueled the fire once again by giving statements to the media in which he called Colombia a "narco-democracy." This label gave new strength to the politicization of drug trafficking and furthered international pressure on Colombia as well.

To summarize, the "political phase" of drug trafficking was diverse, erratic, and self-destructive. It is impossible to speculate as to what the fate of the traffickers would have been had they decided not to participate in the political arena. They probably would have kept business going, but sooner or later confrontation with the state would have become unavoidable. The pressure of public opinion, together with U.S. demands, would have forced confrontation with the Colombian government. The fact that some traffickers did opt to become enemies of the state and others to act as false friends (Orozco 1992) eventually proved insufficient for the survival of traditional trafficking organizations. No doubt, the enormous accumulation of capital in so few hands was overwhelming for small-time criminals who found themselves transformed into petty kings in their regions and into actual threats to state stability, having accumulated so much power and such capacity to corrupt, finance, and buy both property and consciences. They aimed too high and got a conclusive response: many of the surviving members of these organizations are in jail.

Violence and political entanglement were not the only side effects of the Colombian drug trade. Tthe traffickers' investments and spending spread through some sectors of society, fostering a certain degree of upward social mobility. Money laundering, in particular, made it possible for more than a few people to earn a great deal because they belonged to the right social networks. Established businessmen and financial firms, as well as new and competent traders, were thus able to improve their fortunes while at the same time being part of a process whereby Colombian society became less "aristocratic" and more plebeian. This, is turn, reinforced the old fears on the part of the "submerging class" of being invaded or replaced by the "emerging class."

As a result of the production processes, the coca-growing regions experienced an enormous influx of labor for the cultivation, harvesting, and some of the processing of raw materials. Some of the producers were able to make enough to settle down as landowners and coca growers. Others just survived as paid harvesters of the leaf. Coca, then, also stimulated a horizontal social mobility that has converted the southwestern slopes of the country into highly populated areas, with the foreseeable negative consequences on the ecology of an extremely rich biological reserve inappropriate for agriculture.

Thus although drug trafficking did stimulate upward social mobility, it also decisively contributed to a further concentration of property, especially in the agrarian sector. Many of the former traffickers were of peasant origin, and by buying land they enhanced their renown among their fellow peasants; but at the same time they were laundering their fortunes and ensuring their future. Many traditional landowners welcomed the opportunity to sell their land, whether because they did not have the money they needed to make it productive or because pressure from guerrilla groups prevented them from personally tending to it. The result has been a kind of agrarian counter-reformation. In fact, even when drug traffickers have died, the state has been unable to repossess the land and distribute it to facilitate some kind of property democratization.

From Drug Lords to *Traquetos*: The Present Situation

As a result of the dismantling of the drug cartels, trafficking has experienced radical changes in structure, changes that have coincided with transformations in other phases of the business. According to police intelligence sources, there are between 250 and 300 trafficking organizations in Colombia. Their leaders are some of the former cartels' second-rank members: bodyguards, accountants, technicians, gunmen *(traquetos)*,[8] former leaders' relatives, or simply new drug businessmen who benefited economically from the destruction of the cartels.

The new organizations are smaller, closed, and secret, which means less business management capacity and a need to abandon some of the most profitable aspects, such as retail distribution in some U.S. cities. The new traffickers have also been forced to develop new routes, international alliances, markets, and export modalities.

These organizational changes have also coincided with key transformations of the business itself. The first is the transfer of coca leaf production to Colombia. In part as a result of eradication efforts in Peru and Bolivia—which included, in Peru especially, the capture and shooting down of small airplanes transporting coca base and paste—Colombians opted to grow new, more robust varieties locally, The result has been a substantial increase in the Colombian coca-growing area and therefore in exports. According to the most authoritative sources, the total cultivated area grew from 37,000 hectares in 1995 to 122,000 in 1999, and potential production increased from 60 to 520 tons (Rocha García 2000).

The second change has to do with the new type of alliance established with Mexican traffickers. Even though these contacts were already at work when the old drug lords were alive (Kenney 2000), the new arrangements seem different. Indeed, the new exporters have decided to partially abandon distribution in U.S. territory, a task they have left to the Mexicans, who control more extensive and efficient distribution networks.[9] Besides, they have proceeded to negotiate with the Mexicans in kind, reducing both their revenue and their risk of being captured by U.S. authorities.

As an expert on Mexican drug trade has pointed out, "The dismantling of Colombia's Cali group in 1995–1996 created new opportunities for Mexican traffickers, who began to develop their own wholesale and retail operations in the United States. Bypassing now-weakened Colombian operators, they also started forging direct links to coca leaf farmers and processing laboratories in Bolivia and Peru" (Smith 1999). At the same time, some Peruvian traffickers have become independent from the Colombians and have developed their own production and export networks (Lupsha 1994). Thus Colombians are no longer the main direct suppliers for the U.S. market; to the contrary, their position has become more and more subordinated to the Mexicans and others. There are also hints that Chilean, Argentinean, and Brazilian markets are increasingly being supplied by Peruvian and Bolivian exporters. Nevertheless, Colombians keep their dominant role as wholesalers for both the Mexican and European markets, where they have established alliances with local trafficking organizations, especially those from eastern Europe. They have also opted for diversifying their routes, now privileging the use of the Pacific Ocean, less populated and less watched than the Caribbean. At least for some time, innovation will benefit them: they have gained an advantage over those countries' authorities.

All these changes reflect an important capacity on the part of the criminals to adapt to new business conditions and to learn new survival strategies. They also illustrate an enormous paradox, since while Colombian production is evidently growing and worldwide drug use has not slowed, Colombian drug organizations seem more atomized and therefore weaker.

As far as their attitudes and behavior are concerned, these new traffickers seem to have learned the lessons of their predecessors and are avoiding making the same mistakes. They do not attempt, at least openly, to meddle in the political process, even if some of them do interfere with the local administrations in their regions. Some of them are more educated than the former traffickers and have developed strategies, methods, and techniques aimed at making the business more dynamic, sneaking away from law enforcement (Kenney 1999) and blending in better in their respective regions. This means avoiding sumptuous and suspicious consumer habits, following behavior patterns that do not make them excessively visible, and developing personal presentation techniques to make them appear to be legal businessmen. Great estates with luxurious buildings, fine horses, expensive cars, and beautiful women now seem to be a thing of the past. They attracted too much attention from Colombian and U.S. authorities.

These changes are of interest in several ways. In the first place, they throw doubts on the hypotheses about drug-trafficking groups as unitary organizations combining business with pretensions to political power, and in this sense as serious threats to national security and democracy. From the preceding description it is clear that the new drug-trafficking organizations, being independent, small, clandestine, and with a limited capacity to act, are above all economic lawbreakers and would not aspire to gain political power or dominate the state. The most remarkable evidence of this is the apparent decrease in opposition to extradition; new traffickers seemingly prefer to avoid being identified, captured, and remitted to the United States rather than to openly oppose extradition through violent means.[10]

Second, the nature of the organizations does not appear to play a fundamental role in the dynamics of drug trafficking. For big, godfatherlike organizations, or small or medium-size independent entrepreneurs, the new picture shows strong fragmentation accompanied by a great capacity to adapt to conditions created by national or international authorities, to the degree of centralization of corruption in different countries, and to the changing dynamics of international markets.

"Narco-Landowners" and the Paramilitary

Drug trafficking still plays a central role in the Colombian political process, even though some of the members of the new type of drug organizations do not seek to play a direct political role. Their political dimensions are more clearly expressed by their financing of some of the paramilitary organizations. In this practice they act more as extreme right-wing landowners than as drug traffickers. Indeed, paramilitary groups, organized by the cartels to defend their rural properties in guerrilla zones, grew to become enormous armed bands that soon surpassed the agrarian interests of landowning drug lords. After being trained by British and Israeli mercenaries in skills such as settling disputes and eliminating enemies, the numerous paramilitary organizations started to unify around the ruthless struggle against guerrilla organizations. Though some of these bands are still at the service of drug lords, some others have assumed a dynamic that has turned them into big, right-wing armies, relatively independent from the drug lords, which are conducting a struggle against subversion, in defense of the state and social order.

The paramilitaries have thus passed from the private to the public sphere (Cubides 1998) and have become one of the main axes of armed confrontation in Colombia. Moreover, the autonomization process of the main paramilitary organization has even allowed its principal military boss to publicly declare himself against drug trafficking. This, nevertheless, has not been an obstacle for traffickers, other landowners, and extreme right political forces to continue to finance the paramilitaries.

This last point deserves further commentary, since it is clear that this pattern of political activity has had a paradoxical consequence: through the financing of the paramilitaries, the traffickers have established political relationships with the traditional landowners and many of the entrepreneurs and members of the upper classes that also contribute to paramilitaries. Thus these traffickers have solved some of the obstacles to their social legitimation. In the traditional struggles described above they acted on their own, advancing their own interests. Now, through the paramilitary movement, they contribute to the defense of the interests of a major fraction of society and are no longer politically isolated.

However, during the recent peace negotiations in which these bands have engaged with the Colombian government, the U.S. government, the Colombian press, and independent analysts have publicized that the most conspicuous leaders of the paramilitary movement are themselves drug traffickers. It seems clear that they are directing their efforts to be recognized as political actors and thus to obtain some degree of legitimacy and favorability through the negotiations. The greatest obstacle to this maneuver is that the U.S. government has declared them traffickers and has demanded that they be extradited to the United States.

The Forms of Demand

The places where paramilitary armies have settled have also become cocaine- and poppy-growing regions. As a result, the paramilitary have become a third coca-revenue-demanding force, after the traffickers and the FARC guerrilla groups. Thus a growing demand in the international consumer market has consolidated the three main internal sources of demand and the dynamics of drug trafficking in Colombia in general—and, simultaneously, consolidated armed conflict.

The complexity of these demand structures has striking consequences. First, as has been described throughout this chapter, Colombia stands as the major cocaine exporter in the world and thus draws and concentrates the attention of law enforcement agencies both inside the country and in the consuming countries. Second, the "armed demand" represented by FARC and the paramilitaries means that cocaine is key to both right- and left-wing extremist groups engaging in the armed conflict. FARC represents a powerful source of demand—forced or voluntary—mainly for the direct producers located in the areas under their control. And the paramilitaries perceive the potential for huge fortunes both from direct producers located in their areas and from the landowners, traffickers or not.

But, third, the dynamics of "armed demand" differentiate it from the more normal pattern of international drug trade: this new pattern implies the establishment of a close relationship between the irregular Colombian armies and the international organizations that control the arms trade. The result is a new basis for interlocking two of the most powerful and deadly types of organizations in the world today.

Coca and poppy have thus become the main stimulants for both the drug-trafficking business and the armed conflict that crosses over and menaces the institutional stability and democracy of Colombian society. In this sense, the future of the country depends on the possibility that the democratic forces can eliminate the drug business and settle the armed conflict through peaceful negotiations. The outcome of these two processes will determine whether Colombia continues in its current turbulent and critical mode or becomes a less violent and more democratically ruled society.

Notes

1. U.S. Bureau of Narcotics, *Traffic in Opium and Other Dangerous Drugs for the Year Ended December 31, 1957* (Washington, DC: U.S. Government Printing Office, 1958), 22, quoted in Sáenz Rovner (1996).

2. *El Espectador,* May 22, 1959, 3, quoted in Arango Jaramillo and Child 1984. Most probably there is an error, since the U.S. agents involved must have belonged to the FBN (Federal Bureau of Narcotics) and not the FBI (Federal Bureau of Intelligence).

3. U.S. Bureau of Narcotics, *Traffic in Opium and Other Dangerous Drugs for the Year Ended December 31, 1961* (Washington, DC: U.S. Government Printing Office, 1962), 26–27, quoted in Sáenz Rovner (1996).

4. U.S. Congress, House Committee Rules and Administration, *Hearings to Create a Select Committee on Narcotics Abuse and Control before House Committee on Rules and Administration,* 96th Cong., 2nd sess., 1980, 70, cited in MacDonald (1988).

5. France Press cable originating in Lima, published in *El Tiempo,* September 19, 1968, quoted in Rosselli (1968: 1).

6. See also Dan Gardner, "Losing the War on Drugs," *Ottawa Citizen,* September 5, 2000.

7. Sidney Zabludoff, "Colombian Narcotics Organizations as Business Enterprises," in *Economics of the Narcotics Industry Conference Report,* ed. U.S. State Department of State Bureau of Research and Intelligence and the Central Intelligence Agency (Washington, DC: U.S. State Department and Central Intelligence Agency, 1994). In his testimony to the U.S. justice system, Guillermo Pallomari, systems and accounting chief for the Rodríguez Orejuela brothers' organization, stated that the organizations had "divisions," each with its own area of responsibility: intelligence, politics, finances, arms or security, legal issues, and drug trafficking. See Kenney (1999). The best analysis of the Colombian traffic organizations in terms of their entrepreneurial character is the work of Krauthausen and Sarmiento (1991).

8. *Traquetos* are in charge of drug lord security and foe elimination. The expression has been generalized to include several types of second-rank members of trafficking organizations.

9. Known annual exportation of Colombian cocaine to Mexico has increased from one ton in 1985 to thirty tons in 1990, twenty-eight tons in 1994, and more than sixty-five tons since 1995 (Rocha García 2000).

10. This does not, of course, keep some traffickers from seeking to pressure the judges in charge of their extradition processes. Moreover, it cannot be denied that some of these judges' lives are threatened. Nevertheless, the possibility of traffickers succeeding in their objective of paralyzing the justice system is much more remote than it was during the last decade.

References

Abadinsky, Howard. 1997. *Organized Crime.* 5th ed. Chicago: Nelson-Hall.
Arango Jaramillo, Mario. 1988. *Impacto del narcotráfico en Antioquia.* Medellín: Multigráficas.

Arango Jaramillo, Mario, and Jorge Child. 1984. *Narcotráfico, imperio de la cocaína.* Medellín: Editorial Percepción.

Asociación Nacional de Instituciones Financieras. 1979. *Marihuana, legalización o represión.* Bogotá: Fondo Editorial ANIF.

Baum, Dan. 1997. *Smoke and Mirrors: The War on Drugs and the Politics of Failure.* Boston: Little, Brown.

Bertram, Eva, Kenneth Sharpe, and Peter Andreas. 1996. *Drug War Politics: The Price of Denial.* Berkeley: University of California Press.

Camacho Guizado, Álvaro. 1988. *Droga y sociedad en Colombia: El poder y el estigma.* Cali: CIDSE/CEREC.

———. 1993. "Villa Pujante: Une 'narcocratie' régionale." In *La planète des drogues,* ed. Alain Labrousse and Alain Wallon. Paris: Seuil.

Cañón, Luis. 1994. *El patrón.* Bogotá: Planeta.

Cubides, Fernando. 1998. "De lo privado y lo público en la violencia colombiana: Los paramilitares." In *Las violencias, inclusión reciente,* ed. Jaime Arocha, Fernando Cubiles, and Myriam Jimeno. Bogotá: Centro de Estudios Sociales de la Universidad Nacional.

Gómez, Hernando José. 1988. "La economía ilegal en Colombia: Tamaño, evolución, características e impacto económico." *Coyuntura Económica* 18, no. 3.

Gootenberg, Paul. 1999. "Reluctance or Resistance? Constructing Cocaine (Prohibitions) in Peru, 1910–1950." In *Cocaine: Global Histories,* ed. Paul Gootenberg. New York: Routledge.

Gugliotta, Guy, and Jeff Leen. 1990. *Kings of Cocaine.* New York: Harper.

Henman, Anthony. 1980. *Mama Coca.* Bogotá: El Áncora Editores–Editorial Oveja Negra.

Kenney, Michael. 1999. "A Summary of Guillermo Pallomari's Testimony in the 1997 Operation Cornerstone Trial of Michael Abbell and William Moran." *Transnational Organized Crime* 5, no. 1, Documentation section.

———. 2000. "La capacidad de aprendizaje de las organizaciones colombianas de narcotráfico." *Análisis Político,* no. 41 (September-December).

Kleinknecht, William. 1996. *The New Ethnic Mobs: The Changing Face of Organized Crime in America.* New York: Free Press.

Krauthausen, Ciro, and Luis Fernando Sarmiento. 1991. *Cocaína & Co.* Bogotá: Coediciones Instituto de Estudios Políticos y Relaciones Internacionales/Tercer Mundo.

Lupsha, Meter. 1990. "El tráfico de drogas: México y Colombia, una perspectiva comparada." In *Economía y política del narcotráfico,* comp. Juan G. Tokatlian and Bruce Bagley. Bogotá: Ediciones Uniandes-CEI Uniandes-CEREC.

———. 1994. "Nets of Affiliation in the Political Economy of Drug Trafficking and Transnational Crime." In *Economics of the Narcotics Industry Conference Report,* ed. U.S. Department of State Bureau of Research and Intelligence and the Central Intelligence Agency. Washington, DC: U.S. State Department and Central Intelligence Agency.

MacDonald, Scott B. 1988. *Dancing on a Volcano: The Latin American Drug Trade*. New York: Praeger.

Medina, Carlos. 1990. *Autodefensas, paramilitares y narcotráfico en Colombia*. Bogotá: Documentos Periodísticos.

Musto, David. 1993. *The American Disease*. New York: Oxford University Press.

Naylor, R. T. 1995. "From Cold War to Crime War: The Search for a 'New National Security Threat.'" *Transnational Organized Crime* 1, no. 4:37–46.

Orozco, Iván. 1992. *Combatientes, rebeldes y terroristas: Guerra y derecho en Colombia*. Bogotá: Instituto de Estudios Políticos y Relaciones Internacionales/Temis.

Reuter, Meter. 1993. "Después de selladas las fronteras: ¿Podrán las fuentes nacionales sustituir las drogas importadas?" In *El combate de las drogas en América*, comp. Peter H. Smith. México: Fondo de Cultura Económica.

Rocha García, Ricardo. 2000. *La economía colombiana tras 25 años de narcotráfico*. Bogotá: Siglo del Hombre Editores and United Nations Office on Drugs and Crime.

Rosselli, Humberto. 1968. *Historia de la psiquiatría en Colombia*. 2 vols. Bogotá: Editorial Horizontes.

Sabbag, Robert. 1990. *Ciego de nieve: Traficando con cocaína*. Barcelona: Editorial Anagrama.

Sáenz Rovner, Eduardo. 1996. "La prehistoria del narcotráfico en Colombia. Serie documental: Desde la Gran Depresión hasta la Revolución Cubana." In *Innovar: Revista de Ciencias Administrativas y Sociales*, no. 8 (July–December).

Smith, Peter. 1999. "Semiorganized International Crime: Drug Trafficking in Mexico." In *Transnational Crime in the Americas*, ed. Tom Farer. New York: Routledge.

Téllez, Pedro Claver. 1993. *Efraín González: La dramática vida de un asesino asesinado*. Bogotá: Planeta.

Thoumi, Francisco E. 1994. *Economía política y narcotráfico*. Bogotá: Tercer Mundo Editores.

Tovar, Hermes. 1999. *Colombia: Droga, economía, guerra y paz*. Bogotá: Ediciones Temas de Hoy.

Vélez, Luis Guillermo, Gloria Cecilia Tamayo, and Jorge Pérez. 1980. "La cocaína y la marihuana en Colombia, 1972–1978." *Temas administrativos: Revista Universidad EAFIT Escuela de Administración, Finanzas y Tecnología*, no. 39 (July–September).

Walker, William O., III. 1989. *Drug Control in the Americas*. 2nd ed. Albuquerque: University of New Mexico Press.

Colombia

In Search of a New Model for Conflict Resolution

Daniel García-Peña Jaramillo

Daniel García-Peña Jaramillo presents a detailed history of the two models that have guided the peace negotiations to date in Colombia, concluding with his vision for a "third model," more adapted to the present domestic and international context, which could form the foundation for a successful peace process. He draws on firsthand knowledge of the process from his years as acting high commissioner for peace, his role in the Samper administration, and his continuing involvement in the peace process. The first of these models had its genesis in the Betancur administration's negotiations with the Fuerzas Armadas Revolucionarias de Colombia (FARC, Revolutionary Armed Forces of Colombia) in the early 1980s. Betancur acknowledged for the first time that the guerrillas were social and political actors whose grievances were rooted in social inequalities and backed by ideological interpretations of history. His administration put forward a broad agenda that was meant to address the perceived roots of the conflict. Despite important advances, its downfall was its informal style and the failure to reach out broadly to important political and social actors outside the executive branch. In the second half of the 1980s, the Barco administration inaugurated the second model, adding greater institutional formality to the process and focusing negotiations on a narrower agenda, targeting the reincorporation of the guerrillas into political life. These negotiations, however, continued to exclude the legislature, civil society, and the international community. Samper and Pastrana in turn incorporated some elements of both models, but Samper was hamstrung by constant political crises, while Pastrana never quite resolved the tension between the two models. Given the breakdown of all these talks and the return to a more military phase of the conflict under Uribe, García-Peña argues that a third model must emerge once the moment for negotiations returns. This model must be marked by ever broader social participation, increased attention to the norms of humanitarian and human rights laws, consideration of regional autonomy for areas under guerrilla control, the inclusion of the paramilitary in the process, and attention to both the broad and the narrow agendas of the earlier two models. At the same time, he recognizes that the hope for productive talks is dim until the parties have once again exhausted their military options.

The term *complexity* is often used to describe the internal war in Colombia. One of the world's oldest ongoing armed conflicts, it entails multiple, very well-armed actors on both the extreme left and the extreme right, yet the vast majority of casualties are unarmed civilians. The causes of the war are very Colombian, deeply rooted in the nation's political and social history; nonetheless, the internal conflict is intricately linked to several key international factors. It combines elements usually associated with the conflicts of the Cold War era, such as ideologies that espouse national liberation and social revolution, with issues that are part of the so-called new global agenda: terrorism, narco-trafficking, organized crime, small arms proliferation, human rights, humanitarian relief, migration, and the environment. Colombia is Latin America's oldest and most stable formal democracy, but an entire political party has been practically killed off by political violence, and many opposition leaders are either in exile or under armed protection.

However, almost as old and as intricate as the war itself are attempts to end it through political means. Since the first formal steps toward reaching a negotiated settlement were taken during the term of President Belisario Betancur (1982–86), the governments of all of the ensuing presidents— Virgilio Barco (1986–90), César Gaviria (1990–94), Ernesto Samper (1994–98), and Andrés Pastrana (1998–2002)—have attempted to bring the war to an end through dialogue.

These two decades, which Colombians refer to as the "peace process,"[1] have produced some significant, albeit partial, successes and several valuable lessons in peace building, but also many failures and frustrations. The breakdown of the most recent stage of peace talks that took place during the

Pastrana administration left a strong sense of failure and contributed greatly to the election of President Alvaro Uribe (2002–06), who campaigned on his hard-line views regarding the war. Since his inauguration, he has set out to change the balance of power on the battlefield through the use of military force, with the stated objective of creating better conditions for negotiations in the future.

Just as the war in Colombia is a dramatic case study for the "new wars" of the post–Cold War era (see Kaldor 1999), the peace process and the specific forms it might take in the future could well be a fascinating laboratory to study the "new peaces" required for the new millennium. This chapter will attempt to analyze some specific aspects of the past in order to explore the different alternatives for peace in the future.

Each of the previously mentioned presidential administrations has had its particular style, faced very different political conditions, and developed over the years diverse and often conflicting focuses toward the issue of peace. These policies, in turn, were met by different responses from the insurgent groups, whose strategic objectives, nature, size, and military strength also saw significant changes over time. (See table 4.1 for the full names of the armed groups in Colombia and their participation in peace talks.)

The peace process has had its distinct stages and mixed results. However, I will argue that over the years the evolution and interplay between government policy and insurgents' responses have produced two distinct historical models for conflict resolution. The first was molded during the Betancur years and was coauthored by the FARC, while the second was the result of the Barco administration's dealings with the M19. Even though since then there have been variations of the two and attempts at designing alternatives, the two often conflicting models have continued to predominate. (See table 4.2 for significant peace accords signed over the years.)

I will also contend, later in the chapter, that over the years and despite the many setbacks, there have been important elements of progress and evolution that in the future could come to constitute a new third model for conflict resolution. This model would include new factors, such as a more active role for civil society, greater concern from the international community, and the effects of the growing intensity of the war itself, particularly its increasing levels of degradation—attacks on civilians, kidnappings, and other forms of combat distinct from classic warfare—that have led to a high toll on human life and democracy. (See table 4.3 for a summary of the three models.)

Table 4.1
Armed Groups in Colombia and Their Participation in Peace Talks (as of December 2002)

Acronym in Spanish	Name in Spanish	Name in English	Year Founded	Participation in Peace Talks	Date of Demobilization/ Current Status
FARC	Fuerzas Armadas Revoluionarias de Columbia	Revolutionary Armed Forces of Colombia	1964	Jan. 1983–Oct. 1987 June 1991–Mar. 1992* July 1998–Feb. 2002	Still active
ELN	Ejército de Liberación Nacional	National Liberation Army	1964	June 1991–Mar. 1992* Sept. 1994–June 2002**	Still active
EPL	Ejército Popular de Liberación	People's Liberation Army	1967	July 1983–Dec. 1985 Jan. 1990–Feb. 1991 June 1991–Mar. 1992*	80% demobilized in 1991; remaining 20% still active
M19	Movimiento 19 de Abril	19th of April Movement	1974	July 1983–June 1985 Jan. 1989–Mar. 1990	Demobilized in 1990
PRT	Partido Revolucionario de los Trabajadores	Revolutionary Worker's Party	1984 (broke off of EPL)	Apr. 1990–Jan. 1991	Demobilized in 1991
MAQL	Movimiento Armado Quintín Lame	Quintín Lame Armed Movement	1984	June 1990–Apr. 1991	Demobilized in 1991
CGSB*	Coordinadora Guerrillera Simón Bolívar	Simon Bolivar Guerrilla Coordinator	1987	June 1991–Mar. 1992*	Disbanded in 1993
CRS	Corriente de Renovación Socialista	Current of Socialist Renovation	1991 (broke off from ELN)	Nov. 1993–Mar. 1994	Demobilized in 1994
AUC***	Autodefensas Unidas de Colombia	United Self-Defense Groups of Colombia	1996	Does not apply	Still active

*The CGSB was an umbrella organization that was formed in 1987 by FARC, ELN, EPL, M19, PRT, and MAQL, but by the time it held talks with the government in Caracas in 1991 and Tlaxcala in 1992 it was reduced to the FARC, the ELN, and a small remnant of the EPL.
**Although constantly interrupted by suspension and long pauses, formal and informal talks and contacts were held with the ELN during almost all of the Samper and Pastrana administrations.
***Although the Uribe administration is currently undergoing talks with the AUC, it has not yet recognized them as a political actor, nor have any of the administrations analyzed in this chapter.

Table 4.2
Significant Peace Accords Signed, 1984–2002

Name (and Place)	Date	Parties
La Uribe Accord (La Uribe, Meta)	Mar. 28, 1984	Betancur government, FARC
Corinto Accord (Corinto, Valle)	Aug. 23, 1984	Betancur government, M19
El Hobo Accord (El Hobo, Huila)	Aug. 24, 1984	Betancur government, EPL
Final Peace Accord (Santo Domingo, Cauca)	Mar. 9, 1990	Barco government, M19
Final Peace Accord (Ovejas, Sucre)	Jan. 25, 1991	Gaviria government, PRT
Final Peace Accord (Bogotá, DC)	Feb. 15, 1991	Gaviria government, EPL
Accord on the Agenda (Caracas, Venezuela)	June 6, 1991	Gaviria government, CGSB
Final Peace Accord (Bogotá, DC)	June 26, 1991	Gaviria government, MAQL
Final Peace Accord (Flor del Monte, Sucre)	Apr. 9, 1994	Gaviria government, CRS
Draft Accord of Viana (Madrid, Spain)	Feb. 9, 1998	Samper government, ELN*
Gates of Heaven Accord (Mainz, Germany)	July 15, 1998	delegates civil society, ELN
Agenda for Change for Peace (Caquetania, Caquetá)	May 6, 1999	Pastrana government, FARC
Roles for the Encounter Zone (Havana, Cuba)	Dec. 14, 2000	Pastrana government, ELN
Los Pozos Accord (San Vicente del Caguán, Caquetá)	Feb. 9, 2001	Pastrana government, FARC
Accord on Humanitarian Exchange	June 2, 2001	Pastrana government, FARC
San Francisco de la Sombra Accord (San Vicente del Caguán, Caquetá)	Oct. 5, 2001	Pastrana government, FARC
Accord for Colombia (Havana, Cuba)	Nov. 24, 2001	Pastrana government, ELN

*Never ratified by ELN Central Command.

The Betancur/FARC Model

Upon taking office in August 1982, Betancur presented his peace initiative, which was based on the premise that the internal armed conflict being waged with the rebel groups since the mid-sixties had objective causes rooted in a long history of social inequity and political exclusion, as well as subjective causes—ideological considerations that led to opting for armed struggle as the means of achieving revolutionary transformation of society. By recognizing the rebel groups as political and social actors, he deemed

Table 4.3
Summary of Models for Conflict Resolution

Elements	Betancur/FARC Model	Barco/M19 Model	New, Colombian Model
Scope of agenda	Broad (social and political structural reforms as basis for insurgents' transformation into political party)	Limited (guarantees for political and economic reincorporation of insurgents)	Integral (social and political structural reforms, as well as disarmament, guarantees for political and economic reincorporation of all ex-combatants and those affected)
Prioritization	Reforms first, disarmament later	Disarmament first, reforms later	Reforms and disarmament simultaneously
Timetables	Clearly defined for cease-fire, ambiguous with regard to political objectives	Clearly defined for demobilization, not defined for reforms	Clearly defined
Cease-fire	Result of bilateral agreement as first step in process, with inadequate verification and undefined objectives	Unilateral, precondition to begin talks, localization of guerrillas in defined areas	Result of bilateral (or multilateral) agreement as first step in process, localization in defined areas, with international verification and clear linkage to timetable and results
Demobilization/ reintegration	Gradual transition into UP, but with no precise parameters or mechanisms for reincorporation, or for demobilization or disarming	First reincorporation program, with mixed results and limited to ex-combatants	Reincorporation of all ex-combatants, victims, and regions most severely affected by the conflict
Institutional mechanism	Informal, mixed civil society/government (Peace Commission)	Formal, midlevel (presidential advisor)	Formal, cabinet-level (high commissioner), National Peace Council
Intermediaries	Peace Commission (mixed civil society/government)	None	United Nations, group of friends, international personality
International humanitarian law	No role	No role	Key role, by way of special humanitarian agreements, before and during peace talks
Role of civil society	Intermediary role of Peace Commission was key, but on the whole civil society's role was limited, largely symbolic	Marginal role in negotiation (*mesas de trabajo*) but extremely significant role in the broader context (National Constituent Assembly)	Central, decisive role (National Peace Council/ National Convention/ National Constituent Assembly)
Role of military	Excluded from policy making and talks	Informed of policy making, excluded from talks	Included in policy making and talks
Paramilitaries	No role	No role	Active, direct, participation in separate scenario, connected to process with insurgency
International participation	No role	No role	Active, formal role as mediator and guarantor
USA	No role	No role	Active, formal role as mediator and guarantor

them worthy of being the state's legitimate interlocutors in seeking a negotiated end to the armed conflict. This radically differed from the position held by all previous administrations since the 1960s, which had refused to grant the guerrillas the status of political insurgents, treating them as simple bandits and common criminals. In his first months in office Betancur received quick approval from Congress for a broad and unilateral amnesty for the hundreds of jailed rebels as a gesture of goodwill to generate confidence. Although originally intended to lure the M19 into talks, it ended up attracting the FARC's attention first.

Given the pioneering nature of Betancur's new peace policy, his initial approaches were guided more by his personal convictions and intuition than by a well-thought-out strategy. Nevertheless, Betancur did establish three foundational strategies that would guide future administrations in the making of peace policy: talks with the guerrillas, political reforms, and social and economic relief.

He ratified the Peace Commission that had been created under his predecessor, Julio César Turbay (1978–82), but transformed it from a mere advisory body into an intermediary with the insurgents. He also expanded its membership from twelve to forty in order to include a broad range of people representing all aspects of Colombian society.

But his peace plan did not reflect a common agenda taken on by his administration as a whole. The Peace Commission was not a part of the executive branch, nor did it formally belong to the president's office. In fact, John Agudelo, who served as president of the Peace Commission from early 1983 to the end of Betancur's term, was never on the government payroll, did not have an office (he worked out of his own law firm), and reported to no one but the president himself. This very noninstitutional and often informal manner of doing things was quite adequate in the early stages of establishing preliminary contacts and initial confidence building, particularly with the FARC, but later proved fatal when what was needed was commitment on the part of the state as a whole.

The Betancur/FARC model took its most concrete form in the La Uribe Accord between the Peace Commission and the FARC, signed in March 1984. Although agreements were also signed with the M19 and the EPL in August of that same year, their contents were very similar to the FARC accord and had the same basic structure. While the agreement with the FARC lasted for over three years, the one with the M19 held up for less than one year, and that of the EPL only a little over a year.[2] For this reason, the principal interlocutor of the Betancur government was the FARC, making them de facto coauthors of that very significant first stage of the peace process.

The agreement established a bilateral cease-fire, originally set for one year but later extended for almost two and a half, and established various commissions for its verification. During this period, the government committed itself to pushing through Congress a series of political and social reforms that included important aspects of the political system, as well as the social structure, particularly with regard to agrarian reform and land rights. In the meantime, the FARC would gradually transform itself from an illegal fighting force to a legal political party: the Unión Patriótica (Patriotic Union) or UP, created in 1985. However, the specific timetables and procedures for the transition were fuzzy, and there was no talk of disarming the insurgents or of reincorporating them into civilian life.

Although the Peace Commission included symbolic participation of representative members of civil society, in the end the process was centered on bilateral talks between the government and insurgents. In fact, the principal contribution of the M19 and EPL in their respective agreements was the "National Dialogue," which was intended to reflect the diversity of Colombian society and encourage citizen participation beyond that of the armed actors. The concept was a radical break with the bilateral nature of the La Uribe Accord and in practice was never realized, since the process quickly was broken off.[3] Likewise, the EPL proposed that a national constituent assembly be chosen in order to rewrite the nation's constitution.

These proposals not only reflected interesting ideological differences and the specific political emphasis of each organization but also were part of a sort of rivalry that erupted among them with regard to the peace process. This competition was especially acute between the FARC and the M19, both of which jostled for the limelight. Equally significant was the very radical reaction of the ELN rejecting Betancur's peace encores from the start as a trap that betrayed the revolution. It is good to remember that during those years the triumph of the Sandinistas in Nicaragua was still fresh in the minds of the insurgents and victory looked within reach in El Salvador. The stiff opposition to the peace process expressed by the ELN led to their growth after critical years of near-annihilation.

Likewise, it led to the creation of several dissident splinter groups that broke off due to their opposition to the talks with the government. These included groups such as the PRT, which broke from the EPL, and the Frente Ricardo Franco, from the FARC. Another new group, the Quintín Lame (or

MAQL), made up of native indigenous combatants, also appeared. All of these armed groups that rejected the peace process came together to form the first unified guerrilla front, led principally by the ELN. Later, as the M19 and the EPL broke off talks in 1985, they each joined, and when the FARC in 1987 did as well, the CGSB was formally created.

Colombian society reacted in different ways to the peace process. It received massive support at the beginning, expressed in different forms, such as the painting of peace doves all over the country as a sign of solidarity and support. However, popular enthusiasm was not sustained and was unable to transform itself into effective political action. On the contrary, Betancur quickly lost the backing of the traditional political parties, including his own Conservative party. The powerful hierarchy of the Catholic Church never agreed with the president's policies and often spoke out against them. The business community did not take part either, and they did not hide their discontent. Local economic and social elites in various regions of the country felt betrayed by the central government and opted for creating paramilitary groups.[4]

Even within the state itself,[5] there were many discrepancies. The other branches were rarely consulted, and few policies were actually carried out. Although in principle the peace policy, as mentioned earlier, was three-pronged, in practice little of it became reality. In the realm of political reform, only one of the ten bills presented to Congress was approved: the direct election of local city mayors. Even though this proved to be quite important, it fell far short of original expectations. In the area of social relief, the Betancur administration did create the PNR (National Rehabilitation Plan) as an innovative instrument for generating social development in impoverished and conflict areas. However, funding was insufficient and it was unable to get off the ground.

Most significantly, the armed forces were excluded from policy making on the issue of peace. Many political analysts consider this exclusion the underlying motivation for the army's violent response to the M19 seizure of the Palace of Justice in downtown Bogotá in November 1985, in which over a hundred people were killed, including all of the Supreme Court justices. The incident has been widely viewed as a twenty-four-hour coup d'état that practically put an end to the Betancur stage of the peace process. Shortly thereafter, the paramilitary groups, then legal self-defense groups that were never considered or included in the policy, the talks, or the accords, were principally responsible for the political genocide of the UP,[6] with the help and complicity of many members of the armed forces. This extremely significant and tragic reality weighs heavily not only on the consciousness of the members of the security forces directly involved but also on that of the political system as a whole. It also has a great deal to do with the way that the FARC currently views any negotiation process.

The Betancur/FARC model had several other limitations and omissions. The verification commissions were never given a precise and doable mission or adequate infrastructure and logistical support to carry out their tasks successfully. Soon mutual accusations of cease-fire violations led to controversies that could not be resolved. Instead of generating the intended climate of confidence, the verification process led to just the opposite. In addition, other crucial aspects were never clearly defined. Most of the talks took place in the FARC headquarters, the so-called Casa Verde, which was a de facto demilitarized zone, without any written agreement on the matter or explicit legal basis.

The international context was unfavorable as well. Not only were rebel insurgencies still in an uproar, but the Cold War was again heating up, especially in Central America, because of the Reagan Doctrine. The U.S. ambassador to Colombia, Lewis Tambs, coined the term *narco-guerrilla* just days before the signing of the La Uribe Accord, which was interpreted as a torpedo aimed at the process. U.S. antagonism, coupled with the rigidity of Cold War spheres of influence, made it simply impossible to think of any international participation in the peace process in Colombia.

However, reinforcing the pioneering nature of the Colombian process, Betancur did meet with the M19 leadership twice abroad, in Spain and in Mexico, although the respective governments did not participate formally in the meetings, which were quite informal. Furthermore, seeking to gain breathing room abroad and to garner support for his efforts at home, Betancur also actively worked for the creation of the Contadora group, in which Colombia, Venezuela, Mexico, and Panama worked to promote a peaceful solution to the wars in Central America, completely contrary to the military hard line of the Reagan administration.

In summary, the Betancur/FARC model opened many unexplored paths in Colombia and the region, but at the same time circumstances and historical conditions may have been unripe. It laid the groundwork for future efforts but also left many wounds and a mistrust that has been difficult to overcome.

The Barco/M19 Model

In 1986 Barco was elected president, in great part as a reaction against the general perception of failure of the previous administration's handling of the peace process. Even the losing candidate from Betancur's own Conservative party, Alvaro Gomez, distanced himself from the incumbent's peace policy. Barco spoke of a "hand held out, with a steady pulse," to refer to the new tone in which his administration planned to deal with the issue of peace, and upon taking office he introduced several changes.

First of all, being highly critical of the informal nature of the Betancur style, Barco moved to institutionalize policy making and the political instruments with regard to peace. The semi–ad hoc Peace Commission was disbanded, and the Office of the Presidential Advisor for Normalization, Rehabilitation, and Reconciliation[7] was created, reporting directly to the president. Even the name, which avoided using the term *peace*—so identified with the previous administration—reflected the determination to disassociate itself from the past. The new office began to assemble a team of young scholars from several universities to think about policy. This group not only would produce some of the most influential future peace negotiators but would introduce two years later the basic elements of a profound policy shift that would lead to the creation of the second historical model for conflict resolution.

However, in the meantime, many things stayed the same for the first half of Barco's term. In fact, the cease-fire established in the La Uribe Accord continued, although quite shaky, for over a year of the new administration. Furthermore, despite visible changes in style, form, and name from the Betancur years, Barco's policy maintained many fundamental elements of continuity, albeit out of the public eye. He too viewed the rebels as insurgents, shared the idea that the war had social and political root causes, and thought that it should end through dialogue.

Likewise, his peace policy maintained the three dimensions of his predecessor's. However, he differed greatly in his priorities: while Betancur put talks with the rebels first, political reform second, and economic relief third, Barco completely reversed the order. The PNR, abandoned and left without funds after its creation by Betancur, was put back on the drawing board and then implemented, given ample resources, and elevated to the top of the government's agenda by Barco. His initiatives on the political front would come a little later, were more sporadic, and often went further than those proposed by his predecessor, although they were even less successful.

But this reorganization of priorities went far beyond a mere reshuffling of policies. Rather, it indicated clear conceptual distinctions. For the Barco team, the state should unilaterally assume the lead in pushing through the needed social and political reforms, which should not necessarily be the result of negotiations with the insurgents. To its credit, the Betancur administration put forth its own reform agenda early on in the term, long before it had negotiated anything with the guerrillas. But it was generally perceived that the one major reform achieved, the direct election of mayors, was more the product of the talks with the FARC than action by the administration or the state.

However, it was not until September 1988 that these conceptual distinctions would actually be formulated into a new policy, with the Barco team's unveiling of its "Peace Initiative." And just as the FARC helped mold Betancur's peace policy, the coauthor of the new Barco policy was the M19, which had reappeared on the national scene months earlier with the spectacular kidnapping and subsequent release of Alvaro Gomez, which they used as a platform for reopening peace talks.

After having gone through a severe loss of prestige after the Palace of Justice tragedy, a series of military blows that saw several of their top leaders killed, and intense internal debates, the M19, under the leadership of Carlos Pizarro, had recovered militarily. However, within the insurgent movement's unification process, it was clear that the M19's role would continue to be limited and greatly overshadowed by that of other groups, especially the FARC. Furthermore, the M19 knew that its strengths lay more in the national political arena than in the war in the mountains, and it decided to pursue secret contacts with the government on its own, without consulting its partners in the incipient CGSB.

It was soon apparent that there were several key issues on which the M19 and the Barco team were beginning to see eye to eye. First and foremost, both sides quickly agreed upon the objective of the negotiation: rather than the deeper social and political reforms of the Betancur/FARC model, the talks should focus on the political guarantees that would allow the insurgent groups to give up their arms and transform themselves into legal democratic movements, as well as the terms for reincorporation of the ex-combatants into civilian life.

This significant change in the scope of the process constitutes perhaps the essential difference between the two historical models. Whereas the Betancur/FARC model placed reforms first and disarmament later, the Barco/M19 model reversed the order of priorities. Consequently, and more importantly, the breadth of what was understood by reform was different in the models. While the first encompassed deep structural social, political, and even cultural dimensions, which I will refer to in this chapter as the "broad agenda," the second, which I will call the "limited agenda," focused specifically on the democratization of the political system and guarantees for political and economic reincorporation.[8]

This fundamental agreement on the objective of the process was specifically laid out in the Barco Peace Initiative, which was basically tailored to the M19. Talks began in January 1989 and, after many ups and downs, were finally concluded with the signing of the peace accord in March 1990.

In the Barco/M19 model, the insurgent group's express intention of disarming, as well as a unilateral cease-fire on its part as a sign of goodwill, were basic premises and not results of the talks. Once the initial agreements were reached, demilitarized zones were established to gather all the combatants, who would later be demobilized and disarmed. Most of the negotiation was spent on defining ways to enable the M19's immediate transition to legal political activity after disarming. In what was referred to as "political favorability," innovative one-time-only benefits were granted, enabling the group to tally votes nationwide in order to elect representatives to the otherwise regionally based Congress.

However, as with the Betancur/FARC model, talks were exclusively bilateral, and even though the so-called *mesas de trabajo* were established on several issues, the participation of civil society in the process itself was scant, especially in light of the M19's insistence, back in the Betancur years, on national dialogue.

Although, like his predecessor, Barco had his run-ins with the military, in general it was consulted, and the peace policy was coordinated with the army, which played an important role in securing the perimeters of the demilitarized zones. However, the contribution and collaboration of the other branches of government were not the same. Congress was only rarely consulted during the talks themselves and was responsible for almost breaking off the process when it did not pass key elements of the proposed election reforms, which required amending the constitution and were central to the peace accord. Later, the judicial branch's interpretation of the amnesty laws, which had been passed by Congress, was such that a second law had to be passed to precisely cover the crimes linked to the Palace of Justice tragedy. And as in the previous years, "dark forces" struck again, this time by assassinating Carlos Pizarro aboard a commercial airliner as he was campaigning for president.[9]

However, the M19's stubborn decision to go on with the process—in spite of such severe blows and the lack of concurrence on the part of the state as a whole—paid off politically, as the results of the 1990 elections show.[10] Civil society, in spite of not having been called upon to participate in the negotiation process itself, overwhelmingly supported the peace process. The process was so solid that it continued and in fact matured well into the following administration of President Gaviria.

More significantly, the National Constituent Assembly, which was convoked by popular plebiscite on the same day as the 1990 presidential elections, though not included in the accords as such, was an indirect result of the process with the M19. It was also a response to the broader crisis of the Colombian state, highlighted by the August 1989 assassination by the drug cartels of Luis Carlos Galán, the popular dissident reformer who had returned to the fold of the Liberal party and was by all accounts likely to be elected president the following year. His assassination set off a massive protest movement led by students, middle-class urban intellectuals, and a broad array of social organizations. This coincided with the demobilization of the M19 and, more importantly, with the group's reform agenda. In the elections held in December 1990 to choose delegates to the assembly, the M19 list, led by Antonio Navarro, obtained the highest number of votes, with 27 percent of the total. The National Constituent Assembly, which met from February to June 1991, rewrote the nation's constitution, introducing a broad bill of rights and unprecedented democratic reforms that made it one of the world's most modern and progressive constitutions in several areas.

This rich process of reform, in turn, generated mixed responses from the different guerrilla organizations. In all of them, and within the CGSB as a whole, the reform set off intense internal debates. Four-fifths of the EPL opted for the M19 path and broke with the CGSB. The PRT and the Quintín Lame followed suit. To participate in the National Constituent Assembly, these three organizations turned over their guns.[11]

Such was the reformist momentum that the remaining organizations of the CGSB also expressed their willingness to participate, even though their demands at the time were considered to be unacceptably high by the Gaviria administration.[12] Even once the deliberations were under way, and despite Gaviria's decision to attack Casa Verde on the very day of the election of the National Constituent Assembly, it was the CGSB that insisted upon talks with the government. And once they took place, the first point on the agenda was the relationship with the National Constituent Assembly, which they formally requested the chance to address. Intense debates continued within each of the member groups of the CGSB, especially the ELN, from which would later spring the dissident CRS, which would sign an agreement in 1994 very similar in general terms to those other groups signed in 1990 and 1991 (see table 4.2). Although each of the ensuing processes had its own particularities, all of them followed the basic parameters of the M19 process.

In the Barco/M19 model, there was no role for the international community. However, the Socialist International did participate as an observer to the M19's turning over of their weapons, and the government of Holland served in a similar role with the CRS.

Neither the M19, PRT, Quintín Lame, nor CRS faced the kind of genocide previously faced by the UP. However, in the case of the EPL, infighting with ex-comrades from the FARC and the tiny dissident splinter group of the EPL that stayed on in the armed struggle and viewed those who had demobilized as "traitors" proved almost as fatal. It even led to some of the ex-guerrillas taking up arms again, but this time on the part of the paramilitary organizations.

The topic of these so-called self-defense groups was not dealt with in the talks with the M19 or with any of the other groups. However, the rebel groups did agree with the decision in 1989 by the Barco administration to declare the self-defense groups illegal, given their clear links to narcotrafficking as well as their atrocious record of human rights violations. No clear steps were taken to dismantle these groups or reincorporate them into society, although they were extended the judicial benefits granted to drug traffickers who turned themselves in.

Finally, even though within the respective negotiations the issue took up relatively little time and importance, it is vital to analyze the reincorporation process of the different insurgent groups that opted for demobilization, which has had its very positive lessons as well as some very negative ones. On the whole, the Barco/M19 model was quite successful for groups that had previously decided to abandon the armed struggle and fight for their ideas within democratic structures. Neither the Betancur/FARC model nor the Barco/M19 model was wholly successful in achieving peace for the nation, but over the years the two models have continued to hang on even to this day.

In fact, during the first part of the Gaviria years, while on one track the Barco/M19 model was being negotiated and implemented with the EPL, the PRT, and the Quintín Lame, the government simultaneously made an agreement with the CGSB in Caracas that was closer to the "broad agenda" of the Betancur/FARC model. However, this significant attempt to take up where previous experience had left off ended in frustration when talks first stalled in Caracas in 1991 over the means of establishing a verifiable cease-fire, then broke off in Tlaxcala in 1992.[13]

More importantly, the government's declaration of all-out war, commonly referred to as "integral war" by the mass media, led to an even longer interruption in formal dealings between the government and insurgents than the one that followed the breaking off of the process after the Betancur years.[14] Yet again, it was proven true that failed attempts at peace create as much and even more damage to future peace-building endeavors than escalation of the war itself.

The declaration of "integral war" also drew different reactions from the insurgents. The FARC, after a decade of what they perceived as unwillingness of the government and the establishment as a whole to enter into serious talks on its "broad agenda," decided in its eighth conference in 1993 to put the idea of a negotiated settlement on the back burner and abandon the CGSB so as to act on their own. At the same time, they gave greater priority to beefing up their military capacity, expanding their territorial presence, and improving their finances through kidnapping and taxation of the then still small coca plantations. The ELN, on the other hand, had never participated in any talks before Caracas and Tlaxcala in 1991 and 1992, and it did so alongside its comrades in the CGSB. This experience clearly set off a complex internal process that had its first expression in the breaking off of the CRS but produced its most significant result in the third congress of the organization, held in 1996. The group radically shifted its positions: it now clearly spoke of ending the war through a negotiated settlement and giving higher priority to political work and endorsed the proposal set forth by Manuel Perez[15] of the so-called National Convention,[16] which in many ways took elements of broad social participation from the National Dialogue of the 1980s. These different reactions by the two major rebel groups to the concept of "integral war" planted the seeds for their reactions, years later, to the efforts made under Samper and Pastrana.

The Samper Years: Attempting to Forge a New Model Amidst Crisis

Despite their respective contributions and the partial successes of each, neither of the two historical models was able to put an end to the internal war, yet both have continued over the years and to this day to act as basic points of reference. More significantly, recent years have also led to the appearance and consolidation of key new elements. I will argue that these, added to a synthesis of specific parts of the two historical models, could be the ingredients for a future, third model for conflict resolution.

Some of this process took place during the Samper administration. Given my direct role in that administration, I do not want to focus on myself or turn this chapter into a defense of what was or was not done, but I do wish to attempt to put certain issues into a historical perspective. This is no easy task. Samper's term in office was one of the most critical, eventful, and controversial in Colombian political history, due to the narco-scandal that rocked his administration almost from the onset. The crisis of democratic instability had a profound crippling effect on the government's peace policy and, much more significantly, on the political conditions required to carry out meaningful dialogue with the insurgents.

Nonetheless, three distinct phases can be identified in a study of the peace process. During the first year of the administration, significant policy shifts were proposed and put into practice, while preliminary contacts were established with insurgent groups, but a clash between the civilian and military authorities, which coincided with the so-called 8000 Process—a judicial process that looked into drug money donated to Samper's campaign fund—quickly dashed all hopes.

The second phase, during the second and third years, was marred by the widening of the narco-scandal, an escalation of the war and increasing degradation of its methods, severe blows to the army by the FARC, the expansion of the paramilitary groups, and the creation of their umbrella organization, AUC. These issues almost completely displaced peace in the attention of the public.

A third phase can be observed in the last year of Samper's term, in which preliminary contacts were reestablished with the insurgents: with the FARC, talks on the release of soldiers and marines held captive, and with the ELN, formal talks that led to the signing in Madrid in February 1998 of the Draft Accord of Viana (never ratified) between the government and the rebel group. Later, these talks led to the Gates of Heaven Accord signed between the ELN and representatives of civil society, both of which dealt with the proposal of the National Convention and the application of international humanitarian law. Even more significantly, civil society took front stage, and millions of Colombians, with their ballots, ordered their next president to make peace his top priority in policy.

Over the four years, there was a radical transition in the peace process. Some of the shift had to do with changes in government policy. In Samper's first days in office, the Presidential Peace Advisor's Office[17] was restructured, elevated to cabinet level, and renamed as the Office of the High Commissioner for Peace, taking the process of institutionalization introduced by Barco a step further. Samper broke a long tradition of previous administrations with regard to international humanitarian law by presenting to Congress and gaining quick approval of ratification of the Second Protocols to the Geneva Conventions, which deal specifically with internal conflicts like the one in Colombia. In contrast to the "integral war" of the second half of the Gaviria years, which, for the first time since before Betancur, practically rejected recognizing the guerrillas as political insurgents, the new administration spoke of "integral peace," in reference to the structural, substantive, subjective causes of the broad agenda of the Betancur/FARC model. The Samper team explicitly recognized the rebels as political insurgents and granted two of the ELN's leaders, found imprisoned, the status of political spokesmen and negotiators, enabling them to carry out these roles from their jail cells.

However, much of what did not work well was a result of internal contradictions, exacerbated but not created by the political crisis, as well as key presidential decisions. Alongside the peace initiatives, legal civilian defense groups, the Convivir, were created by the president, despite strong opposition from many of us within the government. The incident at the end of the first year in which the army high command leaked a secret internal memorandum clearly undermined the president's peace policy, but more significantly Samper's backing down from his original impulse to stop General Bedoya in his tracks by removing him on the spot ruined for good his credibility with the insurgents. While the FARC quickly cut off all contacts,[18] contacts with the ELN were maintained in some form or another during almost all of the four years.

Much of what ended up as policy was the result of lessons learned from the past and recognition of the realities of the present. While the government's original plan proposed talks with a unified guerrilla movement, like those that had taken place in 1991 and 1992, by 1994 the CGSB no longer existed for all intents and purposes, and it was necessary to deal with the groups separately. Likewise, it was clear that, after the difficulties faced in the 1980s and the early 1990s in establishing a cease-fire as the first step, it was necessary to seek contacts in the midst of war, with no cease-fire in place.

But the most significant progress of the period came, not from the government peace policy or the insurgents' responses, but from the reaction of civil society to the growing effects of the war itself and a new sense of activism and participation. Redepaz (Network of Citizens' Peace Initiatives), created in the dark days of Gaviria's integral war, organized civic support for a negotiated settlement and against the war. The Catholic Church promoted the creation in October 1995 of the Commission of National Conciliation to serve as an informal intermediary in lieu of formal dealings between government and insurgents. Labor organizations began to actively take part in the peace movement, and significant sectors, like the oil workers, organized important efforts around the issue of natural resources and the peace process. The business community, increasingly feeling the pinch of the war, began to participate for the first time in discussions about peace. And the National Peace Council was created in 1998 in response to demands from civil society for a vehicle for involvement in the peace process.[19] Composed of members of the different branches of government at the national, departmental, and municipal levels, as well as representatives of the different sectors of civil society, the council was designed to serve as an advisory body in policy making to the president that could be called upon to participate directly in the negotiation process.

This growing coalition of different interest groups began to mobilize jointly for specific causes. In October 1997, ten million votes were cast in a symbolic national mandate for peace. This event helped catapult the issue to dominating the 1998 presidential elections, which were decided in great part on whom the voters saw as most likely to make peace. Civil society, with the debate that the term itself generates, had won a new role in the peace process.

Interest in the war and in ways to end it received growing attention not only within Colombia but also from the outside. Two major aspects dominated the international realm. In the first place, the 8000 Process almost completely froze Colombian relations with the United States, bringing them to their lowest point since the incident over Panama a century earlier and isolating Colombia internationally. However, at the same time, within the administration there was a gradual change with regard to the participation of the international community in matters such as human rights and international humanitarian law, as expressed in the signing of a framework agreement with the International Committee of the Red Cross and with the opening in Bogotá of a permanent office of the UN high commissioner for human rights. This gradual opening toward the world also occurred as far as peace policy was concerned. In fact, it was under Samper that the term *peace diplomacy* was first used by the foreign relations minister, and several countries offered to serve as an eventual "group of friends."

One huge void, however, was in the area of the paramilitary groups, whose growth not only was not thwarted by the authorities but in fact was encouraged by the Convivir. The massacre of unarmed civilians was generalized as the paramilitaries' prime modus operandi. The toll on human life and dignity was staggering. Internally displaced persons surpassed the million mark between 1985 and 1995, according to the Catholic Church. The economy began to take a beating as well, as the war caused costly damage and scared off investment.

To summarize, during the Samper years the government peace policy returned conceptually to the broad agenda of the Betancur/FARC model while continuing the process of institutionalization central to the Barco/M19 model. In fact, the peace process was elevated to a higher level and a legal framework was established for future negotiations. The government introduced new elements, such as the principles of human rights and international humanitarian law, recognized a new role for civil society, and began talking about the participation of the international community. However, the highly adverse conditions created by a deep political crisis not only prevented any formal, substantive talks from taking place during Samper's term but, more importantly, greatly contributed to the widening and deepening of the war.

The Pastrana Years: Between Two Conflicting Historical Models

For all of the reasons mentioned above, peace became the top election issue in 1998, and the FARC's identification of Andrés Pastrana as the candidate it would most like to deal with no doubt helped push Pastrana comfortably over the top in the run-off election after he narrowly lost the first round. Even before taking office, as president-elect, Pastrana made good on an election promise to meet directly with the FARC leader, Manuel Marulanda. By doing so he began to introduce a significant new element of direct presidential diplomacy that proved key in reestablishing levels of confidence after so many years of built-up mistrust. Without abandoning the formal institution of the Office of the High Commissioner, he introduced a personal style, reminiscent in a way of the informality and closed circle of the Betancur days.

Although Pastrana had at his disposal an extraordinary group of knowledgeable people, some of whom he called upon for specific tasks, for the most part he seemed often—and especially in critical moments—to rely more on his own instincts and hunches. This explains the audacity and self-confidence that he often showed, especially at the beginning of his presidency, but also the many improvisations, missteps, and costly reversals that indicate the lack of a clearer mapping of a long-term strategy. In that sense, he broke with the tradition, which despite the big differences in focus and opinions had been maintained during the Barco, Gaviria, and Samper years, of a team of academics and technocrats working together on policy making.

Pastrana decided to give priority to the FARC—reasonably so, given its size and historical significance. However, many have argued that the ELN was relegated to second-rate treatment, even though it was clearly more advanced in the peace process at the outset of his administration than was the FARC. The choice may have been in part a result of the need of the new administration to differentiate itself from the previous one. In all incoming presidential administrations it is legitimate to rethink and adjust the policy errors of one's predecessors, introduce new elements, and at the same time maintain the continuity of that which is considered to be going well. For Pastrana, this task was even more sensitive given his high level of animosity toward Samper. It was also ironic that beyond superficial changes of wording, on many issues there were many elements of continuity, not only with his despised predecessor, but with much of what had come before as well. The demilitarized zone that was put in place to begin talks with the FARC was established under the provisions of the 1997 Law 418. That law also fostered the idea that in the rest of the territory, until agreements were signed to the contrary, the war would continue, in accordance with the principle of talking in the midst of the war.

In May 1999, after President Pastrana had met personally with Marulanda in Caquetania, the government and the FARC signed the Agenda for Change for Peace. In its scope and content the Caquetania Accords were clearly inspired by the broad agenda of the Betancur/FARC model and followed the general lines of the La Uribe Accord of 1984 and the Accord on the Agenda signed in Caracas in 1991. Although the issue of international humanitarian law was introduced, it occupied a relatively low priority compared to social and structural issues like employment and the economy. There was no mention whatsoever of disarming or reincorporation into civilian life of the guerrilla fighters, and there was no clear timetable for the rebels' transition to legal political activity.

The Caquetania Accords also included important agreements on procedures, which reflect an evolution with regard to past experiences with the FARC. Most significantly, it established mechanisms for citizen participation, such as public hearings, that would pick up proposals and ideas from common people, as well as a committee to organize the themes that emerged, which served as a bridge for these ideas to reach the negotiating table, where seats were limited to the government and the FARC. Although these procedures signaled greater willingness to open the process, the methodology continued to reflect the more traditional bilateral model, rather than the multilateral scenario proposed by the ELN.

But as important as the Caquetania Accords were, they unfortunately were never fully developed. On the contrary, the process was often interrupted by unilateral suspensions declared by one party or the other.[20] In fact, no agreements were signed during all of 2000, and it was not until February 2001, after another personal meeting between Pastrana and Marulanda to "save" the floundering peace process, that the Los Pozos Accord was signed. It introduced for the first time discussion of a cease-fire and a prisoner exchange, created mechanisms designed to involve other political forces, created a special Commission of Notables to make proposals to the parties about reducing the intensity of the conflict, and called for the creation of a "group of friends" composed of ten nations of the international community to serve as observers.[21]

These adjustments seemed to inject new life into the process. In fact, in June 2001, a historic agreement was reached allowing for a prisoner exchange within the scope of international humanitarian law, the first time the FARC had ever recognized its norms. In September, the Notables handed in their proposals, which called for a thorough overhauling of the talks and a new timetable and for the first time spoke of the need to start talking about the FARC's laying down arms. In October 2001, the San Francisco de la Sombra Accord was signed, in which the parties agreed to begin discussion of the Notables' proposals.

But these steps seemed to be too little too late. Despite the significance of the agreements reached from a historical perspective, they dealt mostly with procedural questions, which, important as they were, did not delve into the substance of the agenda and fell far short of the high expectations that had been held by the public at the outset of the administration. By the end of 2001, Pastrana's popularity had plummeted and his administration was on its last legs amidst an increasingly tense presidential campaign. The international climate after the September 11 terrorist attacks in the United States worsened, with U.S. concerns about the lack of controls on the demilitarized zone growing especially. All these factors contributed to a rapid breakdown of the peace talks. After having overcome a deep crisis at the end of January 2002, thanks in great part to the mediation of the UN envoy and the "group of friends," on the following February 20, after the FARC had hijacked a plane and kidnapped a senator, Pastrana decided to break off talks completely. He ordered government troops to retake the demilitarized zone, ending over three years of intense efforts and hopes of reaching peace through dialogue.

As far as the ELN was concerned, throughout Pastrana's term, as stated earlier, the treatment and attention they were given varied widely. When things seemed to be moving forward with FARC (in 1999, for example), talks with the ELN tended to stall; when difficulties erupted with FARC (for example, in 2000), they often appeared to pick up. The process with the ELN was more complex than that, however, and was characterized from the start of the Pastrana administration by the erratic nature of the on-again, off-again talks, and both sides were responsible for the talks' being frequently broken off.[22] Throughout the rocky process, nonetheless, informal contacts were almost always maintained, thanks to the intermediary role of a special commission of civil society representatives, as well as to the international accompaniment of a "group of friends."[23] But their efforts were unable to overcome the immense difficulties, and near the end of his term, in June 2002, Pastrana permanently cut off all contacts with the ELN.

Critics, and there were many of them, were quick to label the processes with the FARC and the ELN as failures and to speak of "three lost years."

Given his immense public support and the optimum political conditions at the beginning of his administration, Pastrana will be long remembered for the powerful sense of disillusionment and deception that has strongly affected the public credibility of dialogue as a means of bringing the war to an end.

However, a more balanced, long-term look would also show that significant progress was indeed made in several areas and that important new ingredients were introduced or strengthened. A key element that was surely one of Pastrana's major priorities was the participation of the international community in the peace process. Pastrana very skillfully used international concern about the growing effects of the war to garner support for and create awareness about the peace process. At times it was not clear whether the objective was to use international diplomacy to strengthen the peace process or to utilize the peace process as a diplomatic tool to further the image of the country or its president. Nevertheless, during the Pastrana years there was a quantum leap in the internationalization of the peace process.

Special attention must be given to the role of the United States. Pastrana was able to elevate Colombian relations with the United States, which had practically been shut off in the previous administration, to one of their best periods, perhaps ever. However, what began as an active role for the United States in the peace process[24] later became aid to the military and aerial fumigation of coca plantations, as was evidenced in the final version of the controversial Plan Colombia, which was largely perceived as supporting the war more than giving a hand to the peace process.[25]

Another significant characteristic of the Pastrana administration's peace policy was its handling of the armed forces. Although the administration had its moments of friction with the military,[26] on the whole it successfully included the army in the process and received from the military their complete collaboration with regard to the demilitarized zone, about which they had strong reservations but abided by presidential orders. The participation of other branches of government was not as clear and showed signs of contradictions, especially on the part of the Fiscalía (the Prosecutor's Office), which repeatedly expressed doubts about the executive's handling of the negotiations. Congress was unable to find a useful role to play.

A further determining factor that must be analyzed is citizen participation. Since much of the impetus that civil society had acquired during the

Samper years had been energized by the need to mediate between the government and the insurgents to bring them back to the negotiating table, once direct contacts were reestablished under Pastrana there was a widely accepted feeling that society's job had been accomplished. Likewise, the overwhelming popular support that accompanied Pastrana's opening gestures of peace quickly gave way to skepticism and even open opposition from important sectors of Colombian society, many of which had supported the president's election bid. Furthermore, the Pastrana team was rather disdainful of "outside" interference and in fact rarely convoked the National Peace Council, which by law should have met every two months.

There was a great deal of improvisation on the part of the presidential team and a lack of an overall strategy. Nor was a clear reform agenda set forth, as Pastrana had pledged to do in the campaign. Moreover, the administration was not able to resolve basic internal contradictions that suggest that the government itself was constantly wrestling between the two historic models. While much of its official rhetoric and, more significantly, the contents of the agenda signed in Caquetania were distinctly inspired by the Betancur/FARC model, much of the administration's policy and handling of specific issues suggested otherwise. This was evident in a seminar held in Cartagena in April 2001, organized by the U.S. embassy in Bogotá, in which the defense minister emphasized the importance of the guerrillas' disarming as a prerequisite for talks, clearly in the Barco/M19 mode, while the high commissioner for peace later explained that the agenda did not even mention the item.

Similarly, many members of the establishment continued to view peace as simply the disarming and reincorporation of the insurgents and were unwilling to make certain concessions on the social front, continuing to favor policies that would create even greater conditions of inequity and impoverishment. The same confusion between the two models was apparent in the distinction that was frequently cited as a reason why the ELN, which was seen to have been defeated by the paramilitaries—as the M19 had been seen to have been defeated by the army a decade before—was willing to agree to a quick disarmament and demobilization in the style of the Barco/M19 model, while a broader agenda was being discussed with the more powerful FARC, which had not been defeated militarily.

An immense part of the responsibility for the collapse of the Caguán experience, of course, also goes to the insurgency. FARC was unable to project and articulate a clear political message, connect to public opinion, or create the kind of support base required for a peace process to truly move forward. Part of this reflects the predominance of hard-liners within the ranks of FARC and the sidelining during these years of the more "political" figures. Although the FARC, not having signed a cease-fire agreement, could not technically be held to stopping their actions, they did not seem to recognize that their relentless persistence in maintaining the war, often with great civilian casualties—as was the case in the small town of Bojayá on May 2, 2002[27]—simply eroded their already weak popular support. Something very similar could be said about the ELN leadership as well.

The advance or progress of a peace process is impossible to measure either quantitatively or qualitatively, especially in comparison to other moments of the past. "Success," furthermore, is relative and can be considered absolute only once a final peace accord is signed, if then. It could be argued, for example, that Betancur's administration advanced peace even further with the FARC than Pastrana's, since it was able to sign a cease-fire, a goal that this time around was not reached. Likewise, some have said that the agenda agreed upon in Caquetania in 1999 went no further in strict terms than what was signed in Caracas in 1991 and might have even taken a few steps backwards. Whereas the Caracas agreement defined the ending of the armed conflict and disarmament as the final objective of talks, the Caquetania agreement said nothing about what the final objective would be.

While these points may be technically correct and interesting academically, they tend to lose sight of the bigger picture. If the "progress" of the peace process can in fact be measured in broader terms, including citizen awareness, ripeness of political conditions, social support, and possibilities for international cooperation, the Pastrana years did see an unprecedented advance. However, there was never a clear and coherent strategy for the negotiation process as such, and the talks themselves did not produce any real progress on the substantive issues that would permit a truly new model for conflict resolution to arise.

Furthermore, despite the rhetoric to the contrary, the government and the establishment on one side and the FARC and the ELN on the other continued throughout the years of dialogue to privilege the strengthening of the military option over taking the talks seriously. Plan Colombia's helicopters and the ten thousand AK-47s purchased in 2001 by the FARC through Montessinos are examples of each side's duplicity. Peace was used by all sides to prepare for more war.

Toward a New Colombian Model of Conflict Resolution?

The breakdown in 2002 of this last stage of peace talks, added to a history of past failures and frustrations, was a severe blow to the credibility of negotiation as a viable way of resolving the war in Colombia. We have inevitably entered into a period without any real possibilities for serious talks, during which each side will try to flex its military might and put everything it can into getting the upper hand in the armed confrontation, so as to impose more favorable conditions on the next round of talks, whenever they may be.

The stated positions initially set by both sides reflect the hardening of lines: whereas President Uribe insisted on the immediate release of all kidnap victims and a unilateral cease-fire as preconditions for dialogue, the FARC demanded the demilitarization of the Caquetá and Putumayo provinces, upping the ante quite a bit from the five municipalities that were granted in 1998. Although both sides have since then modified their positions on the specific issue of a prisoner exchange, on the fundamental issue of peace conditions remain unchanged.

Nevertheless, it should also be said that the peace process over the last two decades has been a rich experience. Each of the two historical models, Betancur/FARC and Barco/M19, made its respective contributions, and new ingredients and elements were introduced in the Gaviria, Samper, and Pastrana years, although some were not fully developed. All of this suggests that further down the road a new model of conflict resolution building upon the lessons of the past but adjusting to the realities of the present and the future may be possible and necessary to construct.[28]

The complex Colombian War requires an accordingly complex Colombian peace process. Unfortunately, for a new, third model of conflict resolution to evolve in the future, the ongoing dynamic of escalation must develop further. Likewise, several additional conditions must be present or be induced.

Unlike classic "civil wars," where nations are split in two along regional lines, as in the U.S. Civil War, or along ideological ones, as in the Spanish Civil War, the Colombian War is a much more fragmented conflict, intertwined with organized crime and narco-trafficking, where the armed political actors—of the insurgent left, the right-wing paramilitaries, and the state itself—have precarious legitimacy. Even taken together, they do not represent the nation as a whole. Consequently, a central component of the new model will have to be the active role of civil society at different levels and at different times in the negotiation process.

It should be understood that civil society is not uniform and cannot be viewed simply as the mass of innocent victims of the armed actors, as it is often portrayed. Rather, civil society reflects the contradictions and conflicts that characterize a nation fractured by years of war and political violence. It is in this diversity that the wealth and strength of civil society lie, and not, as some would have it, in its supposed unification or homogenization. As important as civil society may be with regard to social and political issues, it can neither substitute for nor repudiate the necessary participation of armed actors, especially in matters—such as cease-fires or troop concentrations—related to the armed conflict itself. It could be argued that the more limited the agenda is, the less important it is for civil society to be present, whereas the broader it is, the more necessary it becomes.

Civil society also participates in different ways and is not always reflected in the negotiation process as such but rather in other spheres of the larger peace process. It is simply not a matter of having civil society "sit at the table" as a third party alongside the government and the guerrillas. For example, the most significant arena for citizen participation in the processes of the early nineties was not the peace talks with the insurgent groups that decided to demobilize but the wider dynamics that evolved around the National Constituent Assembly. These other fora, however, must be closely connected to the negotiation of the armed conflict as such, as the experience of the other guerrilla groups of the CGSB, which felt left out of the constitutional process of 1991, demonstrates.

The cases of the Central American nations offer interesting reference points. In El Salvador, the negotiation took on a classic bilateral form between the government on one side and the Farabundo Marti National Liberation Front (FMLN) on the other; both had high degrees of social representation and legitimacy. In Guatemala, on the other hand, where the different forces of civil society felt less represented by the rebels and the government, it was necessary to establish a parallel body, the Assembly of Civil Society, that played a dual role as a sort of consultant to the negotiating table, formed bilaterally by the government and the Unidad Revolucionaria Nacional Guatemalteca (URNG), and as a kind of ratifier of the agreements reached at the table. This plural body, however, proved insufficient as an expression of societal concerns, as was shown by the negative results of the

1999 national referendum, which had the boomerang effect of eroding the legitimacy of the peace accords instead of strengthening them.

It is my view that in Colombia, given the even lower degree of social representation of the illegal armed actors and the still fragile legitimacy of the state, it will be necessary to chart a course of even more ample social participation in the peace process, beyond the scope of both the Central American cases. In negotiations with the FARC and the ELN during the Pastrana years, there was a subtle tendency toward opening a more participatory role for civil society, much more pronounced and decisive in the case of the ELN. Even though neither was able to adequately constitute itself in an effective and socially accepted means of citizen participation, it is significant that both processes at some point showed concern and expressed the need to establish better links with society and its diverse expressions. However, civil society is also quite fragmented, divided, atomized, persecuted, and terrorized by the war. While it has shown great ability to mobilize people power and enormous resilience and capacity to generate new leadership, it is still weak and disorganized and reflects the many rips in the nation's social fiber.

The Los Pozos Accord exemplifies how the "participation of civil society" was more rhetorical than real. There can be no better and more graphic expression to illustrate the classic archetype of bilateralism than the picture of two men, the president and the legendary guerrilla chieftain, meeting alone under a tent, like two generals back in the days of chivalry, deciding the fate of an entire nation. The agreement they signed did not mention or even play lip service to civil society, completely ignoring the numerous expressions and letters of support that civil society had produced in those tense days preceding the encounter. The overwhelming political effect of the meeting, symbolized in the hugs and handshakes, was undeniable and would indicate that even though neither the government nor the FARC can truly argue to represent the Colombian people, when they come together to work jointly for peace, their legitimacy, popular backing, and degree of social representation increase dramatically. This should at least lead us to not overemphasize or overplay the magnitude and scope of civil society representation and instead to place it in a more realistic context.

But what the final breakdown of the talks during the Pastrana years seems to indicate is that the essentially bilateral nature of the negotiation model simply was inadequate given the complexity of the national crisis. It is therefore imperative that, for the new model to one day be able to produce lasting and sustainable peace, society must have clear scenarios and specific objectives for its participation to be effective.

The National Peace Council, although it has not been fully developed or implemented since it was created, can be revived and reformed if necessary as an institution that can bring together the different groups and people that represent Colombian society. Although the ELN's National Convention has yet to be more than a sketchily detailed proposal, many of its components correspond to the basic premise that civil society must play a formal and deciding role in a peace settlement. Likewise, the proposal made in 2001 by the Commission of Notables that focused on linking the cease-fire with the specific objective of convoking a new National Constituent Assembly as the final stage of talks with the FARC was interestingly reminiscent of the Barco/M19 model.

Civil society, in all its diversity, must also be able to further its organizational capacities and reach the necessary levels of commitment, decision making, and empowerment to express its will and have it respected. An important part of this has to do with the political arena. After the genocide against the UP in the late 1980s and the frustration of the ADM19 (Alianza Democrática, the political movement founded by the M19 and others after demobilization) in the early 1990s, the absence of a democratic left within the legal spectrum of party politics fueled the armed conflict, giving credence to the insurgents' claim that opposition in Colombia could be exercised only through the armed struggle.

Consequently, the appearance and relative early success of the Polo Democrático[29] in the 2002 elections should be seen as a significant step toward reversing this historical deficiency in Colombian democracy. Unlike previous attempts, the Polo Democrático was not born out of the insurgency; rather, it reflects the growing autonomy and independence of social organizations, intellectuals, and progressive political movements and their distancing from the rebel groups. At the same time, if it can continue consolidating itself as a large, modern, and viable political alternative, the Polo Democrático may in time lure the guerrillas toward the political process with visible evidence that playing within legal bounds is possible in Colombia and that they have a place in democracy without their arms.

This implies another fundamental transformation required to consolidate the new model, since peace, despite the discourse of being a "state policy," has continued over the years to be largely a "presidential policy." First, it must truly widen its reach, with the making and implementation of peace policy an integral part of all of the branches and components of the state. The armed forces are especially important. Traditionally excluded from policy making, at best informed, and totally excluded from the talks themselves, the military should be directly and actively involved in all phases, including, very significantly, at the peace table. Furthermore, strategic continuity is required to bridge the gap between one administration and the next: peace needs to move beyond the category of "state policy," building consensus in the whole society, to be elevated to the level of "public policy."

This, in turn, responds to an understanding of peace building in Colombia as a process extended in time, which has a protracted history and a very long way to go. This complexity can be expressed in a relatively simple equation:

Government Policy + Guerrilla Reaction + Societal Engagement = Peace Process

Creating and sustaining political support for the peace process is essential for its feasibility. The highly volatile nature of "public opinion" and the fragility of civil society was evident during the Betancur/FARC period, as enormous social and political support for Betancur's peace policies at the beginning fizzled into nothing right when it was most crucial. Something very similar occurred with Pastrana. In the case of the Barco/M19 process, even though civil society played only a marginal role, public support grew ostensibly as the peace agreements began to transform into tangible and visible realities, carrying over into the National Constituent Assembly and into the Gaviria administration.

As mentioned earlier, before public support can be garnered for a future stage of the peace process, current war strategies must first be exhausted and fail, leading to what some have called a "mutually hurting stalemate." But in the meantime, and amidst the escalation of the war and its increasing degradation, much can be done to prepare for and foster a climate once again favorable to a negotiated settlement. The democratic development of the organizations of civil society on the social front, the consolidation and growth of the movements like the Polo Democrático on the political front, strategic thinking and planning on realistic postconflict scenarios on the public policy front, and the building of international support networks for peace are all vital tasks that require a long-term perspective.

Another key component of the future emergence of a new model, and of creating a political and social support base, is the gradual application of the ethical values and norms of conduct of international humanitarian law, as well as those of international human rights law. Given the probability of an even greater increase in the barbarity of the war and the likeliness of a lengthy peace, the implementation of international humanitarian law by the way of special, ad hoc agreements, as a first step toward a fuller respect for human rights, becomes a moral and political imperative. Nevertheless, for all parties the political payoff weighs more than humanitarian values. For special, ad hoc agreements on the implementation of international humanitarian law to be possible, they must produce benefits for both sides: political recognition for the insurgency and the freeing of kidnapped victims for the government, for example.

The outcome of internal processes within the insurgent groups is another key component in determining the feasibility for any future dialogue. Just as the breakdown of talks in the early nineties led to a leadership change in the FARC, giving the hard-liners the upper hand, we will have to wait to see if this time a similar shift takes place, possibly allowing for a repositioning of the more political wing.[30] Within the ELN, recent experience confirms that its traditionally complex consensus decision making by the five-man central command, coupled with the fact that no one has yet been able to replace Manuel Perez at the helm, continues to often lead to erratic political leadership and ever-shifting positions.

One more condition needed for the new model is a new relationship between the processes of the FARC and the ELN. From an understanding of their distinct natures, sizes, and conditions, their historical differences and present rivalries, and the particular rhythms of their internal processes and of their dealings with the government, it is necessary to work toward the eventual convergence of the two into a common trajectory, or at least a coordinated one. The issues to be discussed in each have different order and emphasis but cover identical material. Therefore, the solutions and agreements must also be the same. How and when this coordination can begin to occur remains unclear, but for any of this to ever take place government, insurgents, and civil society must all set it as a common goal.

Within the AUC there has been great confusion and uncertainty since internal strife between the "narco" and "counterinsurgent" wings led to a formal breakup that appears now to be an attempt at reorganization, made even more complicated by the fact that its top leaders are currently wanted for extradition by the United States on charges of drug trafficking. During the campaign, the candidate Uribe spoke of negotiating with the paramilitaries as political actors, adding yet another aspect of uncertainty to the entire issue.

To try to predict or project what the future of peace in Colombia will look like is not easy, especially with the grim forecast for peace in the short term, and carries with it huge limitations given the high degree of unpredictability of events here. But to look toward the future, one must think ahead and to imagine at least some possible scenarios.

First, we should assume as a basic premise that peace will entail deep structural changes in social and political terms, changes that will first require legal and constitutional reforms and then go far beyond to affect society and culture as a whole. Issues that are at the root of violent social conflict, such as land ownership, macroeconomic policy, the use of natural resources, and energy policy, must all be serious debated and redefined. This does not mean that a "socialist revolution by decree," as someone once put it, is necessary before peace can be achieved. But it does mean that the Colombian political system and society must do some serious upgrading to meet the standards set even by liberal bourgeois democracy. Far from achieving the Bolshevik Revolution, Colombia today needs to first think about the French Revolution.

This leads one to envision an major redistribution of political power that will probably include formal recognition of local guerrilla control of significant portions of territory and greater regional autonomy, without ever considering the notion of a Yugoslavia-style disintegration of national unity. On the contrary, power sharing is much more likely than breakup.

Another huge and extremely touchy area in need of reform and redefinition is that of defense and security, including the armed forces. Not only will their doctrine, makeup, and functions be matters of negotiation and of major redesign, but it is likely that integration of today's rebels into some form of national security force will be required. Whether that will be as part of the army, as has been suggested by ELN leaders, in separate units, or in a whole new body remains to be seen. Furthermore, after decades of conflict there are those on all sides who have developed skills in the use of arms and have opted for the military profession (in a broad understanding of the concept) and would probably prefer to remain in some form of military service once the war is over, even if given an attractive opportunity to return to civilian life.

It will be also necessary to view this transition as a long process, with a probable period of adjustment that could take five to ten years, of what could be called a stage of an "armed peace."[31] It is clear that given the long history of unfilled promises and political genocide, the rebels—and this goes for both the FARC and the ELN—see their military power as their only leverage to monitor and press for the implementation of agreements, as well as a guarantee of personal safety for their members and sympathizers.

For this reason, another key ingredient of the new model is the need, based especially upon the Barco/M19 experience, to think about and plan for the colossal task of reincorporating back into civilian life thousands of ex-combatants who do wish to leave military life, ex-combatants from all the armed groups, legal and illegal: the army, police, guerrillas, and paramilitaries. This process must take into account human, family, social, gender, regional, and economic components and not only the needs of individuals, as was the case in the first stages of the reinsertion process of the early 1990s. Rather than efforts to turn peasants into businesspeople, which failed miserably a decade ago, different models of alternative development and more democratic forms of the organization of production within the parameters of a free-market economy will be needed, such as cooperatives or social development zones, where tax credits and public funding can create incentives for investment in historically deprived areas. Opening up real equal opportunity is today far more important for furthering the democratization of Colombian society than nationalizing industry.

One of the major questions about the future, and one in which the present has provided probably the fewest answers, concerns the paramilitaries. Their growth in size, strength, and capacity to spread terror is overshadowed by the extremely significant fact of their evident rise in social acceptability and outright support, as well as growing political legitimacy and public appeal. The paramilitaries, or self-defense groups, as they call themselves, are neither the simple extension of a clear policy of state terrorism, as the rebels affirm, nor completely independent and autonomous actors that arose from the need of peasants and farmers, absent an adequate state response, to protect themselves from the abuses of the guerrillas. This complex phenomenon is somewhere in the middle, with elements from each of the two extreme interpretations but with many other components too.

It seems obvious, though, that for peace to be complete and lasting it must include all those who are involved in the war. And whether the paramilitaries are catalogued as independent actors or not, political or not, legitimate interlocutors or not, they are undeniable actors in the war. The question, then, is not whether they should be invited to participate in the negotiation process but when and under what conditions. It is my view that at least two conditions must be met before they can viably be included in the process.

First, the state's policy and action with regard to these groups must lead to a credible and demonstrable separation of what is legal from what is illegal and should be the target of the most vigorous law enforcement. In his first year President Pastrana took the most significant steps in this direction of any president since these groups were declared illegal more than a decade ago. Yet given the gigantic dimensions of the threat to the legitimacy of the state and to the peace process itself, his measures fell far short of being sufficient.

Second, there must be significant progress in the process with the guerrillas for the thought of inclusion of the paramilitaries in the peace process to be even considered. As they themselves repeat time and time again, the paramilitaries see themselves as a product of the guerrillas' war; consequently, peace with them must also be a result of peace with the rebels. This, however, does not mean that international humanitarian law cannot be discussed with them or that they cannot be obligated to respect its principles and norms. According to Article Three in all the Geneva Conventions, as groups who take part in the armed conflict, they are required to abide by international standards and can even enter into ad hoc agreements to implement those standards, without this entailing any alteration of their legal status or any form of political recognition. Whatever treatment is eventually given to these groups and whenever it is given, it should be clear that their reincorporation into civilian life is necessary.

This, of course, leads to yet another immense area for future definition on which today's reality still sheds little light: impunity, punishment, and due justice. It is clear that given the unthinkable level of atrocities that have been perpetrated by the paramilitary groups, the mere discussion of possible pardons or amnesties raises some very delicate questions and issues that go far beyond the boundaries of Colombia, especially in the new context of the International Criminal Court.[32] We too must face the dilemma that all postconflict societies have had to confront and develop their particular way of resolving the tension between the need to forget—which is required for reconciliation—and the equally important need to punish the guilty—without which peace becomes only a cover-up for impunity and wounds that never heal, as Chile today can attest. How to forgive without forgetting?

But for the success of the peace process and for the consolidation of a new model of conflict resolution that can lead to real and sustainable peace, even more important than punishing paramilitary atrocities is dismantling paramilitarism as a logic, a practice, and a system. The one key ingredient of the new model is the participation of the international community. Despite the many shortcomings of the Pastrana years, in the cases of both the FARC and the ELN it was shown that the role of the international community can be multifaceted and can include accompaniment, facilitation, mediation, cooperation, and technical support. The new realities of the reaches of international law regarding gross violations of human rights will no doubt weigh heavily on how the Colombian peace process one day enters into its final stages.

The current international climate of the "war on terrorism" has already had profound effects. On the one hand, the United States has included the AUC on its list of terrorist organizations, alongside the FARC and ELN, which have long been on it, while the European Union for the first time in history has placed the FARC and the ELN on its list, and Mexico has shut down the FARC office that for years served as the base for their international front. The role of the United States in Colombia will continue to be central, of course, and has already seen a significant shift of immense implications. For years, the ever-growing security assistance from the United States was strictly limited to counternarcotics activities, and not to counterinsurgency, for fear of falling into a Vietnam-like quagmire. After 9/11, the mood in Washington shifted quickly toward extending the reach of the aid to include "antiterrorism," the new terminology for what used to be counterinsurgency. For now it seems likely that Uribe will find support for his war effort in this new international context, much as Pastrana found support for peace in the prior one. Although today it seems highly unlikely, the United States must someday understand that in Colombia the best way of fighting terrorism or narco-trafficking is by eliminating the war—and that the U.S. role in continuing or stopping the war is absolutely central.

Nonetheless, Uribe has left an interesting opportunity slightly open, which might be very useful in the future, by asking for the good offices of the United Nations in attempting to reestablish talks with the FARC. For the insurgents, shut out as never before from the international arena, this means retaining a shred of recognition as political actors, and for the government it is useful for now to "delegate" that task. With the ELN, low-key, initial contacts have continued, under the auspices of Cuba.

Final Thoughts

Joaquin Villalobos, the Salvadoran guerrilla leader, has stated that in a first stage of the negotiation process, which is the longest, peace is merely a tactic within a strategy of war. Then, once the negotiation begins taking on a dynamic of its own beyond the original intentions of the parties, the process enters a new stage in which war becomes a tactic in a strategy of peace. Later, in the final stage, which is ironically the shortest, once the process has matured and solidified, war becomes an obstacle to peace, and the new phase of national reconciliation can begin.

It would appear that, despite the many elements of progress in the past two decades of the peace process, Colombia has been unable to get past the first stage. Our history has clearly shown that every time peace-building efforts are broken it is harder to start up again and much, much costlier for human life and the nation as a whole. While many Colombians feel that we have touched bottom, the potential is still great for violence to spiral even further downward.

The Uribe administration has apparently gone back to the days of intensifying the war even more, to level the playing field, so that the beleaguered state can have a fighting chance and the guerrillas, once militarily defeated, can be forced to negotiate terms for their surrender, rather than have to deal with the complicated and costly matter of social and political structural transformation.

Tragically for all, the insurgency appears to be doing and thinking the same. It too appears to believe that it can ratchet the confrontation up several notches, pushing the regime even further toward collapse, which combined with the economic ills and social unrest of all of Latin America, especially the Southern Cone, can lead to new levels of instability and even popular insurrection. Furthermore, in the post-9/11 international context of increasing U.S. intervention and in light of not having been able to create the strategic conditions for a civil war, the FARC feels that it can now transform the armed conflict strategically into a "patriotic war" with regional implications given Venezuela's "Bolivarian Revolution" and Indian and other social movements in Bolivia and Ecuador.

I confess to be highly skeptical of both sides. I do not think that either one can qualitatively change the equation through its current military strategies. Unfortunately, the tragedy of the Colombian War is that it is unwinnable: the army cannot defeat the insurgents by force, and the rebels cannot take power through arms. In military terms, given the terrain of Colombia, the fluid and nomadic nature of guerrilla warfare, and the lessons of history, it is very hard for the government to show concrete results or define victory, since there are no strongholds to bomb, cities to retake, or precise targets to attack. Other than the capture of one of the top guerrilla commanders, it is hard to think of tangible and credible indicators of "turning the tide." The same goes for the insurgency. However, I may be wrong and one of the sides may indeed impose itself over the other. Only time will tell.

If neither is able to "win" the war, probably later rather than sooner Colombia will find itself once again restarting the peace process. But for this current phase of increasing conflict to develop into the final act of the almost epic saga of this seemingly endless war, a new model for conflict resolution must arise. It must be able to adjust to the burdensome and seemingly outdated need of redressing historic injustices that most societies have resolved decades, if not centuries, ago. But it must also have the high-tech sophistication required to incorporate such a diverse network of interrelated elements, more and more connected with a large variety of global concerns. Such a mammoth task can be accomplished only with the teamwork of a great many people over a long time against apparently insurmountable odds, a challenge that only the Colombian people as a whole, with the help of their friends in the world, can meet.

Notes

1. I will use the term *peace process* to refer not only to the different rounds of talks that have been held with the insurgents but also to the broader process within society as a whole.

2. The cease-fire with the FARC lasted from May 1984 to October 1987; with the M19 from August 1984 to June 1985; and with the EPL from August 1984 to December 1985.

3. It can be argued that many of elements of the idea were recovered more than a decade later—by the ELN, ironically.

4. See the work done on the subject by Romero (2003).

5 Throughout this chapter, I will use the term *government* to refer to the executive branch, and the term *state* to refer to the sum of the branches of government.

6. Between 1986 and 1994, nearly 3,500 leaders of the UP were selectively assassinated, including two presidential candidates (Jaime Pardo in 1987 and Bernardo Jaramillo in 1990), constituting what the Organization of American States has accepted calling "political genocide."

7. Other significant *consejerías* (presidential advisors' offices) were created at the same time, two of the most significant and pertinent being the Offices of Human Rights and National Security.

8. The differences between the various processes have been classified in several ways by Colombian scholars. Jesus Antonio Bejarano (1995) often spoke of the "substantive agenda" to refer to the Betancur-FARC agreements, which he compared to those in Central America, whereas he called the Barco–M19 agreements the "operational and procedural agenda" and also used the expressions "agenda for peace" and "agenda for demobilization" to mark the difference. Otty Patiño, one of the founders of the M19 guerillas, has used the term *open agendas* to refer to those, like the one agreed upon in 1999 in Caquetania, that do not have a clearly preestablished final objective, and *closed agendas* to refer to those that determine from the onset disarmament and reincorporation as the goal. According to Rafael Pardo (1996), the agreements with the M19 produced a "political agenda," whereas those with FARC have revolved around a "social agenda." Others have written on the differences as well. See Bejarano (1995), Pardo (1996), Cepeda (2001), and Valencia (2002).

9. The paramilitary boss Carlos Castaño confessed to having been responsible for Pizarro's murder, although he stated that he did it at the request of powerful people within the establishment, whose names he did not reveal (Aranguren 2001: 39–51).

10. In the 1990 presidential elections, the M19 candidate Antonio Navarro obtained 12 percent of the vote.

11. The EPL was given two representatives. The PRT and the Quintín Lame were each given one representative, who could present proposals and take part in deliberations but had no vote.

12. The CGSB proposed a list of twenty-two members, which would be added to the seventy that were to be elected by direct vote on the national level.

13. The round of talks in Caracas, Venezuela, were held from June to November 1991 and then resumed in Tlaxcala, México, in March 1992. Days later, talks were again suspended, and they were officially broken off in October of that year.

14. It took four years after talks were broken off with FARC in 1987 to restart them in 1991, and six years from the time they broke off in 1992 until they started again in 1998.

15. Manuel Perez was a Spanish priest, a disciple of liberation theology, who joined the ELN in the late 1960s. Upon becoming its leader in the early 1980s, Perez was responsible for the group's military, political, and economic resurgence and was key in forging the unity of the insurgencies during the years of the CGSB. Before his death in 1998, he moved the ELN toward seeking a political solution to the armed conflict.

16. The National Convention is the ELN's proposal for a broad, multilateral forum of social and political participation, including that of the ELN itself, that would serve to draw up the structural reforms required to achieve peace.

17. The name was shortened by Gaviria.

18. With the FARC, formal talks were never held. In the first phase, all contacts were indirect or by letter (not even radio contacts were held). Later, in 1997, talks were held, but strictly to agree upon procedures for release of soldiers. A few informal, unofficial, and off-the-record meetings were held with the group's International Front in Mexico.

19. Other important instruments were created as well, such as the Law 418 (1997), which gives legal backing to a broad range of peace policy components, including the demilitarization of various zones and the possibility of granting temporary permission to jailed rebel spokesmen to leave their jail cells to fulfill their roles as negotiators.

20. While the FARC suspended talks on several occasions because of what it considered to be the government's failure to abide by its pledge to dismantle the paramilitary groups, the government withdrew from talks as a result of the "collar-bomb" incident, which later was proven unrelated, and the hijacking of a plane, by an escaped FARC convict, to the demilitarized zone.

21. The group was composed of Norway, Spain, Cuba, Switzerland, France, Sweden, Venezuela, Mexico, Italy, and Canada.

22. A quick chronology of just the major events illustrates this point:

October 12, 1998: The government and the ELN commit to ratify and continue what was established in the Gates of Heaven Accord.

October 18, 1998: The ELN is responsible for the tragic deaths of seventy people in Machuca, and the government suspends talks.

February 1999: Talks resume in Caracas; the ELN requests a demilitarized zone, the government refuses, and talks are quickly broken off again.

April 19, 1999: The ELN hijacks Avianca flight and kidnaps the forty-six people aboard.

May 30, 1999: The ELN kidnaps over 143 church-goers in Cali.

April 25, 2000: Talks resume, and Pastrana announces the granting of an "encounter zone."

July 23, 2000: A meeting is held between the government, the ELN, and civil society to discuss implementation of encounter zone.

September 17, 2000: The ELN kidnaps seventy people at the eighteenth kilometer outside Cali.

December 14, 2000: The government and the ELN agree to the rules and regulations for the encounter zone.

April 19, 2001: The ELN suspends talks because of the failure of the government to create an encounter zone.

June 2001: Contacts resume on the Isla de Maragarita in Venezuela.

August 7, 2001: Pastrana suspends talks.

November 19, 2001: Talks resume in Havana, Cuba.

November 24, 2001: The Accord for Colombia is signed in Havana.

January 27, 2002: A peace summit is held between the government, the ELN, and civil society in Havana.

June 2, 2002: Pastrana permanently breaks off all contacts with the ELN.

23. The "group of friends" of the ELN process, created before the group formed by the FARC process, was composed of five of the same countries: Norway, Spain, Cuba, Switzerland, and France.

24. In fact, U.S. State Department officials, at the request of the Pastrana government, met with FARC representatives in Costa Rica in December 1998.

25. Eighty percent of the $1.3 billion went to the security forces.

26. The resignation of the defense minister in protest against the prolongation of the authorization of the demilitarized zone in early 1999 set off a flurry of resignations by top generals who supported him, all of which were later refused.

27. On this occasion, a "cylinder bomb," supposedly directed at a group of paramilitaries hiding in the town, exploded in a church sheltering innocent civilians, killing 119 of them, including 47 children.

28. See table 4.3 for a summary of the two historical models and the third, new model.

29. The Polo Democrático is a broad coalition of independent reformers, leftist parties, labor unions, and demobilized insurgents that came together in 2002. In the congressional elections it elected 9 (out of 102) senators, 3 of whom (Navarro, Moreno, Gaviria) were among the top five vote-getters nationwide, and 9 (out of 165) representatives in the House, including 4 of Bogotá's delegation of 18, the best numbers the Left has had at least in a decade. In the May presidential elections, the Polo Democrático's candidate Lucho Garzón finished a surprising third place, out-polling such powerful contenders as Noemí Sanín, and obtaining over 7 percent of the vote, also a record for the Left in recent years.

30. In fact, since the breakdown of talks, two of the FARC's key political figures, Alfonso Cano and Pablo Catatumbo, have given several press interviews after a long silence during the Caguan years.

31. The term, as far as I know, was coined in El Salvador to refer to the period between the signing of the agreements and the actual turning over of weapons, months later.

32. Although Colombia ratified the Rome Statute, in the last days of its term the Pastrana administration, with the assent of the incoming president, evoked Article 124, which allows for a seven-year delay in the application of the statute with regard to war crimes.

References

Aranguren, Mauricio. 2001. *Mi confesión: Carlos Castaño revela sus secretos*. Bogotá: Editorial Oveja Negra.

Bejarano, Jesús Antonio. 1995. *Una agenda para la paz*. Bogotá: Tercer Mundo Editores.

Cepeda, Fernando, ed. 2001. *Haciendo paz*. Bogotá: Ancora Editores.

Kaldor, Mary. 1999. *New and Old Wars: Organized Violence in a Global Era*. Stanford: Stanford University Press.

Pardo, Rafael. 1996. *De primera mano*. Bogotá: CEREC/Norma Editores.

Romero, Mauricio. 2003. *Paramilitares y autodefensas, 1982–2003*. Bogotá: Editorial Planeta/IEPRI.

Valencia, León. 2002. *Adiós a la política, bienvenida la guerra*. Bogotá: Intermedio Editores.

The Peace Process in Colombia and U.S. Policy

Cynthia J. Arnson

Arnson presents a detailed account of the ups and downs of the Colombian peace process during the Pastrana administration and the role of U.S. policy in that process. Empirically, her account is backed up by behind-the-scenes interviews with senior government officials and extensive knowledge of the history of negotiations between the Colombian government and the FARC and ELN. Theoretically, Arnson refers to advances in the theory of conflict resolution. She argues that during the Clinton administration there was a major disconnect between the U.S. realization that there was no military solution to the conflict and the actual policy measures taken, which primarily addressed the military aspects of the problem. Moreover, she finds there was plenty of blame to go around for the failure of the peace process during the Pastrana years: the guerrillas often did not seem serious about peace negotiations, the paramilitaries did what they could to sabotage the talks with the guerrillas, the Pastrana government lacked a coherent approach, and U.S. policy was misdirected when not counterproductive. Ultimately, she concludes, the fate of a future, comprehensive peace process depends on the Colombian government's willingness to combat violent actors on the left and the right and on a shift in the focus of U.S. and other policies to create the conditions for peace by "insisting absolutely on combating paramilitarism, pursuing economic policies to enhance equity and expand economic opportunities beyond alternative development, supporting efforts to engage the FARC politically and diplomatically, and finding those aspects of a reform agenda, including agrarian and tax reform, that the United States can support."

On the night of February 20, 2002, Colombian President Andrés Pastrana ended a three-and-a-half-year peace process with Colombia's largest and most powerful guerrilla group, the Revolutionary Armed Forces of Colombia (FARC). Addressing the nation, Pastrana denounced the FARC's hijacking earlier that day of a civilian airliner and the kidnapping of Senator Jorge Eduardo Gechem Turbay, president of the Senate's Peace Commission. He ordered the Colombian military to retake a large demilitarized zone known as the *despeje*, ceded to the FARC at the beginning of the peace dialogue. "It is not possible," he said, for the FARC "on the one hand to sign agreements, while putting a gun to the head of innocents on the other."[1]

The collapse of the peace process with the FARC—and eventually with the smaller National Liberation Army (ELN)—presaged a new and more deadly round of violence in Colombia's thirty-seven-year internal armed conflict. The FARC stepped up an urban bombing campaign in mid-2002, seeking to undermine the governability of the country by staging relentless attacks on the economic infrastructure and issuing death threats against regional and municipal authorities throughout the country. All this took place against a backdrop of surging growth in the size and territorial presence of paramilitary groups. The deteriorating security situation in Colombia in 2001 and 2002 had a decisive impact on the country's May 2002 presidential elections, producing an unprecedented first-round victory for the conservative candidate Álvaro Uribe Vélez. Uribe's pledges to double the size of the army, increase military spending, and create a vast civilian support network for the armed forces resonated with a war-weary population disgusted with a peace process that not only had failed to produce results but had witnessed an escalation of guerrilla abuses, particularly kidnapping, as well as burgeoning attacks on the civilian population by all armed actors.

The end of peace negotiations with the FARC also coincided with and accelerated a major shift in U.S. policy toward Colombia. This shift had begun in the wake of terrorist attacks on Washington and New York on September 11, 2001, as the country mobilized to fight a global war on terrorism.

Although both the FARC and ELN had been officially designated by the State Department in 1997 as foreign terrorist organizations, U.S. assistance to Colombia had been directed toward and justified solely in the name of counternarcotics. This was principally for two reasons: (1) Colombia was the source of some 80 to 90 percent of the cocaine and a large share of the heroin consumed in the United States; this was a highly salient political issue domestically and reflected the focus of U.S. antidrug programs in the 1980s and into the 1990s on reducing the supply of illegal drugs coming from abroad; and (2) the administration, Congress, and the public had shied away from direct involvement in Colombia's counterinsurgency war, given widely reported human rights abuses by paramilitary groups linked to the armed forces. Between the poles of drugs on the one hand and human rights on the other stood another uniquely American fear, of becoming bogged down in a Vietnam-style quagmire, given Colombia's long history of political violence and the multiplicity of armed actors challenging the state.

Three changes during the administration of President George W. Bush demonstrated the significance for Colombia of the shift in U.S. global priorities. First, as the peace process floundered and the war heated up, the State Department added the principal paramilitary group, the United Self-Defense Forces of Colombia (Autodefensas Unidas de Colombia or AUC), to the list of foreign terrorist organizations. This initiative, announced on September 10, 2001, had been discussed for months within the administration. Whatever the precise rationale for the AUC's terrorist designation, it appeared at least in part to respond to criticism within and outside the U.S. government that the United States exercised a double standard by condemning terrorism of left-wing guerrillas while ignoring that of right-wing paramilitaries. Second, in February 2002, before the collapse of talks with the FARC and as part of its annual foreign aid request, the administration asked Congress for military assistance to train and equip Colombian troops to protect an oil pipeline frequently targeted by the guerrillas. This represented the first time in over a decade that U.S. aid was to be used explicitly for counterguerrilla operations and reflected a growing view in Washington that more needed to be done to help the Colombian government fight the war, not just narcotics. Third, and of greatest significance, in March 2002, after the end of the peace process with the FARC, the administration asked Congress for authority to use aid previously appropriated for antinarcotics for counterterrorism purposes in Colombia.[2] The effect of this change was to make hundreds of millions of dollars in counternarcotics funding available for fighting the war. "Colombia is not part of the global war on terrorism," State Department spokesman Richard Boucher stated in announcing the initiative, part of a wider supplemental aid request. But "President Pastrana's February 20th decision to end his long-standing efforts at a peace process with the Revolutionary Armed Forces of Colombia has put a new focus on counterterrorism in Colombia."[3]

This chapter examines U.S. policy in Colombia with a particular focus on the peace process between the Pastrana government and the FARC guerrillas.[4] It explores U.S. initiatives, primarily during the administration of President Bill Clinton, that aimed specifically at advancing the peace process, as well as the way that pursuit of a negotiated settlement to the conflict interfaced with other U.S. objectives, principally counternarcotics. A central premise of this chapter is that there was a significant disconnect between the view broadly held within the U.S. government—and perhaps still held during the Bush years—that there was no military solution to Colombia's conflict and the specific measures undertaken to advance a peaceful settlement. Key policies, particularly counternarcotics, were never decided within the context of the peace process, even though the antidrug policy itself ultimately came to be justified in the name of peace. That counternarcotics remained the central driver of U.S. policy influenced the composition of aid packages as well as the way U.S. policy was perceived abroad, creating a backlash in Europe against what many saw as a militaristic U.S. approach and for several years activating European governments on behalf of a peaceful settlement that would address the root causes of conflict.

A focus on U.S. policy vis-à-vis the peace process should not obscure the fact that the central dynamic of that process was a Colombian affair. Numerous Colombian analysts have criticized the negotiations during the Pastrana years as deeply flawed in conception and execution, consisting of unilateral and unreciprocated concessions (the granting of the *despeje* or demilitarized zone without any form of domestic or international verification) absent a coherent government strategy or experienced team of negotiators. Added to this assessment was a widely held conviction that the FARC itself was not seriously interested in negotiations and was simply using the talks to buy time. Many of these criticisms appeared vindicated following the collapse of the peace talks with the FARC. At the same time, however, with the exception of several short-lived initiatives discussed below, the United States did little to positively shape the environment—political or military—in which the peace talks took place or to make the pursuit of a negotiated settlement a key priority around which other goals would coalesce.

The Peace Process during the Pastrana Years: An Overview

A brief overview of major benchmarks since the late 1990s helps to put the debate over the management of the peace process, as well as FARC attitudes, in perspective. The peace process foundered during the better part of the administration of Ernesto Samper (1994–98), following a scandal linking his presidential campaign to the Cali drug-trafficking cartel. The guerrillas deemed the Samper government too weak and illegitimate to deliver on commitments made at the peace table, and formal talks were suspended during most of his administration. By the 1998 presidential campaign, the effects of the war on the economy and everyday life—driven home by guerrilla kidnappings, the destruction of infrastructure and investor confidence, growing paramilitary violence and human rights abuses, and reversals for the armed forces in several key battlefield encounters—had become so disruptive as to thrust the issues of war and peace to the top of the national agenda. Conservative Party candidate Andrés Pastrana made the pledge to negotiate an end to the decades-long conflict the top issue in his campaign and traveled to the jungle before his inauguration to meet with the FARC founder and leader Manuel Marulanda. The initiative met with resounding popular approval. Once in office, Pastrana acceded to guerrilla demands that the talks take place inside Colombia and ordered the November 1998 demilitarization of five municipalities in southern Colombia, a depopulated rural area roughly twice the size of El Salvador.[5]

Peace talks were set to begin in January 1999. Pastrana traveled to the *despeje*, only to be stood up when Marulanda, citing concerns for personal security, failed to appear. In the days and weeks immediately following that meeting, and in what appeared as a deliberate attempt to sabotage the talks, paramilitary groups carried out a wave of brutal massacres. The FARC demanded action against the paramilitaries as the price of continuing the dialogue. In April, Pastrana dismissed two generals—Fernando Millán Pérez and Rito Alejo del Río—linked to paramilitary activity. Another two resigned or were dismissed later in the year.

Following some progress in crafting a provisional agenda, the talks broke down again in July 1999. At issue was the government's post facto demand that the FARC permit international verification within the *despeje*, something that the FARC refused. Formal talks finally opened in October 1999 on a twelve-point agenda that placed priority on perhaps the thorniest and most difficult issue: Colombia's socioeconomic structure.

The international community took on a limited role in the peace talks—something initially resisted by both the government and the FARC—when UN Secretary-General Kofi Annan named the veteran Norwegian diplomat Jan Egeland as special adviser for international assistance to Colombia.[6] Reflecting the ambivalence of the parties, as well as the Colombian government's express desire to generate international support for aid to Colombia, Egeland's mandate was vague, structured around serving as a "focal point for the United Nations system" in mobilizing international resources for human rights, alternative development, and peace-building activities.[7] In practice, Egeland was a facilitator of contacts but not a moderator or negotiator, limiting the UN's involvement.

At Egeland's initiative, top FARC commanders left their jungle retreat and toured several European capitals in February 2000, a trip that exposed the guerrilla leaders to European social democracy as well as to extensive criticisms of their human rights record and involvement in drug trafficking. Then, in March, a group of Colombia's most important private sector leaders traveled to the *despeje* to meet with the FARC, emphasizing their commitment to a negotiated solution and discussing agrarian and social policy.[8] The FARC's response to such initiatives was to promulgate "Law 002," requiring Colombians with assets of $1 million or more to pay a "peace tax" or face kidnapping.[9] Pastrana's initial peace advisor, Víctor G. Ricardo, abruptly resigned in April 2000, facing a barrage of criticism of the peace process. He was replaced by the Pastrana confidant Camilo Gómez.

Efforts to engage the FARC in dialogue with the international community and Colombian civil society continued in June 2000, when representatives of European governments, Japan, and the United Nations met in the *despeje* to discuss alternative development for peasants engaged in coca cultivation. But the talks fell into crisis again in September 2000, when a rebel prisoner escaped from jail, hijacking a plane and forcing it to land in the *despeje*. The government demanded that the prisoner be returned to government custody; the FARC refused. The talks were suspended again in November 2000, following a meeting between Colombian Interior Minister Humberto de la Calle and the paramilitary leader Carlos Castaño, head of the AUC. De la Calle's meeting was prompted by the AUC's kidnapping of several Colombian legislators. The FARC again demanded proof of government action against paramilitaries, whose numbers and brutality had escalated during the previous two years and whose growing strength and independence constituted a decisive impediment to progress in the talks.

The November 2000 rupture put the peace talks on the brink of total collapse. Using the imminent expiration of the *despeje* as leverage, Pastrana demanded a meeting with Marulanda to discuss the future of the peace process. At a meeting in the town of Los Pozos, Caquetá, on February 9, 2001, the two signed an agreement intended to accelerate the talks, establish concrete mechanisms for action against paramilitary groups, devise measures to humanize the conflict, and provide a greater role for the international community.[10] In a demonstration of the interest of the international community in keeping the peace process alive, the United Nations and close to two dozen countries in Europe and Latin America—but not the United States—sent representatives to the *despeje* for another meeting with the FARC on alternative development issues in March 2001. According to one European participant, the meeting was poorly organized and unfocused.[11] Yet it underscored the political point that peace and development, not counternarcotics, would galvanize foreign, especially European, participation in Colombia.

Over the course of the following year and until their definitive breakdown in February 2002, the peace talks took place amidst surging violence by both the guerrillas and paramilitary groups, plummeting approval ratings for Pastrana,[12] and hardening opposition from within the armed forces. With one exception opposed by the military—a prisoner exchange agreed to in June 2001—the talks failed to move forward in any substantive area, including discussion of a cease-fire and measures to reduce the conflict's devastating impact on the civilian population.

Periodic reauthorizations of the *despeje* constituted, in essence, a decision every few months over whether to continue or end the peace process, focusing a spotlight on the negotiations' meager results and galvanizing pressure to end the talks. FARC behavior contributed directly to this pressure. In July 2001, for example, the FARC kidnapped three Germans, including a government aid worker, thereby targeting nationals of a government designated as one of the "group of friends" of the peace process. That same month, in a direct affront to the United Nations, the FARC kidnapped the former governor of Meta province, Alan Jara, from a UN vehicle carrying the senior representative of the UN Development Program based in Colombia. Then, in August 2001, Colombian authorities arrested three members of the Irish Republican Army who were accused of training the FARC in the use of explosives and urban terrorism, fueling accusations that the demilitarized zone was a safe haven for illegal activities and war preparations.[13] In an episode that deeply reverberated throughout Colombian society, the FARC in September kidnapped and executed Consuelo Araújonoguera, a beloved former culture minister and wife of the Colombian attorney general. In the outpouring of anger following her murder, fully 61 percent of Colombians polled by the leading Bogotá daily *El Tiempo* said the peace talks should end, and only 23 percent favored their continuation.[14]

Rather than abandon the talks on which he had staked his presidency, Pastrana renewed the *despeje* in October, following an eleventh-hour agreement with the FARC that it would instruct its combatants to end kidnappings and give priority to discussions of a cease-fire.[15] At the same time, Pastrana issued new restrictions prohibiting foreigners from visiting the *despeje* without the government's permission and authorized the military and police to step up air, land, and riverine control around and above the zone. FARC leader Marulanda responded by ordering his commanders not to meet with the government unless military operations around the zone ceased and by again demanding action against the paramilitaries: in the month of October alone, troops of the United Self-Defense Forces of Colombia (AUC) had killed over thirty-five people in two separate massacres, one committed just seven miles from a major military base.[16] Prosecutions of military officers accused of fomenting paramilitarism had languished in the second half of the year under a new *fiscal general* (attorney general) criticized by human rights groups as well as the United Nations for compromising judicial independence in the fight against impunity.[17]

With the peace talks in deep disrepute—and candidates for the May 2002 presidential elections vowing a harder line against the guerrillas—a vast majority of Colombians applauded Pastrana's decision in early January 2002 to end the peace process, giving the FARC forty-eight hours to abandon the *despeje*. A last-minute effort by the United Nations, foreign ambassadors, and the Catholic Church aimed at avoiding Colombia's descent into full-scale war brought the negotiations back from the brink of collapse. An accord signed on January 20 referred to the perennial issues of kidnapping and paramilitarism but for the first time set a concrete deadline of April 2002 for a cease-fire.

Explanations for what happened next vary, but the facts themselves are undisputed: on February 20, FARC guerrillas hijacked a civilian airliner headed for Bogotá, taking hostage Senator Jorge Eduardo Gechem Turbay, nephew of a former president. One interpretation of the hijacking was that it constituted a deliberate effort to sabotage the negotiations once a concrete cease-fire deadline was on the table. Another interpretation held that the FARC was simply conducting business as usual, committing serious violations of international humanitarian law as if they had no bearing on the peace process.[18] Regardless of the interpretation, such an egregious assault on a civilian target—during an electoral campaign in Colombia and following the September 11 terrorist attacks involving airplanes in the United States—made continuation of the peace process politically untenable. In an emotional speech to the nation late on the night of February 20, 2002, Pastrana lashed out at Marulanda for his "arrogance and lies," ordering the armed forces to retake the *despeje* and ending the peace process on which he had staked much of his presidency.[19]

The preceding narrative helps illustrate several central dynamics of the peace process during three-and-a-half years of the Pastrana administration: the failure of the FARC to reciprocate government initiatives with gestures of its own; the failure of the government to adopt a coherent strategy to advance peace, including failing to mount a serious effort against paramilitary groups; the impact of violence against civilians on the legitimacy and viability of the peace process; and the primacy in the negotiating agenda—at the FARC's insistence—of complicated socioeconomic issues, including but not limited to alternative development in drug-producing zones. U.S. policy intersected with those dynamics, shaping and being shaped by the progress or the lack thereof at the peace table. But even with the unveiling of Plan Colombia just prior to the launching of formal peace talks between the Colombian government and the FARC, it would be a mistake to ascribe undue influence or responsibility to the U.S. government for what took place in the peace process. Although advancing peace was never a central driver of U.S. policy, in many ways the direction of influence between countries may have been the reverse: the fits and starts of what took place in Colombia served to isolate the peace process's early and most ardent boosters within the Clinton administration and to confirm the views of its harshest critics that, given the FARC's military and economic strength, there were no conditions for negotiations in the first place.

U.S. Initiatives in Support of Peace

During the Clinton years, the view that a negotiated settlement was possible and desirable in Colombia was a direct consequence of the wars in Central

America and more specifically El Salvador. Just as many senior officials responsible for Central America policy in the 1980s had had experience in Vietnam, for generational reasons, many senior policy makers in the State Department with responsibility for Colombia had spent a good part of their careers dealing with issues of war and peace in El Salvador. These included Acting Assistant Secretary of State for Inter-American Affairs Peter Romero, in the mid-1980s the State Department's desk officer for El Salvador and later chargé d'affaires of the U.S. embassy in San Salvador; Director of the State Department's Office of Andean Affairs Philip Chicola, political counselor, deputy chief of mission, and chargé d'affaires of the U.S. embassy in San Salvador during and immediately after the negotiated settlement to the civil war; and Undersecretary of State Thomas Pickering, U.S. ambassador to El Salvador during the Reagan era, who pushed for a crackdown on death squad violence in 1983, presided over the first years of a bipartisan consensus in the United States over El Salvador following the 1984 election of President José Napoleón Duarte, and participated actively in the United Nations–brokered peace talks in their final phase in 1991.[20] Although the State Department was by no means the only bureaucratic actor in the Colombia debate—in several respects it was weaker and more fragmented than other parts of the U.S. government—it had an important role in framing the public and political dimensions of policy, including priorities beyond counternarcotics.

The negotiated resolution of the Salvadoran conflict—and the subsequent talks that ended Guatemala's war in 1996—shaped several key perceptions regarding the Colombian peace process once it had attained prominence during the 1998 Colombian presidential campaign. Central among these perceptions was the potential for politically engaging insurgents in the post–Cold War era in order to end internal armed conflicts through negotiations. To this was added a view widely held within the State and Defense Departments and the National Security Council: that there was no possibility of defeating the Colombian guerrillas militarily within a realistic time frame, given the Colombian state's historical absence from large parts of the countryside, deficiencies in the armed forces' doctrine, budget, and capabilities, and the guerrillas' growing strength in numbers, capacity, and territorial presence. Even though Clinton administration officials felt politically and economically constrained to limit U.S. assistance to Colombia to counternarcotics, an implicit assumption was that the modernization and professionalization of the military for antidrug purposes would positively affect their other roles and missions.[21] To the extent that military issues entered the U.S. debate over the peace process, officials spoke of restoring "balance" in the military equilibrium between the government and insurgents, thereby creating incentives to negotiate.[22] This stands in stark contrast to the U.S. experience in Central America, where the explicit purpose of counterinsurgency aid to the Salvadoran government was to reduce the guerrillas to the level of "banditry" and where the purpose of assistance to counterrevolutionaries fighting in Nicaragua was to topple the Sandinista regime (see Arnson 1993).

As the peace process achieved higher salience in the Colombian political debate, the U.S. government undertook three concrete, albeit limited, initiatives to advance the prospects for peace. Independent of and for the most part prior to the unveiling of Plan Colombia, these were (1) the fostering of high-level dialogue among Colombians over strategies for peace and policy reform; (2) the opening of direct contact with the FARC in December 1998, at the request of the FARC and the Colombian government; and (3) the financing of discrete projects to provide quick-impact relief to civilians in conflict zones and to contribute to the intellectual framework for achieving peace. These initiatives will be discussed in turn.

The "Houston Process"

Even before war and peace became the central issues in the 1998 presidential elections, a "civilian mandate for peace" had garnered ten million votes during Colombia's 1997 municipal and departmental elections. Believing that the situation in Colombia had reached a turning point, U.S. officials in the political section of the embassy in Bogotá sought a way to foster a discussion among Colombians, "setting a table where Colombians of good will from the far left to the far right can meet and talk in open dialogue about how to cure the problems that plague their benighted land." The goal, in essence, was to "provoke the Colombian political class to acknowledge and act on three principles: (1) Colombian political will is decisive . . . ; (2) Colombia needs to forge its own national strategy: political, economic, social, and security . . . ; (3) Colombia is a rich country. By and large it is going to have to finance its own salvation" (McBride 2000: 216–17). Members of the political section rejected the view that Colombia's problems could be solved from the outside. Instead, the embassy officials saw their role as catalysts for a discussion among Colombians.

Some eight months before Pastrana's inauguration, in January 1998, the embassy sponsored a first meeting in Houston, Texas, on the "lessons of war" in dealing with insurgencies around the world. Between 1998 and 2001, the U.S. embassy sponsored a total of six large gatherings on issues related to the peace process.[23] Because of the unique *poder convocatorio* (convening power) of the embassy (at times in conjunction with major Colombian institutions and the media), the meetings attracted top-level participation from across Colombian society and the international community: the armed forces, the private sector, trade unions, political parties, government ministries, universities, foreign embassies, the United Nations, and so on.[24]

The U.S. embassy's involvement in such an endeavor was enough of a departure from what Colombians had come to expect from U.S. policy that many openly wondered, "What do the gringos really want?" "The answer— although few may believe it," wrote Joseph McBride (2000) of the embassy's political section, "is that they are trying to help Colombians find their own solution to their own problems using their own resources. It is as simple as that" (217).

While the impact of such gatherings is difficult to measure, in Colombia the meetings conveyed an important message of U.S. backing for the peace process. In addition, they provided a venue for debate among a cross section of Colombians that rarely found themselves in the same room. The proceedings from several of the meetings were widely covered in the Colombian press. At one point, edited videotapes of the sessions were broadcast on Colombian television and shared through an intermediary with the FARC and ELN fronts.[25]

Contacting the FARC

If one view of the U.S. role in the peace process had the U.S. government serving as honest broker in a dialogue among Colombians, another envisioned a more proactive role. At the request of the Colombian government, which was itself responding to a request from the FARC, two midlevel State Department officials secretly met with senior guerrilla leaders in Costa Rica in December 1998. The meeting was held despite the FARC's 1997 designation as a foreign terrorist organization for its involvement in attacks on U.S. citizens.

Although what was said at the two meetings has not been disclosed publicly, State Department officials justified it as providing an opportunity to press the FARC on the case of missing Americans, express support for the peace process, and insist on the primacy of U.S. counternarcotics objectives.[26] According to a knowledgeable U.S. official, the FARC indicated that it was prepared to work with the Colombian government on the case of the missing missionaries and, further, that if any U.S. citizen were kidnapped or taken hostage, the FARC would work quickly to have him or her released. Although controversial within the administration, the meetings went well enough that the State Department decided in early 1999 to hold a second meeting in March or April.[27]

Then, in late February, three U.S. indigenous rights activists were abducted by gunmen in Colombia's Arauca province, near the Venezuelan border. Suspecting FARC involvement, State Department officials contacted the guerrillas, using channels set up at the Costa Rica meetings. The FARC privately conveyed that one or more of their units was responsible and promised that the Americans would be released in a matter of days.[28] Just following that admission, however, the three activists were executed, their bound, blindfolded, and bullet-ridden bodies discovered just over the Venezuelan border on March 2, 1999.

What the murders reflected is open to several interpretations, all of them negative for the FARC.[29] One explanation centered on the lack of command and control of the FARC's high command over regional guerrilla fronts, thus calling into question the FARC leadership's ability to deliver its rank and file in a peace process. A darker interpretation held that the murders reflected a division between the FARC's civilian and military leadership and constituted a direct attempt to sabotage the incipient dialogue with the United States. Coincidence or not, the commander of the unit responsible for the murders, Germán Briceño (alias "Granobles"), was the brother of the FARC's top military strategist Jorge Briceño, a.k.a. "Mono Jojoy." In April 2002, "Granobles" and five other FARC members were indicted for murder by the U.S. Justice Department, which requested their extradition from Colombia.[30] A few weeks later, Colombian prosecutors in Bogotá indicted Jorge Briceño himself for the murders of the U.S. citizens.

The political firestorm that erupted in 1999 over the killing of the three Americans ended all contact with the FARC, and cooperation in bringing the perpetrators to justice became the sine qua non for reentering a dialogue. Republican critics of the administration had a field day, attacking the State Department for "sitting down at the table with a group that actively seeks to wantonly kidnap and murder American citizens" and then subpoenaing State Department records related to communications with the FARC.[31] House International Relations Committee Chair Benjamin Gilman (R-NY) accused the administration of "blur[ring] the longstanding U.S. policy of not dealing with terrorists" and said that those in the State Department responsible for such actions should be "held accountable."[32] The FARC, meanwhile, carried out its own investigation of the murders and in May 2000 absolved "Granobles" of responsibility.[33] Pastrana decried the verdict as "nepotism" and a travesty of justice.[34] In perhaps an exaggeration of the level of U.S. commitment to the peace process in Colombia, one official remarked that the murders of the three Americans constituted "the single biggest disaster for those who wanted to move the peace process forward."[35]

Asked in mid-2000 whether the policy of direct U.S. contact with the FARC could change, a U.S. official in Bogotá responded, "I don't know if the political climate in Washington will ever change, absent changes in Colombia. It is not clear what we could do in contact with the FARC."[36] When delegates of twenty-three countries met with the FARC in the zone of *despeje* in March 2001, no representative of the U.S. government attended, despite an explicit request from Pastrana that the United States participate.[37] "If all it means is go down there and chat," explained another U.S. official, "we've already done that."[38]

AID's Office of Transition Initiatives

A third, albeit tiny, area of U.S. government support to the peace process involved the financing of discrete projects in Colombia, overseen by the Office of Transition Initiatives (OTI) within the Agency for International Development (AID) . According to an OTI official, AID's Latin American Bureau, the USAID mission in Bogotá, and the embassy "identified three potential 'openings' for [U.S. government] assistance to the peace process: (1) strengthening the capacity of the High Commission[er] for Peace to examine the different alternatives and positions, and their possible consequences; (2) supporting civil society's ability at the national level to sustain pressure on all actors to continue discussions; and (3) supporting the peace process at the local level" (Kramer 1999: 2). In practice, this meant that OTI responded to requests from the Colombian government for technical support as it established its negotiating positions and that it worked through counterpart organizations, including the Catholic Church and the International Committee for the Red Cross (ICRC), in addressing local needs in areas of high conflict.[39] "The Colombian government has to be seen as responsive to the needs of communities that have been devastated, or there is no chance of a peace process," explained an AID official.[40] Through tiny projects—a sports field, water system, or schoolhouse—OTI aimed to empower local communities, "establishing confidence that there are institutions willing to work with people to help re-build their lives, and restoring their faith that the peace process can yield positive and tangible results" (Kramer 1999: 2).

OTI's initial assessment also recognized a bottleneck involving a lack of communication between Colombia's high commissioner for peace and local officials and civil society organizations that were the intended beneficiaries of newly planned projects. An OTI-sponsored workshop in Bogotá in November 1998 brought together municipal officials in newly designated "peace laboratories" with Colombian officials from a range of government ministries, along with representatives of the ICRC, the church, and civil society. The goal was to involve communities in the decision-making process, fostering a "bottom-up" rather than a "top-down" approach to development in neglected areas.

One of OTI's projects, however, became embroiled in controversy. With the knowledge and support of the highest levels of the Colombian government and the support of the State Department and the U.S. embassy, AID provided indirect funding to a small project in the zone of *despeje*, giving community councils and municipal governments the resources to carry out quick-impact projects. The location of the project—in an area controlled militarily by the FARC but administratively by local officials—sent up red flags throughout Washington and was canceled when officials of other agencies, including the Office of National Drug Control Policy and the Department of Defense, objected. Officials in Washington also derailed OTI's involvement in the dialogue between the Colombian government and community-based organizations, despite the U.S. embassy's support and the interest of the World Bank and Inter-American Development Bank in participating in the discussion over investment priorities. Washington's refusal to permit U.S. government involvement—even indirectly—in projects involving the *despeje* reflected the political limits of support for the peace process.

Carrots and Sticks: Finding a Balance

It is important not to exaggerate OTI's importance within AID overall or the significance of its budget as a portion of U.S. development assistance for Colombia. Nonetheless, the 1998 cancellation of the project in the *despeje* and of OTI's facilitation effort is instructive on several levels. On one level, it illustrates the concern for a potential backlash from committed Republicans on Capitol Hill if U.S. policy were perceived as tacitly accepting guerrilla participation in U.S.-funded initiatives. At a much deeper level, however, it reveals an extreme ambivalence toward the notion of incentives in a negotiating process and thus an ignorance, or at least a misreading, of important advances in the theoretical framework governing conflict resolution. In brief, these changes mark an evolution beyond the concept of a "hurting stalemate" as an objective condition rooted in questions of military balance between contending forces to stress the human elements of perception and choice, particularly regarding strategic decisions governing one's future with and without the conflict.[41] While not discarding the connection between perceptions and some external reality, theorists of conflict resolution in the 1990s have stressed the subjective as well as objective dimensions of choice: in other words, the need to influence minds and not just thresholds of pain. The principal implication of the new theory is that "ripe moments" for a successful negotiation do not just happen but can be created through a combination of inducements and pressures aimed at altering the calculations of the parties (Arnson 1999b: 451; see also Arnson 2001: 41–46).

Key to understanding the Clinton administration's approach to the peace process in Colombia was the unanimity over the need for increased pressure, including military pressure, on the FARC to make the peace process possible. In the words of one official: "The security forces are a shield you need so you can build behind a process that has credibility. . . . You need a sufficiently credible military so that the guerrillas see they are not going to win the war . . . [and] are convinced that their nonmilitary goals can't be achieved through military ends. But neither do you want to create a sense on the part of the army that they can achieve a military victory."[42] Administration policy focused less on the need to foreclose military options for both sides and more on improving the Pastrana government's position through the building of stronger and more effective security forces. Said General Charles Wilhelm, director of the U.S. Southern Command, "[T]actical defeats suffered by the government security forces at the hands of the FARC in recent years have emboldened the FARC and provided little incentive for them to engage in meaningful or substantive peace negotiations with the Government of Colombia (GOC). . . . To improve the GOC's position at the negotiating table, the armed forces must continue to upgrade their combat capabilities and sustain recently observed trends of improved performance on the battlefield."[43] Or in the words of ONDCP director General Barry McCaffrey, "[I]t is hard to imagine peace unless it is based on the strength of the Colombian government."[44]

Aside from the number of FARC military advances beginning in the mid-1990s, of particular concern across the U.S. policy establishment were the economic resources available to the FARC as a result of its involvement in narco-trafficking. Estimates of FARC earnings from the drug trade ranged from about $100 million annually to upwards of $1 billion.[45] According to General Wilhelm, by early 2000 more than half of FARC fronts (and roughly one-fourth of ELN fronts) received "support from, and provide[d] protection to" drug-trafficking organizations.[46] By the end of the year, senior U.S. officials accused the FARC of going beyond their widely acknowledged role in taxing and protecting coca cultivation and processing activities and engaging in cartel-like activities, including the control of export routes.[47]

However one gauges the nature or extent of the FARC role in the drug trade, the very existence of that involvement had important implications for the peace process. Indeed, a number of recent studies of the role of economic resources—diamonds, oil, or drugs—in internal armed conflicts have pointed to the singular difficulty of resolving such conflicts and to the transforming nature of wealth and greed on insurgent organizations originally defined by ideology or ethnic grievance.[48] In the Colombian case, U.S. officials appear to have been divided over whether "the FARC was so deeply involved in drugs that it was a criminal enterprise, philosophically not disposed to negotiations,"[49] or whether the involvement with drugs was, as the FARC itself claimed, negotiable—in essence, that income from the drug trade was a means to an end and could terminate with the advent of peace.

The distinction was important, as the U.S. government had long maintained a position of not negotiating with narco-traffickers except over issues of surrender to justice.[50] But even those philosophically predisposed to consider negotiations with an insurgent group were alarmed by the drug connection. "If the FARC was earning $200 million a year, what were the incentives to throw in the towel and become potato farmers?" asked one U.S. official rhetorically. "A lot of us came to the conviction that a successful effort to eradicate drugs was also important to the peace process."[51] What happened over the course of the Clinton administration, as a result of the lack of progress in the peace talks, was a blending of two perspectives. One emphasized the need for strengthening the Colombian security forces to build a military "shield" behind the peace process. The other emphasized counternarcotics as essential to weakening the guerrillas and other armed actors, including the paramilitary groups. Nowhere did the two perspectives come together more forcefully than in the U.S. contribution to Plan Colombia, unveiled in September 1999 as a $7.5 billion strategy to revive the Colombian economy, reform the justice sector, advance the peace process, conduct counterdrug operations, and invest in social development.

Plan Colombia

The focus of this chapter could leave the impression that Clinton administration policy toward Colombia had as its central organizing principle the peace process. Nothing could be farther from the truth. While peace, human rights, democratic consolidation, and institutional and economic strengthening figured prominently in stated U.S. objectives, the only issue in Colombia that was portrayed as directly affecting vital U.S. interests was drugs.

That 80 to 90 percent of the cocaine and a growing share of the heroin consumed in the United States came from one country necessarily placed the narcotics issue at the top of the bilateral agenda. This was consistent with the U.S. drug war's original emphasis on supply reduction and continued even when the Clinton administration shifted a greater portion of the counterdrug budget to the effort to reduce demand.

The drug "filter" through which U.S. policy was made, quite apart from whether the issue was viewed in national security terms, defined in large measure who was involved from the various policy bureaucracies in Washington, as well as how they were involved. The definition of the "problem" in Colombia helped select the policy actors, drive the policy choices, and focus the type of U.S. resources. For much of Pastrana's term, that problem was defined as the "explosion"[52] of coca production in southern Colombia, itself a product of perceived drug war successes in neighboring Peru and Bolivia that reduced cultivation there and relocated it elsewhere in the Andes.

Throughout the Clinton years, a group of drug war hawks in the U.S. Congress had pushed the administration to do more in Colombia and supply more sophisticated equipment (particularly Blackhawk helicopters, as opposed to the administration-preferred Hueys), pressures that were for the most part resisted during Clinton's first term. Then the figures on drug cultivation worsened. According to the U.S. General Accounting Office (GAO), coca production in Colombia expanded by 50 percent between 1996 and 1998, despite extensive aerial eradication efforts. Moreover, despite record seizures of cocaine in 1998, there was no net reduction in processing or exporting refined cocaine.[53] According to Colombian government figures, between 1991 and 1999 Colombia's share of hectares in the Andean region devoted to coca cultivation rose from 18 percent to 67 percent. One province alone, the Putumayo, accounted for over 50 percent of the coca grown in the country[54] and was effectively controlled by the guerrillas.

Within the Clinton administration, the single most outspoken proponent of expanded U.S. assistance to Colombia was General Barry McCaffrey, director of the White House Office of National Drug Control Policy. It is notable that during the years of the Samper administration, when U.S.-Colombian relations were in the deep freeze, McCaffrey was the only senior official to travel to Bogotá and meet with President Samper. His 1997 visit sent the strong message that the U.S. interest in counternarcotics transcended other political considerations and constituted an acknowledgment that the Samper administration was making a serious effort on the counterdrug front. In the summer of 1999, he was the first official to propose aid in the $1 billion range, publicly and privately lobbying the State Department to play a more active role in responding to the Colombian crisis.[55]

A full discussion of the origins of Plan Colombia and the U.S. contribution to it is beyond the scope of this chapter.[56] Several general points, however, stand out.

First, administration officials who took the lead in crafting an aid package believed that the Colombian government needed a comprehensive strategy for simultaneously addressing the country's multiple crises, not just drugs. This conviction stemmed in part from an instrumental view that Congress would not support a massive expansion of assistance without such a strategy. Accurate or not, that view was helpful in exerting leverage on the Colombian government to embrace a plan that could garner U.S. support.

Second, the involvement of U.S. officials in pressing for a Colombian strategy significantly altered the original conception of Plan Colombia as a kind of Marshall Plan for the reactivation of rural areas. In his inaugural address, President Pastrana had proposed a Fondo de Inversión para la Paz (Peace Investment Fund) that would finance commitments made at the negotiating table, reconstruct war-damaged infrastructure, invest in alternative development, and address pressing humanitarian needs, particularly of Colombia's massive displaced population (see Arnson et al. 2000: 58–75). Because of U.S. influence, what was originally proposed as a "bank" for the peace table came to embrace military issues centering on the fumigation of drug crops.

Third, the U.S. contribution to Plan Colombia became defined by its largest component: military assistance. Some 80 percent of the $1.6 billion package unveiled in January 2000 was for military and police purposes, including the purchase of sixty-three Blackhawk and Huey helicopters, the training of special army antinarcotics battalions, and other support for drug interdiction and eradication efforts. The amounts for alternative development ($145 million) and for programs to reform the judicial system, protect human rights, and promote the peace process ($93 million) were dwarfed by the military component, limited in part by the absorptive capacity of Colombian government aid agencies, by the disparity in costs between heavy military equipment and, say, training for judges, and by the expectation that the European Union would fund the plan's "softer" side. Nonetheless, the content of the package—for all the rhetoric about multiple challenges and an integrated approach—signaled that U.S. priorities in Colombia had evolved little beyond their traditional concern with counternarcotics. Perhaps the most telling remark in this regard was made by President Pastrana. Responding to fears expressed in Congress that the package paved the way for deepening U.S. military involvement in Colombia, Pastrana told the *Washington Post* that "the aid package the United States [proposes] is not a military package; it's an anti-narcotics package."[57]

U.S. officials appear to have been taken aback by the ferocity of the reaction to Plan Colombia overseas and the degree to which the entire plan became equated with a militaristic approach symbolized by Blackhawks. Faced with such criticism, particularly in Europe, U.S. officials repeatedly explained that they chose to support areas that they thought the Europeans would not and, conversely, that the U.S. Congress would. This explanation might have been plausible except that consultation with European allies and other potential donors to Plan Colombia was at best haphazard and late—some have alleged it did not take place at all. Many of those expected to contribute to a multilateral initiative took offense at its being wrapped in a bilateral U.S. military and antidrug package.[58] Non-U.S. commitments to Plan Colombia hovered around a third of the expected $1 billion mark, producing a public relations debacle for the United States and a significant material shortfall for the Colombian government.[59]

In response to U.S. policy, and in a pattern reminiscent of European and Latin American mobilization against U.S. policy in Central America in the 1980s, several European governments stepped up their diplomatic involvement in the peace process, arguing that it, not counternarcotics, should be the international community's umbrella for involvement in Colombia. The effort to place peace front and center was given a boost in February 2001 when the government and the FARC agreed to the naming of a group of friends of the peace process. Foreign involvement in the peace process reached its apogee a year later, when European diplomats and representatives of the United Nations and Colombian Catholic Church brought the peace process from the brink of collapse by negotiating an eleventh-hour agreement setting a deadline for a cease-fire. European attitudes against the FARC hardened following the demise of the process, but several governments sought to avoid public condemnation of the guerrillas, positioning themselves to be helpful should a process be restored in the future.

Bush Administration Policy

Throughout most of the last year of the peace process between Pastrana and the FARC, the Bush administration remained largely a bystander. In February 2001, President Bush turned down a direct request from Pastrana to send a representative to the March gathering of international delegates in the *despeje*. Bush called the peace process "an issue that the Colombian people and the Colombian president can deal with."[60] Later, sensitive to criticism about a U.S. "boycott" of the March talks, the State Department clarified that the U.S. government did not rule out "some participation in the peace process inside Colombia" should it advance significantly.[61] The rejoinder ducked the real question: whether any peace process in Colombia could advance without significant participation and backing from the United States.

Until the terrorist attacks of September 11, 2001, changed the tone and focus of U.S. policy in Colombia, the Bush administration largely stayed the course set by President Clinton. The administration made two adjustments to its aid strategy in response to criticism of Plan Colombia. The first was to package aid to Colombia within an Andean regional initiative, a way of shoring up Colombia's neighbors and containing the spillover (real and potential) of the Colombian conflict. The second was to redress the imbalance between the economic and military components of the aid package, assigning a greater portion to economic and development aid. In August 2001, a high-level U.S. delegation led by Undersecretary of State Marc Grossman visited Colombia in an effort to assess policy progress and options and to prepare for a September trip by Secretary of State Colin Powell. Nothing said publicly during the August visit would have portended a shift in U.S. priorities. Said Deputy Assistant Secretary of State William Brownfield,

> Under Secretary Grossman emphasized support, continued support of the United States government for the peace process in Colombia. He went so far as to say that he did not see how Colombia could address and resolve the many crises that affect it today without a successful peace process. He said we should be able to keep two ideas in our minds at the same time. On the one hand, support for the peace process; on the other hand, acknowledgment and criticism of one of the parties, specifically the FARC guerrilla movement, for abusing and not respecting the peace process.[62]

When the world changed for the United States on September 11, so did its Colombia policy and the rationales advanced in its name. Within weeks of the attacks, State Department Coordinator for Counterterrorism Francis X. Taylor told a congressional hearing that the FARC was "the most dangerous international terrorist group based in this hemisphere."[63] U.S. Ambassador to Colombia Anne Patterson stated that the September 11 attacks had led the United States to reevaluate its entire strategy regarding international organized crime, including the links between drug trafficking, money laundering, and terrorism. She made an analogy between Colombian guerrillas and the Al Qaeda network, affirming that just as Osama bin Laden did not represent Islam, so Colombian terrorists and drug traffickers were hypocritical in claiming to seek social justice for Colombians.[64] Assistant Secretary of Defense Peter Rodman carefully distinguished between a terrorist organization such as Al Qaeda and the violent actors in Colombia. "Although not considered terrorists with global reach," he said, Colombian groups "threaten regional stability and U.S. interests through transnational arms and drug trafficking, kidnapping, and extortion."[65] Assistant Secretary of State Otto Reich perhaps went the farthest in stripping the Colombian conflict of any political motivations and casting the violence in antiterrorist and criminal terms. "We're not going to engage in counterinsurgency in Colombia because there is no insurgency in Colombia," he told a Washington audience. "What you have is three terrorist groups that operate as organized crime families. . . . These are not insurgents. These are criminals. These are terrorists."[66]

Whither the Peace Process

By the time Álvaro Uribe prepared to take office, both houses of the U.S. Congress had approved legislation broadening the use of U.S. military aid for counterterrorism purposes in Colombia. As in previous years, congressional conservatives were instrumental in pushing for an expanded U.S. commitment to Colombia. The peace process figured little, if at all, in the policy debate; to the extent that it did, it reflected the near-universal conviction that only by weakening the insurgents militarily and strengthening the capacity of the state could future negotiations hope to succeed. President-elect Uribe himself made clear that he held open the possibility of an eventual negotiated settlement. To the surprise of many, he publicly urged the United Nations to stay involved in Colombia. Uribe met with UN Secretary-General Kofi Annan on his first trip to the United States as president-elect in June 2002.

Whether U.S. military aid to Colombia and a concomitant strengthening of the armed forces lead toward or away from the bargaining table will depend in no small measure on one central choice: whether the state reasserts its legitimate authority through equal efforts to combat all nonstate armed actors, left and right, or whether the government turns a largely blind eye to paramilitary expansion as it throws the bulk of its energies into the battle against the guerrillas (principally the FARC). The difficulty, as senior U.S. officials themselves recognize, is that many at the mid- and even senior levels of the Colombian armed forces view the paramilitaries not as the enemy but as a force multiplier.[67] According to one U.S. official reflecting on the Pastrana years, "Much of the problem in the peace process [was] that Marulanda [was] telling the truth, that Pastrana promised he'd do something serious regarding the paramilitaries."[68] Instead, during his four years in office, paramilitary forces more than doubled in size, demanding for themselves a role in future negotiations and exerting growing political influence at both the local and national level.[69]

Despite recognition in Washington that paramilitary groups were part of the problem, not the solution,[70] and despite a studied effort to have policy statements reflect an equal concern with left-wing and right-wing terrorism, actual policy initiatives, beginning with the push into southern Colombia to eradicate coca, remained largely focused on the narco-guerrilla. Probably U.S. pressure was the single most important factor behind initial Colombian government moves to dismiss senior army commanders linked to paramilitary groups. But concrete steps against paramilitary organizations have followed by months or years actions taken against guerrilla groups for the same or similar behavior.

The FARC and ELN, for example, were officially designated as foreign terrorist organizations fully four years before the AUC, despite the State Department's reports for years that paramilitaries were engaged in systematic violence against the civilian population. In March 2002, moreover, following an eighteen-month investigation, Attorney General John Ashcroft formally indicted three FARC members and four other South Americans for conspiracy to smuggle cocaine into the United States.[71] In Ashcroft's words, the indictment marked "the convergence of two of the top priorities of the Department of Justice: the prevention of terrorism and the reduction of illegal drug use."[72] At the time of this writing in mid-2002, no evidence had surfaced of parallel investigations of paramilitary involvement in narcotics trafficking. This was true despite broad, private acknowledgment by administration officials that it was a serious problem and despite a public admission by the AUC leader Carlos Castaño that some 70 percent of his organization's revenue came from the drug trade.

By mid-2002, a policy consensus had emerged in Washington— mirroring a shift in Colombian attitudes—over supporting the Colombian military to carry out counterterrorism and counterinsurgency operations in addition to counternarcotics activities. Major doubts still existed as to whether the Colombian government was raising enough revenue from wealthy elites and devoting enough of its own budget to the war effort. And aid conditions still touched on human rights issues such as the perennial subject of military/paramilitary ties and the public health and environmental impact of coca crop fumigation. But the question of whether and for what purpose to aid Colombia was largely settled, reflecting a new U.S. resolve to combat global terrorism and the placing of the Colombia conflict within those parameters.

Significant questions continued to be raised, however, about whether the policy was working. Coca production in Colombia rose by about 25 percent between 2000 and 2001, for example, despite a doubling of the numbers of acres fumigated under Plan Colombia.[73] Moreover, alternative development programs to induce peasant farmers to switch from coca to legal crops faced "serious obstacles," according to a February 2002 report by the U.S. General Accounting Office (GAO). Chief among the obstacles blocking success were the government's lack of control of coca-growing regions, as well as weak Colombian government institutions to coordinate eradication and development activities.[74] Another GAO report in June 2002 revealed that plans to use Blackhawk helicopters and other military aid had "fallen substantially behind schedule," and that Colombian plans to increase military manpower and defense spending were not going forward.[75]

These difficulties aside, the central problem with U.S. policy in Colombia as it affected the prospects for an eventual negotiated settlement was that an excessive focus on the military dimension—whether to defeat terrorism, "level the playing field," or deprive armed actors of economic resources—precluded thinking about other ways that the United States could be helpful. The difficulty was not with aiding the Colombian government so that it could demonstrate to its armed opponents the impossibility of a military victory and/or negotiate from a position of strength. Rather, it was with the absence of an integrated policy aimed at creating the conditions for peace: insisting absolutely on combating paramilitarism, pursuing economic policies to enhance equity and expand economic opportunities beyond alternative development, supporting efforts to engage the FARC politically and diplomatically, and finding those aspects of a reform agenda, including agrarian and tax reform, that the United States can support.[76] The causes of conflict in Colombia have roots far deeper than the drug trade.

Whatever the domestic U.S. salience of drugs and terrorism, no policy to bring stability to Colombia will succeed until those roots are addressed.

Notes

I would like to extend special thanks to Woodrow Wilson Center Latin American Program interns Marianne Benet, Chris Hale, and Jacqueline Lee for their invaluable research assistance.

1. Text, televised address of President Andrés Pastrana Arango, February 20, 2002.

2. The relevant language from the Fiscal Year 2002 supplemental aid request stipulated that "the term 'counter-drug activities' . . . shall be deemed to include activities in support of the government of Colombia's unified campaign against narcotics trafficking, terrorist activities, and other threats to its national security."

3. Transcript, remarks of Richard Boucher, U.S. Department of State, March 15, 2002, distributed by Oficina de Prensa, Embajada de Colombia, Washington, DC.

4. The chapter does not discuss a parallel process of negotiations with the Ejército de Liberación Nacional (National Liberation Army, ELN), or a subsequent peace dialogue with paramilitaries of the Autodefensas Unidas de Colombia (AUC) during the Uribe government. Substantive talks between the Pastrana government and the ELN were delayed by several factors, including mass kidnappings by the ELN in 1999 and the ELN's demand for a safe haven in largely urban areas in their traditional zone of operations. Talks between the government and the ELN became a higher priority after the collapse of the peace process with the FARC but ultimately fell apart in June 2002. The prospects for peace talks between the Uribe government and the ELN appeared to improve in mid-2004 following an offer by the Mexican government to mediate a peace dialogue. To advance the prospects for negotiations with the paramilitaries, the AUC announced a unilateral cease-fire in December 2002. Talks began formally in July 2003, and a group of over eight hundred paramilitaries demobilized in November of that year. The negotiations became repeatedly bogged down by internal divisions within the AUC, symbolized most forcefully by the April 2004 disappearance of the longtime AUC leader Carlos Castaño. Domestic and international controversy also centered on what to do about AUC involvement in human rights atrocities as well as drug trafficking. The U.S. government, meanwhile, sought the extradition of several key AUC leaders on drug-trafficking charges.

5. The significance of the *despeje* had more to do with its role in providing the FARC a sanctuary for a variety of illegal activities, including drug production and hiding kidnap victims, than with its size per se. According to one senior U.S. official, the zone comprised about 4 percent of Colombian territory and held about 0.25 percent of its population. Interview, March 27, 2001, South Bend, IN.

6. In November 2001, Egeland's deputy, James LeMoyne, was named as his replacement.

7. Egeland was to "serve as a channel between the Secretary-General and the Colombian Government and other relevant actors, and ... consult widely within and outside Colombia on how the United Nations system can best promote human rights, humanitarian assistance, and peace." United Nations, "Jan Egeland Appointed Special Adviser to the Secretary-General for International Assistance to Colombia," press release SG/A/715, December 9, 1999.

8. Top U.S. business executives, including the chairman of the New York Stock Exchange and a founder of America On Line, also traveled to the *despeje* to meet with the FARC, trips cleared with Clinton administration officials.

9. It remains unclear whether Law 002 was a deliberate effort to embarrass Egeland and other supporters of the "Eurotour" or simply a manifestation of the FARC's taking actions seemingly oblivious to international and Colombian opinion.

10. At a follow-up meeting in Los Pozos in March 2001, the FARC and the government agreed to a group of twenty-five European and Latin American countries, in addition to the United Nations and the Vatican, that would serve as a "group of friends." A smaller group of ten countries—Canada, Cuba, France, Italy, Mexico, Norway, Spain, Sweden, Switzerland, and Venezuela—were to serve as a "Facilitating Commission."

11. Interview with European diplomat, Bogotá, Colombia, March 19, 2002.

12. By June 2001, almost three years into his four-year term, Pastrana's approval ratings hovered around 24 percent. See T. Christian Miller, "Colombia, Guerrillas, Agree to Landmark Prisoner Swap," *Los Angeles Times*, June 3, 2001.

13. In April 2002, an investigation by the House International Relations Committee concluded that the arrests of IRA suspects "illustrate a new and dangerous escalation of the FARC's ability to carry out terrorist bombings as well as the reach of global terrorism into the Western Hemisphere." Quoted in JoAnne Allen, "House Panel: IRA Trained Colombian Rebels," Reuters, April 23, 2002.

14. Cited in Juan Forero, "Colombian Leader Has to Decide on Peace Talks," *New York Times*, October 5, 2001, A12.

The FARC also prevented the presidential candidate Horacio Serpa from entering the *despeje* to hold a campaign rally on September 29, 2001. The year ended with yet another episode that inflamed Colombian public opinion: a twelve-year-old boy terminally ill with cancer had pleaded with the FARC to release his father, a police corporal held captive by the rebels. The FARC refused, and the boy died on December 18 without seeing his father.

15. The Acuerdo de San Francisco de la Sombra also committed the parties to study ways to end paramilitarism. Text, "Acuerdo de San Francisco de la Sombra para Concretar y Consolidar el Proceso de Paz," October 5, 2001.

16. United Nations, *Informe de la Alta Comisionada de las Naciones Unidas para los Derechos Humanos sobre la situación de derechos humanos en Colombia, 2001* (E/CN.4/2002), 39.

17. In one particularly egregious episode, Gen. Rito Alejo del Río, who had been cashiered by President Pastrana in 1999, was arrested in July 2001 for providing illegal support to the paramilitaries. Less than a week later, he was released. Under pressure from the new *fiscal general* (attorney general), Luis Camilo Osorio, the head of the Fiscalía's human rights unit, the head of the anticorruption unit, and several others investigating paramilitary cases were forced to resign. Osorio had stated that the work of the office was too focused on paramilitary cases and not enough on the guerrillas. In late October, Hina Jilani, the UN special representative for human rights defenders, publicly accused Osorio of stalling the investigation of human rights cases attributed to paramilitaries. United Nations, *Informe de la Alta Comisionada*, 46; U.S. Agency for International Development (USAID), Office of Transition Initiatives, "Field Report: Colombia," August 2001, mimeo, 1; Juan Forero, "Change and Fear in Colombia Rights Panel," *New York Times*, October 19, 2001, 6; "U.N. Envoy Slams Colombia's New Chief Prosecutor," Reuters, October 31, 2001.

18. Interviews with senior Western diplomats, Bogotá, March 18–20, 2002.

19. "Alocución radiotelevisada del Presidente de la República, Andrés Pastrana Arango," February 20, 2002, mimeo, 5.

20. Mark Schneider, the Agency for International Development's assistant administrator for Latin America, had also been a Peace Corps volunteer in El Salvador in the 1960s.

21. Telephone interview with senior U.S. official, April 16, 2002.

22. In the words of U.S. Southern Command Chief General Charles Wilhelm, "for negotiations to succeed, I'm convinced that the government must strengthen its negotiating position, and I believe that increased leverage at the negotiating table can only be gained on Colombia's battlefields." Quoted in Arnson et al. (2000: 5). A minority spoke of the need to "defeat" the guerrillas in order to defeat the drug trade.

23. Following the initial session in Houston, further meetings were held in Colombia in May 1998 on the lessons of peace; in September 1998 on the role of the media in the conflict and peace; in April 1999 on human rights; in February 2000 on the "business" of peace; and in March 2001 on peacemaking.

24. The guerrillas were not invited. Nonetheless, according to a U.S. official, "we made an effort to get as close as we could" by including representatives of organizations with which the insurgents might have had contact. Telephone interview, May 9, 2002.

25. Interview, March 8, 2001. Because of the ongoing nature of the Colombia policy debate, no U.S. officials interviewed for this chapter—from the State and Defense Departments, White House, Agency for International Development, and U.S. Embassy in Bogotá—agreed to be quoted on the record.

26. Testimony of Ambassador John P. Leonard, Deputy Assistant Secretary of State for Western Hemisphere Affairs, before the Western Hemisphere Peace Corps, Narcotics and Terrorism Subcommittee, Senate Foreign Relations Committee, March 24, 1999, 4. "One of our primary reasons for holding the meetings was to press [the FARC] on the Americans," said a State Department official after news of the meeting leaked in January

1999. "We decided it was better to talk to them and lay out our position than to have no contact. They understand we will have serious problems with them if they don't give us answers on the kidnapped Americans."

27. Interview, March 8, 2001.

28. Ibid.

29. It could also be that the State Department's contacts were simply not as good as believed.

30. Attorney General John Ashcroft announced the indictments, saying, "Today, the United States strikes back at the FARC's reign of terror against the United States and its citizens. Just as we fight terrorism in the mountains of South Asia, we will fight terrorism in our own hemisphere." Quoted in Dan Eggen and Karen DeYoung, "Colombian Rebels Indicted as Terrorists," *Washington Post*, May 1, 2002, 8. A year later, the Colombian national Nelson Vargas Rueda, accused of being a member of the FARC and serving a four-and-a half-year sentence in Colombia for rebellion, was extradited to the United States on charges that he had participated in the murders of the U.S. activists. In an embarrassment to both the Uribe and Bush administrations, the U.S. Justice Department dropped the charges against Vargas for lack of evidence, and he was returned to Colombia in July 2004.

31. Douglas Farah, "House GOP Subpoenas State Dept. on Colombia," *Washington Post*, May 21, 1999, A22. The remark was made by Rep. Dan Burton (R-IN), chair of the House Committee on Government Reform.

32. Rep. Benjamin A. Gilman, "Don't Legitimize Terrorist Groups," *Miami Herald*, March 23, 1999.

33. "Granobles" was reportedly wounded in battle in June 2000 and was evacuated to Venezuela and then Cuba for medical treatment. Alicia La Rotta Morán, "Cooperación con la guerrilla," *El Universal* (Caracas), March 20, 2001.

34. Tom Brown, "Colombia's Pastrana Slams Marxist Rebels," Reuters, May 3, 2000.

35. Interview, July 14, 1999.

36. Interview, April 3, 2000.

37. "It is important that the United States be there to directly exchange points of view," Pastrana told reporters in Washington. "It will be good for the [negotiations] to have the United States there." Norman Kempster, "Colombia Wants U.S. as Peace Talks Partner," *Los Angeles Times*, February 27, 2001.

38. Interview, March 8, 2001. The statement was technically not correct, as U.S. conversations with the FARC took place in Costa Rica, not the zone of *despeje.*

39. U.S. Agency for International Development, Office of Transition Initiatives, Bureau for Humanitarian Response, "Field Report: Colombia," October 1–November 15, 1999.

40. Interview, August 23, 1999.

41. See Zartman (1986, 1995); Hampson (1996); and Arnson (1999a).

42. Interview, July 14, 1999.

43. Statement of General Charles E. Wilhelm, U.S. Marine Corps Commander in Chief, U.S. Southern Command, before the Senate Caucus on International Narcotics Control, September 21, 1999.

44. The remarks were made at a Director's Forum, Woodrow Wilson International Center for Scholars, Washington, DC, May 7, 1999.

45. ONDCP estimated FARC and ELN drug revenues to be between $100 million and $500 million. See statement by General Barry R. McCaffrey, Director, Office of National Drug Control Policy, before the Senate Committee on Foreign Relations, October 6, 1999. The higher estimates came from the U.S. Congress. See statement of Rep. Benjamin A. Gilman in Arnson et al. (2000: 16).

46. Testimony by General Charles Wilhelm before the Senate Caucus on International Narcotics Control and Senate Finance Committee, Subcommittee on International Trade, February 22, 2000.

47. The accusations were made by Gen. McCaffrey and by U.S. Ambassador to Colombia Anne Patterson, who said that FARC and paramilitary units have "control of the entire export process and the routes for sending drugs abroad." In August, a FARC envoy was arrested in Mexico for allegedly negotiating a cocaine-for-arms deal with the Arellano Félix cartel. See Juan O. Tamayo, "U.S. Officials Tie Colombian Guerrillas to Drug Exports," *Miami Herald*, December 13, 2000, 3.

48. See, for example, Berdal and Malone (2000) and the research developed by Paul Collier and others at the World Bank project on the Economics of Civil War, Crime, and Violence. This research, available at www.worldbank.org/research/conflict/papers. htm, culminated in the publication of *Breaking the Conflict Trap: Civil War and Development Policy,* edited by Paul Collier et al. (Washington, DC: World Bank and Oxford University Press, 2003). See also Arnson and Zartman (2005).

49. Interview, March 7, 2001.

50. Asa Hutchinson, administrator of the Drug Enforcement Administration (DEA), reiterated this policy when he stated at a press conference at police headquarters in Bogotá that "we do not negotiate with narco-traffickers unless they simply want to know how to surrender. And then we're happy to inform them of how to do that." Transcript, Press Conference with DEA Administrator Asa Hutchinson at the CNP Headquarters, Bogotá, March 26, 2002, mimeo.

51. Telephone interview, March 13, 2001.

52. The word was General McCaffrey's and resonated throughout the policy debate over Plan Colombia.

53. U.S. General Accounting Office, *Drug Control: Narcotics Threat from Colombia Continues to Grow,* GAO/NSIAD-99-136 (Washington, DC: U.S. General Accounting Office, June 1999), 10.

54. Figures are from Gonzalo de Francisco, in charge of Colombian government alternative development programs in southern Colombia, March 2001.

55. Larry Rohter with Christopher S. Wren, "U.S. Official Proposes $1 Billion for Colombia Drug War," *New York Times*, July 17, 1999, A5; and Serge F. Kovaleski, "McCaffrey Defends Anti-drug Aid to Colombia," *Washington Post*, July 28, 1999.

56. See Presidency of the Republic of Colombia, *Plan Colombia: Plan for Peace, Prosperity, and the Strengthening of the State* (Bogotá: Presidency of the Republic of Colombia, October 1999).

57. Q&A: Colombia's President, "The Guerrillas 'Will Never Win,'" *Washington Post*, February 6, 2000, B1.

58. Interviews with European diplomats, April 6, 2000 (Bogotá), May 18, 2000 (New York), and October 19, 2000 (Washington, DC).

59. See Roy (2002) and the European Union, "The EU's Relations with Colombia," retrieved from http://europa.eu.int/comm/external_relations/Colombia.

60. Quoted in Christopher Marquis, "Bush Promises Colombia Help on Trade but Refuses Peace Role," *New York Times*, February 28, 2001, A7.

61. The statement was by Assistant Secretary of State Peter Romero, as quoted in Karen DeYoung, "U.S. Now Sees Possible Role in Colombian Peace Talks," *Washington Post*, March 9, 2001, A21.

62. "Foreign Press Center Briefing with William Brownfield, Deputy Assistant Secretary of State for Western Hemisphere Affairs on Secretary of State Powell's Trip to Colombia," Federal News Service, September 7, 2001.

63. Taylor went on to say that "the danger presented by the FARC is compounded by activities of the other major Colombian insurgent group, the National Liberation Army (ELN)—a group that also targets Americans—and by the far-right United Self-Defense Forces of Colombia (AUC). Both of these groups are also included on the [Foreign Terrorist Organization] list, and the AUC in particular has a history of extreme brutality." Testimony, Francis X. Taylor, Department of State Coordinator for Counter-Terrorism, before the House Committee on International Relations, Subcommittee on Western Hemisphere Affairs, October 10, 2001, mimeo.

64. Speeches of Anne W. Patterson to the Primer Congreso Panamericano sobre Control y Prevención del Lavado de Activos, Cartagena de Indias, October 24, 2001, and to the annual meeting of the Federación Nacional de Comerciantes (FENALCO), Bogotá, October 25, 2001.

65. Statement, Assistant Secretary of Defense for International Security Affairs Peter Rodman, before the House Committee on International Relations, Subcommittee on Western Hemisphere Affairs, April 11, 2002.

66. Remarks by Assistant Secretary of State for Western Hemisphere Affairs Otto Reich, "U.S. Foreign Policy in the Western Hemisphere," forum sponsored by the Center for Strategic and International Studies, Washington, DC, March 12, 2002.

67. Interview, February 13, 2001.

68. Interview, November 16, 1999.

69. AUC leader Salvatore Mancuso told a reporter that AUC-backed candidates would win at least 30 percent of congressional seats in the March 2002 elections because

"we're making recommendations to the people who to vote for." A statement on the AUC Web site boasted that its sympathizers would make up 35 percent of the new Congress. See Margarita Martinez, "Colombia Paramilitary Boss Speaks Out," Associated Press, February 12, 2002, and "Politics in Colombia: A Democracy, but of Many Warts," *Economist*, March 14, 2002.

70. Secretary of State Colin Powell stated during a congressional hearing that "we have made it clear to President Pastrana—and we will make it clear to the future president of Colombia—that if paramilitaries are given a free hand, this is destructive of our efforts to help you." Statement, Secretary of State Colin Powell to the House Appropriations Committee Subcommittee on Justice, March 6, 2002.

71. Six weeks later, the Justice Department announced indictments against the entire FARC organization and six of its members for the 1999 deaths of the three indigenous rights activists. Attorney General Ashcroft described the FARC as a "fiercely anti-American terrorist organization." Eric Green, "Colombian Rebel Group Indicted by U.S. Grand Jury on Murder Charges," Washington File, Office of International Information Programs, U.S. Department of State, April 30, 2002, retrieved February 1, 2006, from http://usinfo.state.gov/regional/ar/colombia/02043004.htm.

72. U.S. Department of Justice, Attorney General John D. Ashcroft Transcript, News Conference-FARC, Washington, DC, March 18, 2002.

73. George Gedda, "Bush Dismayed by Coca Production," Associated Press, March 8, 2002. Some of the rise was attributed to faulty estimates the year before due to cloud cover. The figures clashed with Colombian government estimates, which showed a decline in coca cultivation.

74. U.S. General Accounting Office, "Drug Control: Efforts to Develop Alternatives to Cultivating Illicit Crops in Colombia Have Made Little Progress and Face Serious Obstacles," GAO-02-291, February 2002, 3, 12–16. See also Scott Wilson, "Battles Deferred; Colombia's Aerial Drug Campaign Showing Its Limits," *Washington Post*, March 6, 2001, A18; and Karen DeYoung, "Colombian Governors Protest Crop Spraying," *Washington Post*, March 13, 2001, A17.

75. U.S. General Accounting Office, "Military Assistance under Plan Colombia Is Substantially behind Schedule," Briefing Paper, June 2002.

76. This would include pushing Colombian elites on the question of reform, as the United States did in El Salvador. Remarks by former Assistant Secretary of State Bernard Aronson, U.S. Institute of Peace, Conference on the Implementation of the Peace Accords in El Salvador, Washington, DC, December 8, 1999.

References

Arnson, Cynthia J. 1993. *Crossroads: Congress, the President, and Central America, 1976–1993*. University Park: Pennsylvania State University Press.

————, ed. 1999a. *Comparative Peace Processes in Latin America*. Stanford: Stanford University Press.

————. 1999b. "Conclusion." In *Comparative Peace Processes in Latin America*, ed. Cynthia J. Arnson. Stanford: Stanford University Press.

————. 2001. "El Salvador and Colombia: Lessons of the Peace Process." In *El Salvador: Implementation of the Peace Accords*, ed. Margarita S. Studemeister. Washington, DC: U.S. Institute of Peace.

Arnson, Cynthia J., et al. 2000. "The Peace Process in Colombia and U.S. Policy." Woodrow Wilson International Center for Scholars, Latin American Program Working Paper Series, no. 246 (May). Retrieved Aug. 4, 2005, from www.nd.edu/~kellogg/pdfs/Arnson.pdf.

Arnson, Cynthia J., and William I. Zartman, eds. 2005. *Rethinking the Economics of War: The Intersection of Need, Creed, and Greed*. Baltimore: Johns Hopkins University Press.

Berdal, Mats, and David M. Malone, eds. 2000. *Greed and Grievance: Economic Agendas in Civil Wars*. Boulder, CO: Lynne Rienner.

Hampson, Fen Osler. 1996. *Nurturing Peace: Why Peace Settlements Succeed or Fail*. Washington, DC: U.S. Institute of Peace.

Kramer, Robert. 1999. "Civil Society's Role in Building a Foundation for Peace." Paper presented at the U.S. Army War College conference, "War and Peace in Colombia: Strategy for Ambiguous Warfare," Carlisle, PA, November 11–13.

McBride, Joseph N. 2000. "America Coping with Chaos at the Strategic Level: Facilitator for Democratic Stability in the Post-Counterinsurgency Era." In *Beyond Declaring Victory and Coming Home*, ed. Max G. Manwaring and Anthony James Joes. Westport, CT: Praeger.

Roy, Joaquín. 2002. "Europe: Neither Plan Colombia, nor Peace Process: From Good Intentions to High Frustrations." Paper presented at the conference "Colombia's Ambiguous War in Global and Regional Context: Insurgency, Transnational Crime, and Terror," U.S. Army War College and North-South Center, Miami, March 24–26. Mimeo.

Zartman, I. William. 1986. "Ripening Conflict, Ripe Moment, Formula, and Mediation." In *Perspectives on Negotiation: Four Case Studies and Interpretations*, ed. Diane B. Bendahmane and John W. McDonald, Jr. Washington, DC: Center for the Study of Foreign Affairs, U.S. Foreign Service Institute.

————. 1995. *Elusive Peace: Negotiating an End to Civil Wars*. Washington, DC: Brookings Institution.

PART TWO

Democracy

Political Reform after 1991

What Still Needs to Be Reformed?

Eduardo Pizarro and Ana María Bejarano

Pizarro and Bejarano detail the condition into which Colombian politics has fallen since the constitutional and electoral reform of 1991. The emphasis on opening the political regime to unrepresented interests has produced an "anarchistic fragmentation and pulverization of party representation," which has led to a crisis of governability. Legislative output is characterized by attention to fragmented particularistic interests rather than to the national interest and the proliferation of candidates and parties paradoxically overwhelms and defeats voter choice. This leads to a dilemma: while openness continues to be essential in order to incorporate those who might otherwise take an antisystem approach, the need for governability and responsiveness demands a concern for the stability and discipline of political parties. Against this background, and with close attention to current research in electoral engineering, the authors evaluate a series of electoral reform proposals and make specific recommendations concerning the reforms they feel are most necessary and appropriate and those they feel are to be avoided. Their reforms are aimed at establishing a "moderate multiparty system" with a limited number of internally democratic and disciplined parties of national scope. They also put forward proposals to improve the performance of the Congress, campaign and party financing, and affirmative action for excluded groups.

Antonio Navarro Wolf, former guerrilla and twice Democratic Alliance M19 (AD/M19) presidential candidate, once stated that the political reform being called for in his country had to be based on maintaining "a balance between pluralism—a virtue of the electoral rules set up by the Constituent Assembly of 1991—and partisan organization, which may be what is lacking here. Such a balance, sustaining pluralism without letting us dissolve into total individualism, would impart a clearer direction to our reform."[1] His opinion reflects the central idea of this essay: any future political reform in Colombia must keep the political system open while simultaneously contributing to the creation of a more coherent, efficient, and accountable political system.

The future of political reform in the country no longer hinges on opening the floodgates of the political system or overcoming the institutional restrictions inherited from the National Front period (1958–74), which tended to favor the two traditional parties. The 1991 Constitution left the floodgates wide open. Paradoxically, the result was that the laxity of the norms established in the 1980s and 1990s not only affected the traditional parties (deepening their already disturbing internal fragmentation) but also had an impact on new movements and political organizations (Pizarro 2001). The Left and other minority sectors with a potential for constituting potential alternatives to the traditional parties found themselves negatively affected by the incentive structure put in place by the new constitution and the 1994 law on parties, both of which tended to reward party fragmentation.

Despite the democratic gains since 1991, the state of Colombian democracy is far from satisfactory. Its shortcomings, however, no longer stem from institutional restrictions but are, instead, the outcome of deeper political problems, particularly the secular weakness and recent decline of the central state's authority.[2] In addition, the democratization process was not coupled with a comprehensive peace negotiation with the entire guerrilla movement, which meant that efforts to reform the political system lacked, as an essential counterpart, a new beginning in the political game in which all significant actors would partake in a democratized setting. We are thus certain that the ongoing armed conflict and the continued weakness of the state continue to pose important limits to the building of a democratic order in Colombia.

For the purposes of this chapter, however, we have concentrated our analysis on the question of institutional reform in the party-electoral arena, for two main reasons: first, because in the last decade Colombia has witnessed a disturbing deterioration of its political parties, the party system, and decision making by the legislature, and second, because any successful peace process with the reluctant guerrilla forces—the Fuerzas Armadas Revolucionarias de Colombia (Revolutionary Armed Forces of Colombia) or FARC, and the Ejército de Liberación Nacional (National Liberation Army) or ELN—will most certainly lead to significant institutional adjustments designed to ease the integration of these groups into democratic life. This time, however, there will be no need to convene a new constituent assembly. In our view, instead of a new overhaul of the political constitution, what is needed is a measured and precise appraisal of the specific institutional adjustments needed (in the electoral system, the law on parties, the rules governing the legislature, etc.) to produce a political system that is at once inclusive and effective.

We start by examining the unexpected consequences of the 1991 Constitution on the political system: the explosion of "microparties" and party factions that has further fragmented and weakened the party system. Part of the solution to this problematic fragmentation of political representation lies in reforming the rules of the political game, most particularly the electoral system. To that end, we have studied the proposals of the Commission on Party Reform,[3] the political reform bills recently discussed in Congress,[4] and observations by various domestic and foreign analysts on these bills and proposals.[5] While placing particular emphasis on these electoral changes, we do recognize that political reform is a much broader endeavor. Thus we also discuss additional reforms needed to democratize the parties, strengthen the opposition, enhance the performance of Congress, overhaul the system of party and campaign financing, and ensure the effective representation of women and minorities. Overall, we wish to emphasize that above and beyond the need to reorganize the parties and party system, any attempt at political reform in Colombia should strive for a balance between the goals of inclusion and governability.

The Dilemma: Incorporation versus Governability

The 1991 Constituent Assembly's point of departure was a negative assessment of the country's political system. Particularly stressed were the restrictions on political competition that remained in place from the National Front era (1958–74) and the long-standing Liberal-Conservative hegemony, which apparently shut out other political forces and served as a stimulus for various forms of extraparliamentary opposition, including the guerrillas. The demands to change this state of affairs were coupled by the need to integrate four guerrilla organizations that had recently negotiated peace agreements with the government: the Movimiento 19 de Abril (April 19 Movement) or M19; the Ejército Popular de Liberación (Popular Liberation Army) or EPL; the Partido Revolucionario de los Trabajadores (Workers' Revolutionary Party) or PRT; and the Movimiento Armado Quintín Lame (Quintín Lame indigenous movement) or MAQL.

Accordingly, the reform of the electoral and party systems was a central concern in the minds of the Constituent Assembly's members. In line with the above assessment, when it came to the parties and the party system, the constitution makers created an institutional arrangement geared toward increasing the system's overall "representativeness." However, in doing so, they did not seek to increase the parties' capabilities to function as political mediators but chose instead to increase the number of political parties and movements present in the political arena. In other words, a "logic of incorporation" predominated in the assembly's decisions on these matters. The provisions in the new constitution and their subsequent legislative developments[6] were based on the creation of a set of extremely lax standards that purposefully sought to promote the inclusion of all political and social forces in the political electoral-game.

"Logic of Incorporation"

This tendency to foster representation by increasing the number of political actors with access to the political arena has its origins in Colombia's particular approach to democratization in the 1990s. Situated halfway between the Southern Cone's transition process, which emphasized democratic recovery, and that of Central America, with its prime concern on bringing in both insurgents (El Salvador, Guatemala) and counterrevolutionaries (Nicaragua), the Colombian constitution makers stressed overcoming the bipartisan hegemony and broadening the political spectrum as the most promising way to deepen democracy. They thus explicitly sought to move from the traditional two-party system to a broader multiparty one.

Three avenues were open to increase the number of parties with access to the system. The first was the establishment of mechanisms of affirmative action intended to guarantee the representation of ethnic minorities and insurgent groups in the legislature. To that end, special districts were created, one for indigenous communities in the Senate and another in the House for Afro-Colombian communities. There were also a few temporary provisions to entice guerrilla groups to lay down their arms. Second, a set of vague guidelines encouraged all social actors to form political parties and movements and take part in the political process. Under the 1991 Constitution not only parties and political movements but also social movements and significant groups of citizens are eligible to play the political-electoral game.[7] Provided they fulfill some minimum requirements, all of the above may present candidates or lists in elections, are entitled to government funding, and have access to the state-run media, especially television, at all times. To ease the way for this array of actors, the constitution and the law devised some extremely flexible standards. These include minimal requirements for the granting of legal status by the National Electoral Council, coupled with a very problematic freedom for parties and movements to endorse a limitless number of lists and candidates. Third, the 1991 Constitution created a nationwide senatorial district designed to increase minority representation in Congress. Minorities are thus able to elect a senator by employing the "dispersed strategy" (Botero 1998) of pooling their votes from different regions of the country.

The overcoming of two-party hegemony and the incorporation of insurgent groups and other social and political forces into the democratic system have yielded positive effects. The remaining problem, however, is that the institutional design did not resolve two additional questions that are key to any political reform intended to strengthen democracy and not just broaden representation: How to avoid party fragmentation? And, relatedly, how to avoid the excessive proliferation of minuscule parties with the concomitant destructuring of the party system? In sum, how to ensure a minimum degree of coherence and effectiveness while opening the doors to greater representation? In fact, the new rules did not impede the disturbing trend toward fragmentation of the traditional parties but actually created incentives that fostered even more fragmentation, increasing it to unforeseen levels. At the same time, the new standards produced incentives that nurtured the growth of alternative parties and movements in a climate favorable to "political dwarfism." Colombia has since then experienced an anarchistic fragmentation and pulverization of party representation. The current phenomenon of "electoral microenterprises" (*microempresas electorales*), which affects alternative parties and movements as much as it does the traditional parties), far from being an instrument for the aggregation of interests, actually contributes to their atomization. In Colombia no party represents a class or a significant proportion of a class or any other significant portion of the electorate. Increasingly, instead, electoral microenterprises represent segmented particularistic interests.[8]

How, then, did the institutional design contribute to the extreme fragmentation of political representation? Two examples should serve to illustrate the phenomenon. First, according to the 1994 party law, a legislator needed only fifty thousand votes or fifty thousand signatures[9] from his or her supporters to be legally recognized as a party by the National Electoral Council. Because of this relaxed set of standards, the electoral microenterprises *received* free access to television, state funds, and the right to endorse as many candidates and lists as they saw fit in any electoral contest. The consequences were not surprising. It did not take long for all political parties and movements (including the Liberals and Conservatives), eager for the above-mentioned benefits, to create a big, watery pot of alphabet soup— an endless list of political acronyms that only served to differentiate one particularistic faction from the next (see table 6.1).[10]

Added to the party fragmentation and atomization stimulated by Act 130 of 1994, the continuation of the quotient and remainder formula (the

Table 6.1
Parties and Movements Registered with the National Electoral Council, 1990–2004

Year	Number of Recognized Parties
1990	8
1991	22
1994	54
1998	80
	61

Source: National Civil Status Registry. Except where otherwise indicated, all tables have been taken from registry reports.

Hare system) has combined with the freedom of endorsements[11] accorded to each one of these parties to produce a host of negative effects, particularly inimical to the coherence of both the parties and the party system. This combination has raised the "war of remainders" to unprecedented levels, thus fostering the extreme personalism typical of Colombia's system of political representation. As shown in table 6.2, the number of lists presented for congressional elections (House and Senate) has grown at alarming rates in recent years. According to a prestigious commission of international consultants brought in by the Pastrana government, in 1999 Colombia had the most "personalistic" electoral system in the world (Valenzuela et al. 1999: 237).

The consequences of this personalism are most pernicious for the country's political life. In practice, the election of a Congress member depends, not on a party or political movement, but on the candidate's own efforts to obtain resources and project his or her own image. This leads to further

Table 6.2
Number of Lists Registered for Senate and House Elections, 1958–2002

Year	Senate	House
1958	67	83
1960	–	113
1962	97	143
1964	–	192
1966	147	215
1968	–	221
1970	206	316
1974	176	253
1978	210	308
1982	225	343
1986	202	330
1990	213	351
1991	143	486
1994	251	628
1998	319	692
2002	322	883

weakening of an already precarious party system. The legislator-elect feels no obligation to be accountable to anyone, not even to his or her own party. Moreover, the fact that funds are not concentrated in central party treasuries hinders control over the sources of party financing, which is especially dangerous in a country afflicted with corruption and plagued by the penetration of narcotrafficking wealth into political life. Finally, such a degree of fragmentation of representation makes it impossible to build government or opposition parties, erodes any possibility of obtaining a minimum level of party discipline in the legislature, and reduces the possibility of effective control over government spending and performance.

The extreme fragmentation of the party system has also led to a worrisome increase in the "lost vote"—that is, in the number of lists and votes that obtain no representation whatsoever. In 1998, for example, 222 lists (out of 319) did not obtain a single seat in the Senate, despite having received an overall total of 2,540,000 votes.[12] Given the fragmented representation of a multitude of interests, this relative "waste" of votes can contribute to an even greater undermining of the already weak legitimacy of democratic institutions, since a great many interests and social demands are left without representation.

The "Logic of Governability"

The extreme fragmentation of the parties and the party system since 1991 has forced the pendulum to swing back from a "logic of incorporation" to a "logic of governability." While in 1991 the main objective was to include as many as possible in the political game, the reform projects under discussion since 1994 have focused instead on strengthening the parties and party system so as to promote the formation of solid party majorities and minorities in the legislature. In other words, the main concern became how to build enough legislative support for governments while simultaneously fostering the emergence of oppositions capable of carrying out their role as critics and overseers. This, however, entails a dilemma, since on the one hand there is a demand for a more coherent and efficient political system while on the other the FARC and the ELN will probably insist on the strengthening of the "logic of incorporation" as a condition for their integration into democratic life.

Are these two demands then incompatible?[13] From our point of view, bringing together the two logics has to be the crux of any future political reform in Colombia. Even though it is certainly indispensable to keep open the gates that have allowed the incorporation of new political forces into the system, it remains also true that the system urgently needs to respond to the requirements of democratic governability. Striking a balance between these two goals is the key to any future democratic reform. In 1999, the international commission on institutional reform (see Valenzuela et al. 1999) identified three basic challenges for the consolidation of democracy:

> representativeness, responsibility, and capability. Representativeness is perhaps the most serious and difficult, since it affects the very essence of democratic legitimacy. But the other two also contribute to the acceptance of democracy and to its stability. Responsibility refers to the integrity and transparency of public business, including the clarity of a constitutional state's playing rules with respect to its administrative and legal apparatus. . . . Capability is connected with the state's role as administrator of the public sector and regulator of private activity in the interest of the common good. . . . The building of strong and cohesive parties is a necessary condition for governability within a democracy but is not enough in itself. Only when the above mentioned three challenges meet with satisfactory responses does democracy acquire full legitimacy. (215)

In short, what is needed is not just more democracy but better democracy. A democratic system must be not only representative but also able to govern—that is, democratic and effective. Otherwise, the newly created democratic spaces become in large measure fictitious. A political system "besieged" (Archer 1995; Bejarano and Pizarro 2005) by political violence and intolerance as well as deeply divided among radically opposed ideological visions of the polity is not the best scenario for a flourishing democratic life. In sum, any future political reform must open the gates to the full representation of all the interests present in society, while at the same time seeking to ensure that the decision-making process can function adequately.

The Essentials of a Future Political Reform

In 1991, the need to go from a two-party to a multiparty system came under discussion, but one crucial point was never brought up: namely, what type of multiparty system? Both the Commission on Party Reform (created in 1995) and the report written by Valenzuela et al. (1999) expounded the need to avoid the excessive fragmentation of parties (as had occurred in Brazil) or an unbridled multipartism (as in Ecuador). In other words, faced with a choice between the two-party model and the risk of even greater party fragmentation, Colombia would be wise to look toward a new model, a moderate multiparty system, to use Sartori's term (1976: 163). A limited number of parties of national scope, better structured and also more democratic in their inner workings, would combine the demand for wider political representation with the need to create an environment favorable to democratic governability. In what follows we consider some of the most important proposals that were put forth in a series of debates, from 1994 until 2002, about political reform in Colombia. These can be classified as follows: (1) electoral reforms; (2) internal party democratization; (3) the opposition's rights and obligations; (4) reforming Congress; (5) campaign and party financing; and finally, (6) affirmative action mechanisms.

Electoral Reforms

To confront the problems afflicting parties and the party system, the Commission on Political Reform (created in 1995) urged the parties to give their candidates dependable backing, to commit a program thoroughly discussed in advance, and to choose their candidates through participatory mechanisms. [14] To that end, the commission recommended that parties and movements limit the number of lists for election to collegial bodies and that in cases where one person was to be elected (mayor, governor, president) they choose a single candidate through democratic means (popular referendum, broadly representative convention, etc.). In other words, lists and individuals should be encouraged to represent a movement or party unambiguously and to commit themselves to a clear-cut program, which would make them accountable to the electorate for their performance once in office.

The proposals presented by the Commission for Party Reform were limited, however. Indeed, only a minority in the commission welcomed the idea of drastically limiting the number of party endorsements, and the majority won out, approving a watered-down formula in which the number of lists backed by a party could equal no more than half the posts to be filled. Although the new formula represented some progress, it was not a satisfactory solution to the problem of anarchistic splintering of party representation. The real danger was that limiting the number of lists without adding any complementary measures might only aggravate the existing fragmentation, since those left out of the party lists could simply go ahead and set up their own political tents. The cure could be worse than the disease.

National debate since 1994 has led to the shaping of a more coherent model for political-electoral reform, developing a wiser approach to strengthening parties and ensuring minority representation. This reform has four main components: limiting the number of lists allowed to each political party or movement in each electoral district; changing the formula for seat distribution from the present system (Hare) to the d'Hondt system; and, finally, establishing a minimum voting threshold to ensure access to representative bodies. As for the closed and blocked list, the most sensible recommendation seems to be to keep it as it currently stands. In what follows, we take a close look at each one of these crucial changes to the electoral system.

A rule that would permit each party to offer only one list (for Congress, assemblies, councils, and local governing bodies) or one candidate (for the presidency, governorships, mayoralties) aroused a negative reaction in many legislative circles because of the fear of a return to the *boligrafo* system—that is, to parties' elite control of lists and candidacies. It is therefore essential to tie this restriction to a set of democratic mechanisms designed to guarantee that lists and candidates reflect the forces working within the party and not the preferences of the party's top elites.

The absence of any control over a party's use of its label to freely endorse candidates and lists, combined with the current formula for distributing seats (the Hare system), has stimulated the formation of personalistic factions within the traditional parties as well as the fragmentation of all the alternative parties and movements. Accordingly, it has been suggested that introducing the d'Hondt method would be quite appropriate, insofar as this system would encourage party cohesion while not excluding minorities from the political game (De Roux 2000). So here we have an instrument that combines the twin objectives that must guide any political reform in Colombia: the creation of majority governments and the opportunity for minorities to ensure representation.

A third component of this reform would be the introduction of an electoral threshold. In electoral districts of great magnitude, political minorities have a relative advantage, since it is easier for them to obtain political representation. If the electoral district happens to be nationwide—as has been the case with the Senate in Colombia since 1991—this tendency is maximized (Lijphart 1994). To avoid the undesirable fragmentation of representation, thresholds (or minimum vote barriers) have been set up, with varying figures—Holland, 0.67 percent; Germany, 5 percent; Poland, 10 percent. According to Valenzuela et al. (1999), when the magnitude of a voting district is fairly small, a legal threshold turns out to be superfluous. The formula $T = 75/(M + 1)$ shows the approximate equivalent between the magnitude of the district (M) and the "effective threshold" (T) created by the electoral system. This means that a party or movement would find it just as difficult to win a seat in a district with a legal threshold of 7.5 percent as it would in a nine-seat district with no threshold. A two-seat district corresponds to a threshold of 25 percent of the vote (75/3). In a larger district with eighteen seats, the actual threshold would be 4 percent (75/19). The authors of the report thus concluded that introducing a threshold for the House of Representatives would be rather ineffectual, while introducing one for Senate elections would definitely make a difference.[15] They recommended introducing a threshold gradually, starting at 1.5 percent and raising it to 5 percent. At the same time, so as to keep true minority groups from becoming excluded, the special districts (crafted to ensure the representation of indigenous and black communities) should be kept. In addition, Valenzuela et al. (1999) suggested that the *apparentement* (grouping) model[16] could be introduced as a mechanism to ensure minority representation.

Finally, as reported by Valenzuela et al. (1999), different types of ballots produce different results regarding both intraparty competition and the power of the electorate to choose between individual candidates. To combat proliferation of the electoral *microempresas*, Valenzuela et al. (1999) have suggested introducing the preferential vote. This method would allow each voter, besides choosing one of the lists on the ballot, to mark a preferred candidate within that list. This option, however, contains the risk of institutionalizing the *operación avispa*—a dispersion strategy designed by the Liberal Party to snare as many votes as possible by multiplying its congressional lists ad infinitum. Moreover, it would perpetuate a harsh intraparty competition dominated not by party strength but by the prestige of individual politicians, their resources, and their patronage networks.[17] If the country wishes to avoid personalistic dispersal and fragmentation, it would be better served by keeping the present ballot type (closed and blocked), provided two basic conditions are met: that each party presents only one list per district and that the list is drawn up by democratic procedures.[18]

Internal Democratization

Regarding whether the law should concern itself with the internal dynamics of parties, the report filed by Valenzuela et al. (1999) with the Colombian government explicitly states: "We consider it quite appropriate for internal party democratization to be guaranteed constitutionally, particularly in those democratic regimes that have generated exclusion of significant social and political sectors or have been threatened by antidemocratic movements" (224). Drawing on the pioneering experiments in Germany (Act of Bonn, 1949) and more recently Chile, Spain, and Argentina, the authors conclude that democratic procedures must be applied in particular to the nomination of candidates and the drawing up of lists, through mechanisms such as primaries, direct election of candidates by party members, the establishment of nominating committees independent of other party organs, or frequent elections to determine the makeup of party directorates responsible for choosing candidates. Moreover, the recognition of a party by the National Electoral Council should be conditional upon the party's bylaws providing for internal democratic procedures. In addition, the report recommends that parties granted legal status maintain control over the party's name and therefore over those who sign up under it, that a person not be allowed to join two or more competing parties, and finally that no candidate be allowed to campaign under the label of any party other than the one to which he or she belongs.

It is worth noting two things in connection with party democratization. The first is its recent impact in Latin America. As Jorge Domínguez (1995) points out, the resurrection—after major election defeats or organizational splits—of some of the biggest Latin American political parties was achieved through a variety of measures, with internal democratization among the most decisive. "The resurrection of political parties . . . requires (1) the purging of discredited leaders; (2) the democratization and reactivation of internal party life to involve the members themselves in the reconstruction process; (3) a willingness to examine the party's program and commitments" (12).[19]

The second point here is that Colombia already has some significant experience in democratizing candidate choice using some popular selection methods. Indeed, the Liberal Party chose its presidential candidate on two occasions—in 1990 and 1994—through "primaries" of sorts, organized and financed by the National Civil Status Registry and the National Electoral

Council. Candidates for various governorships and mayoralties have been chosen following similar procedures.[20] It seems worthwhile to spend some space discussing the rules of the game established for the 1990 and 1994 experiments to choose the Liberal candidate, inasmuch as they provide interesting lessons for future changes in democratic practices.[21]

The 1990 Liberal Referendum
In the late 1980s, the extreme fragmentation of the Liberal Party and the ensuing risks that internal division posed for the upcoming 1990 presidential election led to the devising of a popular referendum plan. Under it, the individual obtaining an absolute majority of the referendum vote would become the sole candidate. To keep other political groups—non-Liberals—from turning out in large numbers to support a particular candidate, the referendum results would be discounted if the total vote exceeded by more than 5 percent of the number of ballots cast in favor of Liberal lists running for Congress on that same day. The referendum took place on March 11, 1990 (table 6.3). Five days earlier, on March 6, the presidential hopefuls Hernando Dussán, Ernesto Samper, and César Gaviria had made an agreement (the Pacto del Gun), promising that the "party's candidate for the presidency of the republic shall be he who wins the popular referendum with a plurality, on condition that he has at least a one hundred thousand vote advantage over his closest competitor."[22] Jaime Castro also agreed to the

Table 6.3
Liberal Referendum, 1990

Candidate	Number of Votes	Percentage
César Gaviria	2,796,623	51.53
Hernando Durán	1,204,779	22.20
Ernesto Samper	1,028,593	18.95
Alberto Santofimio	232,092	4.27
William Jaramillo	86,683	1.59
Jaime Castro	46,897	.86
Blank ballots	14,563	.26
Void ballots	16,109	.29
Total	5,426,339	100.00

pact, but William Jaramillo and Alberto Santofimio opposed it, claming that such an agreement was neither valid nor legitimate since it had not been approved by a bylaws convention. The debate proved unnecessary since César Gaviria obtained more than 50 percent of the vote, a sweeping endorsement from the Liberal electorate.

The 1994 Liberal Referendum

The second referendum was held March 30, 1994, the same day as the congressional elections. This time, the winner would be the one receiving a plurality of votes regardless of the number or proportion of votes obtained. Because the Liberal Party did not issue party cards, it had to agree once again to an open referendum with no restrictions. That is, all citizens who wanted to help choose the Liberal candidate could vote, even though they could have voted for other parties in congressional elections held the same day.[23] The winner (see table 6.4) would be immediately endorsed by the National Liberal Directorate as the party's sole presidential candidate, and he was authorized to choose a vice-presidential running mate, the only restriction (by party agreement) being that he or she also belong to the Liberal Party. Finally, even though they already had the endorsement of the party leadership, the presidential candidate and his running mate had to be approved by the Liberal Party's National Convention. In addition, both had to accept the outcome of the party's Ideological Conference (which was to meet several weeks later) as the program for their administration.[24] Finally, a three-member ethical tribunal was set up, with the power to object to any candidate it deemed morally unfit. At the same time, to prevent drug-related money from playing a role in the elections, a council was appointed to watch over election financing, and, at the request of the hopefuls on the Liberal Party referendum ballot, another council was set up to safeguard the neutrality of the nominee-selection process.

The rules of the game for the popular referendum met with the approval of six out of the seven hopefuls for the Liberal nomination (Samper, De la Calle, Turbay, González, Sorzano, and Lemos). The six promised to support the winner and endorse the program of the Ideological Convention. Only Enrique Parejo withheld his approval, claiming that holding the referendum and the congressional elections concurrently favored candidates with a previous base of support in Congress. In other words, these candidates had an advantage because they would benefit from a coattails effect.

Summing up, the "popular referendum" device used in 1990 and 1994 to unify a deeply split Liberal Party represents an interesting experiment in giving the party membership some meaningful role in choosing its presidential candidate, one of the main functions of U.S. primaries. However, if Colombia were to pass legislation requiring that presidential candidates be chosen by such a mechanism, it would be essential for all political forces to hold their referendums concurrently.

The Statute on the Opposition

Colombia lacks a tradition of political opposition. The political monopoly granted to the traditional parties by the National Front pacts between 1958 and 1986, combined with the systematic exclusion and elimination of the opposition on the Left, have left the country without an active, legitimate, and loyal opposition. And without a solid political opposition, the prospects of consolidating a full democracy seem rather faint.

Some authors such as Arend Lijphart (1989) maintain that in deeply fragmented societies and in political communities whose democratic systems are not solid or are threatened by instability it would be better to encourage coalition governments than to promote a strong opposition.[25] In

Table 6.4
Liberal Referendum, 1994

Candidate	Number of Votes	Percentage
Ernesto Samper	1,245,283	48.21
Humberto de la Calle	335,155	12.97
Carlos Lleras	202,925	7.85
David Turbay	172,096	6.66
Carlos Lemos	129,983	5.03
Rodolfo González	72,573	2.80
Gloria Gaitán	65,456	2.53
Blank ballots	160,751	6.22
Void ballots	198,475	7.68
Total	2,582,694	100.00

the Colombian case, we argue instead for the importance of a vibrant political opposition to revitalize the country's democracy.

Back in the 1982 election campaign, Alfonso López Michelsen proposed repealing one paragraph in article 120 of the constitution, a provision inserted during the constitutional reform of 1968 to prolong the life of the National Front (FN) coalitional governments until 1986. Commenting on the matter in a televised speech, he stated:

> I believe it is necessary to repeal Article 120 of the National Constitution, which was, at bottom, a clandestine extension of the National Front.... True democracy is debate, it's the existence of an alternative called opposition, confronting the government as it carries out the program it offered to the electorate. Anything else means never winning, never losing, and seeing a lot of alternatives pop up, in the jungle, like our armed insurgents. If we have to impose some solution in the search for peace . . . it seems to me, just as I said in 1958, that the answer is a return to civilized democracy so there'll be winners and losers at the ideological and programmatic levels, not winners and losers at the bureaucratic level. (Quoted in Pérez 1987: 53)

The question is: how do you promote the emergence of a solid political opposition?

Generally speaking, in today's democratic systems it is unusual to find laws specifically regulating the role of the political opposition. In most countries, guarantees for the existence of opposing parties are to be found in the constitution itself. However, in some European countries that suffered greatly under authoritarian regimes, there is special legislation guaranteeing the rights of the political opposition.[26] Since the 1991 Constituent Assembly debates, the idea has been gaining ground in Colombia that, given the country's experience, the country should have rules concerning the exercise of an opposition, legislation that would establish a minimum legal framework without falling into excessive regulation (as in Germany).[27]

To promote the emergence of a strong, vibrant, political opposition, the Commission on Party Reform suggested that a Statute of the Opposition be passed granting the opposition certain prerogatives (access to means of communication, information, rebuttal, consultation, and oversight, among others) and affording it some weighty guarantees by creating a special legal agency to represent the rights of the opposition and political minorities, providing better administrative resources, and allowing greater autonomy for the agencies of "horizontal accountability" (Attorney General's Office and Office of the Comptroller General), the heads of which should not belong to the party or parties in power.[28] We doubt, however, that this would be enough to recreate a legitimate space for the opposition. Given the current levels of political violence in the country, it is unthinkable that a strong political opposition will be able to emerge and thrive. Indeed, bringing an end to the current cycle of political violence is perhaps the only meaningful and by all means the best guarantee for the opposition in Colombia.[29]

Reforming Congress

As Shugart and Mainwaring (1997, 12–14) have so convincingly argued, the power of the president in any presidential system derives, not solely or mainly from the powers granted explicitly in the constitution, but also and to a great extent from the capacity of the president to muster enough support from Congress to accomplish his or her policy goals. The constitutional reforms of 1991 were designed, in part, to solve and prevent the recurrence of "presidential-congressional disharmony." Instead of strengthening the powers of the president, the Colombian constitution makers opted to restore some of Congress's powers and its overall significance within the system of divided powers. Paradoxically, given the influence of Cesar Gaviria during the Constituent Assembly, the new constitution introduced severe restraints to the president's powers and prerogatives, while strengthening those of Congress.[30]

This constitutional reform has turned out to be somehow counterproductive, since the decrease in presidential powers has not been coupled with a strengthening of the parties' coherence or their capacity to muster solid coalitions in Congress. The dismal performance of Colombia's Congress does not necessarily stem from the constitutional division of powers but is instead largely the result of the political parties' increasing fragmentation and the consequent autonomy of the legislators vis-à-vis their parties. We have already discussed some of the crucial electoral reforms needed to reorganize the party system. In addition, some needed changes in the way Congress operates could be introduced with an eye to reorganizing and revitalizing congressional activity. Many have noted that, despite the significant advances in modernizing Congress instituted by the 1991 Constitution and Act 5 of 1992,[31] there still exist enormous inadequacies in the way the legislature operates, affecting the efficiency of its work and harming its public image (Ungar and Andrade 1995).[32]

Broaching the question of the absence of parliamentary discipline, the 1995 Commission on Party Reform stated that Congress could not continue being the simple sum of its individual members but had to become the expression of the parties and movements present in the two houses. Accordingly, the commission considered the creation of legally recognized parliamentary benches. Such benches would organize legislative tasks around coherent partisan identities exhibiting (both inside and outside the halls of Congress) solid and recognizable attitudes on the questions under debate.

In Spain and Mexico, where the law recognizes this institution, legislators join together according to party affiliation or ideological affinity, forming benches headed by speakers and registered with the House steering committees.[33] The minimum number for establishing a bench varies from country to country, with Spain requiring at least fifteen deputies. In that country's Cortes (or parliament) the speakers from the various benches belong to the Spokespersons' Committee, which plays a major role in the scheduling of parliamentary business. It sets up the agenda in consultation with the steering committees, organizes the debates, appoints each bench's speakers for different parliamentary debates (in plenary session or in committee), and decides how long a speaker will have the floor.[34]

This reform could achieve significant results, contributing to party cohesiveness within the halls of Congress, generating a more disciplined legislative activity, and strengthening the identity of parties and political coalitions.[35] If a party or coalition cannot let ten or twenty orators take the floor but must appoint one speaker or a limited number to debate, the parties are forced to seek internal consensus. Moreover, within a government-versus-opposition framework, instituting benches would achieve at least one essential goal: the political guarantees and rights of the opposition could not be abused (as they are at present), since the steering committees of the two houses would not be able to make decisions about the legislative agenda without input from the opposition benches.

Another serious problem facing Colombia's Congress is the quality of the laws it debates and passes. In general, the national media tend to judge the work of a legislature by the number of laws it enacts, without considering the quality and coherence of the measures approved. It is necessary to change this way of looking at the legislature's work and to make substantial improvement in the quality, for the country is overwhelmed with incoherent, scattered, and improvised pieces of legislation, creating the sensation of an endless legislative avalanche that is both massive and useless.[36] It is therefore essential to improve the lawmaking process and the quality of parliamentary debate and to increase legislators' access to legal expertise.

Another improvement that could help enhance parliamentary performance points in the direction of separating the legislative from the administrative functions, both of which now fall to the House and Senate Steering Committees. Indeed, both houses are responsible for managing the operational funds allocated to each branch from the national budget. Putting the two functions together creates a host of problems. First, it brings constant accusations of corruption that are quite damaging to the public image of the legislative branch. Second, the lack of a clear differentiation between the two functions creates unnecessary duties for the steering committees, thus affecting Congress's main tasks—legislation and oversight. It therefore seems desirable to create an administrative unit (serving both houses) along with proper management criteria, which would mean that the steering committees would no longer handle Congress's financial resources.[37]

On another score, Colombia shares with most other democracies the problems stemming from the pressure that large financial and industrial corporations exert on parties and members of Congress through campaign contributions that are not subject to limits or control. These forms of pressure and influence must be regulated in a search for greater degrees of transparency in the relations between the legislative branch and political donors. To that end, the Liberal Senator G. Vargas Lleras presented a bill on the Senate floor in late 1995 with the explicit purpose of regulating the activities of lobbyists in Congress. Under Vargas Lleras's proposed legislation, a potential congressional pressure group would be required to register with the steering committees, stating the purpose of its activity, who it planned to approach and how, and the total amount of its expected expenditures. In addition, of course, strict limitations on contributions from private donors would need to be part of any bill on party and campaign financing.

Another problem confronted by all contemporary democracies is related to the enormous technical and professional support available to executive power (presidential cabinets, ministries, economic planning bodies, etc.), which contrasts sharply with the paucity of technical support available to legislative bodies, a state of affairs that contributes to strengthening executive power while diminishing the effectiveness of the legislature. The experts that the commission charged with making recommendations on political reform (Valenzuela et al. 1999) drafted a set of relevant proposals that the Colombian Congress should consider. Valenzuela et al. point out that the Congress of the United States has several agencies devoted to serving Congress. These include the Library of Congress, the Congressional Research Service, and the Congressional Budget Office. Although the Library of Congress is open to the public, its main priority is to identify, analyze, and summarize the information it has, making it available to legislators through the Congressional Research Service, which is part of the library but works exclusively for the various members and committees of Congress and their corps of consultants. The information supplied by the service must fulfill certain requirements: it has to be objective, professional, nonpartisan, speedily prepared, and confidential.[38] In line with this recommendation, it would seem appropriate for the Congress to confer with the board of directors of the National Archive about creating a special team of legislative consultants and appropriate mechanisms to ensure that all aspects of legislative work benefit from the flow of electronic information.

In another vein, since 1991, one of the main factors negatively affecting the quality of the legislature's work has been the undependability of the elected legislator, who, after serving in Congress briefly, steps aside in favor of the next name on the list, who soon does the same, and so on, down the line. According to an article in *El Tiempo* in 2000, "[O]ver two years of legislative sessions, in the House and in the Senate around 40 percent of the members of Congress have stepped aside so those down the list—the second, third, fourth, even as far as the seventh—can act as short-term legislators."[39] This absurd pattern had its origins in the Constitution of 1991. The constitution makers, in their aim to eliminate the figure of the alternate legislator (or *suplente,* who would share the seat with its principal holder, each serving two years at a stretch, for example), ended up creating this political aberration. Article 261[40] is yet another example of this constitution's tendency to encourage party fragmentation rather than party cohesiveness. In this particular case, the cure was clearly worse than the disease.

In the current war of remainders, the only candidate with a real chance of winning a seat is the one at the head of the list, so political leaders get together and make deals to assign positions on the list. If X is likely to contribute y number of votes (or in some cases, a certain sum of money), X occupies place z on the list, which will give X the opportunity to occupy the seat for a fixed period ranging anywhere from a long stretch down to a month or two. Although replacement is sometimes warranted—for example, in instances of illness or forced exile—the rankings on lists for the Senate of the republic are for the most part based on political or economic considerations. The logic of the system is as follows: electoral *microempresas* usually have a strong regional basis.[41] However, if they want to garner enough votes to get in through the game of remainders, they have to pick up votes here and there in the rest of the country. Various political deals are struck with that goal in mind and end up being translated into a single list and a series of scheduled replacements during the four-year term of the legislature.

This rapid turnover in Congress has devastating effects on the quality of legislative performance. It hinders the formation of a nucleus of trained politicians. It also affects the legitimacy of the legislature—since the replacements were not elected by the people, it is difficult to defend the fact that these replacements legislate on matters of public interest. Finally, these members of Congress usually seek to spend their short time in office making laws that favor their electoral fiefs and neglect matters of national interest. Clearly, then, one of the most urgently needed reforms concerns changing this mechanism of replacement. One possibility would be to end the practice once and for all. If a senator or representative cannot continue in his or her post for whatever reason, the vacancy should be filled via new elections. Another option is to reform the replacement formula, drawing up a set of strict regulations that would allow this institution to fulfill its real purpose.

Campaign and Party Financing

As has been amply demonstrated worldwide in recent years, political parties are one of the main suspects in the fostering of corruption in contemporary democracies, since they manage enormous sums of money with relatively few controls or restrictions. Establishing stricter surveillance and control over sources of party and campaign financing is high on the list of desired changes in many countries now striving to reform their party systems. This is even more urgent in countries, like Colombia, plagued by the curse of drug-related money infiltrating politics.

The literature on the subject puts forth three main goals to be attained via the regulation of campaign and party finances. First, there is the need to render parties and candidates less dependent on the economic powers (legal or illegal) that seek to influence the behavior of elected representatives. Second, there seems to be a demand for greater transparency in the electoral process and particularly a wish to avoid the influence of money from dubious sources, such as drug trafficking and political corruption. Third, there is the intent of creating a leveled field for all the political forces entering electoral contests, since sharp imbalances between them can affect democratic participation and representation (Alvarez 1995; González-Varas 1995).

In 1985 Colombia's Congress approved a timid campaign-financing law. Later, the Constitution of 1991 got more deeply into the subject with new standards that evolved into Act 130 of 1994. But there is a great irony here: when the country finally had a law—albeit not a perfect one—on campaign financing, the system broke down, for in 1994 there was no transparency, no autonomy, much less any relative political equality. Drug-trafficking funds permeated the presidential and congressional campaigns, and two or three major financial groups paid more than 50 percent of the campaign costs for Andrés Pastrana and Ernesto Samper, the two main party presidential candidates, generating deep imbalances in the political contest.

For the future, any Colombian campaign-financing law must take into account six basic issues. First, it is necessary to decide who should be financed—the candidates or the parties. In this regard, there are two main approaches: the U.S. system favors aid to the candidates, whereas the European system favors financing the parties. In Colombia the system is completely disorganized; the act regulating these matters (1994) states that contributions may go to the coffers of parties or social and political movements, as well as to lists and individual candidates. Indeed, it is a model for anarchy-encouraging party fragmentation. In the Colombian case, thus, the European model seems better suited for the purposes of forcing the parties to rationalize the number of lists and candidates they present, stimulating the emergence of a better organized, more effective system of political representation.

Second, it is important to decide how state funds should be distributed. Again, there are at least two approaches to this question. The first entails the distribution of resources according to the number of votes each party has received. Obviously, this method of party financing favors the major parties, penalizing the minor ones; thus it could prove inappropriate for a country like Colombia, which has been trying for some time to broaden the party system and incorporate insurgent forces. According to the second method, resources are distributed equally among all legally recognized parties. This system, apparently fair in its encouragement of minor parties, penalizes parties with greater political representation. The question, then, is how to combine the two systems to arrive at a distribution of funds that, while encouraging the participation of minor parties, can also recognize the representativeness of the major ones. The mixed model provided by Act 130 (which regulates the parties) responds to both requirements, mandating the distribution of a percentage of resources according to the number of votes, with another percentage, much smaller, being distributed equally. However, to maintain this approach, the rules in force will have to be adapted to the demands of political reform.

It is also important to consider who exactly is to be the recipient of party or campaign funds and under what conditions. For example, if the money is handed over to top party officials, they can make it an instrument for elite control. It would be more appropriate to turn the money over to party treasuries, while at the same time establishing firm rules for the internal democratization of the parties so as to ensure that their funds would be distributed democratically.

Another important question regarding party and campaign financing concerns the total amount of state support. According to some, state funding is the ideal alternative to illegal sources (drug trafficking, corruption) of campaign financing. However, we should not harbor many illusions about state financing. In 1974, for example, Italy passed an election law mandating state financing in an effort to stem political corruption. Contrary to expectations, public money did not replace other contributions but was simply added to them. Parties were delighted to receive public help but still went on accepting the usual funds from dubious donors. As Eduardo Posada-Carbó has put it, "Without any great debate, Latin American countries, one after another, have come to the conclusion that public funding of the parties will be a panacea. All we need to do is take a quick look at some of the countries that resorted to state money years ago—Germany (1956), Italy (1974), Japan (1975), Spain (1977)—and it becomes obvious that such measures do not solve the problem of electoral corruption."[42]

Several things are needed before state financing can become a truly viable replacement for questionable financial sources. First, there ought to be a good calculus of the actual costs of political activity. If state contributions are insufficient, there is the temptation to receive funds from other sources. Second, campaign costs in Colombia must be reduced by cutting the maximum length of campaigns, limiting the excessive use of expensive TV ads, and rationalizing the proliferation of lists to stop indiscriminate granting of party endorsements. Finally, it would be worth discussing seriously the feasibility of minimizing election costs by holding all contests on the same day. Some analysts think that this would constitute a return to "rotten fiefs" and political bossism because of the coattails effect, in which presidential elections have the potential to pull in (*voto de arrastre*) congressional and subnational elections. Despite some potential negative effects, the return to concurrent elections would have the bonus of reducing party system fragmentation while also reducing the probability of minority governments.[43]

Fourth, some thought must be given to the subject of the people's willingness to fund political activities. Given that Latin Americans have lived through some two decades of economic crisis and decreased social spending, accompanied by widespread discredit of parties, politicians, and politics in general, it would require a massive educational effort to convince them to go along with large-scale government expenditures to fund political activity. People must be informed about the cost of sustaining a working democracy, and the link between public funding of political activity and the possibility of achieving greater transparency and accountability in the conduct of public affairs must be made evident. Public funds, however, must be complemented by private contributions, with more rigorous controls established concerning the source and amount of such monies.[44] A reliance on state funding alone is clearly undesirable.

Fifth, electoral authorities must be strengthened. The 1991 Constitution gave the post of treasury inspector a mere three-year life span, and with the problems affecting the National Electoral Council, there is a deficit of electoral control and surveillance. Several factors affect the performance of the National Electoral Council (NEC). First, in Colombia, unlike other Latin American countries, the NEC members do not have the status of magistrates but are ordinary party representatives. Second, votes in this body are decided by a two-thirds majority (six out of nine), which is extremely difficult to attain, at least with the current NEC makeup.[45] As a result, both major parties will veto any resolution affecting their interests, which means an almost total lack of effective sanctions for punishable acts. If there is to be a change in the questionable relationship between money and politics in Colombia, it will be necessary to promote the establishment of effective institutions (a Treasury Inspector's Office and a revised version of the National Electoral Council), as well as effective regulations. As for enforcing the latter, tough measures—such as imposing heavy fines or even jail sentences on campaign treasurers who have committed punishable acts, revoking the legal status of political parties involved in financial misdeeds, and barring their candidates-elect (even a president) from assuming office—must be considered.

Sixth, reform of campaign-financing standards must become a basic tool of "institutional engineering" and thus contribute to the restructuring of the party system. Positive incentives could be designed, such as limiting state contributions to parties that present only one, democratically chosen list in an electoral district.

Taking Positive Action

Affirmative action (or positive discrimination) is based on a quota system intended to guarantee the rights of minorities. Positive action is defined in article 4 of the UN Convention on the Elimination of All Forms of Discrimination against Women as the "adoption . . . of temporary special measures aimed at accelerating de facto equality between men and women."[46] It shall not be considered discrimination, but also it "shall in no way entail as a consequence the maintenance of unequal or separate standards; these measures shall be discontinued when the objectives of equality of opportunity and treatment have been achieved." The idea behind positive actions is that they must be taken to reduce the measurable gap between antidiscrimination laws on the books and the persistence of discrimination in everyday life. Indeed, experience teaches that outlawing discrimination does not automatically bring it to an end, since a mere legal ban does not necessarily lead to de facto equality. Cultural factors such as racism and sexism can result in continuing exclusion in some situations. That is why taking temporary measures to correct de facto instances of inequality is appropriately called positive action.

The 1991 Constitutional Convention—picking up on formulas used in New Zealand, Germany, Belgium, and India—approved the allocation of two seats in a closed Senate district for the benefit of indigenous communities. The International Consultants' Report (Valenzuela et al. 1999) calls this "positive gerrymandering."[47] The constitution also provides for a special House election district benefiting Afro-Colombian communities. The special district for indigenous communities should be kept, since it has amply demonstrated its benefits. The special district for black communities of the

Pacific Coast should also be made a reality to open a channel of representation for this badly marginalized social sector.

The Commission on Party Reform noted that there were few women in executive positions in the government. In the face of this obvious discrimination, which contrasts with advances made in other countries on our continent, the commission unanimously approved Senator Piedad Córdoba's proposal that at least 30 percent of high-ranking posts at all levels of government be filled by women. This proposal finally became a law of the republic ("the Quotas Act," as it is popularly known). Now the country faces the challenge of translating this law into deed, for the legislation has met with strong resistance from many sectors of national public administration as well as from municipal and departmental offices.

Conclusion

Political reform, which began two decades ago with the popular election of mayors, has begun to change the face of Colombian political life. Today the political system has left behind the legal restrictions that had propped up the two-party system since the National Front days; alternative parties and movements have begun to play an important role in political life; and two-party domination has seen its hegemonic grip loosen in election after election (in large part because of the weakening of the Conservative Party).

Nevertheless, Colombia faces two challenges to political party life. First it has to combat the growing fragmentation of the party system and the excessive personalism of its political system, both of which seriously affect the political representation of a variety of social interests and the coordination among them necessary to produce effective government at every level—national, departmental, and municipal. Second, it needs to achieve a minimum degree of internal order that will guarantee the rights and liberties that make citizenship and democracy meaningful. In one sense, eliminating political violence in the country would be the most meaningful contribution to political reform. Beyond this very basic point, the puzzling question remains: Is it possible to improve democratic governability while simultaneously leaving the gates open so that new political forces (especially the reluctant guerrilla groups, the FARC and the ELN) can finally join the democratic game? To reconcile these two objectives should remain the crux of any future political reform.

Notes

Translated by Julia Shirek Smith.

1. "Entrevista a Antonio Navarro Wolff: De la reforma política y de la política electoral," in *Vía Alterna*, www.viaalterna.com.co/pentrev.htm.

2. We develop this argument further in Bejarano and Pizarro (2005).

3. The Commission on Party Reform was appointed by President Ernesto Samper in mid-1995 and consisted of fifteen members: Horacio Serpa (interior minister), Juan Guillermo Angel and Piedad Córdoba (senators and Liberal Party leaders), Jaime Arias and Omar Yepes (senators and Conservative Party leaders), Carlos Arturo Angel (president of the National Association of Industrialists, ANDI), Orlando Obregón (president of the United Confederation of Workers, CUT), Jaime Dussán (senator), Janeth Suárez (ADM19 representative in the House), Alberto Casas (journalist), Guillermo Páramo (president of the Universidad Nacional), and the political analysts Fernando Cepeda, Javier Sanín, Pedro Santana, and Eduardo Pizarro. Once the commission had finished its work, its chair, Interior Minister Horacio Serpa Uribe, turned its recommendations into Bill 118 (which regulates the financing of electoral campaigns), proposed Constitutional Amendment 05 (which reforms the political constitution), and proposed Statute 118 (establishing the Statute on the Opposition). The three bills were rejected by Congress.

4. A summary of the legislation introduced during the Pastrana administration can be found in Roll (1999). This chapter was originally written in the spring of 2001, well before the current administration of President Uribe began in 2002. Thus it does not include an in-depth analysis of the political reform bill passed by Congress in 2003. That bill included some of the reforms discussed in previous proposals and commented upon here.

5. In particular, we have explored the suggestions put forth in two papers: Valenzuela et al. (1999) and Roland and Zapata (2000).

6. See Title II of the Constitution, "On Parties and Political Movements" (arts. 107–11). As for legislation, see Act 130 of 1994, which establishes "the Basic Statute of Political Parties and Movements, with standards for their financing and for the conduct of political campaigns, and various other provisions."

7. Many constitutions permit only legally constituted parties to run candidates so as to avoid fragmenting political representation. Colombia, on the other hand, has opened up an endless range of political possibilities.

8. An especially interesting case in point is that of "Liberal" Senator Alfonso Angarita Baracaldo. In Congress he represents state retirees, and he monopolizes legislative initiatives that would benefit that social sector. So that there is no doubt about its purpose, his electoral *microempresa* is appropriately named the Social Security Movement.

9. An insignificant figure, given that the number of potential voters in national elections is currently close to twenty-five million.

10. *Note that a fair number of the new parties appearing in this table are simply liberal or conservative factions seeking to obtain the benefits offered by the law.*

11. As noted above, electoral systems generally grant parties the right to propose only one candidate or one list per electoral district. In Colombia, by contrast, electoral legislation allowed parties and political movements to endorse a limitless number of candidates and or lists in each electoral district.

12. National Department of Planning (Departamento Nacional de Planeación), *Cambio para construir la paz* (Bogotá: Presidencia de la República, 1998), 106.

13. Some think these are two mutually exclusive goals and approaches to political reform. See Londoño (1999).

14. This chapter summarizes the main reform proposals made on the subject in Colombia from 1994 until 2002. Legislative Act 01 of July 3, 2003, made some progress especially in certain aspects of electoral reform: it introduced the D'Hondt formula, the single list, and the electoral threshold for both the Senate and the House. It also tightened the requirements for forming a party and forbade the possibility of being affiliated to more than one party. Its application during the 2003 regional and local elections showed some beneficial results: the number of lists and candidates was notably reduced, the parties were strengthened, and democratic governability seems to have improved at the local level. It remains to be seen whether these positive effects will occur again during the national elections of 2006.

15. The recent constitutional reform (Legislative Act 01 of 2003) introduced a minimum threshold of 2 percent for the Senate. For all other representative bodies (city councils, departmental assemblies, and the House of Representatives) the threshold will be equivalent to 50 percent of the electoral quotient resulting from dividing the total number of votes into the number of seats to be provided in each specific district.

16. Through the *apparentement* system, the lists of a collection of minority groups are presented to the voters as separate, but in the assigning of the seats obtained the lists are considered all together, as if there were just one. This system, used in Switzerland, Israel, and Holland, allows minority groups that may not be identical ideologically to join forces so they can gain some political representation. The system does not force these different parties or movements to become one single party, but it does allow them to pool their strengths during electoral contests. These and other mechanisms should be considered in any serious attempt to address the concerns of minority movements that electoral reform could close off avenues for nontraditional political expressions.

17. "[W]e feel that in the present state of Colombian politics combining the single list with the preference vote will not achieve the proposed objectives. Quite the contrary. On the pretext of renovating the parties this measure will allow them to continue harboring the vices they have endeavored to combat," emphasize Senators Viviane Morales and Héctor Eli Rojas in their minority report on proposed Constitutional Amendment 088 of 1998, 19.

18. Despite the risks mentioned, some authors have concluded that the preferential vote (approved in the constitutional reform of 2003) is the only viable option. Given the long tradition of fragmentation in the Colombian party system, it was not easy to engineer an overnight overhaul from extreme atomization to a high level of party control and organization. According to Shugart and others, the preferential vote provided a Solomonic solution: on the one hand, the single list, the threshold, and the D'Hondt formula should be incentives for party regrouping; on the other, however, the preferential vote allowed for some continuation of the party's internal currents and factions. The optimum is not always compatible with the possible.

19. And he goes on: "In Jamaica and Panama, just as in Chile and Argentina, the reinvention of these old parties was accompanied by changes in their programs. A change in party program endures only when it is accompanied by a deepening of internal party life and democratization of procedures." Domínguez's examples include parties on the left and on the right: the Christian Democrats and the Socialists in Chile, the People's National Party in Jamaica, and the Democratic Revolutionary Party (PRD) in Panama.

20. Until 1990, according to a well-established tradition the candidate was chosen at a closed gathering, the so-called Liberal Convention, which brought together only politicians and a few other delegates here and there representing unions and guilds, women, and students. In 1998, for the first time, the Conservative candidate was chosen through a new mechanism, namely a decentralized convention, with meetings held simultaneously in all thirty-three departments of the country. Out of a total of 3,950 votes, Andrés Pastrana received 62.4 percent and Juan Camilo Restrepo, 37.4 percent (*El Tiempo*, February 21, 1998, 2A). In turn, during the same year, the candidate of the so-called *tercería* or "third party" was selected in a poll, with Noemí Sanín receiving 69.9 percent and Antanas Mockus, 25.5 percent (*El Tiempo*, April 2, 1998, 3A). In spite of the novelty of these two approaches, in our opinion neither carries the weight of the popular referendum.

21. In this respect, the 1998 return to naming the Liberal candidate through a closed convention constituted a regression, given the potential for democracy inherent in the popular referendum.

22. *El Tiempo*, March 8, 1990.

23. The absence of any means to identify those belonging to the Liberal Party kept that organization from promoting "closed primaries" in which only its members could vote. There is no doubt that so-called "open primaries" are not the ideal, mainly because of the distortions introduced when voters of any political tendency can participate in choosing a party's candidate. Although the United States has both "closed primaries" (in which only those registered as members of a party can vote) and "open primaries" (in which any voter can participate), any distortion stemming from the latter system is limited since (with the exception of two or three states) the two parties, Republican and Democratic, must hold their primaries on the same day. In this respect,

the Liberal Party's "internal referendum" bears only a faint resemblance to U.S. primaries (Lawson 1997).

24. The potential for promoting "a programmatic candidacy" was frustrated, this time, since three tendencies (the sector that styled itself "neoliberal," the "social democrats," and the "moderate center") came into conflict at the party's Ideological Convention.

25. In that book, *Democracias en las sociedades plurales* (1989; originally published in 1977), Lijphart defended "consociational democracy" as the most suitable and stable model for plural societies. Several years later, he earnestly defended government by consensus for democracies fraught with conflict: "Our analysis will suggest that majority democracy is particularly suited to homogeneous societies and that it works best in such environments, while democracy by consensus is more suitable for plural societies" (Lijphart 1987: 21).

26. See García Pelayo (1986). In particular, see Portugal's Act 59 of 1997, "Statute on the Right to Opposition," and the former German Democratic Republic's February 15 law on political parties.

27. The 1991 Constitution mentions the need to enact a statute on the political opposition.

28. On the basis of the commission's recommendations, Horacio Serpa Uribe, interior minister at the time, presented to the House of Representatives Proposed Statute 118 of 1995, "Which sets out a statute on the opposition." It is interesting to note that during the whole FN period, the attorney general and the comptroller general, both named by Congress in those days, belonged to the party opposing that of the incumbent president (Hartlyn 1993: 123).

29. The recent approval (in December 2004) of a new constitutional reform measure, this time allowing for a one-time reelection of the president, has made the need for an opposition statute even more urgent. In light of this change, the opposition needs even further reassurance that it will be able to count on the guarantees to run in a fair election in 2006 and that President Uribe's government will not use the power of office unduly to ensure his own reelection.

30. For a comparative analysis of this change, see Bejarano (2004).

31. Act 5 of 1992, "regulating Congress, both Senate and House of Representatives."

32. See also Congreso Visible's Web page: http://cvisible.uniandes.edu.co.

33. The manuals on Mexican and Spanish parliamentary law by Berlín Valenzuela and Fernando Santaolalla are required reading on the subject. According to the International Consultancy Report, the bench formula is an essential one, enabling Congress to respond to voter preferences and to form cohesive and stable parliamentary groups, and allowing subjects and interests of national scope to become relevant to the political agenda.

34. Congress is currently discussing a bill that would create these parliamentary benches. This would be an excellent complement to the reforms introduced in 2003, all of which were intended to foster the reorganization of the party system in Colombia.

35. The authors of the Consultancy Report add several recommendations for benches: (1) members of Congress who have figured in the same political plan should not be able to sign up for different groups (this should help discourage "turncoat" behavior); (2) each bench should have rules to guarantee internal democratic participation and to keep discipline among its members, with sanctions imposed on those failing to comply with the group's democratically determined guidelines; a bench may, however, allow members to vote as they choose in certain instances, especially on questions involving morality.

36. "[A] country turning out nine hundred general laws annually cannot be fertile ground for the growth of juridical security," points out Juan Camilo Restrepo in his *El Tiempo* column, November 12, 1995.

37. A proposed constitutional amendment, Amendment 06 of 2000, drafted by a group of Liberal, Conservative, and independent legislators, would establish a privately run legal entity to administer Congress, its members to be named by the Attorney General's Office, the Comptroller's Office, the president of the republic, and the speakers of both congressional houses.

38. In Colombia in 1991, following an exposé in the press on the alarming state of the Library of Congress, the Senate Steering Committee took drastic action to remedy the disorder in which it found the library, transferring the collection to the National Archive. Although the library contained bibliographic treasures as well as vital historical and legislative documents, books and archives were found to be in a state of thorough disorder and neglect. While the move ended the criminal negligence with which the library had been run and abolished a phantom payroll of 250 workers, it did not solve the very serious problem of how to guarantee the flow of information that a legislature needs to conduct its business.

39. *El Tiempo*, August 25, 2000. Rocío Peña, adviser to independent Senator Rafael Orduz, comments that "every six months you see fifty different faces. It's the third one on what's-his-name's list, the fifth from what's-his-face's, and so they get a chance to pass some laws for their regions and then they can collect a pension as retired legislators" (Bejarano et al. 2001: 262).

40. It states: "No popularly elected position to a public body may have a replacement. Permanent vacancies will be filled by unelected candidates on the same list, in successive and descending order of registration."

41. In fact, according to Felipe Botero's careful study (1998), in the last three elections (1991, 1994, and 1998) on the average, about 66.72 percent of a winning senator's vote would come from one department.

42. Eduardo Posada Carbó, "De la financiación de campañas: Amigos de la Casa Blanca," *El Tiempo*, March 5, 1997, 5A.

43. At the very least, some serious consideration should be given to the possibility of reducing the electoral schedule to two main contests: one for national offices (president and Congress) and another for regional and local races (governors, deputies, mayors, and council members).

44. Valenzuela et al. (1999) recommend putting a cap on private contributions: for example, 5 percent of the total that a campaign is allowed to spend. They reason that private financing leads parties to encourage members to take responsibility for the organization's funding (through devices such as quotas for affiliated groups), which deepens a sense of belonging.

45. According to art. 264 of the 1991 Constitution, "The National Electoral Council shall be composed of the number of members determined by law, which must be no fewer than seven. They shall be elected by the Council of State, for a period of four years, from a nominating list drawn up by legally recognized political parties and movements. The council shall reflect the political composition of the Congress. Its members shall have the same qualifications the constitution requires for judges of the Supreme Court of Justice and shall not be re-electable."

46. United Nations, "Convention on the Elimination of All Forms of Discrimination against Women," 1979, retrieved February 23, 2006, from www.unhchr.ch/html/menu3/b/e1cedaw.htm.

47. The term comes from the U.S. Congress's practice of dividing electoral districts in an underhanded way, in an attempt to benefit a particular political sector.

References

Alvarez, Angel. 1995. "Competencia política, igualdad de oportunidades y financiación de los partidos." In *Reforma de los partidos políticos: Financiamiento y democracia.* Caracas: Fundación Konrad Adenauer/COPRE.

Archer, Ronald. 1995. "Party Strength and Weakness in Colombia's Besieged Democracy." In *Building Democratic Institutions: Party Systems in Latin America,* ed. Scott Mainwaring and Timothy Scully. Stanford: Stanford University Press.

Bejarano, Ana María. 2004. "Actors, Coalitions and Institutional Choice: Explaining the Sources of Presidential Power in Colombia and Venezuela." Paper presented at the annual meeting of the Canadian Association of Latin American and Caribbean Studies (CALACS), Guelph, October 28–31.

Bejarano, Ana María, et al. 2001. "Que hace funcionar al Congreso? Una aproximación inicial a las fallas y los aciertos de la institución legislativa?" Working paper, Estudios Ocasionales del CIJUS, Facultad de Derecho, Universidad de los Andes, Bogotá.

Bejarano, Ana María, and Eduardo Pizarro. 2005. "From 'Restricted' to 'Besieged': The Changing Nature of the Limits to Democracy in Colombia." In *The Third Wave of Democratization in Latin America: Advances and Setbacks*, ed. Frances Hagopian and Scott Mainwaring, 235–60. Cambridge: Cambridge University Press.

Botero, Felipe. 1998. "El Senado que nunca fue: La circunscripción nacional después de tres elecciones." In *Elecciones y democracia en Colombia, 1997–1998*, ed. Ana María Bejarano and Andrés Dávila. Bogotá: Tercer Mundo-Departamento de Ciencia Política Uniandes-Veeduría Ciudadana a la Elección Presidencial.

De Roux, Carlos Vicente. 2000. "La reforma política, la cifra repartidora y las fuerzas independientes." *Revista Foro* (Bogotá), no. 39.

Domínguez, Jorge. 1995. "Los desafíos de los partidos políticos en América Latina y el Caribe." Paper presented at the Conference on Political Parties in Latin America and the Caribbean organized by United Nations Development Program and the Friedrich Ebert Foundation, Cartagena.

García Pelayo, Manuel. 1986. *El estado de partidos*. Madrid: Alianza Editorial.

González-Varas, Santiago. 1995. *La financiación de los partidos políticos*. Madrid: Editorial Dykinson.

Hartlyn, Jonathan. 1993. *La política del régimen de coalición: La experiencia del Frente Nacional en Colombia*. Bogotá: Tercer Mundo Editores-CEI-Ediciones Uniandes.

Lawson, Kay. 1997. "Les désavantages des primaires américaines." In *La sélection des candidats présidentiels*, ed. Claude Emeri and Jean-Luc Parodi. París: Presse de la FNSP.

Lijphart, Arend. 1987. *Las democracias contemporáneas: Un estudio comparativo*. Barcelona: Editorial Ariel.

———. 1989. *Democracias en las sociedades plurales: Investigación comparativa*. Buenos Aires: Grupo Editor Latinoamericano. (Orig. pub. 1977.)

———. 1994. *Electoral Systems and Party Systems: A Study of Twenty-seven Democracies, 1945–1990*. Oxford: Oxford University Press.

Londoño, Juan Fernando. 1999. "Sistema de partidos y régimen electoral: La gobernabilidad contra la democracia en la propuesta de reforma política." *Pensamiento Jurídico* (Bogotá), no. 11.

Mainwaring, Scott, and Matthew Shugart, eds. 1997. *Presidentialism and Democracy in Latin America*. Cambridge: Cambridge University Press.

Pérez, Jesús. 1987. *Gobierno y oposición: Elementos para una reforma del Estado*. Bogotá: Pontificia Universidad Javeriana.

Pizarro, Eduardo. 2001. "La atomización partidista en Colombia: El fenómeno de las micro-empresas electorales." Working Paper 292, Kellogg Institute for International Studies, University of Notre Dame.

Roland, Gerardo, and Juan Gonzalo Zapata. 2000. "Colombia's Electoral and Party System: Proposals for Reforms." Documentos de Trabajo 16, FEDESARROLLO, Bogotá.

Roll, David. 1999. "Ingeniería institucional y dinámica del cambio político en Colombia." *Pensamiento Jurídico* (Bogotá), no. 11.

Sartori, Giovanni. 1976. *Partidos y sistemas de partidos.* Madrid: Alianza Editorial.

Shugart, Matthew Soberg, and Scott Mainwaring. 1997. "Presidentialism and Democracy in Latin America: Rethinking the Terms of the Debate." In *Presidentialism and Democracy in Latin America,* ed. Scott Mainwaring and Matthew Soberg Shugart, 12–54. Cambridge: Cambridge University Press.

Ungar, Elizabeth, and Inés Elvira Andrade. 1995. "El Congreso en la nueva realidad: ¿Modernización o retroceso?" In *En busca de la estabilidad perdida: Actores políticos y sociales en los años noventa,* ed. Francisco Leal. Bogota: Instituto de Estudios Políticos y Relaciones Internacionales/Tercer Mundo Editores.

Valenzuela, Arturo, Joseph Colomer, Arend Lijphart, and Matthew Shugart. 1999. "Sobre la reforma política en Colombia: Informe de la Consultoría Internacional." In *Reforma política: Un propósito de nación. Memorias,* ed. Ministerio del Interior, 209–311. Serie Documentos 17. Bogotá: Ministerio del Interior.

Deepening Democracy by Renovating Political Practices

The Struggle for Electoral Reform in Colombia

Matthew Søberg Shugart, Erika Moreno, and Luis E. Fajardo

How, in the midst of ongoing war and widespread shortcomings in its democracy, did Colombia come to adopt far-reaching electoral reform? In this chapter Shugart, Moreno, and Fajardo explain the change and contrast it with other, failed attempts. They begin with an analysis in comparative perspective of the vices of the former electoral system—deficiencies that had been generating a cry for reform. They find the system an extreme example of arrangements that reward fragmentation and personalization of the electoral arena, deemphasizing issues and programmatic campaigns. They use concrete examples to illustrate the problems the former law generated and to analyze the motivations of the principal actors in the back-and-forth movements on reform. Their analysis of the potential benefits of reform is similarly grounded in theory and illuminated by empirical references. They find that established political actors are reluctant to take on the very features of the law that are most objectionable because they owe their own success to their ability to exploit these features. But the pressure for reform itself is sufficiently strong that some of these actors have sometimes concluded that they must change or pay the price, even though they may dislike

the substance of the change that is being forced upon them. The authors con-
clude by assessing the effects of the new system on political competition and de-
mocracy in Colombia.

Colombia is experiencing a profound social and political crisis. Guerrilla
armies control vast rural territory, antiguerrilla paramilitaries commit serious human rights violations with official complicity often alleged, and large
numbers of Colombians have been displaced internally by the conflict. The
corrupting influence of the drug trade permeates business and government.
The country's crisis has garnered increasing international attention, including a large package of U.S. aid to Colombian security forces as part of the
"war on drugs." While a few critics in the American media and U.S. Congress have decried a possible slide into "another Vietnam," supporters of the
program counter, correctly, that Colombia (unlike South Vietnam in the
1960s) is a functioning electoral democracy.[1] In the midst of all of this, Colombian political leaders have sought to transform political practices by instituting fundamental changes in how the nation conducts its elections. A
substantial portion of informed political opinion in Colombia—inside and
outside government—came to recognize serious flaws in the former electoral system. While these flaws are not themselves the cause of the larger
crisis, reform has been motivated by a desire to bring about "a renovation of
[Colombia's] political customs and the 'initial quota' for the construction
of a plan for a durable peace."[2] In June 2003, after repeated failures, the Colombian Congress finally passed a major electoral reform. The passage of
the reform occurred in the shadows of a comprehensive and complex referendum on political reform promoted by President Alvaro Uribe. As we
detail below, the threat of the referendum—which contained a less fundamental reform of the electoral system but significant reforms in other areas
that many in Congress feared—was critical to motivating Congress to approve a reform of its own. While the referendum was defeated in October
2003, on the same weekend of voting the new electoral system was used for
the first time in subnational elections. Thus Colombia has entered a phase
in which it is making a transition to new political institutions. The passage
of reform is an encouraging sign of the resilience of Colombian democracy,
even while under siege.

   The electoral system of Colombia up through 2002 was an unusual system in which most political parties presented multiple lists of candidates,
but there was no pooling of the votes won by any of a party's various lists.
Most Latin American and European countries use some form of party-list

system, in which legislative seats are allocated in multiseat districts according to votes cast for lists of candidates submitted by political parties. Typically each party may present only one list per district and parties receive
seats proportionate to their votes. Yet in Colombia, each party presented
numerous lists in each district and nearly every legislator would be the only
candidate elected off his or her respective list. Each list stood alone in the allocation process, effectively placing every candidate in zero-sum competition with every other and resulting in no necessary connection between a
party's vote and seat shares.[3] As we shall see, this electoral system undermined party unity and contributed to governance problems. While the electoral system is only one factor affecting the political process, it is one of the
most important factors because it determines how the balance of legislative
authority is divided among competing political forces. The reform passed
by Congress[4] in 2003 requires that each party present a single list in each
electoral district. Seats now will be allocated to parties in proportion to
their votes. *The new system is thus a radical departure from the old one;* in
fact, it is one of the most fundamental reforms of an electoral system carried
out anywhere in the world in the last decade or so.[5] Whereas the old system
undermined the cohesiveness of political parties and provided no guarantee that parties' shares of legislative authority would reflect their collective
voting strength, the new one redresses both of these shortcomings.

Our goal in this chapter is to explain the reform and consider its prospects for improving the widely recognized flaws of Colombia's democracy.
We propose a framework for understanding reform that focuses on both
"inherent" and "contingent" factors. Inherent factors concern the flaws of
the old system, while contingent factors consider actors' interests and calculations that go into the process of approving or rejecting change. We place
special emphasis on the unusual outcome of the 2002 congressional and
presidential elections, which, we argue, broke the long-standing logjam of
the reform process by changing congressional party leaders' calculus of the
costs and benefits of reform.

A Framework for Understanding Reform

In explaining events such as electoral reform, but also social revolutions, accidents, epidemics, and many others, causes may be broken down into *contingent* and *inherent* factors (Eckstein 1980). Explanations of an event based

on contingencies focus their attention on "aberrant" factors that trigger an event; explanations based on inherencies focus on preexisting conditions. For example, a given airplane crash may be explained as a result of pilot error in manipulating controls (an aberrant or contingent factor) or a design flaw in the airplane's control system itself (a preexisting, and thus inherent, factor). Similarly, certain types of electoral systems inherently produce pressures for reform because they are associated with a style of politics that breeds scandal and a widespread perception that the system is "broken." Yet for reform actually to occur, there must be some triggering event—a contingency—that either leads politicians to vote to change the rules under which they are elected or causes them to lose control over the selection of rules. Other contingencies may prevent reform from occurring even when inherent conditions suggest reform would be likely.

There are two distinct classes of contingencies (Reed and Thies 2001; Shugart and Wattenberg 2001a). *Outcome-contingent* factors spur incumbents to vote for reform if they believe they will be better off under new rules: that is, if they prefer the anticipated outcome of the new rules. *Act-contingent* reasons, on the other hand, are present when politicians do not actually prefer the proposed new system but expect to benefit from the act of voting for reform, for instance when public pressure for reform is so strong that politicians feel compelled to vote for it even if they sincerely prefer the existing system. The difficulty with a reform motivated primarily by act contingencies is that shifts in actors' short-term calculations of the consequences of their public statements and actions for or against the reform can undermine reform just as much as they can impel it toward passage.

In this chapter we situate the current Colombian electoral and party institutions within a comparative context, noting that Colombia's old system lay at the extreme "personalistic" end of a continuum between personalistic and "party-centered" elections. As a personalistic system, Colombia has been characterized by notoriously weak and disorganized parties, low issue content of legislative electoral campaigns, and high levels of intraparty competition, all of which are factors inherently associated with scandal and political ineffectiveness (Reed 1994).

After reviewing the inherent factors, we turn our attention to contingencies. We consider the motivations for members of Congress to support reforms, as well as reasons why the reform failed in several previous attempts. Although there is a long history of political reform proposals in Colombia aimed in various ways at strengthening the capacity of political parties to engage in collective action (Sarabia Better 2003), the first official proposal to adopt a system in which each party would be required to present a single list was that of President Andrés Pastrana, elected in 1998. Because—as we shall argue in this chapter—the adoption of a party-list system is crucial to redressing Colombia's extreme political fragmentation, we pick up the story of reform with the Pastrana administration and follow it through to its passage under Pastrana's successor, Alvaro Uribe, elected in 2002. Each of these presidents, despite differences on other issues (notably how to handle the wars), had made electoral reform a part of his campaign platform prior to election. They agreed broadly on both goals (reducing fragmentation) and tactics (threatening Congress with a referendum and even the specter of dissolution if it did not go along).

We note that act-contingent motivations appeared powerful in 1998–2000 but waned thereafter. When public dissatisfaction with politicians is especially high, it is politically dangerous for any ambitious politician to be seen as antireform. However, outcome-contingent motivations presented significant obstacles to reform prior to 2002. Many politicians who might favor reform (even if only for act-contingent reasons) diverged in their preferences over specific provisions that might have harmed their political careers. The key to successful passage of the reform in 2003 lies in the results of the 2002 elections. The victory of an independent, Uribe, with enormous popularity reinvigorated the threat to Congress of being sidelined by a president prepared to go over their heads (thereby reinforcing reform-enabling act contingencies). In the congressional elections of 2002, the number of legislators elected under the "official" labels of the Liberal and Conservative parties was drastically reduced. This event altered the traditional party leaders' calculations of the advantages and disadvantages of reform (changing their outcome-contingent motivations). We develop this argument below, but first we need to set the stage by considering the inherent flaws of the old system, which are what put reform on the agenda in the first place.

Inherent Factors: Problems and Institutional Solutions

The Colombian electoral system in place before the reform of 2003 was an extreme example of a *personalistic* electoral system. That is, it emphasized campaigning for office based on personal appeals by individual candidates far more than the collective appeal of a party program. Personalistic systems inherently produce highly particularistic campaigning—candidates promising relatively small and locally, even individually, targetable benefits to motivate voters—and reduce the capacity of a political system to address national policy challenges. These inherent flaws have been explicitly recognized by the promoters of reform. President Pastrana himself, in a national address on April 5, 2000, in which he unveiled his demand that Congress permit a referendum on the reform proposal, said: "Our political system . . . is marked by a crisis of representation wherein citizens do not recognize their elected officials as the spokesmen of collective interests. Instead, these officials are generally identified as the purveyors of local favors and nothing else."[6] We now review Colombian prereform institutions and the problems associated with them in detail.

Colombian Prereform Electoral Institutions in Comparative Perspective

Electoral formulas may be arrayed on a continuum regarding the degree to which they encourage candidates for legislative office to cultivate either a *party reputation* or a *personal reputation*. A formula that emphasizes party reputation tends to be conducive to promoting a politics based upon strong parties representing the collective interests of groups of citizens. At least that is the case if parties themselves are internally vibrant, by which we mean that democratic procedures exist for selecting leaders and candidates and for debating and developing party policy platforms. This is the ideal that Colombian reformers appear to have in mind. For instance, the official explanation of the goals of the reform includes "stimulating political debate between the different movements and parties . . . centered around proposals clearly identified by the electorate."[7] While all of the various proposals for reform have agreed on the need to enhance the value of party reputation in legislative campaigns, one of the sticking points was over just how far to push this value.

Electoral systems that generate an extreme incentive to cultivate a personal vote tend to be associated with weak parties to the extent that candidates win or lose elections almost entirely on their own entrepreneurial efforts, with the party reputation contributing little. Candidates engage in personal-vote seeking by all manner of activities, from petty things like attending important community and family functions for supporters and distributing bottles of *aguardiente* to lobbying for exemptions from government regulations and taxes for campaign contributors and using their ties to higher-ups in the party or administration to ensure that job-creating factories, mines, or government offices are established in their supporters' neighborhoods. Strong incentives to cultivate a personal vote explain the phenomenon of what in the Colombian political lexicon have come to be called *microempresas*—legislative candidates setting up microbusinesses to finance their own campaigns and mobilize votes independently of the parties under whose labels they run. We now turn to a consideration of different types of electoral system and why the specific features of electoral rules in Colombia have created a highly personalistic system.

Types of Electoral Systems and the Colombian Case

Here we situate the prereform Colombian electoral system within a typology that has been identified in the literature on electoral systems in order to understand the incentives of the old system and how the new system can be expected to alter those incentives. Colombia long employed a proportional representation (PR) formula, as do nearly all Latin American countries. A PR formula allocates seats to lists of candidates in such a way as to make the share of seats won by each list roughly proportional to the share of votes won (in any given multiseat district). This contrasts with the most common alternative to PR, which is the family of plurality/majority systems—usually in single-seat districts, although there are also variants of plurality for multiseat districts. There are several different formulas for achieving PR, but ironically one of them actually contains an element of (multiseat) plurality. This was the formula used in Colombia, and the electoral system in Colombia, while nominally a form of PR, actually functioned like a multiseat plurality system because of the tendency of parties to present numerous "personal" lists rather than a single party list.

Colombia's prereform electoral formula is known as the *simple quota and largest remainders* (SQLR).[8] Under this formula, a given list of candidates wins one or more seats according to the number of quotas *(cocientes)* its vote total contains. The "simple" quota, *SQ*, is indeed simple to calculate: $SQ = V/M$, where V stands for the votes cast in a given district and M stands for district magnitude (the number of seats to be allocated in that district). However, usually the various lists competing in the district do not combine for sufficient quotas to allocate all available seats. In that case, any seats remaining to be allocated after the distribution of quota seats are awarded to the lists with the largest remainders *(mayores residuos)*—that is, their original votes minus votes used up via quotas. This is the plurality element of the system because the remainder seats are awarded, one per list, in descending order, starting with the list with the largest number of remaining votes and continuing until all seats are filled.

Table 7.1 shows the application of the SQLR formula to four hypothetical parties, as identified in the first column. In the second column are the votes for each party, out of a total of 1,000. With nine seats being allocated, the quota (rounded down) is 111 votes. Party A has the votes for four seats by quota, Party B for two, Party C for one, and Party D does not win a quota seat. The fourth column shows each party's remaining votes after the subtraction of the votes "spent" to win the seats by quota. For instance, Party A has spent 444 votes in winning its four seats thus far, leaving it with a remainder of six votes. We can see that only seven of the nine seats have been allocated so far. The remaining two seats will be allocated to the two lists with the most remaining votes, in descending order. The first remaining seat goes to Party B, with its remainder of 78 votes, and the second remainder seat goes to Party D, with its remainder of 75 votes. The last column shows the final allocation of seats to parties, summing the quota seats and remainder seats. The result is approximately proportional, but, with only 44.4 percent of the seats Party A is slightly underrepresented, while Party D, with 7.5 percent of the votes but 11.1 percent of the seats, is considerably overrepresented. While this is only one hypothetical example, SQLR often favors smaller lists, just as demonstrated in the table, and, as we shall see below, this tendency—*permissiveness* to small lists—is very significant in the Colombian case.

The permissiveness of SQLR means that if, for whatever reason, a party opts not to emphasize a unified party label and instead runs multiple lists, it can actually *gain additional seats by having several small lists instead of one large one.* This will be shown with an actual example from Colombia below. When many small lists are running, it is likely that no lists will win sufficient votes to elect more than one candidate, and in this case the system is actually what is called *single nontransferable vote* (SNTV), which is a multiseat plurality formula. Under SNTV, the winners are simply the M candidates with the highest vote totals, which is exactly how SQLR treats lists in the remainder allocation stage. In other words, Colombia's electoral system functions as the personalistic SNTV instead of the more party-centered list PR because parties run multiple lists and few lists win enough votes to elect more than one candidate. Proportional representation assumes that each list represents a distinct party, so that when votes are allocated among lists they are also being allocated among parties. In Colombia, on the other hand, the major parties have not presented *party* lists per se but rather multiple *personal* lists. Under a personal-list system, each list is identified on the ballot not only by the name of a party or movement but also by the name—and, since 1990, the photo—of the candidate who heads the list. Thus the head of each list has the incentive and opportunity to cultivate his own personal vote, and not to emphasize the attributes of his party, because voters are voting not for party lists but for personal lists. The most fundamental aspect of the 2003 reform act is that it changes the system to a more conventional party-list form of PR.

Because the tendency of SQLR to favor small lists rewards a party for having multiple lists, all the various proposals for reform called for abolishing this formula in favor of an alternative known as d'Hondt divisors or the *cifra repartidora*, which we explain below. First, however, we demonstrate how SQLR can devolve into SNTV, using an actual Colombian example.

Table 7.1
Hypothetical Seat Allocation under Simple Quota and Largest Remainders

District magnitude, $M = 9$
Total valid votes, $V = 1,000$
Quota, $q = V/M = 111$

List	Votes by List, v_1	Number of Seats Won by Quota, s_q	Remainder, $r = v_1 - s_q q$	Number of Seats Won
Party A	450	4	6	4
Party B	300	2	78*	3
Party C	175	1	64	1
Party D	75	0	75**	1
Total	1,000	7	—	9

*Largest remainder, wins first remaining seat.
**Second largest remainder, wins second remaining seat.

Table 7.2 shows the actual votes and seats won by the various lists that competed for seats in the House of Representatives in the department of Huila in 1990. The Liberals ran three lists, the Conservatives two, and a third party one. The quota for winning a seat was 36,501 votes (obtained by dividing the total number of valid votes by the magnitude, which was 5). The first step is to assign seats to any lists that have obtained a quota of votes. The only such list is that of Cabrera, a Conservative. After any quota seats have been assigned, the votes spent on the quotas are subtracted from each list's votes. In Cabrera's case, that leaves him with a remainder of 2,011 votes. For each other list, its remainder is equivalent to its original vote total because none has spent a quota's worth of votes. Then any remaining seats are allocated, one per list, to the lists with the largest remainders, in descending order. Because one seat was allocated by quota, four seats remain, and they go to each of the three Liberal lists and a second Conservative list.

Now suppose, as is also shown in table 7.2, that the Liberal and Conservative parties each had run a single list. In this case, the Liberals would win two seats by quota, and the Conservatives one. The Liberal vote total would now be reduced by the subtraction of two quotas' worth of votes, leaving it with a remainder of 18,776. Two seats would remain to go to the lists with the largest remainders; because both the Conservatives and the third-party MNC would have remainders larger than 18,776, each would get a remainder seat and the Liberals would not. Thus, with the same vote totals, the Liberals would win only two seats when running a single list, whereas they won three seats by dividing their vote among three separate lists.[9] Table 7.2 represents only one example in one district, but its outcome is typical of Colombian elections under the personal-list/SNTV system. It shows that by treating the system as if it were SNTV (i.e., running multiple lists) instead of party-list PR, the largest party was able to win one more seat than if it had run a single list. This practice of multiple lists in Colombia has come to be called *operación avispa*, conjuring up an image of a swarm of "wasps" in the form of separate lists that target blocs of voters throughout the district.

The new electoral system enacted by Congress, as well as that proposed in Uribe's (defeated) referendum of 2003, both call for the abolition of SQLR and its replacement by the d'Hondt formula. The bill passed by Congress did not require a popular vote for it to take effect, so the d'Hondt formula was implemented for the subnational assembly elections that took place the same weekend as the referendum. The new law was used in congressional elections for the first time in March 2006. Under d'Hondt successive whole

Table 7.2
An Example of How the Colombian Electoral System Works: Actual and Hypothetical Results from the District of Huila in 1990

District magnitude, $M = 5$
Total valid votes, $V = 182{,}507$
Quota, $q = V/M = 36{,}501$

Party and Name of Candidate at Head of Each List	Actual Allocation, Multiple Personal Lists				Hypothetical Allocation, Single-Party Lists			
	Votes by List, v_1	Number of Seats Won by Quota s_q	Remainder $r = v_1 - s_q q$ (Order of Allocation of Remainder Seats)	Number of Seats Won by List	Votes by List, v_1	Number of Seats Won by Quota, s_q	Remainder $r = v_1 - s_q q$ (Order of Allocation of Remainder Seats)	Number of Seats Won by List
Liberal					91,778	2	18,776	2
Cuenca	34,840	—	34,840 (1)	1				
Triana	33,996	—	33,996 (2)	1				
Mosquera	22,942	—	22,942 (4)	1				
Conservative					65,257	1	28,756 (1)	2
Cabrera	38,512	1	2,011	1				
Caicedo	26,745	—	26,745 (3)	1				
MNC	20,239	—	20,239	0	20,239	0	20,239 (2)	1
Others	5,233	—	—	0	5,233	—	—	—

numbers (1, 2, 3, 4, . . .) are used as a series of divisors. Seats are allocated to the resulting quotients, in descending order. *A critical benefit of d'Hondt is that no party can ever obtain more seats by splitting into multiple lists than it could by running a single list.* Of common proportional electoral systems, d'Hondt is the only one with this feature. Consider the example in table 7.3, which replicates the vote distribution in Huila in 1990 from table 7.2. The Liberals would have won three seats and the Conservatives two. This happens to be the same outcome as under the actual (SQLR) allocation, but here it is obtained by *presenting a unified front to the electorate,* while under the quota-and-remainders system the party could obtain three seats only by splitting into three *avispas* that would seek votes independently. This is a very important point because d'Hondt is sometimes criticized for supposedly favoring large parties. Yet this is so only when compared to SQLR applied to *unified* parties, not when compared to the de facto SNTV system Colombia currently has.[10] In fact, d'Hondt allocation is unlikely to be any more favorable to the largest party than the former system. Indeed, because smaller political forces are likely to cohere more given the incentives of d'Hondt, the proposed system is likely actually to be less favorable to the largest parties than the former system. An outcome like that of the 1994 Senate election, in which the Liberals won 56 percent of the seats on about 53 percent of the votes while various nontraditional forces won only

Table 7.3
An Example of Allocation by d'Hondt (*cifra repartidora*)

District magnitude, $M = 5$
Total valid votes, $V = 182,507$

| Party | Votes | *Quotient Resulting from Successive Divisors* | | |
		2	3	4
Liberal	91,778 (1)	45,880 (3)	30,592.7 (5)	22,944.5
Conservative	65,257 (2)	32,628.5 (4)	21,752.3	
MNC	20,239			
Others	5,233			

Note: Numbers in parentheses indicate seats, in order allocated.

15 percent of the seats on around 20 percent of the vote, is virtually inconceivable under d'Hondt.

The reason a party does not gain from splitting into multiple lists under d'Hondt can be seen by the relative cost of each seat won by each party under d'Hondt versus the same relationship under the SQLR system with multiple personal lists. In the d'Hondt example shown in table 7.3, each seat won by the Liberals was obtained at a cost of 30,592.7 votes (91,778 votes for the party divided by the three seats it won). Each seat won by the Conservatives cost 32,628.5 votes. Not only is the number of votes needed to win each seat the same within any given party, but also the ratio of dearest to cheapest seat in the district (i.e., both parties) is only 1.07:1. Contrast this to the example of actual allocation shown in table 7.2: the Liberals' cheapest seat—the last one allocated in the district—cost the party only about two-thirds as many votes as its dearest seat, and the ratio of most costly seat (won by Cabrera) to cheapest (won by Mosquera) was more than 1.5:1.

Under SQLR, then, a party can win additional seats by splitting into lists that seek to win via remainders instead of more costly quotas. Under d'Hondt, each seat costs a party the same amount, and running more than one list would reduce all its quotients when its votes were divided by the successive divisors, thereby threatening it with a reduced seat allocation. That d'Hondt never permits a party to gain additional representation by splitting into multiple lists means that just adopting d'Hondt (without any other changes, including the legal limit of one list per party) would encourage a substantial increase in the importance of parties over individual politicians in Colombian political competition. We now turn to the problems engendered by the personalism of the former system in the broader political process.

Forms of PR, SNTV, and Degrees of Personalism

As noted above, a PR system allocates votes to lists of candidates, using a formula such as SQLR or d'Hondt. In typical PR systems, each party presents a single list of candidates, such that allocation to lists is the same thing as allocation to parties. In Colombia, however, the multiple lists rendered the system effectively SNTV, which is not a PR system at all but rather a multiseat plurality system. If voters were presented with a single list of candidates in each party—as encouraged by d'Hondt allocation and actually required by the law passed in 2003—the value of party labels would stand to be enhanced. Under SNTV, on the other hand, the value of personal reputation is more important to candidates than the reputation of their parties because the electoral prospects of each candidate, heading his or her own personal list, depend on votes cast for him or her personally.

We consider now a series of factors that affect the degree of personalism of an electoral system. Several features of an electoral system determine its tendency to promote personal or party reputation seeking (Carey and Shugart 1995). On each of them, Colombia's prereform institutions are located well to the personalistic end of the continuum. First is who controls *ballot access and structure.* Personalism is highest if politicians gain access to the ballot on their own accord and do not require party approval to be a candidate. Party centralization is greater if access to the ballot is centralized in the party leadership, and greater still if the ballot structure permits leaders to rank candidates on the ballot. Second is *pooling* of votes. Personalism is highest when votes for one candidate or subparty list among several running for a given party are not pooled, such that a vote for any one candidate or list is a vote exclusively for that candidate or list. Party centralization is increased if votes for any candidate or list are first pooled within the district at the party level, such that a vote for any candidate or list of the party is first counted as if it were a vote for the party as a whole.[11] A third feature is the *type of vote* cast by voters. Personalism is highest when voters cast subparty votes for specific candidates or factions, while party centralization is enhanced if voters cast only party votes.

A final feature is the *district magnitude,* which means the number of legislators elected from a district. As Carey and Shugart (1995) observed, the effect of magnitude is more complex. Its effect depends on whether there is intraparty competition. If there is intraparty competition (as captured by the *vote* variable), then personalism increases with magnitude. If there is no intraparty competition, then party centralization increases with magnitude. Under rules in which voters cast subparty votes, rising magnitude increases the number of copartisans with whom each individual candidate is competing. Thus the share of his party's vote that a candidate needs to win—we can call this the intraparty constituency—decreases as magnitude increases. When the intraparty constituency is small, campaign strategies directed at wooing a core constituency of personal supporters become both attractive and necessary to fend off multiple copartisan challengers. On the other hand, under systems in which voters vote only for a party, increasing magnitude implies a decreasing effect of any one candidate's efforts on his own electoral prospects. With closed lists, the party's preelection ranking trumps ties to voters in determining which candidates are elected.

Figure 7.1 shows a rough approximation of the degrees of personalism of various allocation formulas for multiseat districts,[12] taking into account all of these variables. The position of any given formula along the vertical axis is impressionistically estimated on the basis of the ordinal scale presented in Carey and Shugart (1995), which combines each formula's scores on *ballot*, *pool*, and *vote*. The horizontal axis represents increasing magnitude, ranging from low (but more than 1) to high (around 100 or more). The higher a given country's electoral system is located on the vertical dimension, the higher the incentive to cultivate a personal vote. The effect of increasing magnitude on the personal-vote incentive—rising in systems that entail intraparty competition but declining in those that do not—is also depicted in the figure.[13] Finally, the figure shows how the former Colombian electoral system, as used in both the House and Senate, compares to other Latin American systems.

We now consider how each of these variables applies to Colombia. Crucial to making Colombia's (prereform) formula SNTV is the *ballot* variable. Parties exercise no effective control over nominations, resulting in a great proliferation of lists bearing the party label, especially in the traditional parties. While a law on parties passed in 1994 formally requires that candidates obtain an endorsement (*aval*) from the "legal representative" of the party, in practice the major parties impose few limits on the *avales* they grant. What this promiscuity in candidate endorsements reveals is that the parties themselves are poorly institutionalized, being primarily assemblages of personalistic politicians. Parties, in general, can be viewed as organizations whose stakeholders—rank-and-file politicians—decide how much authority to delegate to leaders (Cox and McCubbins 1993). In Colombia, politicians have chosen not to institutionalize a rationalization of the endorsement mechanism, presumably out of fear that it could thwart their ambitions to run for office under the name of an established party.[14]

With multiple lists instead of single lists endorsed by each party, the voter must vote for one list among several, thus implying a subparty vote. No votes are pooled (or transferred) across lists. The more lists there are, the smaller the share of the party vote won by each list, and therefore the less likely any of those lists is to elect more than one candidate. Then all seats are filled by the remainders procedure, rendering the system essentially SNTV, as shown in the previous section.

Magnitude in Colombia varies considerably from district to district, with the average in the House of Representatives being only around five,

Figure 7.1
Incentive to Cultivate a Personal Vote under Varying Electoral Systems with
Multiseat Districts

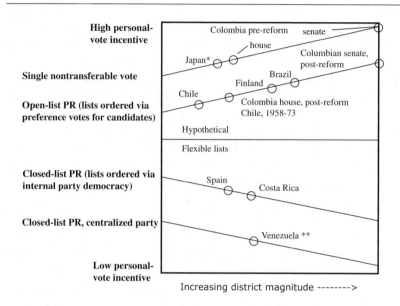

Note: Country labels refer to average district of current electoral system, as of mid-2004, unless
otherwise noted.
*Refers to system in use before electoral reform, implemented in 1996.
**Excluding single-seat districts implemented for about half of all seats in 1993.

while some are larger (up to eighteen). The hundred-seat single national
district for the Senate, on the other hand, places an extremely high value on
personal reputation under the SNTV system, as depicted by its placement in
the far upper right of figure 7.1.

The consideration of these variables allows us to see what various reforms would mean for the level of personalism. An important point is to
recognize that *all of the various proposals debated after 1998 would enhance
the value of party reputation.* This is a very important point, given a major
tug-of-war between Congress and the executive over provisions of the reform bill in 2003, as we review below. During the many rounds of debate on

electoral reform, some commentators actually feared there could be too great a reduction in personalism. For instance, a former director of the Conservative Party worried that the single-list system would generate *camarillas* (Escobar Sierra 1998: 78), vertical networks within parties that compete not for votes but for centrally controlled nominations and list ranks. The *tiranía del bolígrafo,* wherein party leaders gain too much power through their authority to draw up lists,[15] is often decried. In fact, if all Colombia did was move to single lists, the resulting system would be closed-list PR and Colombia would simply be exchanging an extremely personalistic system for an extremely centralized one. In figure 7.1, Colombia's Senate, if elected via closed-list PR, would move from the far upper-right corner to the far lower-right, granting national party leaders potentially more centralized control over members than was ever the case in Venezuela, where excessive centralization of parties was blamed in part for the country's crises in the 1980s and 1990s (Coppedge 1994; Crisp 2000; Martz 1992). Accordingly, most versions of the reform bill have called for internal democratic practices within parties, which would reduce centralization (again, see figure 7.1). A problem, however, is ensuring that internal democracy is institutionalized and subject to effective judicial enforcement.

As a response to fears of centralization or ineffective party democratization within a single list, many versions of the reform bill called for preference votes. Under a preference-vote system, voters are able to vote for one (or sometimes more than one) candidate within the list of their choice. Seats are still allocated first to parties according to the votes received by party lists, but the allocation of each party's seats among its candidates proceeds partly or entirely according to preference votes cast for candidates personally. As noted in figure 7.1, there are many examples of list systems in Latin America, both with and without a preference vote. All of them imply a greater emphasis on party reputation than the SNTV system. Much of the debate in Colombia, as we shall see, has revolved around whether to have a preference vote and, if so, how to use preference votes to allocate seats within lists. The final version that passed Congress in June 2003 actually gives parties the option of employing the preference vote or not. Thus, to take the example of the Senate, with its single nationwide district, some parties could be presenting closed lists (i.e., no preference vote) and hence be located near the bottom right of figure 7.1 in the incentives for their candidates to cultivate a personal reputation. Other parties could present open lists, in which preference votes determine the order of election. The candidates for these parties would still have a very high incentive to cultivate a personal vote; however, even these parties would be able to emphasize their party reputation more than was the case under SNTV, owing to the pooling of all their candidates' votes under the party list.

Figure 7.1 also shows a horizontal line, labeled "hypothetical flexible lists," reflecting the ideal of an electoral formula that splits the difference between open and closed lists. Such lists would be "flexible" in that a party-provided list (as in a closed list) would prevail except in the case of candidates who drew sufficient preference votes to guarantee their election regardless of their rank on the list. We mention this possibility because it was envisioned in some earlier proposals in Colombia. However, in the end, the reform that passed gives each party the option of presenting an open *or* a closed list instead of attempting to combine elements of open *and* closed lists for all parties.

Electoral Personalism and Legislative Particularism

A personalistic electoral system has consequences for the character of campaigns, the structure of the legislature, and the entire policy-making process. In turn, these entrenched patterns of personalistic politics are the greatest obstacles to reforms that would change the character of the political system because current politicians benefit from the current rules. The much-decried clientelism and factionalism of Colombian political parties (Archer 1990; Leal Buitrago and Dávila 1990) is intimately tied to the incentives of SNTV. With the major parties being essentially collections of personal-vote-seeking politicians, candidates who launch their lists invest in their so-called *microempresas,* which function as machines to ensure their personal vote (as noted by Pizarro 1997, 2002). In turn, the multiple endorsements and personal vote for their legislators allows the parties to engage (albeit loosely) in collective action (Gutiérrez Sanín and Dávila 2000), protecting their historically important party labels and maximizing their seats. However, it is important to recognize that this collective action is within the confines of an extremely personalistic electoral system and rarely extends to collective pursuit of a national policy reputation for the party, as would be the case with stronger parties operating within less personalistic electoral rules. We elaborate on these points in this section.

Clientelism as a Means to Organize the Vote

Under SNTV, parties risk committing strategic "errors," in the sense of failing to coordinate their votes effectively across an optimal number of candidates or lists. Indeed, Payne (1968), Latorre (1974), and Hartlyn (1988) all state, in effect, that the error rate is high because a party that presents multiple lists is more likely to displace to other parties seats it could have won. On the other hand, Cox and Shugart (1995) report that the error rate decreased between 1974 and 1990. This suggests that the major parties have adapted to the incentives of the electoral system and can estimate vote totals and distribute votes across their various lists. Table 7.4 suggests that the Liberals and Conservatives have not suffered from running multiple lists—at least before the unusual 2002 elections (which we discuss separately below). It compares the vote and seat percentages for the Liberals, Conservatives, and independents in each of the four Senate and House elections from 1990 to 1998 and provides an "advantage ratio," A, computed by dividing the seat percentage by the vote percentage. $A = 1.00$ indicates full proportionality for the party in question. For the hundred-seat Senate,[16] implemented in 1991, the Liberals' A remained above 1.00 in each election through 1998, although barely in 1998. In the House, on the other hand, A increased in 1998. In fact, the Liberals' seat share in the House remained stable in spite of a fall in its vote share of over three percentage points to less than a majority of votes. It is clear that the party has been capable of using multiple lists efficiently, which implies that its apparatus can mobilize and distribute votes among its many lists. In fact, it was actually slightly underrepresented in 1990, the last election under the departmental districts. This is surprising because the largest party is normally more overrepresented under small district magnitudes, such as before 1991, than in large district magnitudes, such as the hundred-seat Senate district starting in 1991.[17] Evidently the Liberals were advantaged by their ability after 1991 to collect votes for their lists across departmental boundaries,[18] coupled with their ability to distribute their voters across their many lists—we return to this theme below. However, in 2002, the party split and lost its majority status in both houses. We discuss this election separately below, as understanding its unique result is crucial to understanding the passage of political reform.

Table 7.4 shows that the Conservatives also have generally had advantage ratios over 1.00 in the 1990–98 period. However, the "independent" category shows a consistent and severe punishment by the electoral system, with values of A below 0.90 in all cases aside from the first nationwide Senate election. Of course, part of the failure of the nontraditional parties and movements to win closer to proportional representation—and the corresponding bonus for the traditional parties—stems from the fact that the independents are not a single unified force. On the other hand, as we have stressed, neither are the Liberals and Conservatives unified forces; rather, they are collections of lists, each standing alone in the seat allocation process. What the data show is that Liberals and Conservatives have been vastly more successful than the independents at turning the votes received by their respective collections of lists into proportional (or better) seat shares. Partly that is a product of the lack of a common programmatic purpose among the diverse "independent" category, but again, the two traditional parties are likewise hardly noted for programmatic unity. Critically, the impressive ability of the Liberal and Conservatives to translate votes into better-than-proportional representation is a product of the vastly superior access of these parties to the resources—including "pork" and patronage—needed to mobilize votes and allocate them efficiently across multiple lists. And, of course, the traditional parties' long-standing roots in Colombian political history give them a tremendous advantage in managing the distribution of votes across lists. We would add that the clientelism of Colombian politics and the apparent chaos of the process, much noted in the literature, are in fact signs of strategic coordination within a personalistic electoral system. The greater-than-proportional translation of the traditional parties' votes into seats, shown in table 7.4, demonstrates their considerable success at managing the former electoral system. Politicians' success with the system was, of course, a key obstacle to reforming it. In fact, we argue that the dramatic downturn in the traditional parties' electoral fortunes in the 2002 congressional election was a key factor underlying the ultimate passage of electoral reform in Congress.

While most academic works on Colombia[19] suggest that the existence of *microempresas* working for specific candidates indicates the lack of any coordinating mechanism for the party as a whole, in many ways these machines are similar to the personal support networks *(koenkai)* by which Japanese MPs under SNTV ensured that blocs of voters voted for them rather than for copartisans (Baerwald 1986; Hrebenar 1986; Curtis 1988). Colombian politicians long engaged in similar efforts to cultivate personal support networks, including fostering "captive electorates" (Hartlyn 1988: 162).

Organizing the electorate on a clientelistic basis is a means of minimizing parties' strategic errors, as it permits votes to be channeled to specific

Table 7.4

Votes-to-Seats Conversions for Traditional and Nontraditional Political
Forces in Colombia, 1990–1998

Year	Party*	% Votes	% Seats	A**	% Votes	% Seats	A
			Senate			*House of Representatives*	
1990	Liberal	58.6	57.9	0.99	59.2	59.8	1.01
	Conservative	33.2	34.2	1.03	33.3	32.7	0.98
	Independent	8.2	7.9	0.96	7.5	7.5	1.00
1991	Liberal	51.5	56.0	1.09	50.6	54.0	1.07
	Conservative	26.3	24.0	0.91	25.6	26.1	1.02
	Independent	21.9	20.0	0.91	23.7	19.9	0.84
1994	Liberal	52.8	56.0	1.06	52.8	54.7	1.04
	Conservative	27.6	29.0	1.05	26.4	30.4	1.15
	Independent	20.0	15.0	0.75	20.8	14.9	0.72
1998	Liberal	47.3	48.0	1.01	49.4	54.0	1.09
	Conservative	22.5	25.0	1.11	23.6	23.6	1.00
	Independent	30.3	27.0	0.89	27.1	22.4	0.83

Source: Adapted from Gutiérrez Sanín (1998).
*The categories "Liberal" and "Conservative" include various dissident movements within
those larger political forces (for instance, the National Salvation Movement, led by a
dissident Conservative).
**Advantage ratio, A = (% seats)/(% votes).

candidates in exchange for locally or individually targeted benefits (Mc-
Cubbins and Rosenbluth 1993). For instance, Osterling (1989) notes that,
given the large territorial extent of most Colombian districts, "each political
party has tacitly subdivided large districts into various subdistricts each in
a list headed by a different boss" (164). Different lists are also often associated with different organized interest groups that deliver votes to the party.

The existence of specific regional and occupational support groups for
specific candidates does not guarantee an efficient division of the vote but
may contribute to it and is crucial to developing each candidate's unique
personal following. Moreover, the tendency for major-party politicians to
secure votes by offering bureaucratic and budgetary concessions to supporters (Martínez Neira 1998: 53) is consistent with the incentives within an extreme personalistic system to use "pork barrel politics" to divide the vote

(McCubbins and Rosenbluth 1993) and reduce the potential "chaos" of zero-sum intraparty competition.

Intraparty competition, not only in Colombia but elsewhere, has an inherent tendency to reduce the incentives of legislative candidates to campaign on party programs and issue stances. The reasons are straightforward. When candidates of the same party must campaign against each other at the same time as they compete against candidates of other parties, and when they cannot share votes with copartisans, identification with the party label and any programmatic content that it might convey is an insufficient cue to attract votes. Members have little incentive to emphasize a party platform because cultivating the *voto de opinión* (opinion vote), as it is called in Colombia, on the basis of a party program would not distinguish one candidate from others of the same party. Thus party institutions—and associated policy platforms—tend to remain underdeveloped. As Santana Rodríguez (1998a: 17) says, "[E]ach candidate is responsible for his program, finances, and electoral strategy"; correspondingly (with slight exaggeration), "in a strict sense, parties do not exist."

An electoral system that promotes candidates' dependence on their personal electoral machines also tends to promote very expensive campaigns, which in turn tend to enhance the access to the policy-making process of wealthy groups with specific interests. Politicians need resources to differentiate themselves from copartisans. Ensuring the loyalty of blocs of voters requires the expenditure of funds on their behalf. Business groups with a stake in policy outcomes expend resources to ensure that one member of a given party is elected over others, resulting in "a subordination of politics to major economic interests" (Santana Rodríguez 1998a: 18).[20] And of course, in Colombia, another wealthy group that can be courted for financial backing is the illicit drug industry.

Particularism and Executive-Legislative Relations

Legislators' lack of interest in broad national policy has consequences also for the structure of Congress and for executive-legislative relations. If legislators gain their seats not by courting the "opinion vote" but by exchanging clientelistic favors as a means to divide the vote with copartisans, then they will invest in creating a system of patronage rather than a legislature that is active in policy making. They will exchange their own votes with the executive for concessions that aid their reelection or the election of protegees. Executive dominance over the national policy agenda in Colombia has been permitted as long as Congress members are left to pursue their own particularistic/clientelistic goals (Archer and Shugart 1997; Ingall and Crisp 2001).

The relative absence of congressional interest in policy has been recognized for some time by Colombian political leaders. In fact, it was one key factor motivating many of the institutional reforms adopted as part of a new constitution in 1991. Reforms such as reducing the scope of executive emergency powers, restricting congressional delegation of decree authority to the executive, and instituting the possibility of congressional censure of cabinet ministers were among a package of changes meant to empower Congress to tackle national policy matters and rely less on the executive to do so (Nielson and Shugart 1999; Sarabia Better 2003). However, absent a shift in the electoral incentives of legislators, these reforms have not lived up to their potential. Legislators still lack the electoral incentive to become active participants in national policy making, and their tendency to focus on patronage has continued to undermine significant policy reforms sought by recent presidents—and demanded by external lenders—including such matters as restraining fiscal transfers to the regions where politicians court their personal followings.

Shortcomings of the 1991 Constitutional Reform

In 1991 Colombia adopted a new constitution intended to broaden citizen participation. While the constitutional reform process was an important step in the maturation of Colombian democracy, a serious shortcoming was that there were few changes affecting electoral incentives, and the most important one was in some respects counterproductive. No reforms touched upon the system of intraparty competition, while the creation of a single nationwide district for the Senate has proved a disappointment. In this section, we discuss the 1991 reforms—mainly the adoption of a single nationwide Senate district—for the Colombian party system and the subsequent process of electoral reform.

The Effects of the Single Senate District

While the initial opportunity for nationwide campaigning afforded by the new national Senate district produced some Senate lists that won several seats each and had voter support dispersed across the country (Nielson and

Shugart 1999), the incentives generated by the seat allocation rules were so strong that fragmentation and regionalization subsequently reasserted themselves. In fact, from 1994 through 2002 most senators once again obtained the bulk of their support from one region of the country. Moreover, the number of competing lists within each major and some minor parties and movements proliferated (Botero 1998; Crisp and Ingall 2002; Rodriguez Raga 2002). This tendency toward regionally concentrated votes despite a national district in the Senate is perfectly consistent with the electoral formula. Because it is possible, under quota-and-remainders, to win a seat with very small vote shares, and because the multiple-list system permits entry by individual candidates, each heading his or her own list to capitalize on a personal vote, it is easy to win a seat based on regionally concentrated support. This national district combined with the incentive to present personal lists is the very epitome of the *operaciones avispas*.

It would be a mistake to say that the increased internal party fragmentation and the continued regionalization of lists' support bases means that the reforms of 1991 made no difference. Notably, the number of senators in the majority Liberal Party who needed votes from outside their home department about doubled from 1991 to 1994 (Taylor 1997) even as the average geographic concentration of support increased (Botero 1998: 319).[21] Thus the nature of Senate constituencies has changed from exclusively intradepartmental prior to 1991 to potentially cross-departmental afterwards. Even more importantly, the existence of the national district has led to a large increase in the number of senators who are elected on a label other than Liberal or Conservative. These senators usually have a more programmatic (i.e., less clientelistic) constituency. The peak of nontraditional senators under the old rules was nine in 1990. It spiked to twenty in the first nationwide election in 1991, then declined to fifteen in 1994 before increasing again to twenty-seven in 1998 (Gutiérrez Sanín 1998; see also table 7.4). Nontraditional senators—those generally more programmatic in their approach and opposed to the clientelism of the traditional parties—might be expected to be natural supporters of further electoral reform. However, because many Senate seats can be won with very small vote shares, the new Senate district actually ensured that there would be many senators with a vested interest in the status quo—nontraditional and traditional alike. Any reform that would raise the votes needed to win a seat—such as d'Hondt, even alone but especially along with a formal votes threshold—would cost many senators their seats if they did not join forces with larger parties or movements.

The Twin Effects of SNTV and Large Magnitude

The experience of the Colombian Senate election process after 1991 shows us that *operaciones avispas* and individual independent senators are two sides of the same SNTV coin. The party splitting of the *avispas* allows the large parties to "game" the system and win greater-than-proportional representation for themselves. At the same time the system's permissiveness means that some very small parties also obtain greater-than-proportional representation. This result is typical of SNTV, which even in Japan simultaneously promoted a large, long-ruling majority party with "superproportional" representation of small parties (Taagepera and Shugart 1989; Cox 1997).[22] We now explain these phenomena in more detail because understanding them is important both for an understanding of the difficulties of reforming the system and for interpreting what features of the Colombian electoral process are likely to be changed by the new system that finally was implemented for the 2006 congressional elections.

The reason for the so-called superproportionality of SNTV is that when a large party is running multiple candidates or lists in a district and there is no vote pooling (the very definition of SNTV) it has a risk of losing seats to other parties that it could have won for itself. It could have won these seats if it had been able either to pool all its votes (as with a party list) or to manage the distribution of its votes more efficiently across its candidates (or personal lists). The need to be efficient in managing the distribution of a large party's votes is a key reason why SNTV is so favorable to clientelism, for clientelism ensures loyalty of blocs of voters to specific candidates. This difficulty of large parties to manage the votes-to-seats conversion—clientelism is not perfectly efficient, even in Colombia!—favors small parties.

Also favoring small parties is the absence of a threshold of votes required to win a seat. A threshold would be inconsistent with the rules of SNTV because SNTV states simply that the M candidates with the M highest vote totals are winners.[23] It is an electoral rule that awards seats to candidates only on the basis of their ranking in votes relative to all other candidates. It does not reward parties for having a certain share of the vote, as do list PR systems (open or closed), which often have thresholds.

An example will demonstrate what we are arguing about permissiveness for very small parties—both the potential mistakes large parties can make in managing their votes and the absence of a threshold. In Colombia's 2002 Senate election, the last list to obtain a seat had only 0.451 percent of the total valid votes. There is probably no other electoral system in the world that would give a seat to a list with such a small share of the votes. The largest party in 2002 was the Liberal Party, with just over 27 percent of the votes cast. It won twenty-eight seats. However, each of the first five candidates to miss winning a seat was also a Liberal, and none of these missed a seat by more than 0.025 percent of the votes cast (just over 1,500 votes). In other words, if the Liberal Party had had only a slightly more efficient distribution of the votes amongst its lists, it could have won as many as thirty-three seats instead of twenty-eight. With just a very small number of additional votes, these five Liberals might have supplanted the candidates of some minor parties or movements, including the Partido Nacional Cristiano and the Movimiento Progresismo, each of which ran a single list that barely won enough votes for one seat. This is the sense in which the SNTV system is so permissive of small parties as to be superproportional: a large party that is factionalized may displace seats it could have won to a minor party that is more unified.

Thus SNTV is favorable to very small parties, but it also tends to be favorable to the largest parties, paradoxically.[24] Strategies like *operación avispa* and the use of clientelism normally allow the large parties to target their appeals rather efficiently and thus gain an advantage in seat allocation. A governing party is all the more favored because it can use government resources to woo voters to particular candidates. We saw this effect with the advantage ratios for the large parties (table 7.4).

The 2002 election offers a valuable case study in the effects of SNTV. Table 7.5 shows the votes-to-seats conversion for several political parties and movements in 2002. In this election the Liberal Party was disadvantaged for the first time in post-1991 Senate elections. Some very small parties were overrepresented in 2002—such as Renovación Acción Laboral Moral (RALM) and especially Nuevo Liberalismo—while other, larger, parties were underrepresented, such as Equipo Colombia and Colombia Siempre, as well as the Liberal Party. The reason for this erratic treatment of parties was that an SNTV system like that of Colombia *does not reward parties for their overall popularity*. Rather, it rewards them for having candidates (lists in Colombia) that are able to efficiently convert their individual popularity into seats. With no votes pooled from list to list, there is no incentive of a party to maximize votes because doing so does not necessarily maximize seats. Rather, the way to maximize seats is to coordinate the distribution of voters among a party's distinct personal lists.

Table 7.5
Votes-to-Seats Conversions for Political Forces in Colombia, 2002

	Senate		House of Representatives	
Party	% Votes	A*	% Votes	A
Liberal	30.3	0.90	31.3	1.06
Conservative	10.0	1.26	10.9	1.18
Mov. Nacional	4.8	1.22	1.1	0.55
Equipo Colombia	3.3	0.88	2.3	1.07
MIPOL	3.0	1.29	0.5	2.38
Colombia Siempre	2.9	0.66	1.3	1.41
Cambio Radical	2.6	0.76	3.8	1.13
Navarro Wolff	2.4	0.80	—	—
Mov. Popular Unido	2.0	1.02	1.5	0.80
RALM	1.7	1.41	1.1	1.09
Frente Social y Político	1.5	0.68	0.8	1.47
Nuevo Liberalismo	1.0	1.89	—	—
All others combined	34.5	1.05	49.5	0.40

Source: Consejo Nacional Electoral de Colombia.
*Advantage ratio, A = (% seats)/(% votes).

Thus the results in table 7.5 reveal starkly how *the Colombian electoral system treats parties erratically.* In a hundred-seat district, such as Colombia's Senate, we would expect all parties to obtain similar advantage ratios because the very large magnitude normally would produce very high proportionality. However, reading down the column for Senate advantage ratios, in which the parties are listed in descending order by the share of votes obtained, we find no pattern.

Results in the House are even more erratic because of the use of smaller districts, which tend to reward regionally concentrated parties more than those with dispersed support, even in a PR system. When the system is SNTV, the relationship between votes and seats in a system of regional districts is even more unpredictable. Due to SNTV and the smaller districts, the Liberal Party was able to retain its advantage in votes-to-seats conversion in the House in 2002.

Party Sizes under SNTV and the Punishment of Midsized Parties
Yet another notable feature of Colombia's electoral and party system is the large gap between the sizes of the largest and smallest parties. Most PR systems have smaller gaps between party sizes and hence are more competitive. In Colombia in 2002, the sizes of the largest parties in the Senate voting were 30.0, 10.0, 6.4, 4.8, and 3.3. Note the very large gap between the first two parties. Yet nearly 30 percent of the votes was cast collectively for a set of parties (or "movements") that each won just one seat. This shows how favorable the Colombian SNTV system is to very small parties. As noted above, the factionalization of large parties—*operación avispa*—and the presence of numerous very small parties are two sides of the same SNTV coin. Just as large parties act as an umbrella for many personalist campaigns of individual candidates, small parties tend to offer just one list in order to tightly identify their party with their leader. That is, *small parties and large parties alike tend to be made more personalistic by SNTV* precisely because it is an electoral system that counts only personal votes and not party votes.

Table 7.6 draws on data from Colombia's 2002 Senate election to demonstrate this tendency of SNTV to personalize both large and small parties. The Liberal Party's elected senators average a mere 2.2 percent of their party's combined votes. For the Conservative Party, the figure is 6.6 percent. Parties other than the Liberals and Conservatives have senators with intraparty shares of almost 70 percent on average. Those parties or movements that won one seat each have an average share of 93.9 percent, indicating that these parties came very close to having all of their votes concentrated on a single candidate. The concentration of votes implies that the small parties are highly dependent on the vote-pulling ability of a single leader.

The bifurcation of the Colombian party system into internally fragmented large parties and numerous very small parties is not a mere quirk of the 2002 election. In fact, it is typical of SNTV. In the four Colombian elections from 1978 to 1990, the average sizes[25] of the four largest parties in Colombia were 54.6, 37.0, 3.3, and 1.3. There is a very large gap between the top two parties and a far larger one between the second and third largest. Similarly, in Japan under SNTV, the averages for the four largest parties from 1976 through 1986 were 45.9, 19.3, 10.1, and 9.5. While these two party systems differ in important ways (especially in the size of the second party), we find that under both of these SNTV systems there is one dominant party, a second party well behind, and then a large gap between the second- and third-largest parties.

Table 7.6
Internal Party Fragmentation in Colombian Senate Election, 2002

Party	Average Senator's Vote as Percent of His/Her Party's Vote
Liberal	2.2
Conservative	6.6
Movimiento Nacional	14.3
Equipo Colombia	26.8
MIPOL	24.3
Colombia Siempre	41.2
Cambio Radical	26.7
MPU	38.3
RALM	49.6
All	43.6
All except Liberal and Conservative	71.8
All parties that won just one seat	93.9

The political forces that are hurt by SNTV are midsized parties that get squeezed. In fact, they are hurt so much that typically cohesive midsized parties that might offer a viable alternative governing program may not even exist, thus presenting the paradox that the sort of parties that would potentially present policy alternatives are not present to fight for electoral reform. The experience of the M19, an electoral movement founded by demobilized guerrillas of the same name, is instructive. In 1990, its leader, Antonio Navarro Wolff, won 12.6 percent of the vote for president. The M19 then won 26.8 percent of the vote for the assembly that wrote the 1991 Constitution, and Navarro became one of the three co-presidents of the Constituent Assembly. The M19 appeared on the verge of establishing itself as a major alternative electoral force. However, it subsequently behaved like the traditional parties, presenting twelve lists for the 1994 Senate election, in which it saw its votes plummet to less than 4 percent. Even this share should have netted it three or four seats, but with its votes dispersed across several lists it won none.

The M19 came out of the armed struggle with significant internal divisions that underlay the decision to opt for a multiple-list strategy in 1994. First of all, the organization had always had a somewhat loose organizational structure, in part as a reaction to the orthodoxy of other leftist groups. Second, it had lost many of its most prominent high-ranking leaders during the armed struggle, leaving many middle-ranking leaders jockeying for position within the movement (López de la Roche 1994: 300). Recall that under the prereform electoral system a party that presented a single list was of necessity presenting a *closed* list under the name and photo of the candidate who headed the list. Other leaders were unwilling to see the M19 transformed into the personal electoral vehicle of Navarro, whose control over the list in 1991 appears to have generated an internal rebellion that the multiple-list strategy might have been an attempt to placate.[26] Of course, absent the clientelistic resources of the traditional parties, the M19 could not distribute its votes in a way to maximize its seats the way the traditional parties can. So using multiple lists only exacerbated the divisions that already existed and left it with no seats until it regrouped in 1998. After the electoral reform was passed in 2003, Navarro joined with other leftist leaders on a new unified list known as the Polo Democrático Independiente, which represents the very sort of programmatic alternative that was so disfavored by SNTV but is encouraged to organize under d'Hondt party-list PR. In fact, Navarro himself was one of several Colombian commentators and leaders to have gone on record admitting that the failure to implement fundamental electoral reform undercut many of the provisions of the 1991 Constitution that were intended to promote greater accountability of Congress.[27]

We have now reviewed the inherent conditions of SNTV that produce fragmentation and personalization of the legislative electoral process and the consequences these effects have for the functioning of the political system. We have noted that the 1991 constitutional reforms did not address the fundamental flaws of the seat allocation process and that the adoption of a hundred-seat Senate district actually increased fragmentation and personalization, given SNTV. We now turn to the contingent factors that, through several rounds of reform efforts, blocked passage of reform, and discuss the 2002 election as a critical factor in turning contingent factors from unfavorable for reform to favorable.

Contingent Factors: Political Calculations for and against Reform

The shortcomings of the previous system and their recognition in Colombian leadership circles explain why electoral reform was placed upon the Colombian political agenda. However, if inherent factors were sufficient to explain reform, then a change in an electoral system would occur "automatically" when some threshold level of the pathologies of the current system was met. Obviously that is not the case; in fact, such an explanation would strip all the politics out of what clearly, in Colombia, was a highly charged political conflict over reform.

One of the fundamental challenges of reform is that, even when it is widely recognized that a system is inherently flawed, the self-interest of those members who must vote for any change often becomes an obstacle. What would motivate them to change rules that have enabled them to win? The answer may come in the distributive consequences of a reform. That is, some parties or political forces may gain (or lose) more than others in reform. These perceptions of the prospects of reform for specific political careers lie in the category of outcome-contingent motivations. On the other hand, members may vote for a reform that they sincerely oppose on the grounds that they fear political retribution for blocking something that is popular (which may cost them reelection) or because they fear worse consequences if the reform effort shifts to an arena they cannot control (such as a referendum or constituent assembly). These motivations are act contingent. In this section, we turn our attention to the contingencies that have affected the fate of the reform, concentrating first on the Pastrana presidency, when reform failed despite seemingly favorable conditions at the outset, and then turning our attention to the Uribe administration, when reform passed.

Act-Contingent Factors during the Pastrana Administration

Both the president and members of Congress have been motivated by act-contingent factors. The president has tended to push for reform when he would benefit politically from doing so. Congress has supported it when the president has mobilized public support and made an antireform stance politically perilous for legislators. However, prior to 2003, these favorable contingencies always waned before reform could be enacted.

A Campaign Deal on Reform

In the final days of a close presidential runoff race in June 1998, Conservative presidential candidate Andrés Pastrana promised to pursue electoral reform in exchange for a public endorsement from "independent" political figures (Sarabia Better 2003: 125–29). Of the latter, few were as visible as Ingrid Betancourt, a member of Congress who had gained notoriety as a crusader against corruption and whose Senate list had obtained the highest vote total in March 1998. Political reform was an important issue for Betancourt's Verde Oxígeno Party, in part because of the difficulty of nontraditional movements like her own in translating their growing voter support into more Senate seats (as we saw in table 7.4). The party's program director summed up this view: "Assessing the situation, with our core supporters and other independent forces, we conclude that we have been . . . victims of this perverse system."[28]

In other words, at this stage in the process, Betancourt's motivation was outcome contingent, in that she expected to be better off under reformed rules. For Pastrana, on the other hand, the act of promising reform brought its own reward. On May 6, 1998, Betancourt endorsed Pastrana after they jointly signed a "Pact to Transform Political Practices," in which Pastrana promised to hold an "anticorruption referendum" upon taking office. This referendum would ask for popular consent on reforms, including mandating single-party lists.

Upon assuming office, the Pastrana administration was seen by some independents as backpedaling on its campaign promises. Pastrana quickly put aside his initial promise to hold an early referendum. Instead, the government held extensive consultations with traditional congressional leaders, which led to the "Casa Medina Agreement," by which Liberals and Conservatives agreed to support an electoral reform bill that would be introduced for discussion in Congress instead of being presented to the public via referendum.

Pastrana's decision to switch to a congressionally approved reform instead of the referendum was seen by many independents as evidence of the insincerity of his devotion to real political change. Under this view, his campaign promise to hold the referendum was entirely act contingent, an electoral ploy needed to gain the crucial independent vote in the hotly contested election of 1998. However, once in office, Pastrana gave in to the political reality that promoting a reform favored principally by the small number of nontraditional political forces was going to complicate his ability to work with Congress on his policy priorities. Pastrana's own Conservative Party was a minority in Congress, making it potentially very difficult for him to obtain congressional approval of his agenda. (He urgently needed to pass legislation, among other things, on economic adjustment measures and the peace process.) In the first days of his term, Pastrana managed to build a progovernment bipartisan coalition in Congress, baptized as the "Gran Alianza por el Cambio." This coalition incorporated some of the more traditional forces—the very politicians who would be least inclined to back political reform.

In pursuing the reform, Pastrana linked it with the far more controversial issue of the peace process with the FARC guerrillas. In the first half of 1999, as peace talks at San Vicente del Caguán were gaining momentum, an article was added to the political reform bill granting the government wide discretionary powers to conduct peace negotiations. At this point, a quid pro quo emerged among the main actors of political reform. Pastrana would gain powers in dealing with the guerrillas, and clientelist politicians would be assured that the political reform would be less radical than the original referendum-based proposal. An official with Betancourt's party summed up what happened: "Political reform, as initially planned, lost its teeth. In the end, we were faced with a monster. It was such an innocuous reform that the political barons were very happy. It was not going to be an anticlientelist or anticorruption bill, so we had to take the lead to defeat it."[29] The peace process was Pastrana's main priority, and he was willing to sacrifice electoral reform to pursue it.

Pastrana "Goes Public"

In 2000, Pastrana suddenly and dramatically revived the issue of electoral reform by delivering an address to the nation in which he called upon the people to pressure Congress to pass a measure that would convoke a referendum not only on his reform proposals but on dissolving Congress itself and holding early elections. In this gambit, Pastrana appears to have been motivated less by his preference for a new electoral system than by the political points he could score by promoting a "cleansing" of Congress in the wake of a parliamentary corruption scandal revealed by the press early in 2000.[30] Moreover, he could presume that angry voters would particularly punish traditional politicians, especially those from the "official" Liberal Party. The role of voter anger was clearly on the minds of some members of Congress. For instance, Conservative Senator Roberto Camacho said, "To go against public opinion is to commit suicide," given polls showing that 80 percent of citizens would support Pastrana's referendum.[31]

However, Pastrana's "going public" strategy backfired when Liberals, headed by Horacio Serpa, counterattacked by calling for early presidential elections to be held jointly with the new congressional elections.[32] Moreover, early in 2000, the Liberal congressional caucus withheld approval of a crucial economic adjustment package that had been promised to the International Monetary Fund (IMF) by the Pastrana administration a few months earlier. As noted by the newsweekly *Semana*, "The way things are going, there will be not a single bill approved in Congress. The minister of finance himself is aware of this situation, and on his own accord has taken to promoting contacts with members of Congress with the objective of insulating the economy and stopping it from being overwhelmed by the political crisis."[33] Facing this stalemate and a concomitant devaluation of the peso, Pastrana on May 26 decided to withdraw his call for early congressional elections. While he reiterated the necessity of political reform, he noted squarely that the passage of measures required for IMF assistance— including tax reform and rationalization of the fiscal situation of subnational governments—would be a priority.[34]

The Threat from "Below"

The referendum proposed by Pastrana—which would have required the prior consent of Congress—was not the only referendum idea circulating at the time. There was also a citizens' movement, collecting signatures to bypass Congress, that Pastrana had always counted on as his "ace in the hole" to push Congress to support his plan. The prospect of a referendum was summed up well at Pastrana's inauguration in 1998 when Fabio Valencia, then president of the Senate, said, "O cambiamos o nos cambian" (Either we change or they change us).

The 1991 Constitution created mechanisms of citizen initiative, which were codified in Law 134 of 1994, stipulating that 10 percent of registered voters could petition to hold a referendum on a bill that Congress had turned down. There was disagreement as to whether this procedure could be used for a constitutional amendment, although the government claimed it could be.[35] Manuel José Cepeda—who was later appointed to the Constitutional Court—was among those who agreed with the government, and he organized a citizens' movement, Frente Ciudadano por el Referendo, that took to the streets to gather signatures.

However, when Pastrana announced on May 26 that he would no longer insist on the dissolution of Congress as part of his referendum, he pulled the rug out from under the initiative process. A few days after Pastrana's announcement, the planned *Firmatón* events at which the Frente Ciudadano hoped to collect three million signatures netted only around two hundred thousand.[36] While signature gatherers pressed on, they had little chance of success absent presidential support, as noted by *Semana:* "The task will not be easy. It is one thing to have the government as an ally and another very different thing to be left practically alone in the fight."[37] Just as the threat of a referendum taking matters out of their hands helped push Congress to take the issue of political reform seriously, the waning of the threat in the absence of government support reduced one of the more powerful act-contingent motivations legislators faced.

Posturing?

An act-contingent explanation is largely about posturing for short-term political advantage. It assumes that actors do not really support reform for its own sake but fear the consequences of blocking it. Sometimes the fear of standing in the way leads to the passage of major electoral reforms even when those who have to pass them clearly would have preferred a way to avoid the matter. Examples may be found in recent electoral reform histories of Japan (Reed and Thies 2001), New Zealand, and Venezuela (Shugart and Wattenberg 2001a). At other times the benefit derived from the act of voting for reform is not great enough to overcome actors' sincere preference for the status quo.

Outcome-Contingent Factors in the Pastrana Administration

From the start of the Pastrana administration in 1998, there have been several unsuccessful attempts to reform the electoral system. Key political figures have proclaimed the necessity of reforming various rules of the political process, including the electoral system—all the while expressing reservations regarding specific provisions. Furthermore, several, including members of the traditional and "independent" sectors, played critical roles in aborting government-initiated reform efforts between 1998 and 2001. As we noted in the previous section, there were powerful act-contingent reasons for politicians to appear supportive of reform. Nonetheless, politicians are also unlikely to accept any changes that may harm their chances for reelection. That is, politicians, in deciding whether to vote for or against a specific package, assess the likely consequences of specific provisions for their own electoral careers. Such motivations are in the realm of outcome-contingent factors. We review here two provisions of the reform that were most controversial, the threshold and the preference vote.

The Threshold and Concerns of the Independents

Shortly after the 1998 reform bill was presented to Congress, Ingrid Betancourt voiced concerns that the provisions for a threshold would strengthen bipartism, suffocating the many small and "independent" forces that, as we saw in table 7.4, had gained representation in Congress since 1991 (Betancourt Pulecio 1998). As the 1998 *acto legislativo* made its way through Congress, several independents criticized the 3 percent threshold proposed for Senate elections. The main concern was that the threshold placed a burden on smaller, independent parties—who were unlikely to clear the threshold. As one senator told us: "Single party lists and the threshold probably represent a danger for minorities, but that is a risk that must be taken. 'Independents' in the current Congress are like individual atoms affiliated with churches, entertainment, sports, and other movements. One must understand that [some] 'independents' are electoral entrepreneurs *(microempresarios)* just like the Liberals and the Conservatives, and of course they don't want to be erased from the map."[38] This point is reminiscent of our argument above about how *operación avispa* and the fragmentation of the nontraditional movements represent two sides of the same SNTV coin. We would expect that, in the longer run, a threshold would have positive effects on the representation of nontraditional forces, inasmuch as it would encourage them to pool their strength. As we saw in table 7.4, independent forces have frequently received a significantly lower share of seats than of votes. The reason for this is that they are fragmented among many lists that lack electoral coordination. The threshold would be a powerful incentive favoring coordination. However, a threshold also represents a real and immediate threat to many current electoral careers. Personalities unable to subsume their identities within larger parties or coalitions could be swept aside.[39] Thus one of the most important goals of reform—reducing fragmentation—also proved to be one of the major obstacles to reform during the 1998–2002 period.

Fears of Party Centralization and the Debate over the Preference Vote
Many Liberal and Conservative *microempresarios* had vested interests in stalling electoral reform because single party lists invoked images of an earlier era when political bosses had strict control over nominations *(bolígrafo)*. The bill that was defeated in 1999 had called for a preference vote in the form of a flexible list, which, as we noted earlier, is a hybrid of the closed- and open-list concepts. That is, voters could cast preference votes for candidates within a list (as in an open list), but there would still be a party-provided list rank (as in a closed list). Candidates who obtained some stipulated quota of preference votes would be assured of election regardless of how high or low the party had ranked them, while votes cast for the list would be counted as the voters' acceptance of the party-provided rank for the seats not filled by preference votes.[40] Although flexible-list systems can function more like either open or closed lists depending on the precise rules for allocating seats among candidates based on preference votes versus list rank, the proposal was clearly an attempt to split the difference between open- and closed-list principles.

This proposal had raised the ire of traditional politicians because they felt that any provision for party-ranked ballots would increase the authority of party leaders. On the other hand, independents were not enamored of the preference vote even in this limited form because it still implied that old-line clientelist politicians could ensure their seats regardless of how they were ranked on the list (assuming they still obtained nomination). When Pastrana sought to implement electoral reform via a referendum in 2000, his proposal dropped the provision for a preference vote, thus implying a closed list. It is noteworthy that he proposed a flexible list when he sought to pass a bill through Congress, where many traditional politicians were sure to insist on rules that would permit the continued cultivation of their personal votes. Once he shifted the arena to the public in an attempt to bypass Congress, he promoted a more radical change, abolishing intraparty competition in general elections altogether.

Once the arena shifted back to Congress again after the withdrawal of the referendum plan, the government bill again contained a preference vote, but this time it was in the form of an open list, in which the preference votes would be the sole determinant of the order of election from the list. A brief history of the debate in 2000–2001 reveals the continuing intense debate over the preference vote. In 2000, each house passed different versions of the list provision. The Senate version called for voters to have the option of casting a preference vote (implying an open list),[41] while the House passed a provision for a closed list but with mandatory primary elections *(consultas internas)* to determine candidates on each party's list. The House-Senate conference committee *(comisión de conciliación)* reported out, and plenaries of each house approved, a bill retaining the preference vote but appearing to leave open whether it would be a flexible or fully open list.[42]

While *microempresarios* prefer a fully open list, many independents object to it on the grounds that it continues to reward individualistic politicians and does not represent a break with current practice—exactly why the *microempresarios* can accept it. As Navarro Wolff commented in the bill passed by the plenary sessions at the end of 2000, the proposal "does not change clientelism, does not ameliorate vote buying, and favors the two parties, Liberals and Conservatives."[43] Navarro Wolff also claimed that most legislators from the traditional parties will not accept the single-list provision unless accompanied by a full preference vote—anything less would mark too abrupt a change with current practice.[44] In 2001, a proposed modification co-sponsored by several independent senators called for a reinstatement of closed lists with mandatory primaries. The question of the preference vote was never resolved and was one of the causes of the bill's defeat in May 2001. As we shall see next, it very nearly led to defeat again in 2003 before a last-minute compromise attempted to split the difference—not this time by proposing a flexible list but by allowing each party to decide whether to submit an open or closed list.

The 2002 Election and Passage of Political Reform

The 2002 congressional and presidential elections were a watershed in the politics of political reform in Colombia. The most obvious event of this election year was the defection of Alvaro Uribe, a former Liberal governor of Antioquia, from the party. Rather than submit himself to the Liberal presidential primary *(consulta interna)* of September 2001, Uribe announced he would bypass the nomination process and run as an independent in the general election the following May. Uribe's image as a leader who would be tough on the guerrillas and official corruption created a dilemma for candidates registering their lists for the congressional elections that would occur in March. In an election in which Uribe's campaign was threatening to swamp the traditional parties, being identified with the name Liberal or Conservative could be a liability. On the other hand, it could be risky to commit to Uribe's Primero Colombia movement in the event that Uribe faltered. Thus a remarkably large number of candidates with regional or national personal appeal registered lists under new names rather than Liberal or Conservative. The result was that candidates endorsed by the two traditional parties collectively polled barely 40 percent of the vote—by far their worst showing ever in a congressional election.

The 2002 congressional election turned out to be a classic example of what Shugart and Carey (1992) identified as a "counterhoneymoon" election. The traditional honeymoon after the election of a president is the period in which his support surges, and elections held during such periods often produce an increase in the congressional representation of the president's party. On the other hand, in a counterhoneymoon election, a "minor party can seek to demonstrate its value as a coalition partner for the upcoming presidential election" (Shugart and Carey 1992: 257). In this election there were numerous such minor parties (or "movements") presenting themselves with new names as potential coalition partners for Uribe in the upcoming presidential election and in the Congress to support his administration, should he win.

The 2002 congressional election was critical to the subsequent reform process, for it represented the first time in decades that a real cleavage had opened up in a congressional election over identification with a reformist platform. In table 7.7, the 2002 election is compared to the previous six congressional elections that likewise took place in a presidential election year.[45] The table gives the presidential and senatorial[46] vote shares for the Liberal and Conservative parties in each year from 1978 to 1998. The senatorial votes of the (formerly) dominant Liberal Party consistently exceed their presidential votes, as indicated by an "S/P" ratio greater than 1.00. The only exception is 1986, when a "New Liberal" splinter ran under its own label, but it was subsequently reincorporated into the Liberal mainstream.[47] Over the 1978–98 period, the Liberal Party averaged around 53 percent of the Senate vote but only 46 percent of the presidential vote. The Conservatives, on the other hand, tended to perform better in presidential elections than in senatorial, even in years they lost.[48] What this shows us is that in Colombia the congressional elections were hardly responsive to the national trends that animate presidential vote shares. The congressional vote of the Liberal Party was far more stable than its presidential vote, meaning that even in years that would prove to be bad years for the party at the executive level the party's dominance of Congress was usually safe. This result is consistent with the nature of the SNTV system in shielding members from national policy and partisan swings because votes under SNTV depend more on personal connections between voters and politicians than they do on party labels or national issues. This relative absence of any sort of national "pull" on the congressional vote is one of the reasons members of Congress were able to duck responsibility for so long on a national cause such as political reform.

However, in 2002, the unique nature of that election—with a presidential campaign outside the traditional Liberal Party already surging in the polls—allowed national forces to be felt in the congressional campaign. The Liberals' congressional vote plummeted to 30.6 percent, which was almost identical to—rather than the previous average of 6.8 percentage points better than—what the party would get in the presidential election two months later. Arriving at a congressional vote total for parties and movements supporting Uribe is not straightforward, but the parties listed in the notes to table 7.7 include those whose leaders were most associated with Uribe; they combined for just under 14 percent of the votes and seventeen senators (and a similar percentage of deputies). Thus, upon winning a majority of the presidential vote in May 2002 and taking office in August, Uribe would find himself with a substantial, though minority, bloc of supportive legislators elected in his counterhoneymoon. After the election the Liberal Party fractured further, with twelve of its twenty-eight senators and eighteen of its forty-seven deputies defecting from the *oficialista* Liberals to Uribe's coalition.[49] These novel phenomena—a cleavage over national issues affecting the congressional elections and a bandwagon of support behind an independent president—would have profound implications for how the political reform debate would transpire. As we shall see next, these events changed the calculus of both act- and outcome-contingent motivations for members of Congress.

A Renewed Referendum Proposal and Act Contingencies
Those members of Congress who campaigned as *uribistas* had taken a pledge, prior to the election, to support the president (Sarabia Better 2003: 49). Combined with the immense popularity of the new president, this

Table 7.7
Comparison of Presidential and Senate Election Results for Two Leading
Candidates and Their Parties

	Liberal	Conservative
1978		
Senate	55.2	40.0
President	**49.5**	46.6
S/P*	1.12	0.86
1982		
Senate	56.3	40.3
President	41.0	**46.8**
S/P	1.37	0.86
1986		
Senate	49.3	37.0
President	**58.2**	35.8
S/P	0.85	1.03
1990		
Senate	58.5	31.2
President	**48.2**	12.3
S/P	1.21	2.54
1994		
Senate	50.7	18.8
President	45.2	44.9
(runoff)	**50.4**	49.1
S/P	1.12	0.38
1998		
Senate	47.3	22.5
President	34.6	34.3
(runoff)	46.5	**50.4**
S/P	1.37	0.65

Averages (and Standard Deviations) for 1978–1998

	Liberal	Conservative
Senate	52.9	31.6
	(4.4)	(9.2)
President	46.1	36.8
	(8.0)	(13.2)

2002	Liberal	Uribista**
Senate	30.6	13.7
President	31.8	**53.0**
S/P	0.96	0.26

Note: Numbers in bold indicate party or bloc winning presidency.
*S/P is the ratio of Senate percentage of votes to presidential percentage of votes (in first round, in case of two-round election).
**Excludes Conservatives (10.0 percent of the Senate vote), although the party withdrew its presidential candidate and endorsed Uribe. Includes Cambio Radical, Colombia Siempre, Convergencia Popular Cívica, Popular Unido, Renovación Acción Laboral Moral, Voluntad Popular, and Integración Popular. No lists under the Liberal label are included, even though some of these could be classified as *uribista*.

public commitment of support generated a classic act-contingent scenario. These legislators would be judged by their electorates largely by their level of support for the new president. One of Uribe's first acts in office was to follow through on a campaign promise to promote a "referendum against corruption." The exact contours of the referendum proposal changed many times between Uribe's inauguration and the final version that was rejected (on account of low voter turnout) by the Colombian electorate in October 2003. However, some provisions concerning the electoral system remained largely unchanged through several rounds—notably the shift of electoral formula to d'Hondt and the imposition of a threshold, both measures aimed at limiting fragmentation.

In addition to matters of the electoral system, Uribe's proposed referendum covered numerous other issues, including freezes on public expenditures and new regulations for Congress's own administrative arm and for public pensions—all measures that go to the heart of various privileges long enjoyed by members of Congress who seek to use public resources for electoral (or personal) gain. Most alarmingly for non-*uribista* legislators, Uribe also initially proposed that the referendum contain a provision dissolving the current Congress and electing a new one under the changed rules. Thus Uribe was willing to risk a constitutional crisis to carry out what he saw as his "anticorruption" mandate.

As was the case with Pastrana, Uribe was expected to assist a signature drive to force a citizens' initiative on the ballot to carry out his reforms, including the dissolution of Congress. Given Uribe's popularity, the threat carried real weight and prompted Congress to negotiate on a bill to convene a referendum in order to ward off a possibly more radical initiative. As *uribista* Senator Rafael Pardo put it, "Congress all along faced the specter of the president initiating a signature collection campaign for a citizen's referendum, with the rallying cry of new congressional elections, if they did not approve the referendum bill. This motivated Congress, although with some difficulty, to enact the referendum bill. The referendum was approved without enthusiasm by many sectors."[50]

By November 2002—only about three months after his inauguration—Uribe secured passage of a bill containing seventeen articles to be put to popular vote.[51] In the process, however, Uribe dropped the proposed dissolution of Congress, as well as a proposal for unicameralism. This decision to bargain with Congress rather than promote a more radical reform—reminiscent of an earlier decision by Pastrana—was roundly criticized by some sectors, including the left-wing Polo Democrático and the prominent opinion magazine *Semana*, which editorialized that "the government surrendered to petty politics and gave up its intention of dissolving Congress and replacing it with a unicameral body, in exchange for some fiscal policy measures that could have been implemented and enacted by other means."[52] Thus the referendum bill was not as radical as Uribe initially demanded, but it still would be sweeping, contemplating a reduction in the size of each house of Congress, as well as d'Hondt, the threshold, and the fiscal and administrative measures referred to above. The proposal restricted parties from endorsing more candidates than there were seats in the electoral district but was silent on the number of lists. Thus, legally, under the proposal Uribe sought to have the electorate approve, a party in a Senate election could have presented one hundred single-person lists or one list of one hundred candidates, or anything in between those extremes. This would have made for a rather chaotic electoral process, to say the least, with different parties possibly employing different strategies. However, as we noted above, the presence of d'Hondt and the 2 percent threshold would have removed the seat bonus that a party could obtain by splitting. Nonetheless, given how internally divided many Colombian parties are—and the fact that individual lists would have remained closed (i.e., no preference vote)—it is likely that some parties would have presented more than a single list in many districts and taken their chances on the seat allocation process.

The referendum proposal contained no provision for a preference vote. As a result, the restriction on the number of candidates and the electoral incentives of d'Hondt would have threatened to generate conflicts within parties—especially the highly fragmented traditional parties—over which candidates to endorse and at what rank on the list. With a limited number of closed lists in a party, whoever could control the party's process of list formation would determine the congressional composition of the party. Furthermore, given the inevitable conflicts within a party over list formation, the absence of a single-list requirement could mean dissidents would continue to launch separate lists if dissatisfied with their rank on the "official" list. Of course, with d'Hondt, such dissident lists would have markedly less success in translating their votes into seats and could cost the party as a whole some seats. Nonetheless, the threat of defection could greatly complicate the management of intraparty conflict, and some dissidents could be motivated to run separately under the party label. So here enter a set of outcome-contingent motivations that set Congress to work on its own political reform. With the pending referendum and the new status quo it would create if it passed, as well as the changed circumstances for the traditional parties in the wake of the 2002 election, leaders of the traditional parties began to rethink their preferences over electoral systems.

Outcome-Contingent Motivations and the Final Passage of Reform in Congress
The political reform bill that ultimately passed in June 2003 mandates several changes to the electoral system that were debated over the previous years. Most importantly, it coincides with the referendum bill's provisions on the d'Hondt formula and thresholds. However, it goes farther on other aspects of political reform. It explicitly mandates that each party or movement present only a single list of candidates.[53] It also explicitly allows parties to present either open or closed lists. The provisions on a single list and an optional open list can be seen as ways to minimize the possibility—still contemplated in the president's then-pending referendum—that dissidents would launch their own lists. Now they cannot do so and still use the name of the party, and they also may be more motivated to stay in the party if the party's list will be open, rather than closed, because voters rather than party leaders are determining the order of lists.

The bill that passed in June 2003 was an initiative of the traditional parties in Congress.[54] The low credibility of Congress, and the widespread view that it was incapable of reforming itself, led many critics to condemn the reform. It was seen as a threat to the integrity of the referendum—as if the latter must be a more "serious" reform because it was promoted by the president and not by Congress. In fact, some critics blamed Fernando Londoño, the minister of the interior, and the president himself "for all this history of misunderstandings between the presidential referendum and the [congressional] political reform."[55] One of the strongest polemics against the reform bill again came from *Semana*: "The constitutional amendment enacted by an alliance between the Conservative and Liberal parties against *uribistas* and independents does not solve the problem of candidate-based politics. Although the reform reduces the number of parties and lists, the preference vote leaves party atomization untouched. The new political reform will not eliminate *microempresas electorales*, vote trading, legislative indiscipline, or the exchange of support for jobs."[56]

In their own defense, promoters of the reform in Congress argued that their bill actually would go farther and was essential to codify the goals of the referendum itself—specifically the creation of stronger political parties capable of collective action in Congress. For example, Senator Carlos Holguin Sardi, director of the Conservative Party, said, "President Uribe made the referendum proposal a reality, and Congress understood that the referendum needed a complement. The referendum can be considered as only a partial political reform because it refers mainly to the composition and operation of the legislative bodies. Congress realized that there was the need for a complementary bill, fundamentally addressing the electoral and party systems, in order to achieve an integral political reform."[57]

Attempting to look beyond either the disappointment of observers like *Semana*'s editorial writers or the political interests of the Conservative Party leaders, we tend to agree that the congressionally approved bill is in critical respects a more fundamental reform than the one Uribe was promoting via referendum. The single-list mandate and the open-list option promise a major rationalization of the Colombian congressional electoral and party systems. Yet stating that it brings about a rationalization is not an explanation as to why it occurred. For that, we need to look a bit more deeply at the debate and the interests of the major players in Congress.

As was the case under Pastrana, Congress divided—internally and with respect to the executive—over open versus closed lists. The traditional parties tended to favor an open list, due to the investment of their members in cultivating a personal vote under SNTV. *Uribistas,* including the president himself, tended to favor a closed list and a limitation on the number of lists but not necessarily a single list. Many of them vehemently opposed open lists, claiming that a preference vote would just perpetuate the worst of the status quo. However, Uribe's own coalition splintered,[58] with many having their own personal vote to protect. These divisions permitted the traditional parties to prevail on the (optional) preference vote. The depth of division over this matter is best captured by one remarkable statement Minister Londoño made before the First Committee of the House.[59] After branding the bill "regressive, contradictory, and unmanageable," he launched a tirade: "This is a spectacle. Anyone who reads the Colombian Constitution after all this is finished will wonder what it was that legislators were smoking when they approved this bill."[60]

We suspect there was a mix of motives in the administration's opposition to the bill. On the one hand, they appear to have been sincerely opposed to the open list. On the other hand, Uribe probably saw the reform as a threat to the passage of his referendum—stealing the thunder, so to speak. Voters might be less likely to approve a referendum promoted in part as rationalizing the electoral process if Congress had already approved a political reform of its own, and one that in some respects actually went farther. If the referendum were to lose some of its appeal due to the political reform, Uribe could also find various fiscal and administrative provisions contained in his referendum defeated. Given how much of his own prestige he had staked on the referendum, anything that might threaten its passage could threaten the political power of the president himself. In the end the bill passed, but with a compromise that had first appeared in the House version passed in May allowing parties the option to present an open or closed list.

To summarize what transpired in Congress in 2002–3, we would note that the election of Uribe and the president's insistence on a referendum provided Congress with a powerful act-contingent motivation to pursue political reform. Members of Congress feared being swept aside in a process of political reform that a popular independent president was going to pursue with or without them. Unlike previous congressional elections, in which the presidential campaign had little effect on congressional elections, the 2002 election dramatically reshaped the party system. Whatever their sincere preferences on electoral reform, *uribistas* had staked their careers on Uribe's success and would have to deliver for him. Subsequently, the passage of the bill in Congress to adopt a single (optionally open) list resulted from a shift in the preferences of the traditional parties, as well as some defections from Uribe's coalition.

The 2002 congressional election had dramatically altered the traditional party leaders' preferences. Pooling their party's votes looked more attractive when the survival of the party was clearly at stake—a condition that had not yet confronted them under Pastrana. In other words, outcome-contingent motivations finally led traditional party leaders to believe that a party-list PR system was in their interests as long as they could seek preference votes within their party's list. Thus, while various political forces disagreed right up to the end over precise provisions of the reform and may have come to that conclusion through different mixes of act- and outcome-contingent reasons, most considered themselves better off with an alternative to the existing system.

Prospects for the New System

At this point, we have reviewed the inherent flaws of the former system and the political contingencies that led to its replacement. Now it is time to assess the likely effects of the new system, including a brief analysis of the elections of March 12, 2006, the first use of the new electoral system in a congressional election. We will consider the likely effects of the electoral system on both interparty and intraparty competition.

Interparty Competition: The Number of Parties

Colombia has long been regarded as a two-party system, with the Liberals and Conservatives dominating all others. However, this has been a misleading characterization of the congressional party system for most of the past quarter-century. As noted earlier, the average sizes of Colombia's four largest parties over the 1978–98 period were 54.6, 37.0, 3.3, and 1.3. Thus, while there were indeed two major parties, one party—always the Liberal Party—was actually dominant over the others. As we noted, this kind of dominance is inherent in SNTV. So is the atomized opposition, reflected in the large gap between the second party and the rest of the field.

How many parties are we likely to see in Colombia under the new system? When compared to the former SNTV system, the new list-PR system is likely to promote a reduction in the number of parties, over time, from the high level seen in 2002. However, it is unlikely to lead to a return to either a two-party system or a dominant-party system such as Colombia formerly experienced. Let us consider the expected effects of the new system on party-system fragmentation and the 2006 outcome. We will measure fragmentation by the "effective" number of parties, an index that is well established in political science for this purpose,[61] as well as by the actual number of party labels registered for elections and winning representation.

Given the experience of roughly similar proportional-representation systems elsewhere, we might expect the number of parties ("effective" or actual) to settle in the four-to-six range. In the 2006 election, it was higher than this: when calculated based on votes, the effective number of parties (N) was 8.8 in the Senate and 8.6 in the House; on seats, it was 7.2 in both houses. While this is indeed high, the most useful comparison is not with other countries but with the immediate prereform Colombian election. In the 2002 Senate election, the effective number of vote-winning parties was 8.9, approximately what it was in 2006. However, fragmentation in terms of seats was even greater, at 9.3. It is extremely rare (and presumably undesirable) for the N calculated on seats to be larger than the N calculated on votes. That it was so in 2002 only underscores the erratic way Colombia's SNTV electoral system treated parties—exaggerating, rather than reducing, the extreme political fragmentation. As can be seen from a legislative fragmentation in 2006 that is effectively two parties smaller than it was in 2002, despite a roughly similar fragmentation of the vote, the new electoral system has brought about a reduction in overall fragmentation.

In terms of the actual number of parties, the impact of the reform was immediate and dramatic. In the Senate, twenty parties contested the 2006 election, and ten of them won seats.[62] In 2002, 321 lists—mostly with regional bases—ran under sixty-six different party (or "movement") labels (plus sixteen independents). Forty-one party labels and seven independent candidates were represented in the Senate after the 2002 election. Clearly, the new electoral system had an immediate impact, as existing political forces had to realign or have no chance of survival.

Table 7.8 shows the results of the 2006 election. For the first time in Colombian history, a party other than Conservative or Liberal obtained a plurality of seats in one of the chambers of Congress. The Partido Social de Unidad National (Partido de la "U")[63] won 20 of the 100 seats. In the House, the Liberal Party retained plurality status, with 36 of 163 seats. Parties associated with President Alvaro Uribe—including the Conservative Party and La "U"—did well, winning clear majorities in both houses. In assessing the still high degree of fragmentation in the 2006 election, it is worth putting the election in the context of a president seeking reelection as an independent. Uribe was Colombia's first reelection-eligible incumbent president,[64] and just as he did when he won his first term in 2002, he sought his second term without a party affiliation. It is impossible to say whether future presidential candidates will follow a similar path, but if they instead seek a partisan nomination, we can expect party-system fragmentation to decline. As discussed above, we can think of Colombia's electoral cycle as one of "counter-honeymoon" elections, in that the congressional election occurs on a separate date from the presidential election but within the campaign for the latter. With Uribe a strong favorite for reelection to a single additional term and with his not running with any one party, some of the fragmentation of the congressional vote in 2006 can be seen as a virtual "primary" among factions of the *uribista* movement, as various leaders jockey for influence in a second term and for advantage in the eventual succession to carry on Uribe's legacy.

Parties are identified in table 7.8 as to whether they were endorsed by President Uribe or not. As can be seen, there were five separate Uribe-endorsed parties[65] running in the Senate (a sixth, Por el País que Soñamos, got no seats but received 1.7% of the votes), and they obtained, collectively, 61 seats, on 57.8 percent of the vote. While this result indicates overrepresentation, it is important to recognize that the pro-Uribe parties were not overrepresented on account of having presented multiple lists, as would have been the case with the former SNTV system. Rather, they were overrepresented on account of the fragmentation of the *opposition*, including the many parties that failed to clear the new 2 percent threshold. The Uribe-endorsed lists collectively obtained nearly 60 percent of the votes that were cast for threshold-clearing parties, and thus their 61 (out of 100) seats are almost exactly what we should expect from a PR system employed in a single nationwide district.

These parties, plus the Uribe-endorsed National Salvation Movement and Por el País que Soñamos, combined for 90 House seats, or 55.2 percent, on 51.4 percent of the votes. As the column for advantage ratio indicates, some parties were overrepresented and some underrepresented in the House. The reason for this somewhat uneven result is that the House election is carried out in thirty-two self-contained districts of varying magnitudes. Thus the precise regional spread of a party's votes is critical to its overall translation of votes into seats. The most striking aspect of the result is the extent to which this regional variation included many parties that were running in only one or a few districts.

As we noted above, there were twenty parties contesting the election for the Senate. In the House, the number was thirty-nine, of which eleven could be considered "national" parties. We can define a party as "national" if it presents lists in at least twenty House districts, as well as for the Senate. The remaining twenty-eight parties would thus be "regional" parties, and together they obtained about 16 percent of the votes and 21 (13 percent) of the seats. Thus only nine of the twenty-eight regional parties bothered to present Senate lists. In other words, regional politicians generally recognized that the 2 percent threshold would be a barrier to their obtaining Senate representation. However, they also understood that they had good prospects of winning seats in the lower House, and many of them were able to do so under the labels of regional parties. Table 7.8 indicates the number of districts in which parties ran, and for those regional parties that won seats it also indicates the districts in which they won. Aside from one list that ran only in Bogotá and another that won a seat in Valle (where Cali, Colombia's second largest city, is located), these parties have a very distinct "peripheral" character, being concentrated in outlying districts in the south and east, and along the Atlantic coast.

The exact shape of the party system will take some time to sort itself out, especially once Uribe is no longer a candidate in 2010, but it is obvious that the incentives of the new electoral system have already led to defragmenting behavior by political elites at the national level, while retaining space for distinct political forces to articulate some regional interests in House elections. It is also clear that the former character of the party system under SNTV—a single dominant party and a fragmented set of other parties—is unlikely to return. Presumably the reduction in the total number of party labels competing in elections clarifies options for voters considerably over the prereform situation, and thus it can be expected to improve popular accountability of the Congress over time.

Intraparty Competition: *Microempresas* Continuing?

We now consider how the new electoral system is shaping intraparty fragmentation, with reference to the lists presented in 2006 and the election outcome. The first consideration is the extent to which parties choose to present open or closed lists. For the 2006 elections, of the eleven "national" parties identified in the preceding subsection, nine elected to present open lists in the Senate (including all five Uribe-endorsed lists). The pattern was much the same in the House, where about 82 percent of all lists (412 in total, across the thirty-two districts) were open. Only two senators and fifteen representatives were elected from closed lists. Thus, at least in 2006, the new Colombian electoral system can be analyzed as if it were an open-list system, notwithstanding parties' option of presenting a closed list.[66]

Opponents of the open list feared that the preference vote would simply perpetuate the *microempresas* of the old system. However, this view overlooked how the new phenomenon of party vote pooling tends to make parties far less concerned with management of how their votes are distributed among candidates.[67] If parties do not have to manage the vote distribution problem of SNTV—the inherent risk of committing errors of allocation and displacing seats to other parties—then large parties become less a collection of narrow (clientelistic) interests than they were before. A vote for any candidate of the party is beneficial to the party as a whole, unlike under SNTV.

Table 7.8
Results of March 12, 2006, Colombian Congressional Election

Party	Senate		House of Representatives				
	% Votes	Seats	% Votes	Seats	% Seats	A**	Districts***
PSUN (Partido Social de Unidad Nacional—Partido de la "U")*	18.0	20	16.8	29	17.8	1.06	29
Conservative*	16.6	18	15.7	30	18.4	1.17	21
Liberal	16.0	17	19.0	36	22.1	1.16	32
Cambio Radical*	13.8	15	10.7	20	12.3	1.15	24
PDA (Polo Democratico Alternativo)	10.0	11	8.2	9	5.5	0.67	29
PCC (Partido Convergencia Ciudadana)	6.4	7	4.6	8	4.9	1.07	21
ALAS Equipo Colombia*	4.8	5	4.3	7	4.3	1.00	28
Colombia Democrática*	2.9	3	2.5	2	0.5	0.49	22
Colombia Viva	2.5	2	0.03	0	0.0	0.00	10
MIRA (Movimiento Independiente de Renovación Absoluta)	2.4	2	2.7	1	0.6	0.23	30
Apertura Liberal	—	—	2.3	5	3.1	1.33	12 (Bolívar, Magdalena, Vichada)
Movimiento Nacional	—	—	2.0	2	1.2	0.61	2 (Atlántico)
Movimiento Popular Unido	—	—	1.5	2	1.2	0.82	12 (Valle)
Por el País que Soñamos*	1.7	0	1.1	1	0.6	0.56	1 (Bogotá)
Integración Regional	—	—	1.1	4	2.5	2.23	4 (Meta, Nariño, San Andrés)
Huila Nuevo y Liberalismo	—	—	0.9	2	1.2	1.36	1 (Huila)
PAS (Partido de Acción Social)	—	—	0.6	1	0.6	1.02	1 (Sucre)
Moral	—	—	0.4	1	0.6	1.53	1 (Magdalena)

Table 7.8
Results of March 12, 2006, Colombian Congressional Election (*continued*)

Party	Senate		House of Representatives				
	% Votes	Seats	% Votes	Seats	% Seats	A**	Districts***
MSN (Movimiento de Salvación Nacional)*	—	—	0.3	1	0.6	2.04	1 (Caldas)
Participación Popular	—	—	0.2	1	0.6	3.07	1 (Caquetá)
Nacional Progesista	0.1	0	0.1	1	0.6	6.13	1 (Amazonas)
Others	4.8	0	5.0	0	0.0	0.00	
Parties endorsed by President Uribe (subtotal)	(57.8)	(61)	(51.4)	(90)	(55.2)	(1.07)	

Note: All parties that won Senate or House representation are shown. Also shown are all national parties (defined as those that presented a Senate list and a list in each of at least twenty House districts), provided that they obtained at least 1% of the Senate vote. Vote percentages are based on the total valid party vote, from preliminary data available from the Registraduría Nacional de Estado Civil as of March 20, 2006. Special constituencies for indigenous, Afro-Colombians, and citizens abroad not shown.

*Party endorsed by President Uribe.

**Advantage ratio, A = (% seats)/(% votes).

***"Districts" indicates number of House districts in which party ran a list; names of districts indicate those in which the party won its seats (for non-national parties only).

Smaller parties, on the other hand, tend to appear to be more fragmented on the intraparty dimension under open lists than under SNTV, but this appearance is misleading. Under the single-list system now in place they can present many candidates because they no longer need to concern themselves with concentrating their votes on one candidate to ensure winning even one seat. Moreover, various small parties have merged to form larger parties in order to clear the threshold, as we saw shortly after the passage of the reform with the formation of the opposition Polo Democrático on the left and subsequently with Partido de la "U" as a pro-Uribe party.

Table 7.9 provides two indications of intraparty voting behavior under open lists. The first two data columns repeat for both the House and Senate in 2006 what table 7.6 above showed for the Senate under SNTV in 2002: the average member's vote as a percentage of all the votes obtained in a district (nationwide, in the case of the Senate) by his or her party. For the Senate, this intraparty share is loosely related to the number of candidates a list presented, as would be expected, and as can be seen from the relatively high share for the candidates elected from the short lists presented by Colombia Democrática and Colombia Viva. Strikingly, for the Liberal Party, the intraparty share under a 100-candidate open list is actually greater than was the case in 2002 under SNTV, which only underscores how internally fragmented the Liberal Party had become. For other parties that contested both elections, fragmentation is indeed greater in 2006 than in 2002, but, as noted above, the reason for this is that these parties no longer have to limit the number of competing candidates they present because now all their candidates are running on one list, whereas in 2002 parties generally could elect more than one candidate only by presenting each one as the head of a distinct list. In turn, presenting many lists risked spreading their votes too thinly and possibly electing no one. In other words, for the nontraditional parties, the SNTV system artificially lowered intraparty fragmentation at the same time that it inflated interparty fragmentation as new parties emerged to challenge the Liberals and Conservatives. The single open list allows a party to present a slate of candidates that appeal to a more diverse constituency, knowing that a vote for any of these candidates contributes to the total vote and seat share of the party. For the House, table 7.9 shows that intraparty fragmentation is lower than in the Senate—as indicated by the higher average intraparty share for elected members. The reason for this difference is the lower district magnitudes, and hence the smaller number of candidates with whom each member was competing.

The second indicator of intraparty voting behavior shown in table 7.9 is the percentage of votes cast solely for the list. The preference vote is optional for voters as well as for parties. That is, even if a voter favors one of the parties that has presented an open list, the voter is free to give his or her vote simply to the list. Such votes *solo por la lista* count toward the determination of the number of seats a list wins but have no bearing on which of the party's candidates win those seats. That is, these votes have no significance to intraparty competition, as they would if the list type were flexible rather than open.[68] Given that these list-only votes have no practical effect on the identity of a party's elected candidates, the share of such votes is surprisingly high in both houses. For no party is it lower than 15 percent, and for many parties it is 20 percent or more.[69] Most likely, these high percentages of

Table 7.9
Internal Party Fragmentation in Colombian Congressional Election, 2006

Party	Average Congress Member's Vote as % of His/Her Party's Vote		Percentage of Party Votes Cast Solely for the List	
	Senate*	House	Senate	House
PSUN (Partido Social de Unidad Nacional— Partido de la "U")	3.0 (100)	32.8	23.5	24.8
Conservative	3.1 (51)	36.9	17.1	15.4
Liberal	3.2 (100)	36.0	18.5	16.0
Cambio Radical	4.0 (100)	31.9	18.2	18.5
PDA (Polo Demócratico Alternativo)	5.5 (67)	26.4	20.8	19.3
PCC (Partido Convergencia Ciudadana)	7.5 (46)	—	18.3	—
ALAS Equipo Colombia	10.5 (100)	—	20.7	—
Colombia Democrática	18.4 (23)	—	19.7	—
Colombia Viva	18.2 (17)	—	20.2	—

Note: Includes all parties that ran open lists in the Senate and five largest national parties in the House. Figures for the House are averaged across all districts in which the party presented an open list.

*Number in parentheses is number of candidates nominated.

voters choosing not to participate in the ranking of candidates indicates un-
familiarity with a new system and what the *voto preferente*—a completely
new concept in Colombian elections[70]—is. It is also possible that some voters assumed that a vote for the list only was an acceptance of a party-given
order of the candidates on the ballot.[71] There was also a significant effect
(not shown in the table) of district magnitude on the tendency of voters to
cast votes only for the list, rates of which are higher in the Senate and in the
few relatively large House districts than in the many small House districts.[72]
The only party for which the party label itself remained a significant predic-
tor of the percentage of votes solely for the list, after controlling for district
magnitude, was Partido de la "U." This may indicate that this pro-Uribe
party is successfully courting a constituency that values the party label and
what it stands for (i.e., support for President Uribe's policy priorities) more
than the identity of candidates.[73]

The small preference vote shares for the larger parties in the Senate, as
well as the much larger share of voters who chose not to cast a preference
vote, raises the question of the viability of an open-list system for this chamber. The new system permits parties to present a single Senate list with up to
one hundred candidates, which implies a staggering degree of intraparty
competition and bewilderingly long lists of candidate names for voters to
sort through. Rarely have open lists been attempted in such a large district.[74]
As we saw in table 7.9, not all parties chose to run a full slate of candidates
on open lists for the Senate in 2006, perhaps recognizing how unwieldy such
long lists could prove both for the voter trying to find his or her favored candidate and for party leaders trying to exercise some discretion, via the allocation of campaign resources, over which candidates were elected. Notably
the Conservative Party presented only fifty-one candidates and the Polo
Democrático Alternativo only sixty-seven, and some smaller parties presented much shorter lists. Even a list containing fifty to sixty-seven candidates is a very long list. It may behoove Colombian leaders to revisit the idea
of a flexible list—especially for the Senate, although the high percentage of
list-only votes in the House suggests it should be reconsidered for both
chambers. Another possibility might be to stay within the open-list paradigm but regionalize Senate lists.[75] Despite these reservations about the de-
sirability of open lists, we must not lose sight of the very important change
brought about by the new electoral system: parties need not concern themselves with how their votes are distributed across their candidates, thanks to
vote pooling. The number of candidates a party runs and the dispersion of

votes across those candidates will not affect the number of seats that the list as a whole wins in the Senate or any House district. In this sense, the new electoral system, independent of whether parties run open or closed lists, has greatly increased the role of parties in the electoral process and correspondingly reduced the problems of *microempresas electorales* and *avispas*, as they were known in the former system.

Summary of the Effects of the New Electoral System

We have now reviewed the likely effects of Colombia's new electoral system. The introduction of vote pooling reduces the reliance on personal votes compared to the former SNTV system. The new electoral system, consisting of single party lists and proportional representation, appears to be bringing about a rationalization of the party system, evident in 2006 in the dramatic and immediate reduction of the number of different party labels contesting elections and winning seats. Fragmentation in terms of the effective number of parties remained quite high in 2006, and this was partly a result of President Uribe's decision to run for reelection as an independent rather than to form a single party backing him. It was also partly a result of some parties challenging the new 2 percent threshold in the Senate and failing to clear it, and of the numerous regional parties in the House. Nonetheless, the 2006 election was contested around a preelection coalition of parties supporting President Uribe and a set of opposition parties, and over time this emerging realignment of the party system into national blocs is likely to enhance the accountability of Congress for national policy making and to streamline executive-legislative relations.

On the intraparty dimension, voters appear not to have embraced the preference vote in the first election and may not understand its significance. Whether or not over time the percentage of voters abstaining from the ranking of their party's candidates declines, and whether or not further reforms (perhaps to a flexible list) are considered, the new electoral system has ensured that intraparty competition no longer drives interparty competition. That is, the pooling of votes on party lists means that, unlike under the old system, a vote for any candidate within a party—or solely for the party— now contributes to the party's overall seat total. This promises to be the most important aspect of the reform, in that it allows parties to coordinate their political activity and represent the collective preferences of their constituencies far better than was feasible in the prereform system.

Conclusion

Colombia's congressional elections are now played out under a dramatically changed and improved electoral system. The former system was extremely permissive of small political forces, best illustrated by the fact that some senators could be elected with less than half a percent of the national votes. In the traditional parties, this permissiveness took the form of individual candidates with small personal-vote shares, cultivated largely by the provision of government benefits targeted to regions ("pork") or individuals (clientelism), and in fierce competition with numerous copartisans. In the nontraditional parties and movements, this permissiveness meant that many very small parties could gain representation but few could move beyond identification with the personality of their leader. For a small party lacking government connections and attempting to cultivate "opinion" votes, to present multiple candidate lists would be to divide their votes and risk winning no seats. The new electoral system, by mandating a single list for each party and by pooling votes at the party level (nationally in the Senate, and in each district in the House), greatly enhances the ability of parties to act collectively. It does so by doing two important things that the former system did not: (1) ensuring that seat allocations will reflect the distribution of votes by party; and (2) ensuring that a vote for any candidate of a party (in the case of parties presenting open lists) will aid the seat-winning potential of the party as a whole.

Of course, electoral reform is no panacea. Colombian democracy has been troubled by many factors other than its electoral system. Nonetheless, the electoral system is one of the most important features in defining how a democracy functions. The former system undermined political parties and thus reduced legislators' interest in, and capacity for, national policy making. By increasing the role of political parties, Colombia has the chance to develop a more policy-oriented national electoral process: not a guarantee, but the best chance in the past generation or more. In turn, the anticipated greater coherence of political parties should ease the passage of national policy reforms, including those that may be negotiated with demobilizing armed opponents, and it will facilitate the integration of former armed movements into party politics. The rest of Colombia's political progress is in the hands of its leaders and voters, but at least the electoral system has been removed as an obstacle.

Notes

We are grateful to Monica Pachón Buitrago for research assistance and to the many Colombians who kindly consented to be interviewed on the record for this project (and who are acknowledged individually in the notes). We accept full responsibility for our interpretations of their remarks.

1. In recent years, the Freedom House has placed Colombia in the "partly free" rather than "free" category; nonetheless, Freedom House still classifies Colombia as an "electoral democracy."

2. "Exposición de motivos: Proyecto de Acto Legislativo para la Reforma de la Política Colombiana y la Profundización de la Democracia," *Gaceta del Congreso*, no. 215, October 8, 1998, p. 7.

3. This is distinct from the Uruguayan electoral system, in which all of the votes for the lists of a given party *(lema)* are pooled, so that proportionality to parties is ensured.

4. Because it was an *acto legislativo*, which amends the constitution, it was not subject to presidential veto like an ordinary bill.

5. Several democracies have carried out significant reforms of their electoral systems since the early 1990s, but only those of Italy, New Zealand, and perhaps Japan can be considered serious rivals to Colombia's for the title of "most fundamental." See Shugart (2001).

6. "Exposición de motivos."

7. Ibid.

8. In this discussion of the functioning of the former system, we will generally use the present tense for ease of exposition, even though the system has been abolished.

9. The result would be the same if we assumed the Conservatives had continued to run two lists, as in the actual case, while the Liberals had run one.

10. Or, as Cox (1991) put it, SNTV and d'Hondt are "equivalent" in terms of their expected seat bonus to the largest party.

11. Pooling necessarily exists if parties employ a ballot structure in which they control the order of election from a party list. However, pooling can also exist if they do not employ such a ballot, as in "open" lists.

12. Single-seat districts typically imply relatively high personal-vote incentives and are not considered in this analysis.

13. For two empirical studies that find evidence for this differential effect of magnitude on the incentive to cultivate a personal vote, see Crisp et al. (2004) and Shugart, Valdini, and Suominen (2005). The Crisp et al. study includes data from Colombia.

14. Another factor is that there is a proliferation of "movements" using the name of a major party but modified in some way—for instance, Movimiento Nacional

Conservador and Liberales Unidos. These are often headed by a national leader as a means of promoting candidates in his home department. Again, if politicians were interested in rationalizing this process, they presumably could, by passing and overseeing the enforcement of a law regulating the process. By not doing so, national and regional leaders can have a label personally identified with them, while retaining identification with the larger Liberal or Conservative label.

15. The term comes from the Spanish word for ballpoint pen and is thus a reference to the "tyranny" of control being placed in the hands of whoever has the authority to determine the composition of party lists.

16. We ignore here the special seats set aside in each house for ethnic minorities.

17. This result in 1990 was not an isolated occurrence. In no election from 1978 to 1990 did the Liberals enjoy an advantage ratio (A) greater than 1.00. The values for each Senate election from 1974 to 1990 are 1.06, 1.00, 0.98, 1.00, and 0.99. For the House, on the other hand, the increase in A starting in 1991 is expected, given reduced district magnitudes compared to 1990 and before.

18. See Nielson and Shugart (1999) and Taylor (1997) for further discussion of this point.

19. For instance, Payne (1968), Latorrre (1974), Hartlyn (1988), and Osterling (1989).

20. Naturally, elections fought purely between cohesive parties may also be expensive and subject to capture by large economic interests as parties seek to differentiate themselves from one another. The Venezuelan case is instructive in this sense (Crisp 2000; Shugart 2001). The key distinction is that party-based elections *may* be conducted to a very large degree on programs and the ongoing reputation of the party as a provider of national policy, while personalistic campaigns almost never are.

21. In the case of the Conservative Party, data comparing 1994 to 1991 show that the percentage of that party's senators who could have been elected with only those votes won in their home department actually increased.

22. Colombia's case, where Senate $M = 100$, is even more striking than that of Japan, with its low M, because low M is conducive to the overrepresentation of the largest party under any common electoral rule.

23. We could modify that definition a bit to fit Colombian reality, to say that it is the $M - q$ candidates, where q is the number of seats won by quotas and is hence removed from the remainders/SNTV pool. However, in recent elections, q has been no higher than two or three out of one hundred Senate seats, and usually zero in each House district.

24. See also Cox (1996).

25. Measured by percentage of votes in the House.

26. Navarro had nominated many non-M19 candidates to broaden the movement's appeal.

27. Bibiana Mercado, "Renovación o más de lo mismo," *El Tiempo*, April 8, 2000 (quoting Navarro). A similar view was expressed by Santana Rodríguez (1998: 15).

28. Interview with Eduardo Chavez, program director of Verde Oxígeno, February 8, 2001.

29. Ibid.

30. A variety of sources interviewed in Bogotá agreed with this interpretation, including Rodrigo Losada Lora (Universidad Javeriana), Miguel Angel Herrera (Universidad Nacional), Elizabeth Ungar (Universidad de los Andes), and Eduardo Chavez (Verde Oxígeno)

31. Terreros B. Alexander, "Empezó la lucha de poderes," *El Tiempo,* April 9, 2000.

32. "Empezó la campaña presidencial," *El Espectador,* May 15, 2000.

33. "Corte de Franela," *Semana,* no. 940 (May 8–15, 2000): 36.

34. "Presidente Pastrana no insistará en revocatoria," *El Tiempo,* May 27, 2000.

35. "¿Con el pueblo y sin Congreso? Sí o no," *El Espectador,* May 15, 2000; "El referendo, historia de un enredo jurídico," *El Tiempo,* May 20, 2000.

36. "Referendo en la tierra del olvido," *El Tiempo,* July 16, 2000.

37. "La Tregua," *Semana,* no. 943 (May 29–June 5, 2000): 22.

38. Interview with Senator Rafael Orduz (ASI-MCI), February 8, 2001.

39. Interview with Olga Lucia Arjona, aide to Juan Martin Caicedo, February 6, 2001.

40. Flexible lists are common in Europe (e.g., Austria, Belgium, Czech Republic).

41. On this point about how to count votes not indicating a candidate preference, the version passed in 2000 by the Senate said: "Los votos por el partido polítco que no hayan sido atribuidos por el elector a ningún candidato en particular se contabilizarán por la lista presentada por el partido." By contrast, the version that both houses had passed in 1998 said: "Los votos por el partido polítco que no hayan sido atribuidos por el elector a ningún candidato en particular se contabilizarán *en el orden establecido en la lista presentada por el partido*" (emphasis added). The wording from 1998 thus appears to require a flexible list rather than an open list.

42. The version that emerged from the Conference Committee in 2000 said simply (and unclearly) "se empleará el sistema de la cifra repartidora y el voto preferente."

43. Interview with Representative Antonio Navarro Wolff (Via Alterna), February 7, 2001.

44. Ibid.

45. The only congressional election thus omitted is that of 1991, which was an interim election to establish the new Congress mandated by the constitution promulgated that year.

46. Results would be almost identical if we used House vote totals instead.

47. And its leader, Luis Carlos Galán, became the presumptive front-runner for the Liberal presidential nomination of 1990 until he was assassinated in August, 1989.

48. A glaring exception is 1990, when the party split. The Conservative dissident ran under the label of the National Salvation Movement and polled 23.9 percent of the vote. Because this label did not appear in the congressional elections two months before, we could sum the two Conservatives' presidential votes, resulting in 36.2 percent, or

about five percentage points better than the party polled in the congressional election of that year.

49. We derive these numbers from Congreso Visible, an organization that monitors the behavior of Colombian Congress members. See "Mapa político del Senado," retrieved September 11, 2004, from www.andi.com.co/CVisibles/quienes/documentos/bancadasSenado.doc, and "Buscador Legislativo," retrieved Febrary 26, 2006, from http://cvisible.uniandes.edu.co/share/user/listadoCongresistas.php.

50. Interview with Senator Rafael Pardo, August 25, 2003.

51. Some articles were subsequently removed from the referendum by the Constitutional Court in the summer of 2003, but these did not include provisions regarding the electoral system.

52. "En el referendo se concentran la politiquería y los intereses mezquinos," interview with Héctor Pineda, spokesman of the Comite Ciudadano Promotor del Voto por el No, *Semana*, no. 1107 (July 18, 2003), online edition, retrieved February 26, 2003, from http://semana.terra.com.co/archivo/articulosView.jsp?id=71711.

53. It also states that the list may contain no more candidates than there are seats in the district. A version passed by the Senate in the first round simply limited the number of lists per party.

54. It actually combined provisions from one bill promoted by several *oficilista* Liberals and another promoted by various Conservatives.

55. "El que pega primero," *Semana*, no. 1103 (June 21, 2003), online edition, retrieved February 23, 2006, from http://semana.terra.com.co/archivo/articulosView.jsp?id=71118.

56. Ibid.

57. Interview with Senator Holguin Sardi, August 26, 2003.

58. Congreso Visible, "Congreso tomó distancia," *El Tiempo*, June 23, 2003.

59. The First Committee is that to which constitutional amendment proposals are referred.

60. "Nueva derrota del gobierno: Cámara aprueba reforma política en penúltimo debate," *El Tiempo*, June 3, 2003.

61. The "effective" number of parties (N) indicates the number of hypothetical same-sized parties that would render a party system just as fractionalized as are the actual parties of different sizes. It is calculated as $N = 1/[\Sigma(p_i 2)]$, where p_i is the vote (or seat) share of party i, and Σ (Greek sigma) indicates that we sum over all the parties. In other words, N is a weighted index, in which each party is weighted by its own size.

62. In this discussion, we will ignore the special constituencies for indigenous (which exist in both houses) and for Afro-Colombians (in the lower House).

63. This party was made up mostly of dissident Liberals who supported Uribe (himself a defector from the Liberal Party), while the party retaining the Liberal label went into opposition. The new electoral system effectively made it impossible for factions using the same party label in elections to take opposing stances with respect to the executive.

64. Presidents were made eligible for two consecutive terms by a constitutional amendment passed by Congress in December 2004 and upheld by the Constitutional Court in October 2005.

65. In addition, other parties, including Colombia Viva, Convergencia Ciudadana, and MIRA, supported Uribe but did not obtain the president's endorsement.

66. In the House, all of the members elected from closed lists were the only members elected from their list, and most were from regional parties in peripheral districts.

67. Shugart made this point in an editorial in the Colombian newsweekly *Cambio;* see Matthew Shugart, "La reforma política, paso crucial," *Cambio* 6 (June 30–July 6), retrieved February 23, 2006, from www.cambio.com.co/html/opinion/articulos/1199.

68. As explained earlier, in a flexible list parties provide a rank order of their candidates (as they do under closed lists), but this order may be altered if sufficient percentages of the party's voters prefer candidates whom the party ranked lower. Voters casting votes solely for the list, then, are effectively delegating the selection of elected candidates to their party if the list is flexible but to other voters if the list is open.

69. A comparison to Brazil, which has used open lists with an optional preference vote for many years, is instructive. According to data in Samuels (1999: 500) for elections of 1986, 1990, and 1994, the three largest parties over this period had percentages of voters (averaged across chamber districts) electing not to participate in the ranking of candidates that ranged from 1.4 to 19.1 and averaged 9.25. The fourth largest party of this period, the Workers Party (PT), was exceptional, having label-only votes ranging from 22.7 percent to 43.3 percent.

70. Actually, the preference vote first appeared in the departmental and municipal elections of 2003.

71. Parties gave their candidates numbers, and the assignment of these numbers was not random, yet for a voter to accept the party's designation of a given candidate as their "number one" and cast a vote aiding the election of that candidate required the voter to cast a preference vote for the candidate.

72. For lists running in districts containing six seats or fewer the average share of votes cast solely for the list was 16 percent, while for the larger House districts the average was just over 20 percent. A regression analysis on the House lists reveals that the effect of magnitude is statistically significant (at 99 percent confidence). Each additional seat in a district adds about 0.39 percent to a constant value of 14.8 percent in the percentage of voters declining to give a preference vote. (The analysis was performed only on lists that elected at least one candidate; the result is even stronger if the analysis is confined to those lists that elected at least two candidates, where intraparty competition for preference votes is arguably even more important.)

73. When magnitude was not controlled for, the label of Cambio Radical was also significant and that of the PDA was just short of the 90 percent confidence level. The PDA won most of its seats in larger districts, so it is impossible to disentangle magnitude and the value of the label itself as predictors of the tendency of PDA voters to abstain from casting preference votes. Full details of these regression models are available from the senior author.

74. Among the rare examples is Peru, which had a single national Senate district of $M = 60$ and open lists in 1985 and 1990 and a unicameral assembly of $M = 120$ in 1995 and 2000. For 2001, the single chamber was districted, thereby greatly reducing magnitude and hence intraparty fragmentation.

75. This could be done without sacrificing either the national allocation of seats to parties or the ability of party leaders to run nationwide. For instance, there could be ten regional nominating districts, with each party presenting a maximum of ten candidates in each. Parties could be permitted to nominate up to five candidates who would run in every district, with the remainder required to be district residents. Once seats were assigned to parties nationally, seats could be assigned within parties to nominating districts on the basis of the contribution of that district to the party's vote total, and to candidates on the basis of their preference votes. Various formulas could be designed to accomplish the goal of balancing national and regional representation, and, while the formula would be necessarily complex, for the voter it would be simpler than confronting lists with up to one hundred candidates each.

References

Archer, Ron. 1990. "Paralysis of Reform: Political Stability and Social Conflict in Colombia." PhD diss., University of California, Berkeley.

Archer, Ron, and Matthew S. Shugart. 1997. "Presidential Power and Its Limits in Colombia." In *Presidentialism and Democracy in Latin America,* ed. Scott Mainwaring and Matthew S. Shugart. Cambridge: Cambridge University Press.

Baerwald, Hans. 1986. *Party Politics in Japan.* Boston: Allen and Unwin.

Bejarano, Ana María, and Andrés Dávila, eds. 1998. *Elecciones y democracia en Colombia, 1997–1998.* Bogotá: Fundación Social.

Betancourt Pulecio, Ingrid. 1998. "La verdadera reforma es do los Independientes." In Santana Rodríguez 1998b: 93-98.

Botero, Felipe. 1998. "El senado que nunca fue: La circunscripción nacional después de tres elecciones." In Bejarano and Dávila 1998.

Carey, John M., and Matthew S. Shugart. 1995. "Incentives to Cultivate a Personal Vote: A Rank Ordering of Electoral Formulas." *Electoral Studies* 14 (December): 417–39.

Coppedge, Michael. 1994. *Strong Parties and Lame Ducks: Presidential Partyarchy and Factionalism in Venezuela.* Stanford: Stanford University Press.

Cox, Gary W. 1991. "SNTV and d'Hondt Are 'Equivalent.'" *Electoral Studies* 10:118–32.

———. 1996. "Is the Single Nontransferable Vote Superproportional? Evidence from Japan and Taiwan." *American Journal of Political Science* 40, no. 3:740–55.

———. 1997. *Making Votes Count: Strategic Coordination in the World's Electoral Systems.* Cambridge: Cambridge University Press.

Cox, Gary W., and Mathew D. McCubbins. 1993. *Legislative Leviathan: Party Government in the House.* Berkeley: University of California Press.

Cox, Gary W., and Matthew S. Shugart. 1995. "In the Absence of Vote Pooling: Nomination and Allocation Errors in Colombia." *Electoral Studies* 14 (December): 441–60.

Crisp, Brian F. 2000. *Democratic Institutional Design: The Powers and Incentives of Venezuelan Politicians and Interest Groups.* Stanford: Stanford University Press.

Crisp, Brian F., Maria C. Escobar-Lemmon, Bradford S. Jones, Mark P. Jones, and Michelle M. Taylor-Robinson. 2004. "Electoral Incentives and Representation in Six Presidential Democracies." *Journal of Politics* 66 (August): 823–46.

Crisp, Brian F., and Rachael E. Ingall. 2002. "Institutional Engineering and the Nature of Representation: Mapping the Effects of Electoral Reform in Colombia." *American Journal of Political Science* 46, no. 4:733–48.

Curtis, Gerald. 1988. *The Japanese Way of Politics.* New York: Columbia University Press.

Eckstein, Harry. 1980. "Theoretical Approaches to Explaining Collective Political Violence." In *Handbook of Political Conflict: Theory and Research,* ed. Ted R. Gurr. New York: Free Press.

Escobar Sierra, Hugo. 1998. "La paz, fundamental en la reforma política." In Santana Rodríguez 1998b: 75–80.

Gutiérrez Sanín, Francisco. 1998. "Rescate por un elefante: Congreso, sistema, y reforma política." In Bejarano and Dávila 1998.

———, ed. 2002. *Degradación o cambio: Evolución del sistema político colombiano.* Bogotá: Editorial Norma.

Gutiérrez Sanín, Francisco, and Andres Dávila. 2000. "Paleontólogos o politólogos: ¿Qué podemos decir hoy sobre los dinosaurios?" *Revista de Estudios Sociales* 6:39–50.

Hartlyn, Jonathan. 1988. *The Politics of Coalition Rule in Colombia.* New York: Cambridge University Press.

Hrebenar, Ronald J. 1986. *The Japanese Party System: From One-Party Rule to Coalition Government.* Boulder, CO: Westview Press.

Ingall, Rachael, and Brian F. Crisp. 2001. "Determinants of Home Style: The Many Incentives for Going Home in Colombia." *Legislative Studies Quarterly* 26, no. 3: 487–511.

Latorre, Mario. 1974. *Elecciones y partidos políticos en Colombia.* Bogotá: Universidad de los Andes, Departamento de Ciencia Política.

Leal Buitrago, Francisco, and Andrés Dávila Ladrón de Guevara. 1990. *Clientelismo: El sistema político y su expresión regional.* Bogotá: Tercer Mundo Editores.

López de la Roche, Fabio. 1994. *Izquierda y cultura política.* Bogotá: CINEP.

Martínez Neira, Néstor H. 1998. "Buscando gobernabilidad." In Santana Rodríguez 1998b: 51–56.

Martz, John D. 1992. "Party Elites and Leadership in Colombia and Venezuela." *Journal of Latin American Studies* 24:87–121.

McCubbins, Mathew D., and Frances M. Rosenbluth. 1993. "Party Provision for Personal Politics: Dividing the Votes in Japan." In *Structure and Policy in Japan and the United States,* ed. Peter Cowhey and Mathew D. McCubbins. New York: Cambridge University Press.

Nielson, Daniel L., and Matthew S. Shugart. 1999. "Constitutional Change in Colombia: Policy Adjustment through Institutional Change." *Comparative Political Studies* 32 (May): 313–41.

Osterling, Jorge P. 1989. *Democracy in Colombia: Clientelistic Politics and Guerrilla War.* New Brunswick, NJ: Transaction Publishers.

Payne, James L. 1968. *Patterns of Conflict in Colombia.* New Haven: Yale University Press.

Pizarro, Eduardo. 1997. "¿Hacia un sistema multipartidista? Las terceras fuerzas en Colombia hoy." *Análisis Político* 31:82–104.

———. 2002. "La atomización partidista en Colombia: El fenómeno de las microempresas electorales." In Gutiérrez Sanín 2002.

Reed, Steven R. 1994. "Democracy and the Personal Vote: A Cautionary Tale from Japan." *Electoral Studies* 13 (March): 17–28.

Reed, Steven R., and Michael F. Thies. 2001. "The Causes of Electoral Reform in Japan." In Shugart and Wattenberg 2001b.

Rodriguez Raga, J. 2002. "¿Cambiar todo para que nada cambie? Representación, sistema electoral y sistema de partidos en Colombia: Capacidad de adaptación de las élites políticas a cambios en el entorno institucional." In Gutiérrez Sanín 2002.

Samuels, David J. 1999. "Incentives to Cultivate a Personal Vote in Candidate-Centric Systems: Evidence from Brazil." *Comparative Political Studies* 32 (June): 487–518.

Santana Rodríguez, Pedro. 1998a. "Presentación." In Santana Rodríguez 1998b: 9-10.

———, ed. 1998b. *Reforma política y paz.* Bogotá: Ediciones Foro Nacional por Colombia.

Sarabia Better, Arturo. 2003. *Reformas políticas en Colombia.* Bogotá: Grupo Editorial Norma.

Shugart, Matthew S. 2001. "'Extreme' Electoral Systems and the Appeal of the Mixed-Member Alternative." In Shugart and Wattenberg 2001b.

Shugart, Matthew S., and John M. Carey. 1992. *Presidents and Assemblies: Constitutional Design and Electoral Dynamics.* Cambridge: Cambridge University Press.

Shugart, Matthew S., Melody Ellis Valdini, and Kati Suominen. 2005. "Looking for Locals: Voter Information Demands and Personal Vote-Earning Attributes of Legislators under Proportional Representation." *American Journal of Political Science* 29 (April): 437–49.

Shugart, Matthew S., and Martin P. Wattenberg. 2001a. "Conclusion: Are Mixed-Member Systems the Best of Both Worlds?" In Shugart and Wattenberg 2001b.

———, eds. 2001b. *Mixed-Member Electoral Systems: The Best of Both Worlds?* Oxford: Oxford University Press.

Taagepera, Rein, and Matthew S. Shugart. 1989. *Seats and Votes: The Effects and Determinants of Electoral Systems.* New Haven: Yale University Press.

Taylor, Steven L. 1997. "Electoral Reform and the Political Effects of the Post-1991 Colombian Senate." Paper presented at the International Congress of the Latin American Studies Association, Guadalajara, Mexico, April 17–19.

Organized Crime and the Political System in Colombia (1978–1998)

Francisco Gutiérrez Sanín

Gutiérrez explores the relationship between organized crime, principally drug traffickers, and politicians in Colombia, pushing the inquiry beyond the obvious infusion of drug money into political campaigns in exchange for political influence. The question he seeks to answer is simply, "How did each party benefit from the relationship?" Finding that its defining characteristics were its complexity and the excessively high cost to each side, he calls the relationship an "unhappy marriage." Drug traffickers were forced to rely on career politicians for influence. This created a peculiar principal-agent problem, since visible results on the part of the agents would destroy their efficacy as politicians. Politicians thus could take the money but fail to deliver. On the other hand, dozens of politicians—even first-class ones—associated with crime were thrown out of office, imprisoned, or even killed, so the relationship was not a happy one for them either. Gutiérrez uses interviews, journalistic materials, and archival records to build his case, while resorting to microeconomic principles and concepts to make the argument. He concludes that the very nature of the democratic process in Colombia permitted the intrusion of narco-interests into politics and at the same limited their effectiveness. Democracy, he says, is permeable but not vulnerable and remains the best context in which to fight the influence of organized crime on Colombia's leaders.

In the last several decades, the participation of drug cartels and other forms of organized crime in Colombian politics and the ongoing war has been overwhelming.[1] The main institutions—the presidency of the republic, the police, the army, the political parties, the Congress, and the regional-municipal councils—have been subject to the large-scale influence of drug trafficking. The same could be said of the paramilitaries and the guerrillas, although in their case the influence has taken different paths and reached different levels.[2] In response, the less perceptive students of our polity have come up with the notions—and buzzwords—of "narco-democracy" and "Mafioso democracy." Unfortunately, in full accordance with Gresham's law (or Murphy's law, if you will), influential journalists and public policy makers frequently back up their actions and statements with such ideas, and therefore they must be taken seriously. In this chapter, I will try to show why they are inaccurate.

To make my point, I will discuss the relationship between politicians and organized crime (principally drug traffickers) in the last two decades from the standpoint of a simple but crucial question: How did this relationship benefit both sides? As I understand it, this question has not been pursued in a systematic way because it seems to have a fairly obvious answer. Our political system has been fed by enormous resources—mainly but not exclusively money and thugs (see, e.g., Leal Buitrago and Dávila's classic account, 1991)—to develop its activities and exclude de facto or potential competitors. Drug cartels have used politicians to promote or block certain laws—the most emblematic being the extradition bill—and to guarantee impunity through influence peddling at the local, regional, and national levels. This answer is indeed correct—but incomplete. In particular, it confronts us with both empirical and analytical difficulties.

Let us begin with the empirical. The marriage between traditional politicians and narco-traffickers was a rather unhappy one.[3] The narco-traffickers' unhappiness was related to at least three problems. First, the narco-traffickers could easily identify with political newcomers, and some of them attempted to enter the political scene hand in hand with innovative, up-and-coming politicians. They were dazzled by the flaming speeches of these young critics of the system, who preached a sometimes explicit rejection of traditional politics. Second, narco-traffickers themselves were outspoken critics of traditional politicians, whom they considered corrupt and unsound and prone to treason. In fact, an antipolitical stance was a constant in their discourse. In Pablo Escobar's[4] case, it reached obsessive levels. The leaders of the more sophisticated Cali cartel protested periodically that politicians were cheating them. (This was true, by the way, as will be seen below.) Their basic mistrust is illustrated by this conversation between the Cali cartel boss Gilberto Rodríguez Orejuela and his public relations manager, Alberto Giraldo:[5]

Giraldo: This guy Samper seems to be a good friend . . .

Rodríguez: I hope the motherfucker doesn't freak out on his way [up].[6]

Narco-traffickers didn't just express their foul moods verbally. The list of politicians murdered by drug traffickers is long and covers the whole political spectrum (Landínez Suarez, Salcedo Ramírez, and Bautista 1998).[7] But in less extreme cases, when drug traffickers participated openly in public life and on behalf of their own interests, their platforms were generally civic-minded and antipolitical. They included angry denunciations against liberals and conservatives and calls for action against traditional "clientelists" (Gutiérrez 2000). Although some prominent drug traffickers belonged to the traditional parties and took this identity very seriously—Pablo Escobar was a member of the Liberal Party and Gonzalo Rodríguez Gacha belonged to the Conservative Party (Escobar Gaviria 2000)—as public figures they imagined themselves men of action and civic leaders. They felt there was a gulf between them and the garrulous, individualist, and neglectful politicians.[8]

Last but not least, drug traffickers frequently came to the bitter conclusion that the money they were investing to lubricate the state machinery was not being properly rewarded. Their negative evaluation of the services they obtained in return also extended to the state security organizations, although in this domain the results were much more tangible. In any case, differing evaluations by buyers and providers of services led to frequent friction and quarrels.[9]

There are at least two sides to every marriage, and the public lives of many of the politicians married to organized crime were generally "nasty, brutish, and short." Only a few of them escaped from the Hobbesian trap. A look at their biographies reveals a litany of misfortune and sudden falls from grace: prison terms—even before the 1991 Constitution, though especially thereafter, when the probability of being sent to jail increased notably—banishment from the political community, constant threats and intimidation, accidents, kidnapping, family havoc,[10] and death.

I am not suggesting we feel compassion for these characters who so deeply damaged the country and harmed thousands of people. Rather, we should wonder why they became involved in such a dynamic. Let us suppose, credibly enough in this case, that they were completely devoid of normative concerns. Why did they commit themselves to a relationship that, in a relatively short period, could harm their basic personal interests? Was it just hubris? Didn't they know there was a real risk of being punished? Did they peacefully accept risks, knowing the stakes were very high? Were they simply shortsighted? Did they think money coming from illegal business would pay for the years in jail and the banishment from political life?[11] No matter what the answers to these questions might be, and some will be suggested in this chapter, it is clear that, as a group, politicians lost ground and had to face the hostility of many social actors—the mass media and the United States, to mention just two of the most relevant to politicians themselves. They were put in an extremely vulnerable situation. Nobody illustrated this better than one of the most prominent politicians involved in the Cali cartel scandals when he said: "A recent survey pointed out the following answer to the question 'Who is responsible for the Colombian crisis?' Politicians, 46 percent; guerrillas, 15 percent; drug cartels, 10 percent."[12]

This takes us directly to the problem of explaining why politicians and drug traffickers have acted as they have in Colombia. Political regimes are made up of systems and institutions but also of individuals and groups making strategic calculations for their own benefit. Why should both politicians and criminals insist on strategies and interactions that are self-defeating and have prohibitive costs? Here we are facing a simple but powerful paradox: criminals and politicians interacted to satisfy their own narrow interests—in a parody of the famous and infamous *homo economicus*—but ended up destroying themselves.[13] I will try to address this paradox on two interrelated but analytically independent levels, which constitute the two main parts of this chapter.

In the first part, I try to show how the adaptation of the system to new entrants destabilized consociational pacts and procedures. This opened a dramatic divide between the socioeconomic elites and the political elites. In fact, we could say that the historical conditions that made the entrance of the drug cartels onto the political scene possible are the same conditions that constrained their influence. In other words, although democratic institutions are highly permeable, they are not very vulnerable, in the sense that it is easy for illegal actors to penetrate them but difficult to seize control of them. Still another way of putting it is that it is not easy to change democratic rules to benefit only one social actor, whether legal or illegal. In Colombia's case, rather than benefiting one actor, the system evolved in exactly the opposite direction, fostering a tormented pluralism that was extremely costly but no less real for its vicissitudes. The most striking example of this is the Constitution of 1991. It included the main demand of the drug cartels—the prohibition of extradition for Colombians—and at the same time provided the institutional grounds for dismantling the political influence of the Cali cartel leaders, making their prosecution and later arrest possible.

In the second and main part of the chapter, I analyze in detail the contractual dimension of the relationship between politicians and drug traffickers. It is easy to see that every politician was in a principal-agent relationship with his or her own criminal(s). The criminal wanted "his" or "her" Congress member to promote actions that would bring certain results. To get what he wanted, he offered the Congress member certain incentives. However, he could seldom directly learn what the politician had actually done. In other words, he did not know how much effort the politician made to reach the goal, and sometimes he could not even ascertain if any action was taking place at all. He did not have the tools to distinguish between a "good" (loyal and diligent) and a "bad" politician. To use the jargon of the literature, he was confronted with serious problems of moral hazard involved in acting in a "market of lemons" (Akerlof 1970; Kreps 1990). But his situation as principal was worsened by the fact that (1) he lacked a "benevolent court" (Laffont and Martimort 2002) to settle differences with the agent and (2) he himself had incentives to *encourage* the agent to cover his tracks because the efficacy of the agent depended on his ability to conceal himself. Thus "structurally" the relationship implied the exchange of contradictory signals (see below). This hindered the criminal's prospects for finding optimal contractual arrangements.[14]

To understand politicians, on the other hand, one must remember that their visibility as advocates of outlaws put them in jeopardy. They wanted the money from the drug cartels, but at the same time they were not willing to be too active in their defense. Even before the Constitution of 1991, if they had been too involved with illegal business, they could have been relatively strongly punished.[15] After the new constitution took effect the situation became worse. They were facing a collective action dilemma, a "tragedy of the commons." The dilemma is described in a schematic way in table 8.1. All narco-traffickers want "access" to political resources, including influence in decision making, for example. (In the Colombian case, given the extradition issue, they felt they needed it.) But in the process of obtaining access, they risk becoming conspicuous and thus triggering processes that may destroy them: the probability of being punished increases monotonically as their visibility increases.

For simplicity, and to maintain a two-player format, table 8.1 sets the situation of an individual narco-trafficker (Player 1) against all the other narco-traffickers (collective Player 2).[16] To avoid visibility, narco-traffickers (as a group) need to restrain themselves. However, each of them would rather have his or her counterpart exerting self-control while he or she gets unrestricted access. In other words, the best possible individual strategy for each narco-trafficker was to seek access without any kind of self-restraint, relying on the capacity for self-restraint of the others. Lacking central coordination, they became increasingly exposed and wasted all of their political resources. It is well known that the global result of this dynamic is self-destructive, although (or rather because) every agent develops a strictly rational strategy. Politicians who worked for narco-traffickers were in exactly the same situation; if we replace "access" with "capture of illegal rents," the dynamic illustrated in table 8.1 becomes applicable to them.

Table 8.1
The Illegal Actor "Tragedy of the Commons"

Player 1/Player 2	Self-Restraint	No Self-Restraint
Self-restraint	Both players get some level of access, but they are not punished because they are not too visible	Player 1 gets no access, Player 2 gets full access, and both are burdened with the cost of visibility
No self-restraint	Player 2 gets no access, Player 1 gets full access, without costs of visibility	Both players get full access, and are burdened with the cost of visibility

Note: This is a social dilemma if and only if the costs of visibility are high enough. Player 1 is an individual narco-trafficker. Player 2 represents all other narco-traffickers. No self-restraint is the dominant strategy for each individual player.

Furthermore, politicians had many benefactors and social enclaves with contradictory aims. The key expression to describe the history of traditional Colombian political parties in the last two decades might be "divided loyalties." Agents had many principals—a situation somewhat different from the classical catch-all party, as I will try to show throughout this chapter—*and this was actually a requisite of their efficacy as far as the drug cartels were concerned.* This led to a complex labyrinth made of multiple contradictions. It had nothing to do with the image of the hegemonic domination of one group or social caste over the whole of the society, as suggested by the term *narco-democracy* or by a large part of the literature on clientelism and political culture in Colombia.

In my conclusion, I will present a simple argument: Much discourse, a good deal of the social literature on Colombia, and many American policies have been influenced by a deep mistrust of democracy. Therefore, it is necessary to insist on discriminating between the permeability and vulnerability of a political system. Several democratic systems in developed countries—Italy, Japan, the United States—have been pervaded at one time or another by organized crime. I think, however, that if a country can count on two minimal conditions—real political competition and a strong and independent judiciary—narco-traffickers have little possibility of taking over the political system. Competition generates collective action and moral hazard problems, making the marriage between drug cartels and politicians an unhappy one. A functioning justice system increases the probability of punishment, making participation of political leaders in certain activities risky or even irrational. But these democratic "antibodies" act only as limitations to illicit political involvement. To nearly eliminate criminal influence in politics, conditions must be much more stringent and must include a vigilant public, strong social organizations and political institutions, social equity, and real freedom of speech.[17]

Furthermore, actions and discourse aimed at weakening democratic institutions—like Congress and regional and local councils—or at "reinventing the country," and thus getting rid of unpleasant and ugly democratic mediation, are only grist for the mill of narco-criminality. If competition is eliminated from the political system, the informational problems of the drug cartels vis-à-vis the politicians are removed, and the cartels can more easily influence the state. The taming of the judiciary under undemocratic regimes is, of course, also easier. The disclosure of the incidents taking place under the Fujimori-Montesinos rule in Peru seems to support this perception.

Before starting with the narrative proper, a few words on the method of exposition seem to be in order. I have used not only in-depth interviews, press reports, and official documents but also some archived information: congressional, assembly, and city council minutes, and proceedings of the Process 8000—the Colombian equivalent of the Italian "Clean Hands Process." These proceedings demand the deepest critical attention. To save face, politicians accused of misdoing resorted to different stratagems, some of them painfully naive, others quite sophisticated. They often directed public attention to their regional rivals, trying to implicate them as well ("death to Samson and to all his Philistines"). At the same time, these proceedings provide an extraordinarily rich description of how politics is done in Colombia, what kind of social networks support it, and what kind of skills and expectations it fosters. My criteria have been highly conservative, giving credit only to versions corroborated by, or highly compatible with, additional sources. I have also been extremely careful with exculpatory remarks. I will not try the reader's patience with repetitive terminology. The Colombian two-party political system is old (although not venerable). Therefore, I will treat the expressions *traditional* and *historical* as synonyms in reference to the Liberal and Conservative parties. In the case of competitors to the traditional parties, I will use terms such as *renovating forces, third parties, third forces,* and *alternative groups.* I do not make any distinction between the terms *politician, leader,* or *candidate,* on the one hand, and *criminal, drug (narco) trafficker,* or even *Mafioso,* on the other. I know there is a long discussion about the differences in meaning between "organized crime" and the Mafia, et cetera; I take definitional debates very seriously, but I am also aware that on certain occasions (and I suspect this is one of them) they become sterile and boring.

The Mise en Scène: Institutions and Structures

Beginning in 1978, institutional design in Colombia underwent important change at least in three areas. First, there were changes in the field of regulation. The political system between the end of the National Front—the consociational pact in force between 1958 and 1974—and the Constitution of 1991 became a machine, efficiently articulating what was taking place inside and outside the law. This "limited consociational democracy in an uncertain process of change," as Hartlyn (1993) accurately depicted it, functioned as an intermediary mechanism between "formal" and "informal" democracy[18] at several levels:

1. *Inclusion of extrasystemic actors.* This became a relevant public policy issue around 1978. The hope was to co-opt the guerrillas through peace agreements. The scheme, however, expanded to include all the illegal actors, eventually including drug dealers.

2. *Tacit or explicit antisubversive pacts.* In the 1980s, the state lost its monopoly on legitimate coercion by delegating some of that power, as well as by others usurping it. This fostered the conditions for the development of a huge paramilitary army in the 1990s. The delegation of force involved a new (regionalized) consociational model, including old elites, state agents, and organized crime.

3. *Regional pacts.* Some territories, including those in which the state was quite weak, were incorporated into national agreements. This increased the already existing overrepresentation of the less developed and less populated regions in the political system (Gutiérrez 1996).

4. *Tacit incorporation of the emergent elites.* Until the 1990s, important parts of the socioeconomic elites, the mass media, and, indeed, the decision makers in the United States tolerated and even encouraged a lax and at times even benevolent stance toward the emerging elites. They considered the struggle against (narco)corruption subordinate to other objectives (antisubversion and eventually economic adjustment programs).[19] This mood pervaded the relationship between the state and those social actors. All the governments in this period had at best dubious results in the fight against drug trafficking, but until 1994 they could count on U.S. benevolence, or at least aloofness, and the cooperation of diverse power holders in Colombia.

The fall of the Berlin Wall and the demands of economic adjustment began to render "informal democracy" useless and too costly. I am speaking of a phenomenon that is somewhat more than a coincidence and less than an explicit agreement between powerful actors. Indeed, modernizing reforms like those implemented in Colombia were developed all over Latin America, and there is an undeniable family air about all of them. In Colombia, however, three factors strongly influenced reforms: a limited but stable democracy that long preceded them, a growing insurgency, and an extraordinarily powerful organized criminal sector that, having appeared on the national scene by the mid-1970s, actively participated in public affairs.

The architects of the new constitution expected to address the limitations of the existing democracy, insurrection, and criminal transgression through a new social pact. The Constitution of 1991 aimed at an *aggiornamento*, with the hope of limiting or eliminating the coexistence of formal and informal democracy. Thus this chapter covers two periods, before and after 1991, a turning point when the political system's role underwent an important change. After 1991, the political system had to accomplish different functions, and—in theory—it had to fully conform to the law. Within the state, this task of "relegalization" of the political was to be taken on by the judiciary (Uprimny 1996).[20]

Another development in institutional design—directly related to the development of changes in regulation—was the political system's increasing malleability to adjust to a changing reality. I am talking not about a conspiracy (determined by a group or alliance) but about incremental adjustments (like those of a Rubik's cube) that soon became a way of governing in and through instability. Warfare and illegality, especially, triggered continuous adjustments. This encouraged many extrasystemic groups to think of the possibility of making the rules of the game fit their own interests. It also created a large gray area between legality and illegality. Thus, paradoxically, modernization and "formalization" at times offered windows of opportunity to illegal actors. At other times in Colombian history, groups had existed in what we could call a "juridical limbo," where they had been neither condemned nor totally accepted.[21] Now, on top of that informality, two perturbing new elements were added or reinforced: gray areas in which formal rules were difficult or impossible to apply and instability.

This situation led to several outcomes. As far as the relationship with the drug traffickers was concerned, a permanent ambiguity between complicity and negotiation was created. The line separating one from the other was thin.[22] In at least three administrations—Betancur (1982–86), Barco (1986–90), and Gaviria (1990–94)—the government accepted that high-level mediators would send feelers to the drug lords to find out the conditions under which they would start a peace process.[23] Conversations were extremely tortuous, for the governments had little margin to offer something real to their interlocutors or even to acknowledge that they were negotiating at all. Every negotiation was different, but all of them seem to have had two features in common. On the one hand, the Colombian government knew that to fight on many fronts not only was extremely costly but also might prove impossible. There was a high risk of defeat in simultaneously waging too many wars. On the other, there was the feeling that for Colombia the distribution of the costs and benefits of the world war against drugs was grossly unequal. Negotiation was a better alternative for the country, but, in spite of this, foreign forces instigated war. The argument led, for instance, to a principled opposition to extradition in both Congress and the National Constituent Assembly.[24]

Thus the problem of the political (noncontractual) relationships between intrasystemic sectors and the drug cartels was that they developed in an ambiguous context, in which the negotiators, the political class, the army, and the police could suddenly slip into complicity. Under the umbrella of Barco's war against the Medellín cartel's narco-terrorism, the state security organs created bonds with the Cali cartel. The political class was often involved in such events, which frequently had as protagonists alternative forces and angry critics of the traditional parties. Since there was no roll call voting in Congress before 1991, it is difficult to judge how much complicity, bargaining, or conviction there was, for example, in the massive rejection of extradition by the Lower House in 1989.

Incremental adjustments to the institutional framework brought about another outcome. Public opinion internalized these adjustments and posed cyclic demands whenever issues relating to war and violence were at stake. As soon as the costs of negotiation rose or were made visible, angry and belligerent majorities formed. As soon as the costs of war increased, pacifist alliances spread.[25] As far as I can see, there is good evidence in favor of the existence of cyclical majorities when judging the policies of the state regarding the drug cartels. "That week of December 1990, the degree to which Colombians were intimidated by bombs and fed up with warfare became quite evident. Eighty-one point five percent [of the people participating in the survey] expressed their willingness to accept the appointment of extraditable persons [drug lords] as state ministers if this could make the country peaceful again!"[26]

By the mid-1980s it was obvious that there was a generous area of overlap between politics and criminality. There was a criminal turn in politics (we will see to what extent in the next section), and there was also a conscious effort to politicize crime. The interplay between criminality and politics has appeared cyclically crucial in Colombian public life, but it has reached a climax in the last twenty years. Not long ago, a favorite trick of politicians involved with organized crime was to present themselves as victims of a conspiracy or as negotiators speaking on behalf of society. Perhaps this was not just typically Colombian. What was very typical, though, was the amount of evidence and the number of resources politicians could summon to dress up their arguments.

A final fundamental change in institutional design was the massive input of new actors into Colombian politics. Certainly, there were still too many landlords and ranchers in the Congress, but the class composition of both houses abruptly changed. The situation in the regional and local councils was similar.[27] Simultaneously, the nature of party factionalism changed and new resources (money and weapons) flowed into the process. At the beginning of the period, the party factions were big splinter groups (disidencias) that confronted a solid and more or less structured national or regional apparatus. Later, these factions turned into "cottage electoral enterprises" (microempresas electorales)—actually a very inexact term (Gutiérrez and Dávila 2000)—a cloud of small groups that were the party apparatus and had a very fuzzy and tortuous identity (which should not be confused with no identity at all).

Factions became increasingly independent, audacious, and foreign to the world of traditional parties. Since atomistic factionalism became an expression of social mobility and the means for a changeover in political leadership, it spawned brutal intraparty competition. At the same time, it became increasingly difficult for these factions to become bona fide actors in Colombia's formal democracy, for reasons that should become clear by the end of this chapter.[28] The growing fragmentation of the political parties joined the fragmentation of the state and of public policy design. Quite often, state ministries and agencies developed their own strategies, sometimes openly contradicting presidential guidelines. This phenomenon also occurred in the areas of state security and foreign affairs and pervaded the processes of conflict negotiation taking place between the state and the drug cartels.[29]

The changes I have outlined converged to one point: a deep conflict between the political elites on the one side and the socioeconomic elites, the middle class, and the public on the other. Mutual mistrust and exasperation increased during the 1990s. It was not so much the destruction of "bridges of communication" as the "deterioration of the collective relationship."

Certainly, the socioeconomic elites have their "own politicians" (and they are not alone in this regard), but they have come to despise and be afraid of the members of the traditional parties. During the 1994 local elections, upper-class *bogotanos* (capital dwellers) were already voting for nontraditional candidates. Their shift from traditional to alternative preferences was faster than that of any other social sector (Gutiérrez 1995). During the Samper period (1994–98), the disagreement turned into revulsion. The icon of this traumatic rupture was an angry statement made by the Consejo Gremial (composed of industrialists, traders, and landlords) against the government, castigating its lack of responsibility and its endangerment of Colombia's relationship with the United States.[30]

Actors and Contracts

In the last twenty years in Colombia, politicians took at least four basic stands regarding the intrusion of drug cartels into public life. The same person or group was able to combine these positions or alternate between them at different times.

First, there was *opposition*. The most outstanding example is Luis Carlos Galán's Nuevo Liberalismo (NL). NL's opposition is often taken for granted, obscuring the fact that most of its cadres started out as members of the traditional parties.[31] A careful monitoring of the ups and downs of the extradition issue in Congress shows important support for it from the traditional parties, although most of it was given when times were difficult for the drug traffickers.[32] We must also remember that in some regions where the Mafiosi rapidly created enemies as a result of their rash methods, some politicians also battled them (see Gutiérrez 2000).

Second, there was *withdrawal*. It is difficult to calculate exactly what portion of the members of the official Liberal and Conservative parties were not involved with organized crime because in the Process 8000 only a fraction of the people against whom there was incriminatory evidence were actually prosecuted. But even if we suppose that all of them were guilty—and we know for certain that this is not the case—a significant group did not have relationships with drug traffickers. However, many in this group avoided conflicts with narco-traffickers or with politicians that acted on their behalf.

Third, as we have seen above, there was *semiofficial negotiation* (i.e., politicians acting as promoters of a peace accord between narco-traffickers and the state). And fourth, there was *massive contracting with narco-traffickers,* which will be the focus of this section.

To understand this contracting well, we have to turn to the strategies of organized crime. Criminals who wanted to interact with politicians had, similarly, four basic choices: intimidation, opposition, subordination, and infiltration. They sometimes used these strategies together and at other times used them in more or less pure form.

First was *individual intimidation,* meaning open or implicit threats to force politicians to adopt a favorable stance toward narco-traffickers' demands. For a period, Pablo Escobar used this strategy against the enemies of extradition. On April 3, 1990, for example, he kidnapped Senator Federico Estrada Vélez, an important Liberal Party leader in the department of Antioquia. He accused him of being "a resolute enemy of dialogue and peace."[33] Subsequently, he assassinated him.

Escobar bribed politicians in addition to intimidating them, but in this case there was an implicit threat: the worst traitors were those who got money and then shirked. This explains his apparent implacability towards "his" politicians who failed to deliver.[34] Permanent intimidation is efficient only in the short run and in limited spheres of influence. It is not so useful when it comes to handling contractual relations in a modern market economy. In addition, carrying out threats can entail high costs for the narco-traffickers. This explains why Escobar's penetration of the political system was relatively limited (at least in comparison with what the Cali cartel achieved).

Second was *opposition:* that is, denunciation and criticism of traditional politics. The Movimiento Latino Nacional (MLN), a narco-movement from the Eje Cafetero region with a bizarre far-right ideology, peaked between 1984 and 1986. The movement not only made claims against traditional clientelist networks a regular part of its everyday political activity but also tried to block some of the key practices of those networks: manipulation of the payroll, buying and selling of real estate, and misuse of parliamentary aid funds. The outcome was permanent confrontation with the members of the traditional parties, who even signed a formal alliance to oppose the MLN (Gutiérrez 2000).

Third was *subordination,* in which the traditional party structure functioned, but under the direct supervision and control of extra- or semilegal actors. Subordination appeared where entrepreneurs in illegal networks tried to preserve traditional political intermediation but to deprive it of any autonomy through the use of strong intimidation techniques. This pattern seems to have guided the relationship between the emerald dealers and the leaders of the Conservative Party in Western Boyacá (Uribe 1992), where elected leaders apparently took direct orders from emerald dons. A careful and balanced report from the central government observed that "during our visits, we met a member of the departmental assembly and a member of the Lower House who were inside the [emerald] mines of Quípama, presumably carrying out illegal mining [guaqueo]; their dependence on the emerald leaders is evident" (Ocampo, Rangel, and Sánchez de Díaz 1993: 28).

Subordination entails problems, though. It is relevant only in the case of low-level cadres. Skillful and important politicians must have generous elbow room to yield results. This strategy is only useful, therefore, at the regional and local levels, and even then there is no protection from economic or political competitors. For example, in the 2000 elections a prominent emerald entrepreneur enthusiastically backed a candidate for mayor in Otanche—even releasing a flyer publicly announcing his support—but the candidate lost.[35]

A final tactic was *infiltration,* or buying the support of politicians through contracts and other arrangements that implied payment for services. Infiltration was deliberately adopted by the Cali cartel. A long-term strategy, at first it did not galvanize widespread opposition. On the contrary, it was supported by the careful and dense network that linked the interests of the regional and local socioeconomic elites and the Cali cartel. Furthermore, in situations where negotiation, legal advice, and complicity were separated by a very thin line, it allowed for generous use of the ambiguous status of the drug traffickers, who maintained legitimate roles in society even as the authorities began to pursue them more vigorously.

Infiltration thus offered narco-traffickers the most stable bridgehead in the system. The patient labor of the Cali cartel was rewarded with impressive achievements. At least two presidential campaigns, Betancur's (1978), and Samper's (1994), accepted *narco* funding. According to the former accountant of the Cali cartel, Guillermo Pallomari,[36] a very handsome percentage of the cost of the congressional campaigns of the official Liberal Party—Colombia's main political force—was paid by the Rodríguez Orejuela brothers, the leaders of the cartel. Party members included state ministers, general comptrollers, and heavyweights of national politics. Even if we discount inaccuracies due to failure of memory, manipulation, and exaggeration, Pallomari's list—corroborated by the Process 8000—is shocking.

The Conservatives and the third parties were not spared either. It is clear that in the late 1990s the Cali cartel was a reference point in Congress. The enthusiasm of a great many members of Congress with these and other "kind narco-traffickers"[37] was so extreme that in 1994 the Lower House conferred the *Orden de la Democracia*—one of the highest honors given by the Republic of Colombia—on drug lord Justo Pastor Perafán for his "honesty, constancy, and loyalty to the noblest ethical principles."[38] This scary mix of kitsch, unconscious humor, and immorality was one the most salient features of the period.

The drug cartels paid their members of Congress not just for ornamental purposes or for admission to elite social circles (anyway, a quite important objective for them) but for influence on legislation and public policies. They were not so effective in this area, however. A careful review of the attempts of the cartels to produce or block legislation shows the limitations of the infiltration strategy. As we have seen, extradition had strong supporters in the political establishment during the 1980s,[39] when infiltration was already massive, the Constitution of 1991 had not yet been imagined, and the U.S. stance toward both negotiation with drug lords and narco-corruption was lenient. As the situation worsened, the outcome was worse for drug traffickers, as one might expect: they staggered in putting through legislation and striking favorable bargains and encountered ferocious opposition to achieving their major goals.[40] It is worth analyzing in detail the reasons for this relative failure.

First, as we have seen, public opinion, socioeconomic elites, and the United States limited infiltration, though this applies mostly to the period after 1994. Second, there was real and firm opposition to the drug traffickers within the traditional parties, motivated by the conflict of regional interests, by normative concerns, or by both. Third, politicians cooperating with the drug traffickers were playing their own game, an old problem that almost all the Mafiosi in the world have had to cope with. Many of the politicians willing to take dirty money had priorities that potentially put them in conflict with illegal funders. They had to defend their careers and their standing vis-à-vis public opinion, and these considerations entered directly into their decision making. Fernando Botero Zea[41] was quite eloquent in this respect: "I must confess that for me and for my public image it was more profitable to arrest these people [the heads of the Cali cartel] than to reach an agreement with them that they submit to justice."[42]

At the same time, politicians had a relationship to other groups that they had to represent and/or defend. Not infrequently, this implied a sacrifice of the interests of the Mafia. When Samper was suffering through the stormiest stretch of his relationship with the United States, Botero Zea recommended adopting "confidence building measures" (in English in the original), one pillar of this strategy being "to launch a program to militarize San Andrés with a lot of publicity" in order to persuade the United States of the serious nature of the government's intentions.[43] This program affected the interests of the Cali cartel, including *narcos* that were part of Samper's campaign entourage, such as the Sarria spouses. In fact, Samper's government as a whole was more telling than Botero's gestures when it came to showing the outcome of a conflict of interest: Samper became the president of Colombia thanks to a campaign and a party massively permeated by the Cali cartel. When he deemed it necessary, though, he sent the heads of the Cali cartel to jail in order to save his own skin. "He freaked out," as Gilberto Rodríguez Orejuela would put it.

An analysis of the behavior of corrupt politicians shows a landscape that at this point should not take the reader by surprise. The people paid by the cartel eventually avoided decisive confrontations and even turned against its interests. For example, Eduardo Mestre—a Liberal of national standing, convicted in the 8000 Process, and a longtime friend of the Rodríguez brothers—"presented himself before the State Prosecutor's Office as an avatar of the struggle against drug trafficking and a zealous defender of extradition. He pointed to the fact that he had been one of the main defenders of the [extradition] law in the Congress."[44] Another vital contestation terrain for the narco-traffickers was property. The vote over Article 32 of House Bill 113 of 1996 and Senate Bill 19 of 1996 (in Colombia each house numbers the same bills differently) provides an illustration of shirking or at least of foot-dragging. Narco-traffickers clearly had a stronger influence in the Lower House, and they considered the bill—which limited the "extinction of domain," a legal form that allows the state to expropriate property acquired with illegal funds—absolutely vital. Furthermore, they won the vote, by a small margin (the result was reversed in further debates). But even in this case some anomalies can be found.

In table 8.2 the reader will find the results of the vote on Bill 113 in the Lower House, broken down by political affiliation. The "ayes" favored narco-traffickers, the "nays" hurt them. (As I said before, however, many "ayes" were a result of genuine conviction or of a bargaining position.) As could be expected, the political party most infiltrated by narco-traffickers— the Liberal Party—was more inclined to vote "yes" than others were. But all of the parties divided around the issue. A good quarter of the House, forty-eight members of Congress, did not participate in the vote—the favorite strategy of members of Parliament who were compromised by their relationships with narco-traffickers but at the same time lacked the ability, or the will, to take further risks. (Once again, this should not imply that abstainers were on the payroll of the Rodriguez brothers.)

An analysis of individual Congress members involved in Process 8000 reveals interesting details. Jairo Arturo Romero (Conservative) did not attend the session, giving an excuse; José Félix Turbay (Liberal) simply did not show up. Giovanni Lamboglia (Liberal) declared a conflict of interest.

Table 8.2
Vote on Bill 113 According to Party Affiliation

Party/Vote	Yes	No	"Excusa" (Didn't Attend Vote, Giving an Excuse)	"Impedido" (Stated S/he Couldn't Vote Because There Was a Conflict of Interest)	"No asiste" (Didn't Attend Vote)	Totals
Liberal	49	30	5	5	9	98
Conservative	7	19	5	1	21	52
Independent	3	8	1	1*	0	14
Totals	59	57	11	7	30	164

Source: Gaceta 626, December 26, 1996.
Note: I classify as "independent" people who had a seat in the name of a coalition. The votes were counted according to the affiliation at the time of voting. (Viviane Morales was independent and then became Liberal; Íngrid Betancur was Liberal and later turned independent.)
* Valencia Mosquera Agustín Hernando, of the circunscripción especial, seats reserved for ethnic minorities.

Norberto Morales Ballesteros (Liberal) voted "yes." Other House members who lost their seats in following years because of acts of corruption voted in different ways. Emilio Martínez, a Liberal who subsequently would be impeached for embezzlement, voted "no" (no surprise, he systematically went against *narco* interests). Carlos Oviedo Alfaro, a Conservative afterwards convicted of homicide and a narco-traffickers' man, voted "yes."[45] I do not want to exaggerate the number of times politicians went back on their agreements with narco-traffickers; it is clear that the corrupt networks of politicians worked and were useful. At the same time, there was real foot-dragging and a permanent temptation to take the money and then—if the situation got really hot, for example due to U.S. pressure—to avoid further risks. We know that the Cali cartel closely followed the behavior of its politicians, so it was aware of disappointing actions and outcomes.

The fourth reason for the relative failure of the cartels to influence public policy—a reason characteristic of the Colombian context—was that the Mafia had no direct impact on the clientelist networks carefully nurtured by the members of the traditional parties. In spite of all the journalistic ado made about events such as the burial of Pablo Escobar, organized crime's direct influence on politics was quite precarious. In Colombia, these things were measured in votes.[46] The Medellín cartel was rather weak in this area, and its much publicized funding of marginal barrios did not have a significant impact because the very poor in Colombia's big cities rarely vote (and very seldom belong to populist movements). The Mafia's most successful electoral venture by far was the MLN, and at the apex of its influence it had only two members in the Assembly of Quindío, compared to thirteen from the traditional parties. This cannot be considered even a fundamental regional challenge to the two-party system.

Without any need for brokers, the Cali cartel managed to recruit to its service small-time guerrillas, groups of hired assassins, and police officers—a fact consistently hushed up by our anti-Congress demagogues—but it never had its own political party. Indeed, while its influence on some factions was enormous, it was not an insider in the political game; in the world of politics, it needed brokers. It was not that party politics was placed on top of preexisting Mafia networks, as in a stylized Sicilian scenario. Rather, it was that the already strong partisan networks got additional input, but without undergoing substantial transformations in their structure. The basic modus operandi, documented again and again in interrogations, interviews, and newspaper articles, was that the Mafioso gave money to the head of the clientelist network, who in turn distributed it downwards, using his own discretion. The network kept on working as before, just with more money and increased activity. For example, José Félix Turbay said the following about the 20 million pesos he received from a messenger of the Cali cartel:

> I gave 5,000,000 pesos to my uncle Abel Turbay, and I took 15,000,000 to Bolívar Department, where I threw a New Year's party. We gave some of the money to several leaders there, who were supposed to buy some presents with it on behalf of the movement. . . . Among these [leaders], I remember Mrs. NN1, in charge of buying presents for the Turbaco Municipality, NN2, in charge of Cartagena, and NN3, in charge of Carmen de Bolívar. . . . We allocated the money according to the capacity of the municipalities. We gave small quantities to small municipalities. It was a simple calculation based on rules of thumb. There were no exact rules for giving the presents. I gave some of the money to people who came and visited me. Many people came, according to what we are used to doing here, at least in Bolívar, where I am involved in politics.[47]

The exogenous situation of the criminals vis-à-vis the political activity quickly generated an intense problem of informational economy that affected all the links of the chain. The drug traffickers gave money to a political leader so that he or she could be elected—or else it would be a lost investment—but he or she was tempted to siphon off this money for his or her own benefit, thus risking the whole enterprise. Certainly, the tradition of charging "tolls" (fees) for financing seems to be solidly entrenched in the Colombian clientelist tradition. Fernando Botero Zea recalled that when he was the coordinator of Gaviria's campaign east of Bogotá in 1990, "only a few of the political leaders invested all of the money provided by the campaign in the assigned tasks."[48] Drug dealers were not protected from losing money through these practices, as Samper's presidential campaign shows. The same phenomenon can be observed at the micro level. For instance, Jorge Ramón Elías Náder received some funds from the Cali cartel, apparently to finance political campaigns, but he used the money to buy a luxurious apartment for his nephew in Cartagena.[49]

Politicians not only charged "tolls" but also exaggerated their efforts. This happened even with people whose bread and butter depended on the drug cartels. Alberto Giraldo, the public relations man of the Cali cartel, once learned that a high-ranking police officer, who seemed to be open to corruption, was going to be appointed as the director of an institution and was planning to throw an "open house"—the English was used in the original—to celebrate. "Curiously enough, in the first conversation [intercepted by the authorities], Giraldo learned that the appointment ceremony in which the officer was made director had already taken place. Later on, to impress the Rodríguez Orejuela brothers, he lied to them, assuring them that he had attended the ceremony and that he had been invited by the officer to the open house."[50] This kind of case seems to have been common.[51]

Once elected, the politician knew that there was an (implicit or explicit) agenda to follow regarding the cartel. The cartel, in turn, understood that it should not put too much pressure on the politician. Its ideal politician was loyal but discreet so that he or she would not be stigmatized. Being identified as on the take from the drug traffickers meant a dramatic loss of efficacy and influence. As Miguel Rodríguez commented in a conversation intercepted by the authorities: "Listen, buddy, for sure I appreciate Eduardo [a politician in his payroll], but he has never come up with anything. Do the math, brother, and you will see all this adds up to nothing. At the end, *they'll* get the blackball too" (*they* meaning well-connected insiders).[52]

The Mafiosi emphasized the discreet use of their people in order not to burn them out. This meant giving them a free hand to act autonomously, though once in a while they would demand actual results from them.[53] Such an attitude also applied to the state security organs at the national level. (At the local level, the policemen simply took orders from the Mafiosi. This makes the relationship quite different.) Notice the following piece of advice from Miguel Rodríguez Orejuela to Alberto Giraldo when talking about a high-level police officer who apparently wanted to do some business with the cartel but was still hesitating: "You have to give it all, son. . . . Speak to him about love, respect, and distinction. . . . Tell him that we never do things with a sense of reciprocity."[54]

In this context, how could the drug dealer (the principal) establish an optimal contract with the politician (the agent)? The principal had a large number of incentives to select from and carefully monitored the agent's behavior (we know the Cali cartel leaders did precisely that) but generally observed only aggregate results and not individual levels of effort. At the same time, it is clear that the agent had good reasons to minimize his or her level of effort so he or she could keep the money and decrease the possibility of being punished. Aside from the characteristic difficulties of the principal-agent relationship, already studied in political contexts (Fearon 1999; Ferejohn 1986), here we have three additional aspects that make the informational problem of the principal more acute.

First, in this universe there were no tribunals, benevolent courts, or institutions to settle differences. Second, there were no values, norms, or social networks generating trust: drug traffickers, after an erratic start, looked precisely for those politicians who lacked integrity. They had to do so. If not, their "contributions" would have been useless.[55] An agent's lack of integrity was common knowledge; it was a dangerous and useful feature at the same time. Sometimes the roguery of the political leaders they dealt with generated a combination of amazement, reproach, and admiration in the criminals: "That César is a rogue, he is indeed a rogue."[56] Third, as described above, drug traffickers offered incentives to act in a certain direction, but they had to encourage—or at least to tolerate—systematic concealment. In other words, unlike in conventional principal-agent relationships, here the principal offered an ambiguous signal, rewarding or at least tolerating the agent's ability to hide his real level of effort, since an easily interpretable signal might be read not only by the principal but also by the authorities. It is in the context of this contractual ambiguity that we can understand the zigzagging of corrupted politicians, behavior that we have seen in congressional voting and in the attitude of some of the cartel's straw men toward extradition and other issues.

The Cali cartel tried to improve the efficiency of its investments by buying judges. This strategy aimed at reducing the incentives of the politicians to shirk or betray.[57] After the enactment of the Constitution of 1991, however, this became harder.[58] Sometimes drug traffickers got really upset and demanded results. They tried to raise the opaque veil separating them from politicians, as we can see in this dialogue between Miguel Rodríguez and Alberto Giraldo:

> *Rodríguez:* Listen, son, let me tell you something: that's bad 'cause ... It's unfair. ... You have been there. You have spoken. ... You have said, "Here we are." Now, I don't know if you haven't been able to talk to them, and you have been telling us lies, haven't you?

> *Giraldo:* Don't be such an asshole. When have I lied to you?

Rodríguez: Once I got you. You were not telling anything to those motherfuckers. . . . You have to face those people and tell them how things are. . . . Tell them they aren't demanding anything illegal, nothing outside the law. We're decent people who want our lives to be legal. We're people who all their fucking lives tried to help others, right?[59]

Why did the Cali cartel members refrain from the use of systematic intimidation in spite of their frustration? It was not because they did not have a brutal tradition of using violence against commercial competitors and social movements.[60] It was, instead, because the kind of network the cartel wanted to build—a network that would have long-term influence on certain public policies—depended on the voluntary collaboration of political leaders. An impulsive act of violence would ruin many years of work. Additionally, the "official doctrine" of the Cali cartel was that waging a war against the state was not a credible threat.[61] In any case, it had another tool at hand: legal intimidation. Although it paid many bribes in cash, it always tried to hand out some checks and in some cases even gave small gifts using credit cards. Politicians knew the cartel could expose them anytime: there was always proof. (If it had not been for this, the Process 8000 would have encountered many more difficulties.)[62] But even so, the threat was not totally credible, for it could become too costly for the cartel, the principal, to carry out.[63] Thus equilibrium was established: The dominant strategy of the Cali Mafia was to offer bribes, and that of the politicians was to take the money but to shirk their "duties" as soon as the costs of being agents of the cartel mounted.

That is why the final contracts between the *narcos* and the politicians were, from the principal's point of view, highly inefficient (at least according to the available evidence). In this field, there was no neoliberal reform in Colombia. No matter what kind of results they obtained, some politicians got a monthly salary and a Christmas bonus.[64] They were bureaucrats, in the pejorative sense of this word.

The politicians' collective action problems complicated the situation. The political leaders on the cartel payroll did not make common cause with one another. It would have been strange if they had, given the crazily complex landscape of mutually competing factions within the Liberal and—just a little bit more circumspect—Conservative parties. When they were threatened judicially or politically in any number of ways, they tried to build a common front that almost always ended up cracking. While Alfonso Valdivieso was state prosecutor (August 1994–May 1997), his office offered incentives to those who "defected," through plea bargaining, for example. This strategy was very successful.[65] If during the boom of narco-corruption the dominant strategy was no self-restraint, during the Process 8000 debacle—in perfect symmetry—the dominant strategy was to bow to pressure and to turn one's back on other politicians.

For instance, during Samper's administration, Congress members in the majority systematically floated draft bills that would benefit the drug economy. Nonetheless, as soon as public opinion, the justice apparatus, or the United States (or the three of them together) protested in a burst of rage, they backed off. This exasperating dance deeply damaged the country and its institutions. On the other hand, it showed the fragility of the politicians' commitment to the Cali cartel.

There is, however, one episode involving the Mafia that shows the political class keeping solidarity until the bitter end: the accusation and defense of Ernesto Samper in the Congress.[66] This episode is particularly striking because a good number of the Liberal Congress members knew that the president would sacrifice them, if necessary, to save himself.[67] General Prosecutor Valdivieso tried to push through a process to impeach President Samper for having received money from narco-traffickers during his campaign. According to the Colombian Constitution, the Congress had to evaluate if there was sufficient reason to start an impeachment process. Samper was able to gather a comfortable majority to abort the process with an avalanche of juridical arguments, scandalizing the Colombian public—already horrified by his being funded by narco-traffickers—yet again with his legal shenanigans to evade prosecution.

In this case, the explanatory importance of the Liberal identity should not be underestimated. I believe, however, that the most important factor was that the members of Congress could not make a credible threat[68] to defect from cooperation with Samper; if they had broken with him, their situation would have been even worse. Letting the president fall would have triggered a process of incalculable consequences, giving key institutional positions to people who publicly advocated very radical measures for corrupt politicians and creating new incentives for mutually damning accusations. The Congress members had no better strategy than to support Samper, and he was going to betray them whenever necessary.

Why, then, did politicians enter into this dynamic? The first reason has already been discussed: the structure of their interactions favored lack of self-control in a specific sense. They had at the same time incentives to be inefficient and to take unlimited amounts of money. Inefficiency as well as greed could make them fall into the criminal camp, but their greed was not under their (or the drug traffickers') control because, as table 8.1 shows, it was a product of a collective action dilemma.[69] Here we can easily identify a problem of collective overexposure (Dow 2000): each agent takes risks at the level he or she considers acceptable, but the aggregate-collective level of risk leads to disaster. The structure behind this dynamic is a principal-agent structure nested (Tsebelis 1990)[70] with a tragedy of the commons.

There was also much hubris clearly related to the "two sets of incentives" structure of the political system (both before and after the 1991 Constitution) that was discussed in the first part of this chapter. Some leaders believed that they would never be prosecuted or that, in the worst-case scenario, they would have enough resources to politicize their criminal activity. I will state an additional conjecture, though I do not have enough empirical evidence to prove it: in deeply uncertain and permanently unstable environments, politicians become risk-prone and develop high temporal discount rates. In effect, risk-averse politicians migrate to other activities, and those who remain have both the guts and the incentive structure to make very profitable, risky, and short-term bets. Both features *simultaneously* foster their corruption and render them unable to solve their collective action problems.

Divided loyalties also played an important role. Subjectively, politicians felt that in taking money from the Mafiosi they were not going against the system. This has to be understood at two levels. On the one hand, they were convinced that the socioeconomic elites had also accepted (and gotten benefits from) interactions with drug traffickers. They thought of themselves as guests to a party somebody else had organized.[71] It must be admitted that at least in the case of the Cali cartel this is a credible interpretation. On the other hand, in Colombia political campaigns seem to have drifted toward a "shared portfolio" modality in which stakeholders of the most diverse nature can participate. Under these circumstances, politicians were not particular about the possibility of crossing the line of legality. They felt safe if the majority of the actions were in the hands of the right people. People talk about Cocaine Inc.; in Colombia, it is also necessary to speak of Politics Ltd.

How has Politics Ltd. worked? Although the topic goes far beyond the limits of this paper and deserves a separate analysis (Gutiérrez n.d.), it is important to remember that in the context of atomistic factionalism politicians were desperately competing for financial resources. Since there were always huge new resources, competition for money ran amok. Not only the cadres but also many of the voters demanded immediate profit. Thus those with no money were excluded from the game.[72]

Most of the money came from the *grupos económicos* (the three or four enormous clusters of companies that play a dominant role in our economy), regional notables (only they had voters as well as money), and organized crime. I do not want to imply that legal entrepreneurs are similar to illegal ones in any normative or social sense or that there was some kind of coordination between the financing parties or between them and the leaders. As I have tried to show in this chapter, rather the contrary is true. Financing parties became increasingly uneasy about *their* politicians. They did not really know if they belonged to them or not. Actually, segmentation *(compartimentación)* seems to have been a common feature of campaigns in the 1990s. Politicians tried to avoid social or accounting crossovers between the different kinds of money they received.[73]

Furthermore, I believe that corrupt politicians were happy with the money coming from the Mafia as long as they could also get funds from "the decent people" *(gentes de bien)*. Only a few sold their souls outright to the Mafia. This was not a normative but a rational reluctance. "I guarantee, Mr. Magistrate, sir, that those 8,000,000 pesos [gotten from the Cali cartel] did not buy my heart, in the same way that the money coming from the economic groups [Bavaria] or from the businessmen of Sogamoso or Tunja did not buy it either."[74] This generated two axes around which divided loyalties revolved. The first axis had to do with the financial viability of politics and its actual intrasystemic nature: in other words, the ability to win elections (with the exception of Bogotá and perhaps other big cities) and, at the same time, remain inside the bounds of law was in question. It is clear that a significant portion of the local elites—cattle owners who did not pay taxes, cheating entrepreneurs, corrupt contractors—had also "crossed over the line" of the penal code. If you will allow me a *boutade,* a considerable chunk of the Liberal Party represented more or less adequately those who were above the law (the *grupos económicos* and the cattle ranchers in each region), outside the law (the Mafia), and below the law (the members of the clientelist networks who, due to their lack of rights, had to make use of favors or blackmailing). The second axis was related to a fracture between the "representative" capacities (the capacity to get votes) and the "presentative" ones (the capacity to present oneself in front of the cameras, to appeal to public opinion through the mass media). Traditional clientelists were still powerful in the representative dimension but counterproductive in the presentative one. Their votes were relished, but their uncomfortable personas were hidden from public opinion by national leaders. Note that both axes went beyond the typical contradictions of the catch-all party.

Conclusion

The preceding narrative is not an uplifting one. The defeat of the knaves is only partial, as I will underscore below. It is not even a case of "private vices versus public virtues." Here, private vices turned into public catastrophes that in turn caused thousands of deaths, a deep crisis of values, and possibly years of delay in terms of development. But it is a story—and how easily this can be forgotten—of "democratic institutions/public limits." Many works highlight the fact that corruption undermines democracy. Only a few highlight the equally important fact that democracy restricts the power of corruption.

Could we apply such an aphorism even to a tragic, clumsy, and limited democracy like Colombia? My answer is "yes." In the past two or three decades, there have been two considerable changes in Colombia. On the one hand, the entry barriers to the political system have been dramatically lowered. On the other, the system has moved from mediating between formality and informality to a search for institutional clarity. The new openness made possible the massive entrance of organized crime into politics, while the exploration of new institutions made it necessary, since illegal actors started to perceive a credible threat to their power and to search for the means to parry it. I must add to these factors the long tradition of coexistence with illegality among the Colombian socioeconomic elites (as well as among other actors) and of the use of the "combination of all forms of struggle" strategy (Sánchez 1998). Both changes, though, also made life difficult for the Mafiosi. The first created problems related to informational economy and collective action. The second made the justice system more vigorous and independent. The modernization process as a whole strengthened the middle and working classes, whose relationship to illegality was, at least in some regions of the country, distant and critical.

This cannot be taken as an invitation to lower our guard or to believe in a sort of self-regulation that would keep corruption within its "proper limits," as an ex-president once declared with unconscious humor. Mafiosi participation in Colombian public life has been a disaster, and thousands of people, inside and outside the political system, have risked their lives to stop it. Nonetheless, the Colombian case has taught us an important lesson: in spite of being probably more permeable than other systems, democracy is less vulnerable. Democracy can be painfully distorted, but as far as take-overs are concerned it is robust. The cartels, especially the Cali cartel, be-came unbelievably powerful and made many sectors of the system work for them. They penetrated the Congress, the state security organisms, and the presidency itself. Nevertheless, their ability to transform economic re-sources into effective power was limited, partly because many social actors opposed the narco-traffickers. But the patterns that make up the core of democracy itself—separation of powers and political competition—also created multifarious contradictions and dilemmas that rendered the crimi-nals' investment relatively inefficient. We need this drilled into us over and over again.

The practical reverberations of all this have to do first of all with the "siege" on the political system mounted by the general public, a part of the socioeconomic elites, and international actors. The "siege" has brought sometimes extremely positive—and sometimes negative—results. It has played a decisive role in preventing the takeover of the system by organized crime. But occasionally it has weakened democracy itself. The United States, for example, has sent tremendously wrong signals by sparing authoritarian forces whose involvement in narco-corruption is evident. In the Andean re-gion as a whole, including Colombia, much of the public and elites have un-derstood the message and adopted an agnostic attitude—at best—toward democracy. Incidentally, it is symptomatic that some of the accomplices and allies of the Mafiosi hastened to make authoritarian policy proposals on be-half of the anticorruption struggle.

One of the problems with the "natural antibodies" of democracy—political competition and an independent judiciary—is that they generate boom and bust cycles that are difficult to stop if there are no new, positive factors. My hypothesis is that between 1999 and 2001 narco-corruption de-creased, at least at the national level, but that other forms of organized crime maintained a significant—and perhaps even a growing—presence in the political system. I would mention at least two agents: corrupt contractors and paramilitary members (who have their own links with narco-trafficking). My impression is that both are well represented in the Congress. The contractors have already become visible and have taken a couple of beatings (though the results are not as energetic as one would desire). Maybe others will replace them. That would restart a new bloody and costly cycle. To stop the mechanism, we need to strengthen institutional formality and enhance democracy, not destroy it.

Addendum

This chapter was finished in 2001. Every author—at least among those I know—feels pretty uncomfortable after rereading an old paper. I am no exception. But in this case I would use basically the same type of arguments if I were writing today. Actually, I believe that in the last three years several events have taken place that rather confirm my theses. Thus, at my own risk—I know that people who hurry to announce "I told you so" are utterly unpleasant—I would like to be specific about some of the ways in which this "confirmation" has taken place.

Above all, the predicted cycle of penetration-disclosure is currently taking place. The paramilitaries claimed in 2002 that they had captured 35 percent of congressional seats—probably an overstatement, but the actual percentage is alarming anyway—and the peace process in progress between them and the government shows how deeply entrenched they are in the political system (especially at the regional level). At the same time, the political system is exhibiting the same disturbing ambiguities of bargaining and complicity and the same tortuous behavior—trying to circumvent international constraints while verbally accepting them—in face of the dilemmas created by any negotiation with actors that have a double identity, both political and criminal.

The paramilitary leaders who are negotiating with the government—at a snail's pace, as the public has come to learn—are deeply involved in narco-trafficking and other illegal undertakings; some of them are cocaine dons who reinvented themselves through armed politics. Thus, once again, we see the blend of criminality and politics and the ability of certain actors to cross the line that separates one field of activity from another. A careful scrutiny of the operations of the paramilitary in the field, and their relations with elected politicians, would yield a map of tensions and complicities similar to the one I sketched in this chapter.

Last but not least, I feel the chapter has been confirmed by the—again, ambiguous—developments regarding the mutual relationships between criminality, modernization, and democracy. President Uribe (elected in 2002) launched a vast anticorruption and anticriminality campaign and declared his deep engagement with the modernization of the country. The campaign scored some successes. At the same time, two of the crucial "safety devices" that prevented the transformation of permeability into vulnerability have weakened: the present U.S. administration privileges antisubversive motives over anti-*narco* ones and has tolerated a massive illegal infiltration (at the same time sending a strong signal to Colombian economic elites); and the old political system, whose persistence obliged the criminals to act through intermediaries, has loosened critically.

There are additional, growing problems. The Uribe administration has been linked to an effort to decisively weaken the checks and balances of the democratic regime, tilting toward the model of governance, which may be called "strong presidency," that has held sway over the imagination of hundreds of politicians in the Andean region in the last fifteen years.[75] A constant pressure on the judiciary and the stifling of political competition might offer organized crime the sort of opportunities it lacked in earlier years—when it had the clout but confronted social and contractual dilemmas—to qualitatively improve the returns on their investments in politicians. In this regard, the experience of Peru in the 1990s is eloquent enough. Any sensible campaign against criminality and corruption should encourage the independence of the judiciary, open up political competition, and respect the system of checks and balances.

Finally, the territorial control of the paramilitaries has gradually increased and deepened, and as of now there is no plan—sophisticated or not—to curb it. True, Uribe inherited the problem, and today in some regions one can see that the army is harassing paramilitary forces somewhat more scrupulously than before. However, the dimensions of the problem are such that much more energetic actions would be required. It may be that the ongoing peace process will simply legitimize the status quo, allowing the paramilitaries to return to legality without dismantling most of their rackets, illegal businesses, and criminal organizations—not an encouraging outcome for the credibility of the president's anticrime goals. This would put the government in dire straits, as it would highlight the obvious contradiction between the discourse on legality and transparency and the—so far—very disreputable settlement with the paramilitaries.

Notes

This paper presents results of the research project "Violence and the Political System 1978–1998," funded by Colciencias.

1. I will give some essential data and dates about the Colombian situation in this chapter. A complete chronology can be found in Matthiesen (2000). See also Hartlyn (1993) and Gutiérrez (2000).

2. The topic, though, goes beyond the scope of this chapter.

3. I will be using the past tense, since the basic period of my study is from 1978 to 1998. I am not implying that the connection between politicians and narco-traffickers is broken, only that it has been weakened. I will return later to the subject. See also the Addendum at the end of the chapter.

4. The head of the Medellín cartel. In an autobiographic work, his brother, Roberto Escobar, claimed that politicians had corrupted the narco-traffickers (Escobar Gaviria 2000).

5. Gilberto Rodríguez was the strategist and "statesman" of the Cali cartel. His brother, Miguel Rodríguez, was more involved in quotidian affairs. Both were already deep in the business in the 1970s. Alberto Giraldo is a journalist, go-between, and PR person of conservative background.

6. *Semana*, January 8, 1995, 23–31.

7. Nevertheless, the leftists and the independents were punished more severely, if one controls for size of the parties. This is a constant regarding the murder of political leaders and activists in Colombia (Gutiérrez and Dávila 2000).

8. There is also a certain antipolitical tradition among men of action in Colombia. In the 1960s, for example, rural bandits in the service of the Conservative Party in Western Boyacá had a rather turbulent relationship with their political contacts.

9. In 1989, Retired Captain Luis Javier Wanumen was arrested with documents indicating a connection between army members, the drug cartels, and the paramilitary. The Mafioso don Gonzalo Rodríguez Gacha sent his lieutenants to tell the police officers in the station where Wanumen was temporarily being held: "Go to hell. This is not what we're paying for." In other words, he was demanding that Wanumen be set free. However, Wanumen stayed in jail because the police wanted thirteen million pesos to let him go. Rodríguez Gacha thought the maximum should be no more than two million pesos. He said furiously: "Tell them I will waste them if they insist on the thirteen million figure." The police did not back off, however. These statements are taken from a conversation intercepted by the authorities. *Semana*, May 15, 1989, 26–29.

10. A fair number of the people prosecuted in the so-called "Proceso 8000" (the scandal involving the contribution of drug money to the Samper campaign) ended up getting divorced. I have the impression that many of the spouses felt ashamed to be married to politicians. For instance, the husband of Congresswoman María Izquierdo declared, "What do wives ask for money for, especially a wife like María Izquierdo? To waste it in politics!" Then he added, "I always begged her not to get involved in this dirty business." Testimony of Mr. José Rodríguez Piñeros before the Supreme Court of Justice, February 14, 1996.

11. Some politicians stole enough money to live comfortably for the rest of their lives, and the most intelligent of them even saved money. Others were already rich before they took the money from the drug cartels. However, this was not true in all cases, and even where illegal money was effective insurance against professional risks, it is still not evident that politicians' behavior was successfully optimizing—or even satisficing, as game theory would describe it. If they had not been so bold, they could have accumulated much more money without having to put up with public exposure. Therefore, we have to take into consideration additional parameters—e.g., their notion of time—which will be briefly discussed below. There is also an aspect of incommensurability regarding threats: for example, What is the price (not to society but to oneself) of the possibility of losing one's life?

12. Complement to the interrogation of Mr. Fernando Botero Zea, February 14, 1996.

13. This is a far cry from the thesis that Thoumi (2002) attributes to me, without offering a single quotation: "This led Gutiérrez Sanín to argue that traffickers did not get much for their money." No. At the end of the original version of this chapter, I stated the following: "The cartels, especially the Cali cartel, became unbelievably powerful. They made many sectors of the system work for them. They penetrated the Congress, the state security organisms, and the presidency itself. Nevertheless, their ability to transform economic resources into effective power was limited." And what I try to explain is why, despite their "unbelievable" power, (1) they got less that *what they expected,* and (2) they paid very high costs for their large-scale penetration of the political system. In the long run, the most important members of both groups (corrupt politicians and criminals) were not that successful. I claim that this is evidence of collective action and contractual dilemmas, created—among other factors—by democratic institutional design. No more, no less. But even the arguments offered by Thoumi against his straw man do not work very well. He says, first of all, that "while drug moneys can cover a very large share of a political campaign, they are insignificant relative to total drug revenues," which implies that "traffickers are willing to 'throw away' funds to politicians without a quid pro quo." This is a misunderstanding of the problem. Stakes were high not because of the amounts of money involved but because of the importance of the political issues that were being decided (extradition, property rights, etc.). Even then, anybody who has studied organized crime knows that criminals are not fond of being cheated, even when small amounts are involved, because their life and fortunes rest on a reputation of impla-

cability. The idea that narco-traffickers will merrily throw around their money without a quid pro quo is particularly amazing. If *narcos* use their contributions "as jokers that they can pull out when needed," then this is simply a delayed quid pro quo (which, by the way, I look at in this chapter). Thoumi also says: "Many inconspicuous non-extraditable traffickers use their contributions just to gain social recognition." Basically true, but inexact, since, by the very nature of the business, "non-extraditable traffickers" are a rarity. (I deal with this issue as well in this chapter.) But then narco-traffickers should be aware that they are incurring high risks in contributing to politicians because each new contribution makes them less and less inconspicuous, a point that Thoumi fails to notice.

14. According to Lévi's dictum (2000), I will use the logic of this literature in the analysis without offering an explicit model (although formulating a model might be possible and interesting).

15. A common perception is that before 1991 no measures were taken against corruption. This is an exaggeration, although it is true that corrupt leaders could move more freely. However, some were sent to prison (though not banned from political life, as currently happens), including powerful people like Alberto Santofimio Botero, an important politician and presidential alternative *(presidenciable)* in the Liberal Party. There were also sanctions at the regional and local levels.

16. This can be easily generalized to an *n*-player format, in the obvious way (see, e.g., Lichbach 1996).

17. In Colombia in the last five years all of these conditions have deteriorated. To explain why I am providing this heterogeneous list of conditions, which transcend the scope of this chapter. However, I believe the list includes some items necessary for a normatively desirable adjustment of our political system.

18. I am using *informal democracy* in an analogous manner to the way the expression *informal economy* is used.

19. I don't want to imply that the war on drugs in the 1980s was phony. What I want to stress is that (as in a typical exercise of optimization) it was subject to some fundamental constraints, the first of which was the preservation of the stability of the Colombian political system.

20. Of course, there was continuity between the two periods (before and after the constitution), but for politicians the "two-times" framework made a difference as far as what could and could not be done.

21. "El narcocassette del 'Loco' Giraldo," *Semana*, June 28, 1994. This phenomenon appeared before the period we are studying. A good example is the emerald economy, which even today is still in that limbo. Only since the 1970s, however, has it been sufficiently large as to affect the whole political system.

22. This is a quite complicated topic transcending not only the scope of this chapter but also my empirical evidence. See Gómez and Giraldo (1992) and Mathiessen (2000) for an excellent documentation of some of the negotiation processes.

23. At least in Gaviria's case there was a de facto negotiation (Gómez and Giraldo 1992).

24. When I refer to a "principled opposition," I mean an opposition not paid for by the drug cartels or designed to favor them. An important sector of the Left and of the traditional parties attacked extradition. Some of these opponents were principled, and some of them were paid.

25. I know I am not doing justice to the rich and complex subject of cyclical majorities in the Colombian political system, which is key to the understanding of the relationship between violence and democracy in the last two decades (Gutiérrez n.d.).

26. "Todo tiempo pasado," Semana, January 24, 1995, 22–27. In contrast, from 1995 on, there was a growing anger with the drug traffickers.

27. I cannot provide quantitative data in this regard, but I have found exactly the same pattern in almost every clientelist network I have studied. Twenty years ago, local "notables" headed these networks. Later they were replaced, and the networks became disperse and fragmented. Local politics turned into a channel for upward social mobility, providing both large benefits and high risks.

28. I am using the expression *formal democracy* with the idea of making a contrast with the "informal" democracy (as in the dichotomy formal-informal economy) that regulates and incorporates illegal activities.

29. An extreme example of this is as follows: During Barco's administration, Joaquín Vallejo Arbeláez, a well-known figure of Liberal background, believing he was following a government suggestion, and obsessed with the idea of stopping narco-terrorism, worked with the Medellín cartel to write a draft agreement for a negotiated solution. Vallejo handed this document to German Montoya, a close advisor to the president, who thought that the United States—being the world's number one consumer of illegal drugs and having interests in Colombia—should participate in an eventual negotiation. The outcome was that the cartel (not the state, or the Colombian Embassy, or a group of negotiators) was to contract with a lobbying firm to sell the idea to the American public. According to the journalistic account (which, as far as I know, has not been contradicted), the cartel actually hired a lobbyist, but without success. In the end, the government parted company from the initiative. "La bomba del diálogo," Semana, October 10, 1989, 24–29.

30. This would have been unthinkable ten years before. "Se enreda la pita." Semana, October 10, 1995, 38–46.

31. In fact, some drug traffickers tried to win people from the Nuevo Liberalismo, but they were able to co-opt only a few individuals successfully.

32. However, the anti-*narco* social base gave signs of vitality even when there was a quasi-consensus favoring the ban on extradition and negotiation with drug lords. When the subject was discussed in the Constitutional Assembly of 1991, a member of the Liberal Directorate of Antioquia (one of the departments most affected by narco-trafficking and violence) sent a document to the assembly, defending extradition and strong

measures against narco-traffickers. "If the new constitution is not soft on crime—he concluded—and if it gives the executive adequate tools to fight crime . . . and makes a great reform of the Congress . . . Colombia very soon will be admired by nationals and foreigners." Daniel Henao Segura, letter to ANC, January 10, 1991.

33. Flyer produced by the *Extraditables* (those who are subject to extradition), April 4, 1990.

34. "Amistades peligrosas," *Semana,* April 10, 1994, 4–6.

35. By the way, this candidate presented himself as an enemy of the vices and corruption of the traditional political class.

36. Complement to the interrogation of Guillermo Pallomari, Commission of the State Prosecutor in charge of penal investigation 24249, November 14, 1995.

37. "While the Medellín cartel was throwing bombs and killing, this cartel [Cali] was searching for . . . empathy." Statement of María Izquierdo during the complement to the interrogation of María Izquierdo before the Supreme Court of Justice, n.d.

38. Resolution 178, April 7, 1994. Perafán was subsequently jailed and extradited to the United States.

39. Extradition was supported not only by the majority of the Nuevo Liberalismo, its ministers, and its representatives in Parliament, but also by an important part of the official Liberal and Conservative parties.

40. Roberto Pombo, "El año del juicio del siglo," *Semana,* January 16, 1996, 9.

41. Liberal politician, who was minister of defense in the Samper administration until the general prosecutor jailed him for his links with the Cali cartel.

42. Complement to the interrogation of Fernando Botero Zea. State Prosecutor's Commission, February 7, 1996.

43. Complement to the interrogation of Fernando Botero Zea. State Prosecutor's Commission, February 5, 1996.

44. *Semana,* February 5, 1995, 26–29. For a similar line of defense, see also the complement to the interrogation of María Izquierdo, Supreme Court of Justice, December 1, 1996. These are not mere coincidences; at the beginning of Process 8000, some of the most vulnerable Parliament members created a group to study the possibility of carrying out a successful legal defense. The initiative did not prosper due to collective action problems.

45. Not coincidentally, Oviedo can be described as an extreme risk taker. I do not count Yolima Espinosa, because, although at the time of the vote she was involved in the 8000 Process, she was later shown to be innocent.

46. But it must be said that using other criteria they don't fare very well either. Pablo Escobar's burial was crowded but relatively small when compared, for example, to the ceremonies of other public figures who were assassinated in the period. With the exception of the Movimiento Latino Nacional, a regional movement that deserves separate scrutiny (Gutiérrez 2000), the Mafia was not capable of generating massive support or social mobilization.

47. Interrogation of José Félix Turbay, Regional Prosecutor's Office, December 10, 1997. I do not know of any testimony from interrogations or interviews contradicting this basic image. Fieldwork also supports it.

48. Transcription of the complement to the interrogation of Fernando Botero Zea. Regional Prosecutor's Office, January 22, 1996. But evidence seems to show that in 1994 this righteous defender of morality charged his own "toll" to Samper's campaign, around US$1,000,000. What is under discussion is whether this money belonged to the Mafia or not. See, e.g., "Auto de detención por hurto contra Botero Zea," *El Tiempo*, January 24, 2001, 1-5.

49. First instance # 033, Jorge Ramón Elías Náder, Delegate Prosecutor's Office before the Supreme Court of Justice, September 2, 1997. Maybe Náder was lying, and the donation was not given to finance his campaigns but as a payment for services because Náder was one of the cartel's really good politicians. If so, it would undermine the example but not the general argument.

50. "¿Quién es Benitín?" *Semana*, July 19, 1994, 34–37.

51. According to the confusing and ambiguous statements of Father Bernardo Hoyos, ex-mayor of Barranquilla and leader of a nontraditional group vociferous about anticorruption, whose second term as mayor, however, was accused of having been highly corrupt. See "El boleteo del cura," *Semana*, June 27, 1995, 24–25, where Hoyos states that some politicians not only asked for money from the Rodríguezes but also "demanded" it. Hoyos had an interview with the Rodríguez brothers in which they showed him some apparently incendiary documents. The priest's statements threw the heads of the cartel into a tizzy: politicians were not thinking of the public good but only of their own benefit. Miguel Rodríguez Orejuela commented: "You talk to them about one thing, but they do another. . . . Fuck. . . . You should have seen how we had to beg for this favor, and the stuff turned out to be something completely different. . . . But then, one thinks a person like him should be reasonable because of his position . . . that he should not be the protagonist, that he only wants peace, to benefit everyone. . . . And now, one finds out that he only wants to be a star and to fuck us." Conversation intercepted by the authorities, quoted in "Miguel Rodríguez, 'Ya tengo empacada la plata,'" *Semana*, July 18, 1995, 34–37.

52. "¿Quiénes serían?" *Semana*, June 28, 1994, 8–12.

53. The Medellín cartel was much cruder. A congressman told *Vanity Fair* that Escobar did not know how to approach them. According to this version, more colorful for sure than what actually happened, if somebody opposed Pablo Escobar when he was in the Congress, he would offer his opponent a check. "Senators were much too ashamed. They pretended not to know who he was." Quoted in "Una visión gringa," *Semana*, November 24, 1992, 46–53.

54. Rodríguez wanted the officer turn a blind eye for thirty days. Literally, he was "buying time" for the cartel. Notice these kinds of "favors" were also a serious informational issue for the Colombian state and society. In a short time it is difficult to distin-

guish between voluntary paralysis, unprovoked failure, and lack of skills, especially in an institutional context characterized by inefficiency and high levels of uncertainty.

55. At the beginning, they offered money to people who were perhaps unaware they were getting funding from criminals.

56. ¿Quiénes serían?" Most probably, the reference is to a sports leader.

57. This also relates to their efforts to come to a negotiated solution when Gustavo de Greiff was the general prosecutor of the nation (April 1992–August 1994). I will skip the issue here.

58. For example, the cartel bought the general procurator of the nation, Mr. Orlando Vásquez Veláquez, but he ended up in jail.

59. Conversation intercepted by the authorities and quoted in "Medina tiene la palabra," *Semana*, August 1, 1995, 23–31.

60. See in this regard the excellent doctoral dissertation of Joseph Ricardo (1998) which includes ample empirical documentation on the differentiated attitudes and practices vis-à-vis violence within the cartel.

61. In an informal definition, a "credible threat" is, in game theory, a threat that can be implemented by an agent without harming his or her own interests. Here, the Cali cartel thought war against the state would harm its interests. The Medellín cartel, on the other hand, thought it was a feasible alternative.

62. María Izquierdo complained that the Cali cartel leaders had no sympathy for her. In their meticulous accounting, they almost always used initials to identify all of the people they gave money to. In her case, they used her full name.

63. An important precedent was that of Rodrigo Lara Bonilla, a quite popular leader of the Nuevo Liberalismo, and the first minister of justice during Betancur's government. In vengeance, since he was really fighting the Mafia, the Medellín cartel exhibited a check Lara had accepted (apparently without knowing the source) from a criminal. This radicalized Lara's war against the Mafia. He was then murdered, and his murder, in turn, generated a very tough anti-Mafia response fully supported by public opinion. For sure, the members of the Cali cartel had this and other experiences fresh in their minds.

64. "El maletín de Miguel Rodríguez," *Revista Semana*, July 25, 1995, 22–28.

65. Members of Congress who admitted their offenses and denounced other corrupt politicians received a reduction in their sentences (both jail time and fines). The effect on congressional solidarity was devastating. For example, Jaime Lara Arjona admitted receiving more than 300 million pesos from the Cali cartel and in turn named two of his peers, Jorge Tadeo Lozano and Roberto Pérez Santos. His sentence was reduced by one-sixth, though "he hadn't told all the truth." Proceso No. 28802-5 por Enriquecimiento Ilícito y Falsedad Documental, Juzgado Quinto del Circuito Especializado, November 2, 1999.

66. As soon as arrests related to Process 8000 started, fifteen of the Parliament members at high risk created a group to study their options if they were formally

charged. Three hypotheses were debated in the group: (1) "President Samper is going to help us. Ultimately, we are all involved in the same problem." (2) "Samper is going to sacrifice us in order to save his scalp." (3) "Everybody, the president and the Congress members, is lost." "Ave María." *Semana*, January 23, 1996, 22–30.

67. Most probably, this was also the (accurate) view of the drug lords who, in spite of knowing what was going to happen, never defected.

68. See n. 61.

69. Of course, it was their own fault that they lacked normative concerns and took bribes in that situation.

70. This is not explicitly stated in Dow's model. His model operates in an organizational universe and therefore searches for explanations related to lack of internal control. The analogue of this in a nonorganizational universe is a collective action dilemma.

71. According to María Izquierdo, "We all knew President Samper had been a close friend of the Rodríguezes since 1990. Nobody in the high elite of Colombia ignored that." Certainly there is an exaggeration here. What we do not know is how big the exaggeration is. Complement to the interrogation of María Izquierdo, Supreme Court of Justice, February 9, 1996.

72. María Izquierdo complains: "[During the campaign], in every department each one of us had to get funds for the election lunch, for transportation, for all the things people got used to being given by politicians." Complement to the interrogation of Senator María Izquierdo, Supreme Court of Justice, February 12, 1996. The notion of "people getting used to generosity" is a common complaint among politicians and comes up in the course of not only interviews but also campaigns (Gutiérrez 1998).

73. In Náder's case, the main benefactors were Cervecería Águila and the Cali cartel (this pattern reproduced Samper's campaign at the regional level). Náder's son-in-law declares: "I remember that when he told me to fetch those checks in Cervería Águila, he asked me not to mix them up with the ones he had given me beforehand [checks paid by the Cali cartel]. That is the reason why I opened another account." By the way, Náder's case shows clearly how fees were also charged to legal benefactors. Interrogation of Federico E. Meisel de Castro, State Prosecutor's Office/National Unit against Money Laundering, September 15, 1997.

74. Complement to the interrogation of Senator María Izquierdo, Supreme Court of Justice, n.d.

75. Actually, opinion polls consistently show that Colombia's population is less enthusiastic about democracy than any other in the Andes region.

References

Akerlof, G. 1970. "The Market for Lemons: Quality, Uncertainty and the Market Mechanism." *Review of Economic Studies*, no. 54:345–64.

Dow, James. 2000. "What Is Systemic Risk? Moral Hazard, Initial Shocks and Propagation." Working paper, Bank of Japan, Tokyo.

Escobar Gaviria, Roberto. 2000. *Mi hermano Pablo*. Bogotá: Quintero Editores.

Fearon, James. 1999. "Electoral Accountability and the Control of Politicians: Selecting Good Types versus Sanctioning Good Performance." In *Democracy, Accountability and Representation*, ed. Adam Przeworski, Susan Stokes, and Bernard Manin. Cambridge: Cambridge University Press

Ferejohn, John. 1986. "Incumbent Performance and Electoral Control." *Public Choice*, no. 50:5–25.

Gómez, Ignacio, and Juan Carlos Giraldo. 1992. *El retorno de Pablo Escobar*. Bogotá: Oveja Negra.

Gutiérrez, Francisco. 1995. "Tendencias de cambio en el sistema de partidos: El caso de Bogotá." *Análisis Político*, no. 24:73–83.

———. 1996. "Dilemas y paradojas de la transición participativa." *Análisis Político*, no. 29:35–53.

———. 2000. "Politicians and Criminals: Two Decades of Turbulence, 1978–1998." *International Journal of Politics, Culture and Society* 14, no. 1:71–87.

———. n.d. "Organized Crime and the Political System: The Colombian Case." Manuscript in progress.

Gutiérrez, Francisco, and Andrés Dávila. 2000. "Paleontólogos o politólogos: ¿Qué podemos decir hoy sobre los dinosaurios?" *Revista de Estudios Sociales*, no. 6:39–50.

Hartlyn, Jonathan. 1993. "Drug Trafficking and Democracy in Colombia in the 80s." Working Paper 70, Institut de Ciéncies Politiques y Socials, Barcelona.

Kreps, David. 1990. *A Course in Microeconomic Theory*. Princeton: Princeton University Press.

Laffont, Jean Jacques, and David Martimort. 2002. *The Theory of Incentives: The Principal Agent Model*. Princeton: Princeton University Press.

Landínez Suarez, Heráclito, Jorge Salcedo Ramírez, and José Fernando Bautista Q. 1998. *El precio de ser Liberal*. Edición Dirección Nacional Liberal.

Leal Buitrago, Francisco, and Andrés Dávila. 1991. *El sistema político y su expresión regional*. Bogotá: Tercer Mundo-IEPRI.

Lévi, Margaret. 2000. "The Economic Turn in Comparative Politics." *Comparative Political Studies* 33 (August/September): 822–46.

Lichbach, Mark Irving. 1996. *The Cooperator's Dilemma*. Ann Arbor: University of Michigan Press.

Matthiesen, Tatiana. 2000. *El arte político de conciliar: El tema de las drogas en las relaciones entre Colombia y Estados Unidos (1986–1994)*. Bogotá: FESCOL-CEREC-Fedesarrollo.

Ocampo, Myriam, Carlos Rangel, and Teresa Sánchez de Díaz. 1993. *Oficina de orden público y convivencia ciudadana*. Santa Fé de Bogotá: Ministerio de Gobierno.

Ricardo, Joseph. 1998. "Life in a Cell: Managerial Practice and Strategy in Colombian Cocaine." PhD diss., University of Michigan.

Sánchez, Gonzalo. 1998. *Guerre et politique en Colombie*. Paris: L'Harmattan.

Thoumi, Francisco. 2002. "Illegal Drugs in Colombia: From Illegal Economic Boom to Social Crisis." Retrieved September 6, 2005, from http://lacc.fiu.edu/research_ publications/working_papers/working_paper_02.pdf. Tsebelis, George. 1990. *Nested Games: Rational Choice in Comparative Politics*. Berkeley: University of California Press.

Uprimny, Rodrigo. 1996. "Jueces, narcos y políticos: La judicialización de la crisis política." In *Tras las huellas de la crisis política*, ed. Francisco Leal. Bogotá: Tercer Mundo-FESCOL-IEPRI.

Uribe, María Victoria. 1992. *Limpiar la tierra*. Bogotá: CINEP.

PART THREE

Human Rights

chapter nine

U.S. Foreign Policy in Colombia

Bizarre Side Effects of the "War on Drugs"

Arlene B. Tickner

Tickner reviews the main concepts underpinning U.S. foreign policy on Colombia and evaluates the impact of this policy on Colombia's domestic situation and on the drug trade. She argues that U.S. policy is driven by a realist worldview that places drug interdiction and eradication at the forefront of its Colombia policy and prompts the militarization of the fight against the drug trade. She then presents evidence to suggest that this approach has been counterproductive, not only exacerbating the drug problem, which it was meant to combat, but also worsening critical problems that should concern the United States, such as the weakness of the Colombian state, the human rights situation in the countryside, the failure of the peace process and continuation of the guerrilla war, the lack of economic alternatives to illicit crop cultivation, pervasive poverty, and environmental degradation. Her discussion is grounded in historical evidence, including a wealth of personal interviews with key actors, and a theoretical understanding of the state. She concludes by saying that "without a simultaneous strengthening of the institutional expression, and more importantly, a legitimating 'idea' of the state, increased state presence alone will never resolve the problems inherent to state weakness in Colombia." The United States must break out of the realist paradigm in its dealings with Colombia if it wishes to address the broad range of interrelated problems that combine to place it high on the U.S. foreign policy agenda.

309

During the past decade, U.S. foreign policy in Colombia has undergone significant transformations. In a relatively short time, Colombia's status vis-à-vis the United States shifted dramatically: long considered a faithful "ally" in the fight against drugs, as well as "showcasing" Washington's achievements in this camp, the country became widely identified as an international "pariah" during the administration of Ernesto Samper (1994–98), given the narco-scandal surrounding the Colombian president's election. The inauguration of the Pastrana government in 1998 marked the official return to "friendly" relations with the United States, but Colombia became considered a "problem" nation whose spillover effects threatened to generate instability in neighboring countries. The terrorist attacks of September 11, 2001, in combination with the termination of formal peace talks with the Colombian Revolutionary Armed Forces (FARC) in February 2002, created greater alignment between the Colombian and U.S. governments, highlighting the potential "threat" of the Colombian crisis for regional security.

Colombia has also gained a higher priority in the U.S. foreign policy agenda in Latin America. Between 1997 and 2000, military aid to this country increased nearly sevenfold, while high-level governmental officials became much more closely involved in policy planning and oversight. During a mere two-week period in February 2001, six congressional delegations from the United States visited Colombia with the goal of evaluating the implementation of Plan Colombia. Since taking office in August 2002, General James T. Hill, Commander of the U.S. Southern Command, has been to the country on twenty-three different occasions. Undoubtedly, increased concern on the part of Washington policy-making circles has led to concerted efforts to better understand the numerous, interrelated problems involved in Colombia's present crisis. Nonetheless, the enormous complexity of the Colombian case, in combination with the central role that the "drug war" (and more recently, the "war" on terrorism) occupies in U.S. foreign policy toward this country, continues to pose serious challenges to the United States' role in Colombia that have yet to be adequately addressed.

This chapter explores the myriad implications of U.S. policy in Colombia. Given the centrality of counternarcotics activities to U.S.-Colombian relations, I first explore the underlying assumptions driving U.S. strategies to address this problem. Specifically, I argue that the "drug war" is largely the product of a realist worldview that tends to interpret the drug problem through the lens of national security, leading to the use of coercive diplomatic measures designed to elicit cooperation on the part of host countries. I then discuss the practical implications of this interpretation of the drug issue with regard to the evolution of U.S.-Colombian "drug diplomacy" during the Samper and Pastrana administrations, with the goal of illustrating the extent to which Colombian drug policy has responded to U.S. imperatives rather than to the domestic manifestations of this problem. In subsequent sections, I explore problems of counterinsurgency, growing militarization, human rights violations, and state weakening as they relate to U.S. counternarcotics policy in Colombia. In the postscript, I provide a brief assessment of the effects of 9/11 on bilateral relations.

The "Realist" Approach to Counternarcotics

Given the centrality of drug diplomacy to U.S.-Colombian relations, a comprehensive analysis of the implications of U.S. antinarcotics strategies in other policy areas such as counterinsurgency, militarization, human rights, democracy, and state building in Colombia must necessarily begin with a brief discussion of the conceptual assumptions underlying the "war on drugs" as well as the stated national interests at stake in the United States.

Beginning in the mid-1980s, the drug traffic began to occupy a more important place on the United States' domestic and external agenda, given the significant increase in domestic consumption of illegal substances as well as the growth in crime figures associated with the use of drugs.[1] Notwithstanding minor variations in the antidrug policies adopted during the Reagan (1981–89), Bush (1989–93), and Clinton (1993–2001) administrations, the underlying rationale has remained virtually intact (Tokatlian 1995: 119). In April 1986, President Ronald Reagan, through National Security Decision Directive 221, declared that illicit drugs constituted a lethal threat to U.S. national security. Directive 221 mandated direct military involvement of the armed forces in the "war on drugs" and the consequent militarization of U.S. antidrug strategy. Concomitantly, supply-side actions such as interdiction, crop fumigation, and eradication, and demand-side policies based upon the penalization of the traffic, distribution, and consumption of narcotics, began to receive greater priority than rehabilitation and education-based strategies (Bagley 1988; Perl 1988; Pardo and Tickner 2000).

During the Bush administration, the military components of the "war on drugs" were intensified through the Andean Initiative.[2] This initiative also expanded and shifted U.S. counternarcotics activities toward drug interdiction in the coca-producing Andean countries (Bagley 1992; Washington Office on Latin America [WOLA] 1993). In response to what he considered to be an inherent weakness of U.S. counternarcotics policy, Bill Clinton, in his 1992 presidential campaign, pledged to refocus the country's efforts upon demand-based strategies. In early 1993, an exhaustive review of U.S. antidrug strategies conducted by the Clinton administration confirmed suspicions that the Andean Initiative had been largely unsuccessful in curbing the availability of illegal substances in the United States (Crandall 2000). As a result, drug-related assistance for the Andean region was both reduced dramatically and reoriented toward a "source country" strategy based mainly upon crop eradication rather than interdiction. The staff of the Office of National Drug Control Policy (ONDCP) was also diminished from 146 to only 25 individuals. Nonetheless, the 1994 midterm elections in the United States led to Republican Party control of both houses of the Congress, and Clinton's "soft-line" approach to drugs became increasingly criticized. The Clinton administration subsequently intensified and hardened its antidrug strategy in response to such congressional pressure. In October 1998, in fact, the U.S. Congress approved the Western Hemisphere Drug Elimination Act, through which public spending for drug interdiction and eradication efforts was substantially increased.

According to Bruce Bagley and Juan G. Tokatlian (1992: 216), U.S. drug control strategies have evolved within the framework of the realist tradition in international relations. This tradition highlights (1) the predominance of the state, conceived as a unitary, rational actor; (2) the existence of anarchy, understood as the absence of a single source of authority in the international system, and thus the need for states to recur to self-help tactics; (3) the stratification of international objectives between "high" politics (considered to be those pertaining to the strategic-military realm) and "low" politics; and (4) the strict separation between domestic and international politics (Vásquez 1991: 49–55).

From a purely realist perspective, the drug problem would most likely not be considered a significant policy issue in terms of the strategic global interests of the United States. Nevertheless, on a policy implementation level, realism, observed more loosely as a "worldview" that has guided U.S. foreign policy, constitutes an ideological framework (resembling realpolitik) that has informed policy-making circles in the formulation of counternarcotics strategies.[3] The realist worldview predisposes policy makers, and the public at large, to view drug trafficking more as an "external" threat to national security than as a "domestic" problem.

According to David Campbell (1992: 210), "An important dimension of the 'war on drugs' is thus the portrayal—in a manner that replicates almost exactly the formulations of the Soviet threat in the early 1950s—of drugs' danger to the ethical boundaries of identity in terms of a threat to the territorial borders and sovereignty of the state." With the end of the Cold War, the United States lost its most significant "other," the Soviet Union (Huntington 1997: 32); it also lost a clear sense of the national security interests of the United States. Drugs, long considered a threat to U.S. values and society, became an obvious target for accommodating Cold War anticommunist language to the new "drug war discourse." Viewed in this light, the threat represented by illegal drugs in the United States is not an objective condition; rather, narcotics constitute one of the "cognitive enemies" against which U.S. identity attempted to rebuild, albeit only partially, until September 11. In this sense, drugs are seen as endangering the American way of life and social fabric, much like the challenge posed by the communist threat to America's values during the bipolar conflict.

Given the sense of moral superiority that has traditionally characterized U.S. relations with the rest of the world, drug consumption is understood as being prompted by the availability of illegal drugs, which are concentrated, unsurprisingly, in the countries of the periphery; it is rarely seen as a problem originating in the demand for drugs in the United States or in the prohibitionist strategies that have traditionally characterized America's handling of this issue. While this rationale clearly runs contrary to commonsense economic rules of supply and demand, it tends to reinforce the underlying assumption of moral "purity" upon which America's sense of self is partly based (Huntington 1989).

In light of the above considerations, U.S. antidrug policies, based upon repressive, prohibitionist, and hard-line language and strategies, become more comprehensible, given that they express the need to confront this "enemy" or "scourge" with determination. This leads to yet another underlying assumption of realist-inspired drug strategies, crucial to an understanding of how U.S. counternarcotics efforts ultimately tend to undermine progress in other policy areas: external pressure exerted by the United States, primarily through coercive diplomacy, is viewed as one of the most effective mechanisms for guaranteeing cooperation on the part of source countries, with the interests and needs of the drug-producing countries frequently acquiring a secondary status (Friman 1993: 104).

The terrorist attacks of September 11, 2001, and the United States–led retaliation mirror this perspective on drugs. Just as the drug issue fails to conform to typical notions of security and threat from a realist perspective, so September 11 challenges traditional views of international relations. The attacks came from within America's borders, not without, and were perpetrated by nonstate actors with little or no military power. But terrorism, rather than being seen as a diffuse, nonterritorial problem, has been associated by the Bush administration with state-based territories—Afghanistan and the entire "axis of evil"—and personified in figures such as Osama bin Laden and Sadam Hussein. The exercise of military power in countries seen as threatening "freedom" and "justice" in the world constitutes the cornerstone of the U.S. strategy. And the zealous language accompanying the fight against terrorism eerily recalls the Cold War period.

The similarities between the wars on drugs and terrorism and the war on communism notwithstanding, a crucial difference exists: the enemies of these new wars are not readily identifiable, making victory nearly impossible. Hence any explanation of the role of drugs (and terrorism) in U.S. domestic and international politics must necessarily return to the concepts of danger and threat. Although the policies implemented by the United States have failed in reducing the availability of illegal substances—and will most likely be unsuccessful in erasing terrorism from the globe—drugs and, more importantly today, terrorism occupy a crucial discursive function in support of American identities and values. Both are considered lethal threats to U.S. security—and the political costs associated with directly challenging existing policies in Washington are extremely high. At the same time, the need to persevere in the war on drugs has received an additional push from the war on terrorism; the financing of terrorist activities with drug money has received much greater attention in United States policymaking circles in the aftermath of 9/11.

The Role of Drugs in U.S.-Colombian Relations

The ways in which the issue of illicit drugs has been addressed in Colombia derive substantially from the U.S. approach to this problem. Specifically, a great majority of measures adopted in the country to fight the drug trade have resulted largely from bilateral agreements subscribed with the United States or the unilateral imposition of specific strategies designed in Washington. Although this state of affairs shifted somewhat during the Barco (1986–90) and Gaviria (1990–94) administrations, the Samper government (1994–98) inaugurated a return to U.S.-inspired orthodoxy in the drug war that has continued and been reinforced during the Pastrana government (1998–2002).

In the mid-1980s, the U.S. stance toward Colombia became largely predetermined by its international counternarcotics policy (Shifter 1999: 18), given the expansion of drug-trafficking organizations in the country as well as growing concern with consumption levels in the United States. Nevertheless, the administration of Virgilio Barco asserted Colombian independence in relation to the United States, particularly through its explicit emphasis upon foreign economic diplomacy, the expansion of commercial and diplomatic relations with other regions of the world, and the preservation of Colombian autonomy in this realm (Cardona 1990: 8). On the drug front, however, the country inaugurated an unprecedented strategy of confronting narco-trafficking organizations that won Barco praise from Washington as a faithful ally in the "war on drugs."[4]

President César Gaviria also gave priority to Colombia's foreign economic relations. In the area of drug control, Gaviria's policy orientation differed dramatically from the hard-line approach advocated by the Barco administration. The reasons for this shift lie primarily in the social, political, and economic costs of the campaign of terror and violence inaugurated by the Colombian drug cartels to impede the extradition of drug traffickers to the United States.[5] The Gaviria administration's response was to establish a clear distinction between narco-terrorism and the drug traffic, two related but distinct manifestations of the drug problem. "For Gaviria, narco-terrorism, and not the drug traffic, was the principal threat to the country's democracy, and what he was willing to combat" (Matthiesen 2000: 259). In light of these developments, in 1990 the Colombian government enacted a plea-bargaining system in which individuals accused of drug-related crimes would receive reduced jail sentences in exchange for their voluntary surrender and confession of their crimes.[6] Nearly a year later, the 1991 Constitutional Assembly, under significant pressure from the country's drug-trafficking organizations, voted to prohibit the extradition of Colombian nationals altogether.

The escape of Medellín cartel leader Pablo Escobar from prison in July 1992 led to increasing U.S. intolerance of the Colombian government's drug strategy. Although Escobar was ultimately killed in December 1993 by Colombian security forces, the permissive conditions surrounding the Medellín cartel leader's imprisonment, which were brought to light following his escape, led to growing apprehension in the United States concerning the effectiveness of the plea-bargaining system. Washington's uneasiness was intensified in May 1994 when the Colombian Constitutional Court decided to legalize the consumption of certain illegal drugs for personal use. This controversial decision came shortly after a series of public declarations by the country's general prosecutor, Gustavo de Greiff, beginning in late 1993, that the war against drugs had failed miserably and that the consumption and traffic of illicit substances should be legalized (Tokatlian 2000: 68). Together, these incidents led to increasing concern that key Colombian actors had "lost their stomach for the contest."[7]

The Samper Administration and the Breakdown of Bilateral Relations

Although the Gaviria administration's propensity to stray from U.S.-inspired counternarcotics dogma led to a steady deterioration in U.S.-Colombian relations, Colombia continued to be considered a "showcase" for U.S. efforts in the region (Matthiesen 2000: 261–62). Nonetheless, with the inauguration of President Ernesto Samper in August 1994,[8] the bilateral relationship experienced severe breakdown following revelations that his presidential campaign had received financial contributions from the Cali cartel.[9] Called Proceso 8000, the drawn-out series of accusations and denials concerning this allegation polarized the country and irrevocably damaged the legitimacy and credibility of the Samper government on both the domestic and international fronts.[10] Increasingly, the United States began to refer to Colombia as a "narco-democracy" and a "narco-state" rather than a determined "ally."

Nevertheless, following his election, President-elect Samper made a series of statements highlighting his strong commitment to the drug war.[11] In consequence, Washington's initial stance toward the incoming Colombian government was one of pragmatism, in clear recognition of the fact that the two countries needed to work together in the fight against drugs. This attitude was confirmed at an initial meeting in New York between officials from both countries in June 1994. "Having got what they wanted—firm indications that the new Colombian President would not relax the pressure on the *narcotraficantes*—U.S. officials indicated that they would give Samper the benefit of the doubt—for now."[12]

Samper was also given an official U.S. document with a series of new and stricter criteria to be used to evaluate Colombia's antidrug performance in the certification process of 1995.[13] The implicit message set forth in the document was that the Gaviria administration's performance had not been completely satisfactory and that the standards for judging compliance in the future would be applied more stringently. Colombia was subsequently certified for reasons of U.S. national interest in 1995. U.S. pressure led to a series of developments in Colombia's counterdrug policies: in December 1994, Rosso José Serrano was appointed head of the National Police, which subsequently embarked upon an aggressive campaign against corruption in this institution; an intensive antidrug effort was initiated; the main protagonists of the Cali cartel were successfully placed in jail; and crop eradication efforts were intensified dramatically.[14]

Nonetheless, as speculations in Colombia grew regarding Samper's level of awareness and involvement in the campaign scandal,[15] U.S. policy toward the country became markedly more aggressive and intransigent. Although there are divergent opinions concerning whether the U.S. government identified Samper's removal from power as an explicit policy objective,[16] the weakening of the Colombian president clearly became the policy of some, if not many, State Department officials (Franco 1998: 53; Crandall 2000). U.S. policy toward the country thus became inextricably related to the country's own domestic crisis. Direct relations with the Colombian president were precluded altogether, while increasingly the United States attributed the success of counternarcotics activities to its own efforts, in coordination with those of the Colombian National Police and the general prosecutor's office, identified as the only reliable partners in the "war on drugs."[17] Notwithstanding the Samper government's vigorous compliance with the exigencies of U.S. antinarcotics policy, Colombia was decertified in March 1996, although economic sanctions were ultimately not applied.

One month after the charges pending against President Samper were dismissed by the Colombian House of Representatives Accusations Committee in June 1996, Samper's U.S. visa was revoked, in apparent retaliation. Following this decision it became increasingly clear that Ernesto Samper, and not the "drug war" in and of itself, had become Washington's central problem in Colombia. Nonetheless, the Colombian president's weakened stature on a domestic level was considered a prime opportunity for furthering the U.S. counternarcotics agenda in the country through the use of coercive diplomatic measures, namely the threat of economic sanctions.

During 1996, the fumigation of poppy crops nearly doubled from 1995 levels and coca crop eradication efforts were intensified. In February 1997, a counternarcotics maritime agreement, which had been in the works for a long time, was finally signed by the two countries, and the Colombian Congress passed legislation to increase the jail sentences of confessed narcotraffickers.[18] Increasingly, U.S. officials conceded in private that Colombia had complied effectively and decisively in the drug war.[19] The country was nevertheless decertified for a second time in March 1997, and economic sanctions were threatened to pressure the Samper government to comply with an additional list of counternarcotics measures. In response to this U.S. stick, the country went so far as to experiment with the granular herbicide Imazapyr (Vargas 1999), as well as approving a drug assets seizure law. In December 1997, the 1991 Colombian Constitution was also amended to permit the nonretroactive extradition of Colombian nationals. Finally, in March 1998, Colombia was recertified on the grounds of U.S. national interests.

As will be discussed in a subsequent section, it was increasingly clear in 1997 that U.S. policy in Colombia had become utterly counterproductive. Although the Samper administration "accepted perhaps the most prohibitionist strategy" in the history of U.S.-Colombian drug diplomacy (Tokatlian 2000: 76), the overall results of U.S. counternarcotics efforts were dismal in terms of curbing the drug trade itself. On the contrary, Colombia experienced an unprecedented expansion of coca leaf production from the mid-1990s onward (Bagley 2000: 1), which in turn fueled the country's armed conflict. Through its coercive diplomatic strategy, the United States also aggravated an already complex domestic situation by weakening the Colombian government even further. President Samper counterbalanced U.S. pressure by employing a domestic "survival strategy" consisting of political and economic handouts provided to a diverse array of social actors (through increased public spending, contracts, and favors). As a result, public corruption levels in the country increased dramatically, while economic stability was threatened.[20]

The Pastrana Administration: From Pariah to Friend

The election of Andrés Pastrana in 1998 was considered a prime opportunity for reestablishing a cooperative tone to the bilateral relationship. Given the magnitude of the Colombian crisis, as well as the now general perception that Washington's heavy-handed strategy had put excessive pressure on the Colombian state, the United States sought to portray him as a trustworthy ally, in contrast to his predecessor. However, Pastrana attempted to establish a clear distinction between Colombia's domestic priorities, which primarily concerned finding a peaceful solution to the armed conflict, and U.S. interests in the country, based essentially upon the drug problem. During the Colombian presidential campaign, he was in fact the only candidate who explicitly challenged the wisdom of U.S. counternarcotics policies. On June 8, 1998, Pastrana presented a peace plan in which he asserted that the cultivation of illicit substances constituted, above all, a social problem that needed to be addressed through a type of "Marshall Plan" for Colombia (Pardo and Tickner 1998: 24). In an interview in July, the president-elect stated that narcotics, although an important aspect of U.S.-Colombian relations, had "dominated the agenda for far too long" and should be replaced by more important topics such as trade relations.[21]

Before his inauguration, Pastrana met with U.S. President Bill Clinton in Washington. One of his primary goals was to press for an "opening" of the bilateral agenda beyond the issue of drugs. For its part, the U.S. government had already begun talking about the need for a more "comprehensive" approach to Colombia that took into account the multiple factors involved in the Colombian crisis, among them, the armed conflict, weak institutions, paramilitarism, and the social implications of crop eradication (Youngers 1998: 4). During Pastrana's first official visit to the White House in late October 1998, Clinton made an explicit pledge to support the Colombian peace process and to work with other international institutions to mobilize resources to support this objective. The United States also stepped up its military assistance to US$289 million for 1999. Yet one aspect of the peace process met with a certain degree of alarm in Washington—namely, the creation of a demilitarized zone, approximately the size of Switzerland, in five municipalities located in the southern portion of the country, in order to initiate negotiations with the FARC in early November.

Notwithstanding such reservations, in mid-December U.S. government officials secretly met with members of the FARC in Costa Rica to discuss their involvement in the kidnapping of several U.S. citizens and in the drug trade. Undoubtedly, the meeting marked a significant, albeit brief, turning point in the U.S. posture vis-à-vis Colombian insurgent groups.[22] During the same month, however, at a Defense Minister Summit held in Cartagena, U.S. Secretary of Defense William Cohen and his Colombian counterpart, Rodrigo Lloreda, signed an agreement designed to strengthen military cooperation between the two countries. This arrangement paved the way for the training of the first (of several) special Colombian Army counternarcotics battalions, whose primary mission was conceived in terms of the repossession of guerrilla-controlled territories in southern Colombia where coca crop cultivations were concentrated.[23]

In early March 1999, members of the FARC murdered three U.S. indigenous rights activists. According to Phil Chicola, director of Andean Affairs in the U.S. State Department, the murders sent an important signal to Washington in terms of the lack of control exerted by the FARC leadership over its divisions as well as the sincerity of the guerrillas with regard to peace. This event hardened Washington's stance toward the Colombian peace process considerably.[24] This shift was mirrored in Colombia, following the emergence of difficulties in the management of the demilitarized zone, as well as a series of setbacks in the negotiation process.[25] Citing serious discrepancies with the Pastrana government's handling of the peace process, Defense Minister Rodrigo Lloreda resigned. This triggered the resignations of a significant number of high-level military officials, which were later rejected by Pastrana. Undoubtedly, the incident highlighted growing civil-military tensions surrounding negotiations with the FARC.

In August 1999, U.S. Undersecretary Thomas Pickering met with Andrés Pastrana to express Washington's concern with the above developments. Pickering warned the Colombian president that the predominant feeling in the United States was that Pastrana had been too "soft" in his dealings with the FARC and that Colombia's relations with the United States could be impaired if this situation continued unabated. The State Department official also offered the Clinton administration's full cooperation in requesting additional U.S. funding if Colombia could design a comprehensive antidrug strategy (LeoGrande and Sharpe 2000: 6). Unsurprisingly, this visit planted the seed for what became known as Plan Colombia.

The changing domestic climate, as well as growing skepticism among key U.S. officials regarding the viability of the peace process, led to an important shift in the Colombian government's foreign policy strategy. By

September 1999, with the presentation of Plan Colombia in the United States, Pastrana no longer anchored his appeals for U.S. assistance to the peace process. Rather, the drug issue, and the country's inability to confront this problem alone, given the weakness of the Colombian state, became the central focus of the plan. While admittedly Pastrana's "Plan for Peace, Prosperity and the Strengthening of the State" incorporated a wide range of issues considered crucial to the government's peace effort—including economic recovery, judicial sector reform, social development, democratization, and human rights—the fight against drug trafficking was explicitly declared to be the "core" of the Colombian strategy.[26]

In short, following initial attempts to distinguish between domestic priorities (peace) and U.S. concerns (drugs), President Pastrana was forced to resort to a "drug war logic" to secure sorely needed U.S. support. In January 2000, President Clinton proposed a $1.6 billion, two-year aid package for Colombia. Following intense negotiations in the U.S. Congress, the package was finally approved in June. In it Colombia received nearly $900 million between 2000 and 2001 (in addition to $330 million in assistance approved earlier). Although approximately 20 percent of the aid corresponded to economic assistance for human rights, judicial reform, law enforcement, aid to the displaced, and peace efforts, 80 percent of the package was geared toward military and police aid.[27]

The "War on Drugs" and Counterinsurgency

The implications of this type of antinarcotics strategy in a country such as Colombia are multifaceted. To begin with, the definition of the drug traffic as a matter of U.S. national security, and thus "high" politics, implies that drugs occupy a predominant place in U.S. foreign policy objectives in Colombia, to the exclusion of other longer term objectives, including the strengthening of democracy, the defense of human rights, the reduction of poverty, and the preservation of the environment (Perl 1992: 28–29). Official rhetoric aside, "the sad reality is that U.S. policy towards Colombia is hostage to drug war politics in Washington" (WOLA 1997: 44).

In addition to underestimating the importance of other "low politics" objectives not directly related to the drug war, the militarization of counternarcotics activities facilitated greater involvement of U.S. and local armed forces in the internal affairs of drug-producing countries. Following the end of the Cold War, and the peaceful settlement of armed conflict in Central America, the drug problem replaced communism as the primary threat to U.S. national security in the Western Hemisphere. U.S. military assistance to Latin America, in consequence, became concentrated in the source countries, in particular Colombia. Concomitantly, the definition of "low-intensity conflict," a concept commonly used to describe the political situation in Central America during the 1980s, was expanded to include the drug problem in those countries in which drug-trafficking organizations threatened the stability of the state (Corr and Miller 1992: 24). As such, the strategies applied in the 1980s to confront other types of "low-intensity conflict" in the region were simply readjusted in the 1990s to address the "new" regional threat, drugs.

In Colombia, this view of the drug problem, based upon a "drug war" logic, and of the strategies needed to combat it, is especially troublesome, given that guerrilla groups, in particular the FARC, and paramilitaries maintain complex linkages with diverse aspects of the drug trade. On both a conceptual and practical level, then, the U.S "war on drugs" has become nearly inseparable from counterinsurgency efforts in Colombia.[28] Not surprisingly, "[t]hough couched within a counterdrug framework, the elements of Washington's military aid program for Colombia are taken straight from the Pentagon's counterinsurgency handbook for El Salvador" (Leo-Grande and Sharpe 2000: 6).

The conflation of low-intensity counterinsurgency tactics with counternarcotics strategies has been facilitated primarily through the "narco-guerrilla theory" (Zirnite 1997: 7) and essentially represents an attempt to "render the drug war more intelligible on a traditional security register" (Campbell 1992: 212). This term was made popular in the 1980s by former U.S. ambassador to Colombia Lewis Tambs.[29] Notwithstanding the suspected links between guerrilla and drug-trafficking organizations, the fact that paramilitary organizations, most notably MAS (Death to Kidnappers), were created in the early 1980s and financed by drug traffickers in retaliation for guerrilla kidnappings seemed to belie the theory's validity. By the mid-1990s, however, references to the "narco-guerrilla" slowly began to find their way into the official jargon of certain sectors of the U.S. and Colombian political (and military) establishment. Robert Gelbard, U.S. Assistant Secretary of State for International Narcotics and Law Enforcement, referred to the FARC as Colombia's third largest drug cartel in 1996. During the Samper administration, the Colombian president himself began to use the narco-guerrilla label domestically in an attempt to discredit the FARC, given their unwillingness to negotiate with a political figure that the guerrilla organization considered illegitimate.[30] In its relations with the United States, the Colombian government also attempted to convince Washington that the symbiosis between guerrillas and drug-trafficking organizations was real and that U.S. counternarcotics strategies needed to take this relationship into consideration.[31] Similar arguments were formulated by the Colombian military during this period. Nevertheless, the claim that the guerrillas were involved in the drug traffic was generally refuted by the U.S. government.[32]

Until 2000, the United States had never categorically associated Colombian guerrilla organizations with the latter stages of the drug-trafficking process. On November 29 of that year, however, a press statement delivered by the U.S. Department of State directly accused the FARC of harboring relations with the Mexican organization Arellano Félix, one of the most powerful drug cartels in that country, and claimed that "since late 1999 the FARC has sought to establish a monopoly position over the commercialization of the cocaine base across much of southern Colombia."[33] One week later, the U.S. ambassador to Colombia, Anne Patterson, affirmed that both the FARC and the paramilitaries had "control of the entire export process and the routes for sending drugs abroad," were operating as drug cartels in the country, and could thus be requested by the United States in extradition, given existing legislation.[34]

In principle, the "narco-guerrilla theory," as currently employed in Colombia, conveys that (1) the FARC control most aspects of the drug trade, given the demise of the major drug cartels in the mid-1990s; (2) the Colombian state is too weak to confront this threat, primarily due to the inefficacy of the country's armed forces; and (3) U.S. military support is warranted to wrest drug-producing regions, particularly in the south of the country, from guerrilla control. Although to a certain degree true, this description grossly simplifies the Colombian situation. For example, while a consensus exists at present that the FARC derives a significant portion of its income from the taxation of coca crops and paste (Rangel Suárez 2000), there is widespread disagreement concerning the levels of involvement of the FARC in the transportation and distribution of narcotics. Contrary to the claims made by some U.S. government officials, Klaus Nyholm, director of the UN Drug Control Program in Colombia, stated in 2000 that "we have seen no evidence yet that the FARC is directly involved in cocaine production and export."[35] In testimony provided to the U.S. Senate in 2001, the director of the Drug Enforcement Agency (DEA), Donnie Marshall, confirmed that there was no conclusive proof that the FARC was currently operating as an international drug cartel.[36]

The involvement of the paramilitaries in drug-related activities challenges predominant assumptions even further. According to some sources, paramilitary expansion in southern Colombia during the latter months of 2000, particularly in the Putumayo region, where the "Push into Southern Colombia" was concentrated, was largely financed by drug-trafficking organizations in response to FARC-imposed increases in the price and taxation of coca paste.[37] This is not surprising given that the leader of Colombian's main paramilitary organization (the United Self-Defense Force of Colombia, or AUC), Carlos Castaño, personally acknowledged in a televised interview in March 2000 that a large percentage (up to 70 percent) of the AUC's revenues, particularly in departments such as Antioquia and Córdoba, was also derived from the drug trade. Nevertheless, until September 2002, when the U.S. government presented extradition requests for AUC leaders Castaño and Salvatore Mancuso, U.S. counternarcotics strategy in Colombia failed to systematically identify these actors as targets that needed to be combated in the war against drugs.

U.S. policy informed by the narco-guerrilla theory also fails to make a clear distinction between peasant coca growers and drug-trafficking organizations, to the extent that both are targeted equally as "criminals." As a result, the crucial issue of economic, cultural, and social subsistence faced by those marginalized social actors involved in the cultivation of coca is at best a secondary focus of the Colombian national drug control strategy.

Taken together, the above observations constitute only a few examples of the dangers involved in making sweeping generalizations in the Colombian case. Even so, the "narco-guerrilla theory" seems to have increasingly informed some U.S. political and military actors in the search for policy options in the country, while also lending credence to those who argue that counterinsurgency techniques used in other low-intensity conflicts can be used successfully in Colombia. Although the concrete political implications of this shift are still unclear, several general observations are in order. First, growing U.S. identification of armed actors, in particular the FARC, as criminal drug-trafficking organizations (and more recently as terrorist groups) could weaken U.S. support for a negotiated settlement with the guerrillas in the future, as could the fact that the highest growth in coca cultivations during the year 2000 took place in the FARC-controlled demilitarized zone.[38]

Second, the U.S. government's separation of counternarcotics and counterinsurgency to justify dramatic increases in military support for the Colombian armed forces is untenable. Tellingly, U.S. Representative Benjamin A. Gilman, in a letter written to Barry McCaffrey in November 2000 criticizing the militarization of counternarcotics activities in Colombia, suggested the need for public debate concerning counterinsurgency aid to the country: "I have no doubt that after such a public debate, the U.S. would commit to help the Colombian military in its counterinsurgency struggle." General Peter Pace, head of the U.S. Southern Command, also acknowledged that "it is clearly true that many of the guerrillas, if not all, traffic in drugs, so trying to define that line is very difficult."[39] Similar arguments formulated by prestigious U.S. think tanks accompanied this shift. The RAND Corporation (Rabasa and Chalk 2001), in a comprehensive report on U.S. policy in the country, stated that the central problem faced by the Colombian government was regaining control of territories under the influence of parastate actors, in particular the guerrillas. As a result, the report argued in favor of reorienting Washington's Colombia policy toward counterinsurgency, rather than counternarcotics, to resolve this situation.

Militarization and Human Rights

This latter question of the precise nature of U.S. involvement in the Colombian conflict points to one of the most severe challenges to U.S. policy, derived from the human rights situation in Colombia. The U.S. State Department's *Report on Human Rights* for 2001 indicates that political and extrajudicial actions involving government security forces, paramilitary groups, and members of the guerrillas resulted in the deaths of 3,700 civilians; paramilitary forces were responsible for approximately 70 percent of these. During the first ten months of 2001, 161 massacres occurred in which an estimated 1,021 persons were killed. Between 275,000 and 347,000 people were forced to leave their homes, while the total number of persons displaced by rural violence in the country during the last five years alone grew to approximately one million. More than twenty-five thousand homicides were committed, one of the highest global figures per capita, and approximately 3,041 civilians were kidnapped, by far the highest rate in the world.[40]

While Colombian security forces were responsible for only 3 to 5 percent of human rights violations in 2001 (a notable improvement over the 54 percent share in 1993), the report points out that government security forces continued to commit abuses, including extrajudicial killings, and to collaborate both directly and indirectly with paramilitary forces.[41] Notwithstanding efforts undertaken by the Colombian government to strengthen its human rights policy and to combat the expansion of paramilitarism in the country, the results of its strategy have been rather poor; in particular, a significant number of members of the armed forces continue to be connected directly or indirectly to paramilitary activity (Human Rights Watch 2000).

For reasons related to the questionable human rights record of the Colombian armed forces, as well as the Colombian government's unwillingness to denounce this situation publicly, U.S. military assistance to the country was severely limited during a large portion of the 1990s. Nevertheless, during this period the United States continued to provide the armed forces with military training, weapons, and materials. In 1994, the U.S. Embassy in Colombia reported that counternarcotics aid had been provided in 1992 and 1993 to several units responsible for human rights violations in areas not considered to be priority drug-producing zones (Human Rights Watch 1996). As a result, beginning in 1994, the U.S. Congress anchored military aid in Colombia directly to antidrug activities. In turn, the Leahy Amendment of September 1996 sought to suspend military assistance to units implicated in human rights violations that were receiving counternarcotics funding unless the Secretary of State certified that the respective government was taking measures to bring responsible military officers to trial. Notwithstanding the restrictions that applied to the Colombian armed forces, in September 1996 the Clinton administration announced the decision to sell US$169 million in military equipment to the Colombian Army, including twelve Black Hawk helicopters. Commercial arms sales to Colombia also began to increase substantially during this same year (Human Rights Watch 1996: 85). Existing U.S. legislation lacks concrete measures for overseeing the actual use of equipment sold abroad in both types of transactions.

In 1994, during the Samper administration, the Colombian government began to adopt a stronger stance vis-à-vis the issue of human rights. In January 1995, for the first time ever, the Colombian president publicly acknowledged the responsibility of the state in what became known as the Trujillo massacres, which resulted in over one hundred assassinations at the hands of government security forces in collaboration with the hired hands of the country's drug-trafficking organizations. Other measures directly sponsored by the Samper government in this area included the creation of a permanent office of the UN High Commission for Human Rights; the ratification of Protocol II of the Geneva Convention; and the formalization of an agreement with the International Red Cross that enabled this organization to establish its presence in the country's conflict zones.[42] Unfortunately, "Little by little, the novel proposals made at the beginning of the Samper administration became relegated to a secondary status, given the government's need to maintain the support of the military in order to stay in power."[43]

The moderate changes effected by the Colombian government in its handling of human rights issues, in combination with the intensification of the armed conflict and the changing military needs of the country's armed forces, facilitated the signing of an agreement in August 1997 whereby the Colombian armed forces accepted the conditionality imposed by the Leahy Amendment. In the past, the Colombian military had repeatedly refused U.S. military assistance on the grounds that such unilateral impositions "violated the dignity of the army."[44] Nevertheless, the marked asymmetries between U.S. aid earmarked for the Colombian National Police (CNP), which immediately accepted human rights conditions, and assistance designated for the Colombian army in particular constituted a strong incentive for the military to finally accept the conditions attached by the United States to further aid. As a result, U.S. relations with the Colombian armed forces were normalized.

Beginning in 1997, U.S. military aid to Colombia skyrocketed. From approximately US$54 million that the U.S. government gave to Colombian security forces in 1996, U.S. aid rose to US$289 million in 1999. Between 2000 and 2001, the Colombian army received US$512 million, compared to US$123 million earmarked for the police. Until the late 1990s, the CNP constituted Washington's principal ally by far in the "war on drugs," receiving nearly 90 percent of U.S. military aid for Colombia (Isacson 2000: 2). This was due in part to the involvement of the military in human rights violations but was also closely related to the military's reluctance to participate more closely in a "war" that it considered to be of secondary importance, given the generalized climate of armed conflict in the country.[45] However, the aid figures corresponding to the Colombian army and the CNP in the 2000–2001 aid package reversed this trend.

With the approval of the Plan Colombia aid package in June 2000, the U.S. Congress specified that the president had to certify that the armed forces were acting to suspend and prosecute those officers involved in human rights violations and to enforce civilian court jurisdiction over human rights crimes and that concrete measures were being taken to break the links between the military and paramilitary groups. Nevertheless, the legislation gave the president the prerogative to waive this condition if it was deemed that vital U.S. national interests were at stake. As a result, on August 22, 2000, several days before conducting his state visit to Colombia, President Clinton invoked the waiver. Notwithstanding the testimonies of several human rights organizations in early 2001, which showed that little or no progress had been made in satisfying the human rights requirements contained in the aid package, Washington announced its decision to disburse the second portion in January 2001 (Mariner 2001).[46]

Modifications in Colombian human rights policy, characterized by a formal commitment on the part of both the government and the armed forces to denounce and punish human rights abuses committed by members of the military, cleared the way for intensified military aid. In August 2000, in an effort to show the country's determination in combating human rights violations, a new military penal code was approved that allowed for the dismissal of 388 military officials, apparently at the behest of Washington.[47] Several high-level generals figured among these. The great majority of officials were nevertheless dismissed for reasons other than violations of human rights.[48]

In July 2001, General Rito Alejo del Río, one of the generals dismissed a year earlier, was arrested on charges of sponsoring paramilitary groups and of omission of duty in the Mapiripán massacre of July 1997.[49] Del Río's arrest coincided with debates in the U.S. Congress on a new aid package for Colombia and the Andean region. Several days later, however, the general was set free. In an October 2001 visit to Colombia, Hina Jilani, special delegate of the UN General Secretary, accused the Colombian General Prosecutor's Office of laxity in cases such as that of General del Río, as well as highlighting the impunity characteristic of the Colombian judicial system.[50] A Security and National Defense Law passed in August 2001 was also criticized by human rights organizations in the United States and Colombia, given that, among other questionable practices, it authorized members of the military to detain and interrogate civilians without judicial warrants, thus creating permissive legal conditions for the further violation of human rights in the country.[51]

Given human rights restrictions associated with U.S. military assistance, paramilitarism was converted into an alternative, more "effective" means of combating Colombian guerrilla movements;[52] consequently, those violations once committed by government security forces simply shifted toward paramilitary groups. This situation surely constitutes one of the largest "black holes" of U.S. policy toward Colombia. Both the Colombian military and paramilitary groups are combating the same military target, although the latter have been much more successful in containing the territorial expansion of guerrilla movements within the country, given the sheer brutality of the methods they employ. Thus the incentive for directly confronting the paramilitaries and for breaking the links between these and specific members of the military is largely absent and is being provided mainly by the United States through coercive diplomatic action, namely the provision/withholding of military assistance. Nevertheless, U.S. policy continues to be ambiguous in this area, as the use of the human rights waiver clearly testifies, so coercive measures, although marginally effective, have failed to promote sweeping changes in Colombian human rights policies.

U.S. Policy and State Weakening

Inherent to growing U.S. concern with the Colombian situation is the perception that the state has become "weak" in terms of its capacity to confront the domestic crisis and to maintain it within the country's national boundaries. Thus, in addition to combating the drug threat and reducing human rights violations, another goal of U.S. policy is to enable the Colombian military to reestablish territorial control over the country as a necessary step toward state strengthening. To what extent is this diagnosis of state weakness, based upon the capacity of the Colombian state to exercise a monopoly over the use of force, correct? It is my contention that U.S. policy is based upon a fundamental misconception of the Colombian crisis, derived primarily from the "drug war" imperative and the narrow framework within which the problem of state weakness is viewed from the vantage point of realist ideology. To explore this assumption further, a brief discussion of the state will be offered, followed by an evaluation of the Colombian case, as well as the implications of diverse aspects of U.S. policy, specifically in terms of state weakening.

Weak States/Strong States

According to Barry Buzan (1991: 65), the components of the state are (1) a physical base, composed mainly of population and territory; (2) an institutionalized expression of this physical base, consisting of all government machinery, as well as the laws and procedures that regulate their operation; and (3) an "idea of state," embodying a legitimating idea based upon ideology, national identity, and values, among others, shared by wide sectors of the population. This final aspect, the "idea of state," is in many ways the central foundation for a given state's existence.[53] Thus, in cases in which a legitimating idea is not widely held among a given population, other sources of legitimacy, most significantly institutional strength, become crucial to the state's ability to function (Buzan 1991: 82).

Within this context, Kalevi J. Holsti (1996: 83) argues that state strength and/or weakness can be measured essentially in terms of the "capacity of the state to command loyalty—the right to rule—to extract the resources necessary to rule and provide services, to maintain that essential element of sovereignty, a monopoly over the legitimate use of force . . . , and to operate within the context of a consensus-based political community." For Holsti, an additional factor, legitimacy, conceived in both vertical and horizontal terms, must be incorporated into Buzan's conceptual model to account for differing degrees of state strength (84–90). *Vertical legitimacy* refers to the authority of a particular "idea of state" and the state's accompanying institutions, as well as their ability to command loyalty from the population. *Horizontal legitimacy* provides a measure of the inclusiveness of those political arrangements embodied in the state. Both are based upon (1) an implicit social contract between state and society by which the state is entitled to extract resources in exchange for the provision of goods and services, as well as societal participation in public decisions;[54] (2) consensus concerning the rules of the political game; (3) the effective exercise of sovereignty; and (4) the existence of clear distinctions between public service and private gain (98).

Accordingly, a critical factor for explaining state weakness is the question of legitimacy. Weak states (as opposed to strong ones) are precisely those in which a solid national identity, or an "idea of state," is absent or contested by a diverse array of societal actors; sociopolitical cohesion is especially weak; consensus on the "rules of the game" is low; institutional capabilities in terms of the provision of order, security, and well-being are limited; and the state is highly personalized (Buzan 1991; Job 1992a; Holsti 1996). In other words, in weak states vertical legitimacy, measured in terms of the ability of the state to exercise authority, and horizontal legitimacy, or the inclusiveness of political arrangements, are extremely low, making the state a contested entity.

One of the primary results of the lack of legitimacy characteristic of weak states is what Brian L. Job (1992a: 17–18) describes as the "insecurity dilemma": given the highly contested nature of the state, the notion of "threat" is derived primarily from domestic threats to the state's own existence. The state's instinct for self-preservation reduces its institutional capacity to provide security and well-being for the population at large, leading to the increased vulnerability of society as a whole, as well as the further erosion of already low levels of state legitimacy. Compounding this dilemma even further, the lack of state control over the domestic environment, as will be discussed subsequently, also makes weak states increasingly permeable to international pressures, which can in turn exacerbate problems existing on an internal level (Ayoob 1992: 65). Many of these aspects are reflected in the Colombian case and help to explain both the particular dynamics of the country's crisis and the pernicious effects of U.S. drug war efforts.

The State in Colombia

The historical weakness of the Colombian state has been widely documented.[55] Most, if not all explanations offered for state weakness in Colombia are derived primarily from the particular nature of the country's political system, namely the political hegemony of the traditional Liberal and Conservative parties. According to Fernán González González (1989: 10), the emergence and consolidation of the two parties in the mid-1800s replaced many of the integrating functions of the Colombian state. Specifically, in the early stages of the state-building process, the Liberal and Conservative parties constituted the primary channels through which national integration and identification with the "nation" took place, thus allowing the country to overcome the dangers of territorial fragmentation inherent to this period. Francisco Leal Buitrago (1984: 136) claims that the Liberal and Conservative parties in fact constituted the central pillars of the state formation process in Colombia, given their capacity to create a truly national system of ideological identification on the part of the population. The chain of civil wars that culminated in the War of a Thousand Days (1899–1902) facilitated in this sense the "creation of two systems of affiliation and collective identity" rooted in party loyalties (Pécaut 1987: 20).

The elite-controlled bipartisan party structure that came to characterize the Colombian political system supplanted to a large degree the "idea of state" described above, impeding the creation of a sufficient degree of sociopolitical cohesion upon which state legitimacy could ultimately rest, as well as the creation of channels through which state-society relations could take place. As a result the Colombian state never became recognized as a legitimate agent of social unification (Pécaut 1987: 18). Rather, the exclusionary nature of bipartisan politics converted the state into the primary arena for bipartisan struggle and thus social division, in the sense that both the Liberal and Conservative parties, when in power, aspired to exercise total control over the state apparatus to the exclusion of the opposite party. The entrenched nature of the traditional parties also limited the development of class-oriented political organizations by accommodating diverse interests within the bipartisan structure (Tickner 1998: 61).

Clientelism constituted the central mechanism through which this system operated (Leal Buitrago 1984: 140). Although the implications of clientelism for the development of the Colombian political system are multifaceted,[56] several repercussions are of interest here. To begin with, the effective functioning of the clientelist system rested upon the active role of local and regional party bosses; the existence of strong local/regional bases of political ascription and identity largely impeded national integration projects in the country. In addition, clientelism, based upon personal party loyalties, impeded the depersonalization of the political rules of the game, so that the separation of the public and private spheres was also never completed. Finally, the personalism characteristic of the Colombian state tended to blur the division between state and government. Together, these factors acted to weaken the state in Colombia even further.

Notwithstanding these structural constraints, the Colombian state did become a significant regulatory agent beginning in the 1930s. Paul Oquist (1978: 219) argues that during this period the state became an important economic actor, increased its control over strategic pressure groups, and acquired a significant role as intermediary in labor-capital relations.[57] However, the intensification of "la Violencia" between 1948 and 1949, following the assassination of Jorge Eliecer Gaitan in April 1948, led to what Oquist describes as the state's "partial breakdown," characterized by the dissolution of existing institutional arrangements, the total political rupture between the two traditional parties, and the use of high degrees of state repression to compensate for the lack of state legitimacy and territorial presence (Oquist 1978: 236).

Although the power-sharing arrangement contained in the National Front (1958–74) put an end to interparty violence, it also set the stage for the "depolitization" of the bipartisan system (Leal Buitrago 1984: 145), while leaving the economic and social problems at the root of la Violencia intact. As a result, the fundamental question of state illegitimacy was only partially addressed during this period. According to Leal Buitrago (1984: 146–72), the traditional integrating function of the two parties was largely replaced by the integrating role of capitalist expansion in the country. The traditional party loyalties that characterized the bipartisan, clientelist structure up until the National Front consequently gave way to a strict bipartisan control by the state bureaucracy, as well as the economic benefits to be derived from it.

While public spending as a percentage of GNP, one indication of state institutional expansion, grew constantly throughout the duration of the National Front governments, increased public expenditures were heavily concentrated upon strengthening the coercive apparatus of the state, to the detriment of other aspects geared toward the provision of citizen security and well-being (Bejarano and Segura 1996: 12–18). The expansion of the coercive capacity of the state was combined with the nearly continuous use of state-of-siege legislation as an additional means of exercising state control over the national population and territory. As highlighted previously, the insecurity dilemma of weak states typically produces this type of self-defense mechanism on the part of the state.

Given the complete absence of legal authority (state or military) in many regions of Colombia, parastate actors such as guerrilla movements, drug-trafficking organizations, and paramilitary groups became legitimate forms of social organization, force, security, and justice for ample sectors of the population. To a large degree, the emergence of these multifaceted, parallel expressions of political activity and violence, in combination with growing levels of state corruption, produced a second, more severe "partial breakdown" in the Colombian state in the 1980s (Tokatlian 1995: 9).

As a result, the 1991 Constitution sought to restore the legitimacy of the political system by increasing the participation of civil society in diverse decision-making processes, creating more effective mechanisms of state accountability, and incorporating previously marginalized nontraditional groups into the political fold. However, many of the structural problems that initially led to the popular referendum that mandated the Constitutional Assembly remained intact in the post-1991 period (Valencia 1997: 180). This situation was aggravated even further by the narco-scandal surrounding Ernesto Samper's election in 1994.

The U.S. Role

The previous discussion shows that state weakness has been a permanent aspect of Colombian political history. However, during the 1990s the progressive deterioration of the national situation accelerated rapidly. In the section that follows, I argue that the underlying logic of U.S. counternarcotics policy, which has largely predetermined Washington's stance toward Colombia since the 1980s, has played a direct role in this process.

On the simplest and most obvious level, the expansion and consolidation of drug-trafficking organizations in Colombia during the 1980s were intimately related to the growth in U.S. domestic consumption of illegal substances, as well as the repressive policies traditionally applied to counteract this problem. Specifically, both the U.S. demand for drugs and U.S. prohibitionist strategies created permissive external conditions in which the drug business in Colombia could flourish.[58] The appearance of these organizations coincided with unprecedented levels of corruption in the public sphere, the growth in parallel forms of violence, and decreasing levels of state monopoly over the use of force (Bejarano 1994: 58).

The dismantling of the Medellín and Cali cartels in the mid-1990s gave way to fundamentally different drug-trafficking organizations that featured greater horizontal dispersion, kept a low profile, and had a more sophisticated strategy, which made them even more difficult to identify and capture.[59] Part of the void created by the disappearance of these two cartels was filled by guerrilla (primarily the FARC) and paramilitary organizations, which became more directly involved in drug-related activities between 1994 and 1998. In consequence, U.S. drug consumption, in tandem with the country's counternarcotics strategies, exacerbated the Colombian armed conflict, providing diverse armed actors with substantial sources of income without which, arguably, their financial autonomy and territorial expansion might not have been as feasible.

Further, the United States' propensity to interpret the drug problem as a national security issue, in combination with the use of coercive diplomatic measures designed to effectively confront this threat, has forced the Colombian state to "securitize" its own antidrug strategy (Tokatlian 1995: 17–18), in which local problems, related primarily to social and economic development, have often become subordinate to Washington's "war on drugs." The underlying assumption of this "war," inspired by a realist ideology, is that external pressure is a crucial tool for achieving foreign policy objectives in this area and that U.S. power is an enabling condition for the success of coercive diplomacy. U.S.-Colombian relations during the Samper administration, in particular, seem to confirm this fundamental belief, in the sense that President Samper "collaborated" much more vigorously with the United States than previous administrations. Nevertheless, realist-inspired counternarcotics efforts ignore the fact that policy orientations in source countries must necessarily answer to domestic as well as international exigencies (Friman 1993: 126). If domestic pressures are ignored on a systematic basis, growing state illegitimacy and state weakness can result; in an already weak state, this strategy can accelerate processes of state collapse.

In the case of the Samper administration, the U.S. drug decertifications of 1996 and 1997 and the continuous threat of economic sanctions combined with domestic pressures originating from President Samper's lack of internal legitimacy to force the government to collaborate vigorously with the United States. As mentioned previously, between 1994 and 1998 the Colombian government undertook an unprecedented fumigation campaign that elicited impressive results in terms of total coca and poppy crop eradication. Nevertheless, coca cultivation mushroomed during this period. More significantly, however, the fumigation campaign had tremendous repercussions in those portions of southern Colombia where it took place. In addition to provoking massive social protests in the departments of Putumayo, Caquetá, Cauca, and, most of all, Guaviare, guerrilla involvement in the drug trade heightened during this period, and the FARC strengthened its social base of support among peasants involved in coca cultivation (Vargas 1999). The absence of the Colombian state in this part of the country greatly facilitated the assumption of parastate functions (administration of justice and security, among others) by the guerrillas. Paramilitary activity also increased with the explicit goal of containing the guerrilla expansion. The end result of this process was the strengthening of armed actors and the intensification of the Colombian conflict. Although the United States was not responsible for creating this situation, the excessive pressure placed upon the Samper government to achieve U.S. goals clearly made it worse.

According to Holsti (1996: 95), the lack of external state legitimacy can exert a negative impact upon domestic legitimacy as well. In the case of U.S.-Colombian relations between 1994 and 1998, this was undoubtedly the case. Not only was the Colombian president himself ostracized by the United States, both domestically and internationally, but increasingly Colombia became identified as a pariah state within the international community. The political costs of the country's reduced status on a global level were significant. During his entire rule, for example, Samper received only two official state visits to Colombia, by neighboring countries Venezuela and Ecuador. In turn, on an official tour through Africa and the Middle East in May 1997, the Colombian president was greeted in South Africa by the news that President Mandela was unable to meet with him. Equally considerable were the economic costs of this situation. Colombia was precluded from receiving loans from international financial institutions during the time in which the country was decertified by the United States, while U.S. foreign investment there was dramatically reduced.[60]

Following growing evidence that the United States had in many ways aggravated Colombia's domestic crisis, Washington became increasingly sensitive to the issue of state weakness and attempted to develop a more "comprehensive" strategy toward the country when Andrés Pastrana took power in 1998. In part, this shift in U.S. policy explains the United States' initial willingness to adopt a "wait-and-see" strategy regarding the peace process. Given the marked deterioration in the Colombian situation, it became difficult to ignore the clamor of an increasingly strong civil movement for a negotiated solution to the country's armed conflict. Thus, during the first year of his government, Pastrana was able to effectively navigate between domestic pressures for peace and U.S. exigencies on the drug front. Nevertheless, the assassination of three U.S. citizens by the FARC, in combination with growing difficulties in the peace process itself, marked a turning point in both U.S. and Colombian postures and facilitated the ascendance of the "drug war" logic once again.

With the emergence of Plan Colombia in late 1999, as the direct result of the "renarcotization" of the bilateral agenda, the Colombian government was able to circumvent domestic pressures by manipulating information about its intentions vis-à-vis the United States.[61] This was achieved mainly through the publication of distinct versions for public consumption (in both Colombia and Europe), in which peace (and not the "drug war") was adeptly presented as the centerpiece of Plan Colombia's strategy. Public governmental statements negating the strong emphasis placed upon the drug problem in the plan presented to the United States reinforced this idea. When the U.S. Congress approved the Colombian aid package in mid-2000, it became increasingly difficult to sustain this argument, primarily due to the strong military component designated in the package for intensifying the "drug war." Instead, the Pastrana government attempted to highlight the approximately US$200 million earmarked for initiatives related to alternative development, law enforcement, assistance to displaced persons, human rights, and democracy, while shying away from public debate concerning the significant weight attached to the military and counternarcotics aspects of the package.

Although this strategy of misrepresentation allowed the Colombian government some initial leeway in dealing with domestic pressures, the ultimate costs of such a policy were high in terms of their potential for aggravating already considerable levels of antigovernment sentiment among certain sectors of the population, including peasants involved in coca cultivation, displaced persons, and indigenous communities. During the final months of 2000, the implementation of the first stages of the "Push into Southern Colombia" led to an armed strike organized by the FARC, which consisted of cutting off the Putumayo Department from the rest of the country with road blockades. As mentioned previously, paramilitary groups largely funded by drug-trafficking organizations increased their military presence in this region, with the goal of countering the FARC, and as a result violence and displacement of the population intensified.

Following the end of the armed strike, in mid-December 2000 massive fumigation commenced in this portion of the country. According to both U.S. and Colombian official sources, the implementation of this first phase of the coca crop eradication effort had impressive results in terms of the total number of acres fumigated, while a "historic opportunity" was seized to target and destroy large coca plantations.[62] On a local level, however, the repercussions of this initiative were much less positive. An exhaustive study conducted by Colombia's national human rights ombudsman indicates that fumigation activities affected legal food crops in areas in which crop substitution pacts with the government were already in place, in areas in which such pacts were in the process of being formalized, and in areas participating in alternative development projects financed by the Colombian government, the United Nations, and Europe.[63]

The ombudsman's pronouncements were not effective in halting aerial fumigation efforts. In mid-2001, a legal action *(tutela)* was filed by the Organization of Indigenous Communities of the Amazon in which it was claimed that aerial fumigation was causing public health and environmental problems, as well as affecting the cultural integrity of indigenous communities inhabiting the southern portion of the country.[64] Following a provisional court order to suspend all fumigation activities, the judge handling the case ordered their resumption in early August 2001. In addition to indigenous leaders, members of the scientific community in the United States and elsewhere expressed growing concern over the negative health and environmental effects of fumigation in southern Colombia.[65] An evaluation of Plan Colombia conducted by the Colombian general comptroller echoed the above, while also affirming that the aerial fumigation strategy implemented in the country lacked a concrete plan, mandated by law, for mitigating potential negative effects.[66]

Events in southern Colombia evoke earlier mistakes committed during the Samper administration and may compound problems of state illegitimacy and state weakness rather than facilitating state strength. A 2001 alliance established between the governors representing the six departments most affected by the implementation of Plan Colombia (Tolima, Cauca, Nariño, Putumayo, Huila, and Caquetá) seems to confirm this trend. This group of governors staunchly opposed the military components of the plan, as well as criticizing what they considered to be the displacement of the social needs of their respective departments by the exigencies of war (Rodríguez 2001: 17). In addition to formulating demands for voluntary eradication and agrarian reform to the central government, the alliance lobbied the U.S. Congress and established direct relations with European actors. Members of the Colombian Congress themselves proposed alternative strategies for addressing the drug problem in Colombia, ranging from the depenalization of small plots of illicit crops to the legalization of drugs.[67] For its part, the FARC also pointed repeatedly to the military aspects of Plan Colombia, among others, as a pretext for halting negotiations with the government.

Admittedly, nearly all of the examples highlighted above constitute instances of government rather than state illegitimacy. However, the specific nature of the Colombian state, as described previously, tends to blur the distinction between government and state, both in practice and in the eyes of the majority of the country's population. This is largely due to the lack of territorial integration and institutional development that characterizes the state apparatus in Colombia, the absence of social cohesion surrounding the "idea of state," and the marked inequality and exclusion that have characterized the national political system since its inception. As a result, the question of governmental legitimacy derived from the "securitization" of domestic policies in response to U.S. coercive diplomacy in Colombia has increasingly been identified as a crisis of state legitimacy, with which the problem of state weakness has been accentuated.

The specific nature of Colombian governmental/state weakness and illegitimacy is frequently overlooked by U.S. policy makers and policy advisors in the search for options in Colombia, as illustrated by a report issued by an independent task force commissioned by the Council on Foreign Relations and the Inter-American Dialogue. According to this report, "Colombia's multiple problems derive from a weak state," while the country's "core, underlying problem is one of state authority and maintenance of public order" (Independent Task Force 2000: 10–11). "[B]olstering the military capacity of the state" (Independent Task Force 2000: 22) is considered to be a crucial first step toward reestablishing territorial control and providing security to the population, without which the economic and social aspects of the Colombian crisis cannot be addressed. In other words, the report views the establishment of a monopoly over the use of force as a necessary precondition for exercising authority and thus overcoming the weakness of the Colombian state. Nevertheless, as Buzan (1991) suggests, control over the national territory and population constitutes only one of the component parts of the state. Without a simultaneous strengthening of the institutional expression and, more importantly, a legitimating "idea" of the state, increased state presence alone will never resolve the problems inherent to state weakness in Colombia. The absence of state authority in the Colombian case, although partially related to the precarious military capacity of the state, is also the result of low levels of state legitimacy derived from its contested nature. Thus the redress of social, economic, and political inequalities in the country, the building of consensus concerning the political rules of the game, and the "opening" of the state (in other words, the signing of a new "social contract") constitute indispensable aspects of the state-strengthening process in Colombia that have been often overlooked, and at times hampered, by the United States.

Conclusion

The discussion and analysis offered in this chapter suggest that U.S. policy in Colombia has worked largely at cross-purposes in terms of (1) reducing the availability of illegal substances, (2) addressing the problem of human rights violations, and (3) strengthening the Colombian state. In fact, in all of these areas, U.S. actions have in many ways worsened an already grave situation, thus providing powerful examples of how *not* to achieve foreign policy objectives. One of my central arguments is that the realist ideology that has molded U.S. policy, in particular with regard to counternarcotics (and more recently counterterrorism), constitutes an extremely narrow framework in which to address the myriad, complex problems being faced by Colombia at present, given that the question of "national security," defined in a traditional sense, has tended to take precedence over equally significant political, economic, and social considerations.

The implications of the Colombian crisis for regional (in)security are also intimately related to U.S. counternarcotics policy. Following the approval of Plan Colombia in the United States, Brazil, Ecuador, Peru, Panama, and Venezuela have taken more stringent military actions to protect their borders in response to the fear that the Colombian armed conflict and intensified U.S. military involvement are producing spillover effects. Such concerns are clearly not unfounded. In Venezuela, the kidnapping and extortion of inhabitants of the Colombian-Venezuelan border has become a common occurrence. Kidnappings, guerrilla and paramilitary incursions, and the flow of displaced persons from southern Colombia into Ecuador have accentuated the permeable nature of that country's border with its Colombian neighbor. Following the withdrawal of the United States from the Panama Canal Zone, the presence of armed actors in the Darien region, as well as the flow of drugs and arms, also produces increasing alarm (Rabasa and Chalk 2001: 35).

U.S. interpretations of the problem consequently have shifted toward a more "regionalized" approach, as evidenced by the Bush administration's "Andean Regional Initiative" aid proposal for 2002, through which Colombia's neighbors receive more aid than in previous years. In addition to the destabilizing effects of the Colombian situation itself, increased U.S. military presence in Colombia—and in Ecuador, following the establishment of a "forward operating location" at the Manta airforce base[68]—has had the effect of subordinating local security patterns to the security imperatives of the United States. This situation, described by Buzan (1991: 198) as "over-lay," occurs when the "direct presence of outside powers in a region is strong enough to suppress the normal operation of security dynamics among the local states." The effects of "overlay" for Colombia's relations with Latin American neighbors, particularly in the Andean region, are multifaceted: (1) the imposition of U.S. national security imperatives over local concerns supresses the identification of shared regional interests; (2) the high levels of interdependence that underlie the drug issue as a common problem faced by the Andean region have given way to the increasing identification of Co-lombia as the sole depository of this problem; (3) "zero-sum" competition is encouraged, in the sense that Colombia's neighbors perceive the "relative gains" accrued by this country in terms of U.S. aid and the fight against drugs as a potential loss for themselves; (4) regional security dynamics run the risk of becoming entangled in a larger security dynamic, created pri-marily by the U.S. "drug war" logic.[69]

Postscript

The events of 9/11 and America's war on terrorism introduced an additional ingredient to U.S. policy in Colombia: counterterrorism. The Colombian government's termination of the peace process on February 20, 2002, placed Colombia squarely within Washington's new "war on terrorism." Until that day, the government of President Andrés Pastrana had never publicly re-ferred to the guerrillas as terrorists. In a televised speech announcing his decision to call off the peace talks, however, Pastrana made this association explicit. Echoing this change, the presidential electoral battle of 2002 cen-tered on the issues of counterterrorism and war and led to the election of hard-liner Álvaro Uribe on May 26. During his first eighteen months in office, the primary objective of Uribe's foreign policy has been to link the Colombian conflict to the international crusade against terrorism led by the Bush administration (Tickner and Pardo 2003).

The U.S. State Department's identification of Colombia's three princi-pal armed groups as global terrorist organizations, and the FARC and AUC's participation in diverse stages of the drug business, facilitated this process. An immediate effect of this strategy, whose implementation began during the last six months of the Pastrana administration, was the elimination of many of the restrictions associated with the use of U.S. military assistance in Colombia. In his March 21, 2002, request for supplemental funding for the war against terrorism and national security, President Bush requested congressional authorization so that the counternarcotics assistance that Colombia had received through Plan Colombia could be used in the fight against terrorism. As a result, the distinction, admittedly fuzzy, that the United States had maintained between drugs and counterinsurgency was subsequently eliminated. Washington also began to provide direct funding for activities unrelated to drugs. The Bush administration's 2003 budget request for Colombia, which totaled US$605 million, included approximately US$98 million for an oil pipeline (Caño Limón-Coveñas) protection program. This tendency has remained constant in the 2004 and 2005 budget requests for Colombia, which amount to US$547 and $570 million, respectively (Isacson and Stoner 2004).

President Uribe's strict alignment with Washington reflects the conviction that U.S. military assistance is indispensable to the Colombian government's own "war" against terrorism, the cornerstone of its "democratic security and defense policy."[70] In aligning itself with the United States, the Uribe administration's primary goal has been to encourage greater degrees of international involvement—especially by Washington—in the fight against illegal armed actors in Colombia, in particular the FARC. This strategy has been largely successful. In early 2004, the Bush administration requested that the troop cap in Colombia be raised from 800 to 1,400 total, arguing that the strategic offensive initiated against the FARC in mid-2003—Plan Patriota—required additional U.S. military support (Starmer 2004). In May 2004, the House of Representatives passed an amendment authorizing a slight increase (100) in the military personal cap and no increase in the case of private contractors. However, an amendment presented in the Senate to authorize the same increases approved by the House was rejected the following month, and the new troop caps will be determined in conference committee negotiations. The U.S. Southern Command participated actively in Plan Patriota's design and has been a key player in its execution, and the Bush administration is committed to providing approximately US$100 million per year for three years to maintain it.

Primarily due to the AUC's involvement in the drug trade, the United States has also been closely linked to the informal "peace talks" with the paramilitary groups that the Uribe administration initiated in November 2002 and that officially began in May 2004. The U.S. request for extradition of AUC leaders Carlos Castaño and Salvatore Mancuso in September 2002 on charges of drug trafficking led to fears that the talks would become hopelessly entangled in this issue (Tickner and Pardo 2003: 72). But although several other high-level members of the paramilitaries appear on the list of drug traffickers published by the United States in early 2004, Washington has yet to process their respective extradition requests, indicating a certain degree of backing of the Colombian government's attempts to negotiate with the AUC. Contrary to this position, Washington has staunchly opposed any type of rapprochement with the FARC. In June 2004, U.S. Ambassador William Wood expressed the United States' disapproval of a humanitarian exchange with the FARC, adducing that granting any type of benefit to the terrorists could be a catalyst for greater terrorism in Colombia.[71]

Notes

1. Nevertheless, the association of the drug issue with the notion of "threat" began much earlier. For instance, during the 1970s, President Richard Nixon declared that the abuse of illegal substances constituted a "national emergency" and called for a "full offensive" against this plague.

2. During the Bush administration, the U.S. global counternarcotics budget increased 82 percent; funding designated to international antidrug initiatives, primarily in the Andean region, grew dramatically as a result. The Andean Initiative, in contrast to previous antidrug strategies, considered both U.S. and local military involvement in the drug war crucial to the success of U.S. policy. See Washington Office on Latin America [WOLA] (1993: 27–40).

3. See Ashley (1987) and Der Derian (1992) for a discussion of the ways in which realist theory permeates common understandings of the world shared by a wide range of social actors, including policy makers and the media.

4. See Tokatlian (1995) and Matthiesen (2000) for an extensive discussion of Colombian drug policy during the Barco administration.

5. This situation reached its apex on August 18, 1989, when Liberal presidential candidate Luis Carlos Galán was assassinated by gunmen supposedly hired by the Medellín cartel. However, the United States' handling of the Marion Barry drug scandal was also a primary determinant in President Gaviria's decision to shift Colombian drug policy. The decision to sentence Washington, DC's former mayor to a maximum of one year in prison for possession of cocaine was viewed in Bogotá as proof of the laxity with

which the U.S. judicial system handled its own internal drug problem. See Matthiesen (2000: 263).

6. Two key drug-trafficking figures, Fabio Ochoa of the Cali cartel and Pablo Escobar of the Medellín cartel, surrendered in November 1990 and June 1991, respectively.

7. Michael S. Serrill, "Narco-Democracy Now?" *Time,* July 4, 1994, 21.

8. A more comprehensive discussion of U.S.-Colombian relations during the Samper goverment appears in Tickner (2000). My analysis of this period was largely influenced by a series of personal interviews sustained with Rodrigo Pardo García-Peña, former minister of foreign relations of Colombia, between July and September 2000.

9. On June 20, 1994, one day after Samper won the second round of presidential elections, Andrés Pastrana, the Conservative Party candidate, released an audiotape in which Cali cartel leaders Gilberto and Miguel Rodríguez Orejuela were overheard offering several million dollars to the Samper campaign.

10. Even before the eruption of the narco-scandal, the United States viewed Samper with a certain degree of distrust: in addition to having advocated the legalization of marijuana in the late 1970s, in 1981, when he managed the unsuccessful presidential campaign of Alfonso López Michelsen, Samper was suspected of receiving financial contributions from the Medellín cartel (Samper Pizano 2000: 226–30).

11. Michael S. Serrill, "Is It the Last Battle?" *Time,* August 8, 1994, 12.

12. Ibid., 13.

13. Interview with Ernesto Samper Pizano, September 4, 2000, Bogotá. The certification mechanism was created in 1986. On March 1 of each year, the president of the United States must send a report to the Congress in which countries involved in the distinct aspects of the drug trade are classified according to their cooperation in counternarcotics efforts. Three classification options exist: full certification, decertification, and certification for "national interest" reasons. In cases of decertification, the U.S. government can apply different types of sanctions, including the suspension of significant portions of foreign aid not related to humanitarian or counternarcotics purposes. In turn, the country is obligated to vote against all loan requests on the part of the decertified country to the World Bank, International Monetary Fund, and Inter-American Development Bank.

14. Joshua Hammer and Steven Ambrus, "From Bad to Worse," *Newsweek,* October 20, 1997, 14–18.

15. On January 22, 1996, Minister of Defense Fernando Botero provided public declarations implicating Samper in the narco-scandal. Botero's indictment of the president strengthened the position of those in favor of Samper's resignation and exacerbated the government's legitimacy crisis.

16. Interviews with Myles Frechette, former U.S. ambassador to Colombia, May 26, 2000, Washington, DC; Rodrigo Pardo García-Peña, former minister of foreign relations of Colombia, between July and September 2000, Bogotá; Ernesto Samper Pizano, September 4, 2000, Bogotá.

17. See, for example, Robert Gelbard's testimony before the House of Representatives Subcommittee on the Western Hemisphere, June 6, 1996, in which the State Department lauds the arrests of major Cali cartel figures but attributes them primarily to assistance provided by the DEA and other U.S. agencies to the Colombian National Police.

18. "A toda máquina," *Semana*, February 10, 1997, 33.

19. Interview with Myles Frechette, former U.S. ambassador to Colombia, May 26, 2000, Washington, DC. According to Frechette, on repeated occasions he in fact insisted to the State Department that Colombia should not be decertified in 1997.

20. The international financial community began to express concern for the future of the country's economy, in particular due to the size of the fiscal deficit, as well as the growing levels of corruption that Samper himself encouraged in order to remain in power. Nevertheless, one of the greatest ironies of the Samper period is that foreign investment grew considerably, in particular during 1998, in which total foreign investment reached over US$5.5 billion, representing an increase of nearly 80 percent from the previous year (Banco de la República 2002: 8). In contrast, the Pastrana period witnessed significant decreases in foreign investment levels, notwithstanding the Colombian president's positive international image.

21. Cathleen Farrell, "Setting the Next Agenda," *Time*, July 6, 1998, 27.

22. In 1997 the FARC was declared a terrorist organization by the Department of State, and thus conversations with the guerrilla group were in principle prohibited.

23. Douglas Farah, "U.S. Ready to Boost Aid to Troubled Colombia," *Washington Post*, August 23, 1999, A1.

24. Interview with Phil Chicola, May 24, 2000, Washington, DC.

25. In May 1999, following extensive discussions between the government and the FARC, disagreement set in concerning the FARC's rejection of international verification mechanisms. Talks were subsequently frozen until October.

26. Office of the President of the Republic of Colombia, "Plan Colombia: Plan for Peace, Prosperity and the Strengthening of the State," October 1999.

27. The Center for International Policy, Washington, DC, has compiled exhaustive information regarding U.S. military aid to Colombia. See this institution's Web site, www.ciponline.org, for further information.

28. In the mid-1990s, before U.S. military assistance to Colombia began to rise, government officials openly admitted that counternarcotics and counterinsurgency were essentially the same in the Colombian case. In fact, in an interview conducted by Human Rights Watch with Barry McCaffrey, then head of the U.S. Southern Command, McCaffrey conceded that they constituted "two sides of the same coin" (Human Rights Watch 1996: 85).

29. Following the discovery of a sophisticated cocaine laboratory in the Caquetá Department (nicknamed "Tranquilandia"), Tambs accused the FARC of sustaining direct links with drug traffickers.

30. Interview with Ernesto Samper Pizano, September 4, 2000, Bogotá.

31. Interview with Juan Carlos Esguerra, former defense minister and Colombian ambassador to the United States, November 3, 2000, Bogotá.

32. Juan O. Tamayo, "U.S. Officials Tie Colombian Guerrillas to Drug Exports," *Miami Herald*, December 13, 2000.

33. U.S. Department of State, "Colombian Rebel Connection to Mexican Drug Cartel," statement by Richard Boucher, spokesman, November 29, 2000. One day earlier, Drug Czar Barry McCaffrey also gave a news conference in which the FARC were accused of being involved in maritime shipments of drugs.

34. Tamayo, "U.S. Officials." Following the terrorist attacks of 9/11, as will be discussed in the Postscript, the U.S. government has reformulated and recycled such accusations and threats within the global war against terrorism (Patterson 2001: 46-49).

35. Robert Collier, "Rebels' Grip Tightens," *San Francisco Chronicle*, December 18, 2000, A1.

36. "Aumenta coca en el Caguán," *El Tiempo*, March 1, 2001, 1–2.

37. Robert Collier, "Paramilitaries Keep Nation in a State of Terror," *San Francisco Chronicle*, December 18, 2000, A11.

38. Ibid.

39. Jared Kotler, "Colombia Drug-Fight Troops Gear Up," Associated Press, December 10, 2000, electronic version.

40. U.S. Department of State, *Report on Human Rights: Colombia 2001*, Bogotá, March 2002. The U.S. State Department's 2003 report concludes that notwithstanding improvements in homicide, kidnapping, political and extrajudicial murder, and massacre and displacement figures, the overall human rights record of the Colombian government continues to be poor. U.S. Department of State, *Report on Human Rights: Colombia 2003*, Bogotá, March 2004.

41. U.S. Department of State, *Report on Human Rights: Colombia 2001*.

42. See Gallón (1997) for a more extensive discussion of Colombian human rights policy during the Samper administration.

43. "Aliados y distantes," *Semana*, March 3, 1997, 31.

44. "La otra certificación." *Semana*, July 14, 1997, 44.

45. See Juan G. Tokatlian (1995: 33–55) for an evaluation of the military's marginal role in counternarcotics activities in Colombia.

46. Since 2001 the waiver has been invoked yearly, attesting to the lack of compliance on the part of the Colombian government.

47. "Purga en F.M. sí fue pedida por los E.U," *El Espectador*, November 5, 2000, 8A.

48. "Sólo 49 militares salieron por D.H.," *El Espectador*, November 12, 2000, 4A.

49. One hundred members of the paramilitary forces seized the town of Mapiripán and tortured and killed approximately thirty inhabitants suspected of sympathizing with the guerrillas.

50. "Del Río aleja a ONU y Fiscalía," *El Espectador*, November 4, 2001, 6A.

51. "Indígenas rechazan fumigación de cultivos ilícitos en sus territorios," *El Tiempo*, August 7, 2001b. Tellingly, the Colombian National Human Rights Ombudsman considered the law unconstitutional. However, antiterrorist legislation that was approved in 2003 by the Colombian Congress and that will most likely be passed into law during 2004 authorizes precisely these measures.

52. Alejandro Reyes Posada, "Geografía de la guerra," Lecturas Dominicales, *El Tiempo*, October 17, 1999, 5.

53. Although the "idea of state" developed by Buzan constitutes a useful and interesting concept, it does not sufficiently emphasize that such legitimizing ideas are necessarily the expression of specific social relations and historical processes. Max Weber (1997: 1047–94), among others, has responded to the question of precisely which of these relations and processes lead to the "idea of state," arguing that the modern state is the direct result of the process of rationalization of domination characteristic of capitalism.

54. For Juan J. Linz (1978: 18–23), this specific aspect of state legitimacy is strongly based upon both the efficacy and the effectiveness of a given regime in identifying and implementing solutions to fundamental problems facing a given political system.

55. See Oquist (1978), Leal Buitrago (1984), Pécaut (1987), and González González (1989).

56. See Leal Buitrago and Dávila Ladrón de Guevara (1991) for a thorough analysis of the role of clientelism in the Colombian political system.

57. In the Colombian case, Alfonso López-Pumarejo's "Revolución en Marcha" (1934–38) provides the best example of the changes in the nature of the state described here.

58. See Tokatlian (1995: 1–10) for a more extensive discussion of this topic.

59. Joseph Contreras and Steven Ambrus, "Fighting the New Drug Lords," *Newsweek*, February 21, 2000, 8–13.

60. As noted previously, however, total foreign investment in Colombia actually rose during the Samper administration and was accounted for mainly by British investment in the oil industry and Spanish investment in the financial sector.

61. The two-level games approach to diplomacy highlights the fact that statesmen must usually respond to both domestic and international pressures surrounding specific issue areas. When such pressures fail to coincide, statesmen must seek ways of reconciling them. The manipulation of information concerning specific agreements is one means of doing so. See Moravcsik (1993: 15–25).

62. David Adams, "Plan Colombia Gets off to a Rocky Start," *St. Petersburg Times*, February 11, 2001.

63. Defensoría del Pueblo, "Informe defensorial no. 1 de la Defensoría Delegada para los Derechos Colectivos y del Ambiente: Fumigaciones y proyectos de desarrollo alternativo en el Putumayo," February 9, 2001.

64. "Pastrana firmó ley de guerra," *El Tiempo,* August 16, 2001.

65. See www.tni.org for a series of articles related to this topic.

66. Contraloría General de la República, *Plan Colombia: Primer informe de evaluación* (Bogotá: Contraloría de República, 2001).

67. "Críticas a proyecto de ley para legalización de drogas," *El Tiempo,* August 22, 2001.

68. In December 1999, the Ecuadorian and U.S. governments signed a ten-year agreement whereby the United States was granted use of the Manta air force base to conduct counternarcotics air surveillance and reconnaissance missions. The agreement allows up to four hundred U.S. military personnel to be stationed at this forward-operating location, which, in addition to three others located in Curacao, Aruba and El Salvador, forms part of a network of U.S. military bases in the region.

69. See Tickner and Mason (2003) for a more detailed explanation of the overlay concept.

70. Presidencia de la República de Colombia and Ministerio de Defensa Nacional, "Política de defensa y seguridad democrática," June 2003, retrieved from http://alpha. mindefensa.gov.co/index.php.

71. "E.U. en contra de intercambio," *El Tiempo,* June 16, 2004, 1–6.

References

Ashley, Richard K. 1987. "The Geopolitics of Geopolitical Space: Towards a Critical Social Theory of International Politics." *Alternatives,* no. 12:403–34.

Ayoob, Mohammed. 1992. "The Security Predicament of the Third World State: Reflections on State Making in Comparative Perspective." In Job 1992b, 63–80.

Bagley, Bruce. 1988. "U.S. Foreign Policy and the War on Drugs: Analysis of a Policy Failure." *Journal of Interamerican Studies and World Affairs* 30, nos. 2–3:189–212.

———. 1992. "Myths of Militarization: Enlisting Armed Forces in the War on Drugs." In *Drug Policy in the Americas,* ed. Peter H. Smith, 129–50. Boulder, CO: Westview Press.

———. 2000. "Drug Trafficking, Political Violence and U.S. Policy in Colombia in the 1990s." Mimeo.

Bagley, Bruce, and Juan G. Tokatlian. 1992. "Dope and Dogma: Explaining the Failure of U.S.-Latin America Drug Policies." In *The United States and Latin America in the 1990s: Beyond the Cold War,* ed. Jonathan Hartlyn, Lars Schoulz, and Augusto Varas, 214–34. Chapel Hill: University of North Carolina Press.

Banco de la República. 2002. *Indicadores económicos 2001.* Bogotá: Banco de la República, Imprenta Nacional.

Bejarano, Ana María. 1994. "Recuperar el estado para fortalecer la democracia." *Análisis Político,* no. 22 (May–August): 47–79.

Bejarano, Ana María, and Renata Segura. 1996. "El fortalecimiento selectivo del estado durante el Frente Nacional." *Controversia* (Centro de Investigación y Educatión Popular), no. 169 (November): 9–34.

Buzan, Barry. 1991. *People, States and Fear: An Agenda for International Security Studies in the Post-Cold War Era.* Boulder, CO: Lynne Rienner.

Campbell, David. 1992. *Writing Security: United States Foreign Policy and the Politics of Identity.* Minneapolis: University of Minnesota Press.

Cardona, Diego. 1990. *Evaluación de la política exterior de la administración Barco.* Documentos Ocasionales, no. 16 (July–August). Bogotá: Centro de Estudios Internacionales.

Corr, Edwin G., and David C. Miller Jr. 1992. "United States Government Organization and Capability to Deal with Low-Intensity Conflict." In *Low-Intensity Conflicts: Old Threats in a New World,* ed. Edwin G. Corr and Stephen Sloan, 17–45. Boulder, CO: Westview Press.

Crandall, Russell. 2000. "The Eagle and the Snowman: U.S. Policy toward Colombia during the Presidential Administration of Ernesto Samper (1994–1998)." PhD diss., Johns Hopkins University.

Der Derian, James. 1992. *Antidiplomacy.* Cambridge: Blackwell.

Franco, Andrés. 1998. "La cooperación fragmentada como una nueva forma de diplomacia: Las relaciones entre Colombia y Estados Unidos en los noventa." In *Estados Unidos y los países andinos, 1993–1997: Poder y desintegración,* ed. Andrés Franco, 37–80. Bogotá: CEJA.

Friman, H. Richard. 1993. "Neither Compromise nor Compliance: International Pressures, Societal Influence and the Politics of Deception in the International Drug Trade." In *The Limits of State Autonomy: Societal Groups and Foreign Policy Formulation,* ed. David Skidmore and Valerie M. Hudson, 103–26. Boulder, CO: Westview Press.

Gallón, Gustavo. 1997. "Diplomacia y derechos humanos: Entre la inserción y el aislamiento." In *Colombia: Entre la inserción y el aislamiento,* ed. Socorro Ramírez and Luis Alberto Restrepo, 202–31. Bogotá: Siglo del Hombre Editores-IEPRI.

González González, Fernán. 1989. "Un estado en construcción." *Análisis* (Centro de Investigación y Educación Popular), no. 53 (May): 5–12.

Holsti, Kalevi J. 1996. *The State, War, and the State of War.* Cambridge: Cambridge University Press.

Human Rights Watch. 1996. *Colombia's Killer Networks: The Military-Paramilitary Partnership and the United States.* Washington, DC: Human Rights Watch.

———. 2000. *Los lazos que unen: Colombia y las relaciones militares-paramilitares.* Washington, DC: Human Rights Watch.

Huntington, Samuel P. 1989. "American Ideals versus American Institutions." In *American Foreign Policy: Theoretical Essays,* ed. G. John Ikenberry, 223–57. New York: HarperCollins.

―――. 1997. "The Erosion of American National Interests." *Foreign Affairs* 76, no. 5 (September/October): 28–49.

Independent Task Force. 2000. *Toward Greater Peace and Security in Colombia: Forging a Constructive United States Policy.* Report of an Independent Task Force, Council on Foreign Relations, Inter-American Dialogue.

Isacson, Adam. 2000. *Getting in Deeper: The United States' Growing Involvement in Colombia's Conflict.* International Policy Report, February. Washington, DC: Center for International Policy.

Isacson, Adam, and Eric Stoner. 2004. "Highlights of the Bush Administration's 2005 Latin American Aid Request." Memorandum, Center for International Policy, February 10.

Job, Brian L. 1992a. "The Insecurity Dilemma: National, Regime and State Securities in the Third World." In Job 1992b, 11–35.

―――, ed. 1992b. *The Insecurity Dilemma: National Security of Third World States.* Boulder, CO: Lynne Rienner.

Leal Buitrago, Francisco. 1984. *Estado y política en Colombia.* Bogotá: Siglo XXI Editores.

Leal Buitrago, Francisco, and Andrés Dávila Ladrón de Guevara. 1991. *Clientelismo: El sistema político y su expresión regional.* Bogotá: IEPRI, Tercer Mundo Editores.

LeoGrande, William M., and Kenneth E. Sharpe. 2000. "Two Wars or One? Drugs, Guerrillas and Colombia's New *Violencia.*" *World Policy Journal* (Fall): 1–11.

Linz, Juan J. 1978. *Crisis, Breakdown and Reequilibration.* Baltimore: Johns Hopkins University Press.

Mariner, Joanne. 2001. "The Clinton Administration's Stealth Waiver of Human Rights Protections for Colombia." February 8. Retrieved February 26, 2006, from http://writ.news.findlaw.com/mariner/20010208.html.

Matthiesen, Tatiana. 2000. *El arte político de conciliar: El tema de las drogas en las relaciones entre Colombia y Estados Unidos, 1986–1994.* Bogotá: FESCOL-CEREC-Fedesarrollo.

Moravcsik, Andrew. 1993. "Introduction: Integrating International and Domestic Theories of International Bargaining." In *Double-Edged Diplomacy: International Bargaining and Domestic Politics,* ed. Peter B. Evans, Harold K. Jacobson, and Robert D. Putnam, 3–42. Berkeley: University of California Press.

Oquist, Paul. 1978. *Violencia, conflicto y política en Colombia.* Bogotá: Instituto de Estudios Colombianos.

Pardo, Diana, and Arlene B. Tickner. 1998. "La política exterior en el proceso electoral colombiano." In *Elecciones y democracia en Colombia 1997–1998,* ed. Ana María Bejarano and Andrés Dávila, 17–34. Bogotá: Fundación Social, Departamento de Ciencia Política, Universidad de los Andes, Veeduría Ciudadana a la Elección Presidencial.

————. 2000. "El problema del narcotráfico en el Sistema Interamericano." In *Sistema Interamericano y democracia: Antecedentes históricos y tendencias futuras,* ed. Arlene B. Tickner, 291–309. Bogotá: OEA, CEI, Ediciones Uniandes.

Patterson, Anne W. 2001. "Las nuevas relaciones entre Estados Unidos y Colombia." *La Revista de El Espectador,* no. 68 (November 4): 46–49.

Pécaut, Daniel. 1987. *Orden y violencia: Colombia, 1930–1954.* Bogotá: Siglo XXI Editores, CEREC.

Perl, Ráphael. 1988. "The US Congress, International Drug Policy, and the Antidrug Abuse Act of 1988." *Journal of Interamerican Studies and World Affairs* 30, nos. 2–3:133–60.

————. 1992. "United States Andean Drug Policy: Background and Issues for Decisionmakers." *Journal of Interamerican Studies and World Affairs* 34, no. 3:13–37.

Rabasa, Angel, and Peter Chalk. 2001. *Colombian Labyrinth: The Synergy of Drugs and Insurgency and Its Implications for Regional Stability.* Santa Monica, CA: RAND.

Rangel Suárez, Alfredo. 2000. "Parasites and Predators: Guerrillas and the Insurrection Economy of Colombia." *Journal of International Affairs* 53 (Spring): 577–601.

Rodríguez, Omar Roberto. 2001. "La alianza del Sur." *La Revista de El Espectador,* no. 27 (January 21): 16–17.

Samper Pizano, Ernesto. 2000. *Aquí estoy y aquí me quedo: Testimonio de un gobierno.* Bogotá: El Ancora Editores.

Shifter, Michael. 1999. "Colombia on the Brink." *Foreign Affairs* 78 (July–August): 14–20.

Starmer, Elanor. 2004. "Lifting the Cap: Bush Administration Seeks to Expand U.S. Military Personnel in Colombia." May 12. Retrieved September 13, 2005, from Americas Program, Interhemispheric Resource Center Web site: http://americas.irc-online.org/reports/2004/0405expcolombia.html.

Tickner, Arlene B. 1998. "Colombia: Chronicle of a Crisis Foretold." *Current History* 97 (February): 61–65.

————. 2000. "Consecuencias indeseables de la política exterior estadounidense en Colombia." *Colombia Internacional,* nos. 49/50 (May–December): 39–61.

Tickner, Arlene B., and Ann C. Mason. 2003. "Mapping Transregional Security Structures in the Andean Region." *Alternatives* 28, no. 3:359–91.

Tickner, Arlene B., and Rodrigo Pardo. 2003. "En busca de aliados para la 'seguridad democrática': La política exterior del primer año de la administración Uribe." *Colombia Internacional,* nos. 56–57 (September–June): 64–81.

Tokatlian, Juan Gabriel. 1995. *Drogas, dilemas y dogmas.* Bogotá: TM Editores, CEI.

————. 2000. "La polémica sobre la legalización de las drogas en Colombia, el presidente Samper y los Estados Unidos." *Latin American Research Review* 35, no. 1: 37–83.

Valencia Villa, Hernando. 1997. *Cartas de batalla: Una crítica del constitucionalismo colombiano.* Bogotá: CEREC.

Vargas Meza, Ricardo. 1999. *Fumigación y conflicto: Políticas antidrogas y deslegitimación del Estado en Colombia.* Bogotá: TM Editores, Acción Andina.

Vásquez, John A. 1991. *El poder de la política del poder.* México: Gernika.

Washington Office on Latin America. 1993. *¿Peligro inminente? Las fuerzas armadas de Estados Unidos y la guerra contra las drogas.* Washington: DC: WOLA.

———. 1997. *Losing Ground: Human Rights Advocates under Attack in Colombia.* Washington, DC: WOLA (October).

Weber, Max. 1997. *Economía y sociedad.* Bogotá: Fondo de Cultura Económica.

Youngers, Colletta. 1998. "Waging War: U.S. Policy toward Colombia." Paper delivered at the annual meeting of Latin American Studies Association, Chicago, September 24–26.

Zirnite, Peter. 1997. *Reluctant Recruits: The U.S. Military and the War on Drugs.* Washington, DC: Washington Office on Latin America (August).

Human Rights

A Path to Democracy and Peace in Colombia

Gustavo Gallón

Gustavo Gallón, director of the Colombian Commission of Jurists, brings his considerable knowledge of and passion for the human rights situation in Colombia to this chapter. Gallón argues that the intractable nature of the Colombian conflict has its origin in three misunderstandings about the crisis: (1) by failing to grasp the true nature of the crisis, and (2) by ignoring the responsibility of the Colombian state and successive governments for its violence, participants and observers have (3) failed to understand the possible solutions to the conflict. The Colombian crisis, the author argues, is one of human rights. The guerrilla fighting, drug trafficking, and paramilitary activities that are often perceived as being the core of the conflict are in fact all traceable to a root problem, which is the "lack of institutional commitment to credibly protect and respect the human rights of the entire population." The author provides abundant details of the current human rights situation in Colombia to support the claim that the crisis has human rights violations at its core. He strongly criticizes the view that the state is an (or the) innocent victim of lawless violence, exposing its complicity at all stages of the progressive degradation of the Colombian situation since the mid-1960s. In particular he highlights the state's close relationship to paramilitary groups, its failure to follow through on human rights commitments, and its current effort to further militarize society by enlisting civilians in the fight and giving the military greater latitude in law enforcement activities. Finally, he persuasively argues that, to break the vicious cycle of war and human rights violations, the government must craft a policy that places human rights at the core. To begin to resolve this conflict, the government must prevent human rights violations, punish past ones, strengthen key institutions like the courts, guarantee minimum levels of economic, social, and cultural rights, and foster a more inclusive political environment for all Colombians. To end the war, he says, Colombia must build democracy now, not later.

Colombia, like many other countries in the world, is a beautiful nation with honest, hard-working people and a wealth of natural resources. Yet at the same time, Colombia, unlike many other countries, has been tormented by a deep-rooted human rights crisis since its very inception. Far from being resolved after centuries, Colombia's crisis has worsened severely over the last two decades of the twentieth century. If Colombia is able to overcome this serious human rights situation, it could become a very attractive place to build a prospering society.

Three main misunderstandings regarding the crisis in Colombia make it difficult to successfully redress the situation. The first concerns the nature of the crisis—that is, its diagnosis. Many people, both within the country and abroad, believe that what is happening in Colombia is a problem of violence generated by drug trafficking. Other people think that violence in Colombia originates primarily or only with the guerrillas. Still other observers are convinced that Colombia is a violent society because of the violent nature of most of its members. These views are simplifications of a more complex problem that cannot be understood if it is not seen as what it is: a very serious crisis of human rights. What Colombia is suffering is the result of the lack of institutional commitment to credibly protect and respect the human rights of its entire population. Obviously, this lack of institutional protection and respect is aggravated by factors like the violence perpetrated by drug traffickers or guerrillas. Moreover, the existence of drug traffickers and guerrillas in Colombia is one of the outcomes of that lack of protection and respect. But the hard core of the problem is the human rights crisis and not the particular expressions of violence that aggravate that crisis or are among its consequences.

The second misunderstanding concerns the responsibility of the Colombian government—the Colombian state, more precisely—in this crisis.

Due to the existence of democratic practices in Colombia, some journalists, policy makers, scholars, and ordinary citizens see the state as a victim of the crisis rather than a protagonist deeply involved in it. The state itself, in the analysis that each Colombian government since the 1970s has made of the crisis, promotes this image of victim. This misunderstanding is intimately related to the first one. If the focus is put on drug traffickers or guerrillas, it is natural that the state is seen as a victim. But if the focus is put on the lack of institutional respect and protection that characterizes the Colombian situation as a human rights crisis, the responsibility of the state comes sharply into focus. Another factor also emerges clearly when the Colombian crisis is looked at in this way: the existence of the paramilitary groups, created originally by decision of the state, then made illegal but—to say the least—tolerated and not pursued with the clear intention of eliminating them. The activity of paramilitary groups in Colombia—which tends to be ignored when the problem is not understood as a human rights crisis—is the clearest evidence of the responsibility of the state in such a crisis, but it is not the only one. The state's responsibility is also evident in the illegal and violent actions committed by state agents against the civilian population for many years, as well as in legal but arbitrary decisions and activities that have been repeatedly undertaken by successive Colombian governments under the state of exception. The state is also notorious for not following through on its responsibility to provide decent levels of social, economic, and cultural rights. Their absence is a very important component of the human rights crisis.

The third misunderstanding concerns the solution to the crisis and is also intimately related to previous misunderstandings. If Colombia's main problem is drug trafficking, the source of all kinds of violence, and if the Colombian state has no responsibility for that violence, what must be done is to help the Colombian government combat drug trafficking. Similarly, if the problems of Colombia are reduced to the existence of guerrillas and of an internal armed conflict, and if the Colombian state is seen to have no responsibility in that conflict, what must be done is to help the Colombian government put an end to the conflict through peace negotiations or military action. But if the crisis in Colombia is considered as what it is—that is to say, a human rights crisis implicating the state as responsible—one must request that the Colombian state fulfill its national and international duties on human rights. This is the only way to overcome the crisis, strengthen democracy, and build peace, making Colombia strong enough to solve its other problems, such as drug trafficking.

This chapter tries to deal with these three misunderstandings by first describing how serious the human rights crisis is; then analyzing how crucial the responsibility of the state is and how it has tried to interpret the situation in order to be seen as a victim; and then proposing the adoption and implementation of a suitable and committed human rights policy as the surest way to overcome this tremendous but surmountable crisis. The participation of the international community, as well as that of the people of Colombia, is very important in this task. Particularly significant is the contribution that citizens and governments from the European Union, Latin America, and the United States can give to identify the Colombian crisis as a human rights crisis and to help provide solutions emerging from this understanding.

Colombia's Crisis Is One of Human Rights

Colombia's human rights crisis is characterized by a high level of sociopolitical violence, as well as violence resulting from common crime, impunity, and social inequity. These problems have also become embedded in the broader panorama of this country's history of human rights violations.

High Levels of Sociopolitical Violence

At present, Colombia has considerably high levels of sociopolitical violence,[1] a phenomenon that has plagued this country for some time. Close to twenty people are killed each day for sociopolitical reasons. Between 1988 and 1997, an average of ten sociopolitically motivated deaths occurred per day in Colombia. This means that the situation has become worse since 1998, dramatically doubling the already high figure of killings reached during the 1990s.[2]

Many of those twenty deaths correspond to individuals killed, not in combat, but on the streets, at work, or at home: fifteen per day between 2000 and 2002, eight per day between 2002 and 2004. They were killed or forcibly disappeared for being political activists, trade unionists, peasant activists, human rights workers, journalists, or indigent homeless persons. The remaining five or twelve of those twenty deaths were the direct consequence of the armed conflict (soldiers, guerrilla members, and noncombatant civilians caught in the crossfire).

Between 2000 and 2002, almost 85 percent of murders committed out of combat were attributed to paramilitary groups and state agents, and just over 15 percent to guerrilla groups. Between 1988 and 1997, 70 percent of out-of-combat murders were attributed to state agents and paramilitary groups and 30 percent to guerrilla groups. That means that the shift from ten socio-political killings each day to twenty was mostly due to the increase in killings attributed to paramilitary groups. Since 2002, more than 75 percent of these murders have been ascribed to paramilitary groups and state agents and about 25 percent to guerrilla groups.

The level of political violence has clearly gotten much worse over the last twenty years (see table 10.1 and figures 10.1 through 10.3). In 1980, one hundred people were killed for political reasons. In 1985, that figure had risen ten times, to one thousand. By 1988, the yearly toll was over four thousand. From 1988 to 1997, the number of politically motivated killings remained practically the same: between three thousand and four thousand lives per year. Thus the deterioration of the situation from 1988 and 1997 was accompanied by a stabilization of an extremely high political homicide rate. Unfortunately, this rate has increased once again since 1998, hitting levels close to seven thousand per year since 2000.

Colombia has also had a very high rate of kidnappings (see table 10.2 and figure 10.4). During the bulk of the 1990s, approximately 1,200 people were kidnapped each year, for an average of three persons per day. Since 1998, this rate has also risen dramatically. In 2000, there were more than 3,700 people kidnapped, an average of almost nine per day. In 2001, there were about 3,000; in 2003, more than 2,000. Approximately half of these kidnappings have been attributed to guerrilla groups and 10 percent to paramilitary groups. Several cases from the remaining 40 percent (attributed mostly to common criminals) have been ascribed to present or former state agents.[3]

Clearly, the overall human rights situation in Colombia has continued to deteriorate in recent years. The huge increase in paramilitary groups is one of the main causes of this degradation, with consequences such as the systematic murder of human rights defenders and the enormous rise in the ranks of internally displaced people.

Paramilitary Groups

In the context of the aforementioned entrenchment of political violence at high levels since 1988, and its subsequent upsurge in 1998, there has been an

Table 10.1

Evolution of the Human Rights Situation and Sociopolitical Violence in Colombia, 1980–2003

Year	Extrajudicial executions and political homicides	Forced disappearances	Extrajudicial executions and homicides of socially marginalized persons (a)	Subtotal of victims 4=1+2+3	Deaths in combat and crossfire	Victims of sociopolitical violence: dead and missing 6=4+5	Daily average of sociopolitical dead and missing 7=6÷365	Total homicides in common crime	Daily average of homicides in common crime 9=8÷365	Total violent deaths (b) 10=6+8	Total daily average of violent deaths 11=10÷36	Total victims of sociopolitical violence + total violent deaths 12=6÷10
	1	2	3	4	5	6	7	8	9	10	11	12
1980	92	4		96	21	117	0.32	9,005	24.67	9,122	24.99	1.28%
1981	269	101		370	95	465	1.27	10,248	28.08	10,713	29.35	4.34%
1982	525	130		655	69	724	1.98	9,856	27.00	10,580	28.99	6.84%
1983	594	109		703	173	876	2.40	8,845	24.23	9,721	26.63	9.01%
1984	542	122		664	225	889	2.44	9,805	26.86	10,694	29.30	8.31%
1985	630	82		712	386	1,098	3.01	11,801	32.33	12,899	35.34	8.51%
1986	1,387	191		1,578	362	1,940	5.32	13,732	37.62	15,672	42.94	12.38%
1987	1,651	109		1,760	313	2,073	5.68	15,346	42.04	17,419	47.72	11.90%
1988	2,738	210	273	3,221	1,083	4,304	11.79	16,796	46.02	21,100	57.81	20.40%
1989	1,978	137	364	2,479	732	3,211	8.80	20,101	55.07	23,312	63.87	13.77%
1990	2,007	217	267	2,491	1,229	3,720	10.19	21,600	59.18	25,320	69.37	14.69%
1991	1,829	180	389	2,398	1,364	3,762	10.31	25,110	68.79	28,872	79.10	13.03%
1992	2,178	191	505	2,874	1,602	4,476	12.26	25,125	68.84	29,601	81.10	15.12%
1993	2,190	144	161	2,495	1,097	3,592	9.84	24,042	65.87	27,634	75.71	13.00%
1994	1,668	147	277	2,092	1,009	3,101	8.50	23,543	64.50	26,644	73.00	11.64%
1995	1,831	85	371	2,287	1,049	3,336	9.14	22,062	60.44	25,398	69.58	13.13%
1996	1,479	168	169	1,816	1,131	2,947	8.07	23,695	64.92	26,642	72.99	11.06%
1997	2,199	222	143	2,564	1,283	3,847	10.54	21,532	58.99	25,379	69.53	15.16%

Table 10.1

Evolution of the Human Rights Situation and Sociopolitical Violence in Colombia, 1980–2003 (continued)

	1	2	3	4	5	6	7	8	9	10	11	12
Year	Extrajudicial executions and political homicides	Forced disappearances	Extrajudicial executions and homicides of socially marginalized persons (a)	Subtotal of victims $4=1+2+3$	Deaths in combat and crossfire	Victims of sociopolitical violence: dead and missing $6=4+5$	Daily average of sociopolitical dead and missing $7=6÷365$	Total homicides in common crime	Daily average of homicides in common crime $9=8÷365$	Total violent deaths (b) $10=6+8$	Total daily average of violent deaths $11=10÷36$	Total victims of sociopolitical violence ÷ total violent deaths $12=6÷10$
1998	1,812	260	150	2,222	1,463	3,685	10.10	19,411	53.18	23,096	63.28	15.96%
1999	2,298	340	244	2,882	1,479	4,361	11.95	20,087	55.03	24,448	66.98	17.84%
2000	3,901	629	321	4,851	1,730	6,581	18.03	19,959	54.68	26,540	72.71	24.80%
2001	3,854	494	256	4,604	1,965	6,569	18.00	21,271	58.28	27,840	76.27	23.60%
2002	3,536	462	387	4,385	3,420	7,805	21.38	21,032	57.62	28,837	79.01	27.07%
2003	3,231	421	259	3,911	2,430	6,341	17.37	23,523	64.45	29,864	81.82	21.23%
Total	44,419	5,155	4,536	54,110	25,710	79,820		437,527		517,347		

Sources: Inter-congregational Justice and Peace Commission (CIJP), Bogotá, *Information Bulletin*, vols. 1 to 8.

CINEP (1995).

Human Rights and Political Violence Database of CINEP and Justice and Peace (BCJP), *Noche y Niebla* (Night and Fog Review), Panorama of Human Rights and Political Violence in Colombia, Bogotá, BCJP, nos. 1 to 28, July 1996 to 2003.

Revista Criminalidad (Criminality Review), Bogotá, 1980 to 2004.

Torres et al. (1982).

Giraldo (1988).

Permanent Committee for the Defense of Human Rights, *Press Bulletin*, Bogotá, 1981–91.

The newspapers *El Colombiano, El Espectador, El Tiempo, Diario del Sur, El Heraldo, El Liberal, El Meridiano de Córdoba, El Meridiano de Sucre, El Nuevo Día de Ibagué, El País, El Universal, Hoy Diario del Magdalena, La Libertad, La Nación, La Opinión, La Tarde,* and *Vanguardia Liberal.*

The magazines *Semana, Cambio,* and *Cromos.*

Written denouncements in the files of the Colombian Commission of Jurists.

Notes:

a. Due to information problems, data on homicides and extrajudicial executions of socially marginalized persons before 1988 are not included.

b. Total and average daily violent deaths do not include deaths that occurred in road accidents.

Figure 10.1
Extrajudicial Executions, Sociopolitical Homicides,
and Forced Disappearances outside Combat, 1980–2003

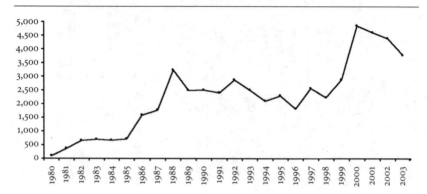

Source: Figure 10.1 was prepared using data from Table 10.1, Column 4.

Figure 10.2
Deaths in Combat and Cross Fire, 1980–2003

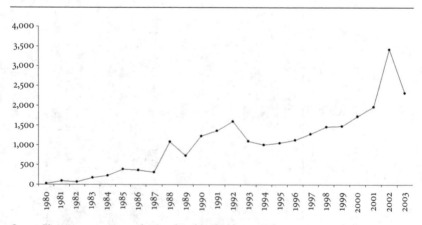

Source: Figure 10.2 was prepared using data from Table 10.1, Column 5.

Figure 10.3
Extrajudicial Executions, Sociopolitical Homicides, Forced Disappearances outside Combat, and Deaths in Combat and Cross Fire, 1980–2003

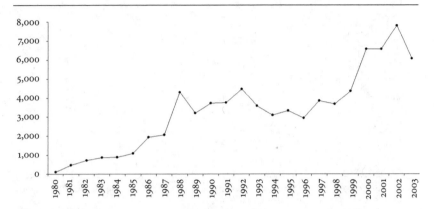

Source: Figure 10.3 was prepared using data from Table 10.1, Column 6.

Table 10.2
Hostage-Takings and Kidnappings Perpetrated by Guerrilla Groups, Paramilitary Groups, and Common Delinquents, 1990–2003

Years	Number of kidnappings
1990	1,282
1991	1,717
1992	1,320
1993	1,014
1994	1,293
1995	1,158
1996	1,608
1997	1,986
1998	1,609
1999	1,991
2000	3,706
2001	3,041
2002	2,963
2003	2,058

Source: National Police, Criminology Investigation Office.

Figure 10.4
Hostage-Takings and Kidnappings Perpetrated by Guerrilla Groups,
Paramilitary Groups, and Common Delinquents, 1990–2003

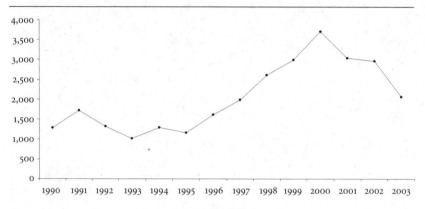

Source: Figure 10.4 was prepared using data from Table 10.2.

ominous change in the makeup of the actors taking part in this phenomenon. In the 1990s, paramilitary group involvement in acts of sociopolitical
violence rose substantially, in a change that was gradual yet systematic.

There has been a progressive and enormous increase in paramilitary
group involvement in political violence since 1993, accompanied by an
equally progressive and significant decline in actions attributed to state
agents. More than 50 percent of noncombatant acts of political violence in
1993 were attributed to state agents, with less than 20 percent attributed to
paramilitary groups. Year after year, this proportion shifted to the point
where it totally reversed. More than 50 percent of political killings in 1996
were attributed to paramilitary groups and less than 20 percent to state
agents.

This change in levels of involvement has continued to evolve. Since
1997, more than 75 percent of politically motivated murders were attributed
to paramilitary groups, less than 5 percent to state agents, and almost 20
percent to guerrilla groups.[4] In 2000, almost 80 percent of these murders
were attributed to paramilitary groups, close to 5 percent to state agents,
and more than 15 percent to guerrilla groups. In 2003, following the launching of a process of negotiations between the government and paramilitary

groups, murders attributed to the latter showed a relative reduction (to 69 percent), and those attributed to state agents registered a relative increase (to 7 percent), as did those attributed to guerrilla groups (to 24 percent). This represents a serious and important shift in violence and human rights violations over the past decade, a sharp rise in paramilitary actions combined with an equally sharp fall in actions directly attributed to state agents. The change denotes a worsening situation and makes its control that much more difficult.

Some Colombian authorities claim that this phenomenon is the result of a policy oriented toward guaranteeing respect for human rights by the armed forces.[5] Unfortunately, there are issues that make it hard to accept this conclusion. First, despite the aforementioned changes, there continues to be strong evidence of ties between the armed forces and paramilitary groups, evidence that has continued to emerge during the few last years. High-ranking officers have been investigated and indicted by the Prosecutor General's Office (Fiscalía)[6] for being involved in massacres perpetrated by paramilitary groups with the complicity of the armed forces. When witnesses of mass killings by paramilitary groups have been able to speak after the fact, they have substantiated that the army and/or the police have supported these acts, either by being present or by deliberately and suddenly withdrawing from the scene. In fact, there have been no reports of any paramilitary group that does not have the support or at least the tolerance of the armed forces (Inter-American Commission on Human Rights [IACHR] 1999). The government argues that these are isolated cases and that they do not mean that there is a general policy involving the armed forces as a whole. Though this may well be true, it is beside the point, which is that cases like these arise so frequently and uniformly in various regions of the country that they indicate the existence of repeated, strong, and significant relations between the armed forces and paramilitary groups. The natural result of such ties is joint activity.

A second issue makes it difficult to conclude that the reduction in the number of allegations of state agents' direct involvement in human rights violations over the last few years is a direct result of their greater respect for human rights. That issue is the reluctance that the police and military forces have shown toward taking action against paramilitary groups. During the Pastrana administration, the Ministry of Defense argued that the armed forces had captured approximately nine hundred members of paramilitary groups between 1998 and 2000. Yet the official figures fail to indicate how many of these individuals were captured by virtue of arrest warrants issued by the Prosecutor General's Office.[7] In fact, the former prosecutor general, Alfonso Gómez Méndez, revealed that by the time he finished his term in mid-2001, his office had issued hundreds of these warrants that the armed forces had not acted on. In most cases, paramilitary agents have been captured by the armed forces almost by chance (i.e., they have been detained in an unplanned confrontation with state agents and not as a result of operations organized to serve arrest warrants issued by the Prosecutor General's Office). No paramilitary leaders have been pursued by the army or police forces. The deputy commander in chief of the army stated in 1999 that pursuit of paramilitary forces was not one of the duties assigned to the armed forces under the Colombian Constitution.[8] Since the 1980s, several Colombian presidents have announced their intentions of organizing a special task force of one thousand special state agents for the specific purpose of combating paramilitary groups. None of these task forces have materialized. Given these and other circumstances, it is difficult to conclude that state agents are truly committed to confronting paramilitary activities in Colombia.

The truth is that the total number of people killed every year for sociopolitical reasons in Colombia did not go down in the 1990s, though the direct involvement of state agents in such killings has apparently decreased. The reduction of criminal actions directly attributed to state agents has been more than compensated for by a rise in acts perpetrated by paramilitary groups, with the evident tolerance, complicity, or acquiescence of state agents (IACHR 1999).

Murders of Human Rights Defenders and Other Social Activists

Another factor that has made the situation degenerate further is the brazen multiplication in the number of murders of human rights defenders and peace activists in recent years. Since 1996, an average of more than one defender has been killed each month. Between July 1996 and May 2003, at least ninety-four human rights defenders (including leaders of indigenous and Afro-Colombian communities) were assassinated or forcibly disappeared in Colombia. In cases in which the generic assailant was known, about 61 percent were attributed to state agents—7 percent as the perpetrators and 54 percent by paramilitary groups acting with the tolerance or active participation of state agents—and approximately 9 percent were attributed to guerrillas. The remaining 30 percent were attributed to unknown armed groups.[9]

Attacks against trade union leaders are also alarming: between January and December 2003, eighty-six were victims of homicides and forced disappearances. In cases in which the generic assailant was known, about 33 percent were attributed to paramilitary groups with active participation or omission by state agents, 3 percent were attributed to state agents, 1 percent to guerrillas, and 57 percent to unknown armed groups. Other social sectors (such as peasants and indigenous peoples) and professionals (such as journalists and members of the judiciary) also continue to be victimized.

There are several factors that put activists at risk and that the state has failed to take any effective action to curtail. One is the stigmatization of human rights defenders, who are constantly accused by state agents, without any evidence, of working for the guerrillas.[10] Another is the false and uncontrolled information about them kept in intelligence archives. A third factor is the free activity of paramilitary groups, which continue to grow and which are the main perpetrators of crimes against human rights defenders. Finally, the prevailing impunity allows state agents, paramilitary groups, and guerrillas to attack human rights defenders without being concerned about the consequences of their actions.

The government is also trying to limit the activities of human rights organizations. There is a bill in Congress aimed at regulating international cooperation and controlling, in this way, the work of nongovernmental organizations (NGOs).[11] The bill requires that NGOs list their programs in a "Register of Activities" organized by a governmental agency and that those activities be in conformity with priorities established by the Foreign Affairs Policy and the National Plan of Development. The governmental control outlined in the draft bill aims to eliminate the liberty of action recognized by the constitution for private initiatives like those of NGOs.

Due to the magnitude of the aggressions against human rights defenders, the UN special representative to the secretary general on human rights defenders, Mrs. Hina Jilani, carried out an official visit to Colombia in October 2001. During her visit, she transmitted some concerns to the Colombian authorities. After the mission, she wrote a detailed report and presented it to the UN Human Rights Commission in April 2002. In that report, she formulated clear and pertinent recommendations to be implemented by the state in order to substantially improve the situation of human rights defenders and social activists.[12]

Forced Displacement

In recent years, another telling sign of the worsening situation has been the colossal rise in forced displacements, which is directly related to the upsurge in paramilitarism. More than three million persons have been displaced since 1985, many silently and individually. Over the last decade, cases of collective or mass displacements have become increasingly common: thousands of people have had to abandon whole towns out of fear due to recent massacres or threats of the same in areas near their homes. These effects are felt by men, women, and children, especially the latter two groups, since over 50 percent of the internally displaced population are female and over 53 percent are minors.

By 1995, 130,000 persons were displaced annually, followed by 180,000 in 1996 and 250,000 in 1997. Since 1998, over 300,000 additional individuals have been displaced each year. In 2001, about 360,000 people were displaced, which means around 1,000 internally displaced persons per day on average. In 2002, 400,000 more people were forcedly displaced. In 2003, there were more than 200,000 new displaced people.[13]

Colombian authorities have not implemented a serious policy to aid displaced people. Several public policies have been formulated since 1995, yet none has been coherent in and of itself. The result has been greater confusion and neglect of these individuals.

Legislation was finally adopted in 1997[14] to define the state responsibility regarding internally displaced people. Unbelievably, the government took an additional three and a half years to adopt an executive decree[15] needed to enact that law, and even then only partially. Displaced people had to bring suit against government before the Constitutional Court, which then ordered the government to enact the decree, setting a maximum period of six months to do so.[16] The UN secretary general's special representative for internally displaced people, who visited Colombia in 1994 and in 1999, recommended on both occasions the necessity of adopting such measures to achieve a coordinated policy to provide integral aid to victims of forced displacement in the country.[17]

High Levels of Common Violence

Politically motivated violence represents less than 15 percent of all violence in Colombia, with overall violence currently at a record high. In 1980, there were approximately ten thousand homicides per year. That figure rose to over twenty thousand in 1988, and there have been close to thirty thousand murders per year since 1991. Colombia has one of the highest rates of violent death in the world, sometimes reaching approximately eighty homicides per one hundred thousand inhabitants per year.[18] The inordinately high levels of insecurity and common violence are such that they will most likely survive the end of the armed conflict.

High Levels of Impunity

It is widely recognized that there is almost total impunity for human rights abuses in Colombia. Cases are rarely investigated or tried, and most of those that do go to trial are transferred to the military courts, which have been repeatedly criticized as biased in intergovernmental reports from the United Nations and the Inter-American system. When violations are investigated in ordinary courts, prosecutors or judges must often face threats and attacks by state agents and paramilitary groups.

Impunity for human rights violations is another clear sign of a broader phenomenon of impunity that affects the whole justice system in Colombia. Even the most optimistic official studies report that less than 10 percent of common crimes are solved and perpetrators sentenced in this country. The more pessimistic studies assert that the real figure is no greater than 0.5 percent. In any case, there is an increasing consensus that "legal mechanisms have not been really effective in achieving timely resolution of social conflicts" and that "abuses of the state of emergency [for combating drug trafficking and rebellions through exceptional judicial mechanisms] have robbed the judiciary of its ability to resolve daily conflicts properly."[19]

Some efforts to overcome impunity were made in previous years. A special unit dealing with human rights was created in the Prosecutor General's Office after the mid-1990s. Committed prosecutors have developed some courageous investigations. However, there are few results to show for this hard work. Several prosecutors and court employees have been killed or threatened by perpetrators, and some of those who escaped being murdered had to leave the country. The efforts of the Human Rights Unit during the 1990s were not backed enough by the various administrations. There was no governmental will to fight against impunity and to pursue state agents

and paramilitary groups violating human rights. In August 2001, this situation became worse with the appointment of a new general prosecutor. He
dismissed important court officials who were investigating serious cases
against prominent military figures and introduced changes in the Human
Rights Unit that weakened its capacity to carry out such investigations. The
new orientation of the General Prosecutor's Office has raised serious concerns both at the United Nations and in the Inter-American system.[20]

High Levels of Inequity

At first glance, the poverty rates and levels of satisfaction of basic needs
seem to have improved in Colombia during the 1980s. The truth is, however,
that the country is still suffering from a deep-rooted social exclusion that
has long been a problem. This exclusion is reflected in the general poverty
level (affecting approximately 60 percent of the population) and the absolute poverty level (affecting more than 20 percent of the inhabitants). It is
also seen in the tremendous inequality of land distribution (under 10 percent of all landowners possess more than 90 percent of all arable land)
and in the obvious conditions of inferiority of most indigenous and Afro-
Colombian people. In these three overall areas—poverty, land ownership,
and ethnic marginality—the situation of women is particularly dishearten-
ing.[21] The situation is even more dramatic in some regions of the country,
like the Pacific coast of Chocó, where general indices of exclusion are huge
and whose specific rates of satisfaction of basic needs are considerably lower
than the national average, which is itself precarious.

The widespread acquisition of landed estates by drug traffickers since
the 1980s has aggravated the problem of inequality in land distribution and
made it more difficult to achieve an equitable redistribution. It is estimated
that more than 40 percent of lands in what is commonly known as the "agricultural frontier" are now in the hands of drug traffickers-*cum*-large landowners.

Moreover, coca leaf production in Colombia's Amazon region has en-
snared many who have been excluded politically or economically from the
nation's heartland. This has deepened the pattern of colonization of outlying areas that resulted in the aftermath of Colombia's political violence in
the 1940s and 1950s. The solution to this problem is not at all easy due to its
social, ecological, and political implications nationally and internationally.

The Fallacy of the State-as-Victim Theory: Underacknowledgment of the Human Rights Crisis in Colombia, Combined with Unwillingness to Tackle It

The seriousness of the Colombian human rights crisis is due not only to high levels of violence, impunity, and inequity but also to the weak acknowledgment of the crisis by Colombian administrations and to the government's unsatisfactory efforts to redress the situation. These deficiencies are related to similar shortcomings in how the Colombian case is interpreted by certain key actors from the international community and the media. Some of those limitations have been overcome, but many actors are still confused about the nation's situation, and this confusion weakens their ability to demand that the Colombian authorities take the appropriate measures to respect and protect the inhabitants of the country.

At least five main periods in the human right crisis in Colombia since the mid-1960s can be identified by looking at two factors: (1) modalities of reluctance in acknowledging the crisis (i.e., the different ways adopted by the government to elude its responsibility for the crisis); and (2) the different types of limited action undertaken by the government to deal with systematic human rights violations. The common thread through each of these periods is the Colombian government's attempts to present itself as a victim forced to react to violent actors who threaten the state and society or as a victim unable to control such violent forces. In both of these views, the government has not fully recognized its own responsibility for perpetrating violations and for not being sufficiently diligent in preventing them. This lack of recognition of state responsibility has been at the bottom of the limited and inadequate action the state has taken in face of the human rights crisis—when it has taken any action at all. The view of the Colombian state as victim of the human rights situation has also colored requests made by the international community to the Colombian government, diluting the strength of pressure to protect human rights and honor its international commitments. The state-as-victim theory has gone through different versions in Colombia, which are outlined below.[22]

Mid-1960s to Mid-1980s: The State as Victim of Social Indiscipline

The first period characterized by limited acknowledgment of and response to the human rights situation in Colombia extended from the mid-1960s to the mid-1980s.[23] The main characteristic of this period was that the existence of human rights violations in the country was not recognized at all by the top authorities. Alleged cases of political killings, torture, arbitrary detentions, or absence of due process were explained as "isolated cases." The government issued frequent appeals to the whole society to gather around and support the authorities in their fight against the dangerous forces threatening state institutions. For the most part, the allegedly dangerous forces targeted in this way were social movements made up of peasants, workers, or students. Some were political opposition groups. Of course, guerrilla groups—which have existed in this country since the 1960s—were painted by the government as a permanent danger. Drug traffickers were added to this list in the late 1970s. To combat all these enemies, the government exercised extraordinary powers granted through the declaration of states of emergency (or states of siege), allowing it to suspend constitutional guarantees for extended periods of time, during which state security forces were provided with ideal conditions for continued human rights violations in "isolated cases." The country was governed under these types of measures three out of every four years on average (i.e., 75 percent of the time) between the 1960s and the 1980s.

With few exceptions, the international community as a whole did not intervene against this systematic practice of human rights violations. Of course, many international human rights NGOs became progressively more and more involved in criticizing this arbitrary use of power, especially after the late 1970s. The IACHR, an intergovernmental institution, also expressed its concern in the early 1980s. Nevertheless, the major international bodies belonging to the UN system remained inactive regarding the deteriorating situation during this period.

There were some reasons for this passivity. The international human rights system was less developed than it is today. The perception of the Colombian situation was clouded by other issues in the Americas that were considered to be more serious (i.e., dictatorships in the Southern Cone and civil wars in Central America). The Colombian human rights community was also less developed than it is today and was not very confident in its dealings with, nor very active regarding, intergovernmental bodies. Amidst these elements, which muddied the waters and made it more difficult to acknowledge the existence of serious violations in Colombia, the nation's authorities were then still able to take advantage of the internationally accepted idea that Colombia was the oldest and most stable democracy in Latin America. Ironically, this "democracy" was almost constantly governed under a state of exception.

This made it possible for the Colombian government to be perceived internationally as a victim fighting its internal enemies to protect democracy, especially within the context of the Cold War. Consequently, no significant action was undertaken by the government to acknowledge and to act against human rights violations in this period.

Mid-1980s to Mid-1990s: The State as a Victim of Drug Trafficking

A second important period can be identified ranging from the mid-1980s to the mid-1990s.[24] One of the main differences between this period and the previous one was that the authorities recognized, or were forced to recognize (albeit in limited terms), the existence of a cause for concern regarding human rights violations occurring in Colombia. Several official investigations were opened against members of the armed forces involved with paramilitary groups. As a result, the oversight agency, the Inspector General's Office (Procuraduría),[25] revealed in 1983 that more than 150 officers had actively cooperated with those illegal groups. One of Colombia's security boards that report directly to the President's Office, the Administrative Department of Security (DAS), released a report in 1989 showing strong ties between high-ranking military officers and paramilitary leaders, as well as the involvement of the former in massacres and other horrendous crimes.

Pursuant to these admissions, the government did take some actions regarding human rights issues, though such efforts were still limited in scope. Colombia's administrations did not refrain from using state-of-emergency powers. In fact, the country was governed under state-of-siege measures from April 1, 1984, to July 5, 1991. Nevertheless, the armed forces were partially restructured, and for the first time since the 1950s a civilian was named minister of defense in the late 1980s. Similarly, since the late 1980s the deputy inspector general *(procurador delegado)* for the military forces is supposed to be a civilian, with the mandate of carrying out disciplinary investigations of members of the armed forces. This was a position formerly reserved for high-ranking military officers, whose impartiality in such matters was not necessarily credible. In addition, in 1989 the government suspended a norm that had been established in 1965 and had been used to provide a legal basis for the existence of paramilitary groups.[26]

These measures and other similar decisions were based on the assumption that perpetrators acting as state agents would automatically or progressively be weakened if they lacked the official support of the civilian government. Unfortunately, with rare exceptions, this assumption was not backed up with effective actions for prosecuting such perpetrators. Though the government ordered the creation of a specialized task force to fight paramilitary groups,[27] to be made up of one thousand policemen under the personal direction of the national chief of police, this force was never actually created. The administration put more effort into altering the official language used to discuss human rights issues than into organizing concrete plans to block the actions of human rights violators and punish them.

The shift in official human rights language marked the government's decision during this period to accept the legitimacy of the human rights approach and marked a significant difference from the previous period, when a simple mention of human rights was automatically categorized as a subversive act by a government that refused to recognize the occurrence of serious violations in this field. As such, this modification in the official stance on human rights was an important change, but one that was insufficient to redress the situation.

In keeping with this point of view, substantial innovations in the area of human rights were included in the new constitution approved in 1991 (see Gallón 2005). Peace agreements were achieved with five guerrilla groups from 1989 to 1994.[28] Those and other significant results would not have been possible without this changed mind-set and language. The change allowed the authorities to see that negotiating with armed enemies was politically possible and that there were outcomes to the conflict beyond defeat, imprisonment, or death. It also allowed Colombian society to accept that a state built on a foundation of human rights could be accepted as upholding democratic principles, instead of being rejected as an attempt to weaken the government. Yet the government did not take the necessary steps to provide decisively for the arrest and prosecution of state agents and paramilitary groups involved in numerous, systematic, and ongoing human rights violations. The military justice system was left untouched by the government in this period, though reform was obviously necessary to prevent impunity for crimes committed by members of the armed forces. The ordinary justice system, on the other hand, did not receive sufficient state protection from alleged perpetrators under its investigation, nor did it receive enough cooperation from the police and the army to enforce decisions, especially arrest warrants, filed against violators.

Furthermore, the official acknowledgment of the existence of a human rights problem in Colombia during this second period did not imply that the government recognized the state's responsibility in this tragedy. As in the prior period and in keeping with the official point of view, the state continued to present itself as a victim of the human rights situation and not as an actor perpetrating serious violations. The difference between these two periods is that, in the second, responsibility for the whole situation was artificially attributed almost exclusively to a single sector: drug traffickers. Between 1984—with the assassination on March 31 of Minister of Justice Rodrigo Lara Bonilla, on the order of the infamous drug baron Pablo Escobar—and 1993, with the killing of Escobar in Medellin, the main official explanation for violence and human rights violations in Colombia was that these were violent acts perpetrated by drug traffickers.

Without a doubt, drug traffickers did arrange many murders and organize terrorist actions specifically to block judicial or police actions against them and to force the Colombian government to refuse extradition requests from the United States. They also killed many people involved in drug trafficking to "settle accounts" or to resolve disputes between illegal competitors. Some drug traffickers were also involved, along with members of the armed forces, in developing new paramilitary groups or strengthening some of the existing groups, which had been created by the armed forces starting in the 1960s. Nevertheless, setting aside for the moment the violence drug traffickers committed as part of paramilitary groups, the deeds attributed to drug traffickers in their fight against the state (i.e., murders of former collaborators who had betrayed them or the killing of competitors) were more obvious but considerably less numerous than rampant sociopolitical murders and other human rights violations. The people being killed each day by state agents, paramilitary groups, or guerrilla forces—especially peasants from isolated rural areas—were not interesting topics for coverage by the national or, particularly, the international media. A bomb set off by Pablo Escobar in a supermarket parking lot or on a crowded plane, on the other hand, invariably drew full coverage, making a huge impact on public opinion domestically and abroad. This type of reporting distorted the perception of the human rights crisis in Colombia, obscuring state responsibility and the participation of state agents and paramilitary members—other than drug traffickers—in the bulk of the violations.

This distortion served the needs of the Colombian administrations, which fought diligently during this second period to block in any possible way the involvement of the international community as observers of the treatment given to the human rights crisis. This was one of the state's top priorities. For many years, they were successful, due to the prevailing perception of the Colombian state as victim of drug trafficking and of the human rights crisis as the logical result of institutions weakened and a society threatened by drug traffickers. This view was held by several key member states of the United Nations at that time. The ever-growing number of political killings and the persistence of impunity for them, even after the end of the terrorist era in which drug traffickers like Pablo Escobar had reigned, finally made it clear that systematic human rights violations in Colombia did not begin or end with drug trafficking and that the killings and impunity would not end if the illegal drug trade weakened or even disappeared.

Mid-1990s: The State as a Victim of Institutional Weakness

A third period of reluctant acknowledgment and reluctant action regarding the human rights situation in Colombia came about in the mid-1990s.[29] For the first time, the government in power—the Samper administration—recognized that the situation was dire and that the country needed the support of the international community to overcome the crisis. This recognition was hesitant and not always consistent, however, because at times the government would react against concrete decisions made by international bodies. The state also tried to put the bulk of the blame on guerrilla groups and not on its own agents, painting the guerrillas as the main actors responsible for the severity and extent of the situation as a whole. As a result, important work was done in the area of legislative decisions concerning human rights, yet little was accomplished in terms of actual measures against specific individual perpetrators, many of whom were able to promote or support the shocking increase of paramilitary groups from within the state during those years.

In 1994, the government ratified Additional Protocol II to the Geneva Conventions on humanitarian law. The armed forces had opposed this approval for seventeen years, arguing that it would imply the recognition of the "belligerent status" of guerrilla groups, even though the protocol explicitly states that this possibility is excluded. Other decisions were taken by the government without the consent of the armed forces. In 1995, on behalf of the state, the president took responsibility for a horrendous series of massacres committed between 1989 and 1991 by military and paramilitary forces in the town of Trujillo. This recognition was made before the Colombian people and the IACHR and resulted in the dismissal of an army colonel who had organized and carried out the atrocities. The generals in the military reacted strongly to this decision. In 1996, the UN Human Rights Commission decided to ask the high commissioner for human rights to open a permanent office in Colombia with the twofold mandate of observing the situation and aiding the authorities and Colombian society in improving human rights conditions. The decision was made with the agreement of the government, ignoring the opposition of the high commanders of the armed forces. The office opened in 1997 and beginning in 1998 has issued an annual public report on the Colombian situation to the Human Rights Commission.[30] In 1996, the Colombian Congress approved a bill recognizing the binding nature of decisions regarding human rights violations in Colombia made by the IACHR and the Human Rights Committee of the International Covenant on Civil and Political Rights.[31] This bill established a judicial and summary procedure to define the monetary damages that must be paid to victims by the Colombian government in cases decided by the aforementioned agencies. This bill was also adopted without the consent of the high commanders of the armed forces.

The staunch opposition of the military to these and other decisions concerning acceptance of international bodies' involvement in Colombia's human rights situation does much to explain the inconsistencies observed on the part of the government during this period with respect to specific decisions or recommendations put forth by those agencies. It is also the reason behind the Colombian government's blind insistence that the Inter-American and UN systems explicitly declare—and condemn—the full responsibility of the guerrilla groups for the country's human rights situation. In 1995, Colombia's president publicly criticized a sentence issued by the Inter-American Court in a case of forced disappearance perpetrated by military and paramilitary forces. According to the president, the court should have done more to come out against violations committed by guerrilla groups instead of harping on acts performed by state agents. This remark flies in the face of the legal jurisdiction of the court, which is not permitted by the Inter-American Convention on Human Rights to pass judgment on cases committed by private groups. Evidently, the president was under pressure to ignore this minor legal detail and attack the Inter-American system as a way of mitigating the negative reaction of the Colombian armed forces to the court's important decision.

In fact, the mandate of international intergovernmental bodies, such as the IACHR and the UN Human Rights Commission, does include the consideration of violations and abuses committed by guerrilla groups and other private actors in their general reports on specific countries. Pursuant to the specific guidelines used in issuing these reports, those organizations have done so in their reports on Colombia. These accounts reflect not only the implementation of the guidelines but the consequence of undeniable guerrilla participation in approximately 30 percent of political killings in Colombia during most of the 1990s (and 25 percent in the early 2000s). It also includes very sensitive violations of fundamental rights, such as kidnappings and indiscriminate attacks on the civilian population, as described in the first section of this chapter. Yet the serious responsibility of guerrilla groups for violating the fundamental rights of Colombians cannot be used to discount or reduce the government's responsibility to protect those rights against violations committed by its own or private agents, including guerrilla groups. In this third period, the recognition of the human rights crisis in Colombia and the actions taken to address it were limited, due to the government's insistence that the international community exonerate the state from its responsibilities by blaming guerrilla groups. This was an argument that the government expressed on many occasions and in many different ways. Fortunately, it did not succeed in this attempt, which was clearly improper, given the nature and duties of international human rights bodies. Nevertheless, it did reduce the strength and scope of decisions made by the Inter-American system and the United Nations. These were the far-reaching effects of this new version of the state-as-victim theory.

The negligence of the government in acknowledging the situation was reflected in its erratic actions regarding human rights. In particular, there was no policy set up to rein in or fight paramilitary groups. On the contrary, these groups were significantly strengthened during the period: their membership grew from about one thousand to four thousand, and up to twelve thousand later, during Pastrana's administration. The territory in which they were active also increased, especially in the northern part of the country, as did their coordination, through the formation of an illegal organization called the United Self-Defense Groups of Colombia (Autodefensas Unidas de Colombia). This marked growth took place under the equally marked inactivity of the authorities, with, at times, the public support of local military commanders. At the national level, the government promoted legislation to legalize the paramilitary groups once again, giving them authorization to bear weapons of war, as had been the case in the past. Under the misleadingly euphemistic name of "coexistence cooperatives" *(cooperativas convivir)*, these groups were theoretically to be put under the supervision and control of an agency of the Ministry of National Defense. The Constitutional Court realized that this type of supervision had not been effectively enforced and ruled once again, as it had in 1989, that paramilitary groups were unconstitutional.[32] This important decision led the government to change its policy, and it took key measures to prevent the existence of "legal" paramilitary groups.

During this period, the government also tried to resurrect the practice of governing under a state of emergency to take advantage of the extraordinary powers granted to the armed forces. The administration's first attempt in this direction, in August 1995, was declared unconstitutional by the Constitutional Court. Under the pretext of reacting to the assassination of an important leader of the Conservative Party in November 1995, the government attempted once again to declare a state of emergency. The second time around, the Constitutional Court did not initially block the decree, and the government was able to grant exceptional powers to the armed forces, such as the right of making arrests without a warrant or forcibly occupying private property with military personnel. Fortunately, the Constitutional Court, on examining the case more closely, decided that there was no justifiable connection between the unfortunate and reprehensible murder of the Conservative leader and some of the exceptional powers granted to the armed forces and therefore ruled for their revocation.[33] The judicial investigation into the killing has since indicated that the crime was organized by members of the armed forces, ironically enough, by members of the very same body that would have benefited from the exceptional powers granted under the state of emergency brought on by the crime.

These inconsistencies were clearly the result of conflicting tendencies regarding human rights policies within the government. Nevertheless, they were probably also due in part to the Samper administration's desire to earn the support of the armed forces in the face of the political ostracism experienced after Samper was indicted in mid-1995 for having received campaign contributions from drug traffickers in 1994. For the next year and a half, through late 1996, when Congress decided to absolve the president of any wrongdoing connected to these accusations, government policy was subordinated to the more urgent goal of keeping the president in power and having him acquitted. This also explains why the government felt freer to rethink certain human rights issues in 1997 and 1998, after the storm had passed.

Two draft bills bear special mention in this regard: a new military criminal code and new legislation against forced disappearances, which were finally criminalized. The first bill required that human rights violations be brought before the ordinary justice system and not the military justice system, as per a Constitutional Court decision of 1997.[34] The second, the formal recognition of the criminal nature of the forced disappearance of individuals, was needed because it was not recognized as a practice that occurred frequently in Colombia and was not considered by the law to be a crime. Prosecutors and judges, as a consequence, faced serious legal difficulties in investigating and trying such acts. The opposition of the armed forces to legislation against forced disappearances had been very evident over the prior ten years. Five draft bills regarding this issue had failed since 1988 because of the active (and sometimes public) opposition of high-ranking members of the military command. At the end of the Samper administration, the sixth draft of the bill on this issue and a draft of the new military criminal code had been submitted to Congress for approval.

Late 1990s: The State as a Victim of the Armed Conflict

The fourth period of government response to the human rights crisis in Colombia was characterized by a significant and renewed effort to prove that state agents are not responsible for the country's undeniably severe situation.[35] If official versions during this period were to be believed, state agents were the victims of a situation caused by two crazed or criminal groups that were destroying the nation: the guerrillas and the paramilitaries. The spin was as follows: both groups had connections to drug trafficking because they protected coca or poppy growers in their respective territories, thereby profiting economically by extortion payments from producers. Both groups also frequently took part in processing or trading cocaine and heroin. Consequently, if state agents bolstered their efforts to eradicate coca and poppy crops, both guerrillas and paramilitary groups would be weakened and then defeated, either through armed combat or after peace negotiations. Therefore, the only thing that the Colombian authorities needed from the international community was economic and political support for strengthening military operations and social programs to put an end to drug production in the country. Once this was achieved, the government expected human rights to improve automatically in Colombia.[36]

The plan of action that followed this interpretation of the facts did not necessarily have to be implemented in any particular order (i.e., starting with crop eradication, followed by armed combat and/or peace talks). On the contrary, these actions could be put into effect in any order or simultaneously. In fact, the Pastrana administration started by proposing and developing a peace process with guerrilla groups: first with the Revolutionary Armed Forces of Colombia (FARC) in 1998 and later with the National Liberation Army (ELN) toward the end of 2000. At the same time, the government garnered the support of the United States in the form of military aid and equipment, complemented by some social and institutional programs. This approximately one-billion-dollar package, known as Plan Colombia, was approved by the U.S. Congress in early 2000.[37] After Israel and Egypt, it was the third largest foreign military aid package granted by the United States.

The Pastrana administration considered the economic, military, and political support of the United States more important than the international cooperation of the UN Human Rights Commission and the IACHR. The international agencies' reiterated recommendations concerning the need to act against paramilitary groups—the authors of almost 80 percent of sociopolitical killings, committed with varying degrees of complicity by state agents—and strengthen the capacity of the Colombian system to bring perpetrators to justice fell on deaf ears. This attitude limited the effectiveness of the Permanent Office of the High Commissioner for Human Rights, established with the agreement of the Colombian authorities in 1997. Instead of seriously implementing the UN and IACHR recommendations, official government efforts focused on developing a sophisticated publicity campaign to convince U.S. authorities that the Colombian government was meeting the human rights requirements established by the United States, some of which were prerequisites for releasing monies authorized under Plan Colombia. To lend credibility to its publicity campaign, the government issued decisions and took action as proof of its willingness to redress the human rights situation. Unfortunately, these were no more than small-scale cosmetic measures that did not express a serious commitment to human rights protection. Consequently, they did not result in any reduction in the level of violations.

On August 12, 1999, the government announced the adoption of an important policy on human rights and humanitarian law. It included the creation of a special task force to fight paramilitary groups, similar to the one announced ten years earlier. As was the case with the first plan, this one did not become a reality, though the government reiterated, from time to time, its intentions of creating such a group. Instead of actually following through, the administration (and the Ministry of National Defense) preferred to publish statistics showing that it had captured hundreds of paramilitary members. These figures did not indicate how many of these individuals had been captured by the armed forces. The only paramilitary leader put in jail was captured by the Prosecutor General's Office without the support of the army or the police. The then prosecutor general also deplored that arrest warrants issued by that office for paramilitary members were not carried out by the armed forces.

The human rights and humanitarian law policy announced by the government in August 1999 included support for the draft bill on forced disappearances presented to Congress by the previous administration. That bill was approved by Congress in December 1999. Nevertheless, contradicting its own supposed commitment, the president then vetoed the bill and tried to suppress its enactment as law, especially the standard instructions that human rights violations and forced disappearances be brought before the ordinary justice system and not before the military system. Fortunately, the Congress reacted firmly and preserved the bill, in its sixth draft in twelve years before Congress. Thanks to the congressional reaction and to political gaffes committed by the government during discussion of the veto, the essential elements of the bill were salvaged.

The other draft bill on human rights presented by the previous administration had to do with the adoption of a new military criminal code and was also approved by Congress in 1999. Yet before it was passed, the government authorized the military high command to negotiate with Congress a substantial change to a key article of the proposed code. The article originally stipulated that all human rights violations were automatically outside the jurisdiction of the military justice system and were the responsibility of the ordinary justice system. The version of the article proposed by the military and eventually approved by Congress stated that jurisdiction would be determined on a case-by-case basis by analyzing whether the violation in question was committed in the course of fulfilling one's duty. Thus the "new" rule was actually the same old rule that the military justice system had always applied to refuse to send human rights violations to the ordinary justice system. This "new" rule also went against the already mentioned ruling handed down by the Constitutional Court in August 1997, which made clear that every human rights violation should be brought before the ordinary courts and not before the military tribunals. The military high command also convinced Congress to modify another article of the draft bill that originally enumerated human rights violations that would always be outside the jurisdiction of the military justice system, detailing crimes such as rape, forced displacement, and involvement in paramilitary groups. Under the weakened version, specific mention of those crimes was suppressed. As a result, if the August 1997 Constitutional Court decision does not take precedence—and it is not always respected—the crime of rape committed by a soldier could be considered behavior that was part of his normal duties.[38]

In that 1997 decision, the Constitutional Court had ordered the military courts to transfer all cases of human rights violations that they were then trying to the ordinary courts. None of the more important or renowned cases, including those eventually decided by international bodies, like the IACHR or the UN Human Rights Committee, were transferred to ordinary courts. In mid-2000, human rights groups made a formal petition to the president of the republic to request his compliance with the Constitutional Court's decision, insisting that his military commanders (who were acting as military judges) not impede that order by accepting or keeping cases of human rights violations in their jurisdiction. The president denied this request, arguing that the military judges were independent of the executive branch. Nevertheless, one month later, the president signed a brief letter announcing that the new military criminal code, which had been approved in 1999, had finally gone into effect in August 2000. He stated that he hoped that from then on military judges would abstain from dealing with cases of human rights violations, such as forced disappearances, genocide, or torture. That letter (or some other similar instrument) was one of the six human rights prerequisites established in Plan Colombia for the release of U.S. military aid to the Colombian government. Two days after this letter was made public, the U.S. State Department officially certified that the Colombian government had fulfilled that condition and proceeded to waive, "for national security reasons," the other five conditions, authorizing the disbursement of the promised funding to the Colombian government. This is a clear example of human rights decisions made by the government during this period simply as part of a publicity campaign.

Even after the letter signed by the president regarding this issue was made public, the most important cases of human rights violations remained in the military courts. In February 2001, a general was sentenced by a military court to forty months in jail for having been responsible "by omission" for the massacre committed by paramilitary groups of forty-nine people in a southern Colombian town called Mapiripán. The conclusion that the general's responsibility in this matter was one of simple "omission" is a stretch of the imagination. More than two hundred paramilitary fighters arrived equipped with weapons at the military airport in the city where the general was based before continuing on to Mapiripán by river to perpetrate the massacre. They remained in the town for a full week, during which time a colonel warned the general about what was happening, yet the general did not react or intervene in any way. Under these circumstances, the military court found the general innocent of having collaborated with paramilitary groups and of complicity in the massacre. Afterwards, the general's conviction was trotted out by the authorities as unquestionable proof of their commitment to human rights. Though it is true that this was the first time that a general had been convicted of human rights violations in Colombia, the refusal of the military justice system to refer the case to the ordinary justice system was nothing less than a bald-faced contradiction of the Constitutional Court order. Furthermore, his absolution on the more serious and easily provable of the charges he faced is evidence of the persistence of a great degree of impunity during this period.[39]

This particular general was dismissed from service, along with two other generals, in May 1998. A fourth general was dismissed in August 1998. Subsequently, three of the four generals were formally accused by the Prosecutor General's Office of having links with paramilitary groups. The government, however, did not order the initiation of a judicial investigation against them, nor did it support the investigation undertaken by the Prosecutor General's Office. The military justice system appealed the decision to try these cases in the ordinary justice system, without any reaction from the government. The general interpretation of these dismissals was that they had been ordered at the request of U.S. authorities. The government never admitted that the generals had been dismissed due to human rights violations. The lack of any official acknowledgment of the reasons for the decision (i.e., indicating that this was a government measure to improve the human rights situation) provoked negative reactions within the armed forces and Colombian society. By trying to avoid being labeled disloyal to its soldiers, the government missed a great opportunity to strengthen its capacity to implement a firm and decisive policy of respect for and protection of human rights.

An additional 388 members of the armed forces were dismissed in October 2000. Their dismissal was initially presented by the media and by the U.S. State Department as evidence of the purification of Colombian institutions through the elimination of human rights violators. Yet the Colombian government officially denied this explanation. The minister of defense admitted some days later that approximately fifty of the officers who had been removed had joined the ranks of paramilitary groups. The administration's attitude in this case was as erroneous as it had been in the case of the three generals. None of the dismissed officers was brought to justice after being fired. The government missed out on another opportunity to clearly demonstrate to the public that human rights violations went against the principles and aims of state institutions. Any possible positive subliminal effects were offset by the negative impact of the decision being interpreted at the time as unexplained, unfair, and incomplete.

At the same time as its human rights publicity campaign, the government undertook a process of peace talks with the main guerrilla group in the country, the FARC.[40] These efforts were significant but also ambiguous. They were important because they could have created a path to a political solution to the armed conflict; they were ambiguous precisely because that path was not paved with a serious human rights policy. Without doubt, the continued guerrilla attacks—many of which truly were and are horrendous—against the population during this process discredited it. Yet the government's reluctance to adopt effective policies to prevent and punish human rights violations also caused its credibility as a negotiator determined to achieve a fair agreement to deteriorate. After beginning in late 1998, the talks were suspended by the FARC several times due to their complaints regarding the government's tolerance of or inaction toward the increasing violations perpetrated by paramilitary groups. Under these circumstances, both parties not only tried to strengthen a negotiated solution but also expected at the same time to legitimize their respective positions in a new and stronger phase of armed confrontation. The government decided to end these talks in February 2002 because important sectors of society were increasingly expressing their opposition to continued talks without concrete results.[41]

During the peace talks, neither the government nor the guerrillas tried to hide the ambiguity of the process. Guerrilla groups continued to increase their attacks, territorial presence, and military capacity. The government implemented a plan to "modernize the armed forces" that included new weapons, more efficient troops, and legal reforms to allow them more autonomy. In late 2000, Congress approved a "National Security Bill" promoted by the Ministry of Defense.[42] The bill authorized the armed forces to capture individuals without arrest warrants and instituted new mechanisms of impunity in favor of members of the armed forces. The bill was also one more attempt to revive the legalization of paramilitary groups by authorizing the development of national security and defense activities through private vigilante and security services "under the control of the Ministry of Defense." The intention was to establish that it was the duty of all residents of Colombia to cooperate with "national power" to obtain what were called "national objectives."

This kind of proposal does not seem strange compared to other practices implemented in Colombia during the second half of the twentieth century. Similar initiatives were undertaken during the state-of-emergency regime in effect from the 1960s to the 1990s. At that time, other, even more ambitious proposals were also inspired by the "National Security Doctrine" that governed the Southern Cone military dictatorships during the 1970s. Though such measures could have been contradictory with the then ongoing process of peace talks, they were also the natural result of the aforementioned ambiguity. Above all, they are one of the most possible outcomes of the state-as-victim theory. If the state is indeed the victim of violent actors threatening the society and the government, one solution to this weakness is to strengthen the state, albeit through authoritarian measures. This is not an innovative recipe for change, and it certainly is not a solution that has worked in the past.

Early 2000s: Transforming the Alleged Victim into an Avenger

The National Security Law adopted in August 2001 was declared unconstitutional by the Constitutional Court in April 2002.[43] The court found that such a law was contrary to the basic principles of democracy and rule of law, especially because of its aspiration to merge society and state and militarize them under the pretext of providing security and development to the population. According to the court, all societies have the right to organize a national security system but must respect essential notions violated by the 2001 law, such as the principle of separation of powers, the distinction between civilians and combatants, a certain degree of autonomy for civil society vis-à-vis the government, and the predominance of civilian over military authorities.

Despite the striking down of the National Security Law, its adoption in August 2001 signaled the beginning of a new period in which the Colombian authorities have been trying to go further in the implementation of the state-as-victim theory.[44] The previous periods were characterized by the Colombian government's attempts to avoid condemnation for the human rights crisis and to get international assistance under the pretext of developing institutions to protect human rights. The attitude of the government in this new period is more oriented to obtaining the active involvement of Colombians and of the international community in supporting measures allegedly aimed at providing security rather than worrying about human rights concerns.

This is what Alvaro Uribe's administration, elected in May 2002 and inaugurated the same year in August, is trying to do. The new government has created a network of informants, some of them paid by the armed forces, as a way to develop active cooperation between civilians and security services. The final goal of this initiative is to integrate the whole society of forty-four million people into this network, so that those who are not informants can be considered enemies by the official forces of the state. Another idea with a similar goal is the incorporation of a new force of half-time "peasant-soldiers" who are civilians for part of the day and members of the army for the other part. Women are also targeted in this plan. One of the issues included by the government in a draft referendum presented to the Congress in August 2002 was the creation of a "social service with military instruction," obligatory for both men and women, that would replace the current obligatory and male-only military service. The referendum was defeated, but the initiative was included in a bill presented to the Congress.[45]

The problem with measures like these is that they can increase the level of insecurity instead of reducing it. Many people fear that a network of informants made up of nonprofessionals would be a dangerous source of misinformation. The risk is even bigger if the informants are paid without formally belonging to—and being subject to the disciplinary controls of—the state security services. This informal network, as well as the category of "peasant-soldiers," can be an illicit door through which members of paramilitary groups might be massively incorporated into official state forces. A policy genuinely aiming to provide security must firmly confront all violent actors. When some of them are tolerated or protected, insecurity becomes higher, at least for those who are usually their preferred victims.

In a similar way, a security policy in a country like Colombia must confront first and most urgently the armed combatants. The new government declared a state of exception on August 11, 2002, and authorized all soldiers and police agents to arrest, without judicial warrant, all civilians that they arbitrarily suspected of having criminal plans. This authorization was based on the conviction, explicitly revealed by the government, that one of the main obstacles to fighting the criminal groups was that they were "hidden within the civilian population."[46] According to the Inspector General's Office, security did not improve significantly and many irregularities were committed against the civilian population under this state of exception that was in force until April 29, 2003.[47]

At the same time that it plans to implement this dangerous security policy, the government intends to reduce or eliminate several institutions and mechanisms to protect human rights that were created or strengthened by the 1991 Constitution. One of them is the *tutela*, a judicial resource allowing any person to request from any judge protection against possible violations of fundamental rights. The judicial decision must be taken within ten days. The government wants to prohibit the application of this action to judicial sentences (even though the sentences are accused of violating due process) and to the denial of social and economic rights. Other institutions and legal regulations in danger, as a result of these proposals, are the competence of the Constitutional Court, the Ombudsman's Office (Defensoría del Pueblo), the local officers for human rights in each municipality (*personeros municipales*), and the time limits and the judicial control of the state of exception (see Colombian Commission of Jurists [CCJ] 2003b). The first minister of justice and internal affairs announced his intention of abolishing the constitutional principle of the social rule of law. In his own words, the whole Constitution of 1991 should be broken "into one thousand pieces" (Londoño Hoyos 2001).

One important piece of the 1991 Constitution has already been broken: the prohibition against military forces exercising judicial power over civilians. On December 10, 2003, the government obtained congressional approval of a constitutional reform that allowed members of the armed forces to act as judicial police officers, authorized to arrest civilians, interrogate them, collect evidence, and carry out other judicial functions that could decisively influence the direction of trials and the rulings of judges. The reform also authorized administrative authorities to carry out detentions, registration of domiciles, and interception of communications without judicial warrants. They were authorized as well to force inhabitants of particular regions in the country to formally inform them, for military purposes, of all circumstances concerning their private life, including domicile, activities, and family.[48] The government insisted on pushing through these constitutional changes, ignoring numerous and explicit recommendations made by international bodies that warned that the changes were contrary to basic human rights principles and to the Colombian state's international obligations and commitments.[49] It seems that the government is more committed to reestablishing, in a stronger way, the antidemocratic principles, objectives, and mechanisms contained in the unconstitutional National Security Bill.[50]

Thus the prevailing policy of this new period is deepening the erroneous theory of the state as victim in a very authoritarian way. The government feels that it has extensive support from the Colombian population to go in that direction, on the basis of the 53 percent of voters who elected the new president on the first round of voting. But most of the people who voted in favor of President Uribe did not ask him to dismantle the protective institutions included in the 1991 Constitution. On the contrary, they requested protection because the Colombian administrations have not consistently protected the rights of the Colombian people for many decades. They were reacting especially against the failure of the peace talks held for more than three years by the Pastrana administration without concrete results, as was mentioned in the previous section. Similar opposition can be expected and expressed later if this policy increases the level of insecurity and human rights violations, as it seems will be the case.

The government is so sure that it will not lose popular support that it is proposing to change the constitution to allow the consecutive reelection of President Uribe to a second four-year term in 2006. Yet the government is repeating the same mistake made by the Pastrana administration in promoting peace negotiations that may end in serious failure. This time the negotiations are being held not with the guerrillas—and particularly not with the FARC—but with paramilitary groups. But, as with the previous government, the negotiations are not grounded on a consistent policy of human rights and humanitarian law. To the contrary, they are based on an open challenge to principles of justice and legality. For more than a year and a half, from the start of the process in December 2002 until July 2004, when it inaugurated a demilitarized zone for the meetings, the government frequently met and negotiated with paramilitary leaders under judicial orders of detention, without any action to acknowledge, carry out, or even first suspend those orders. The president also promoted a bill with the acknowledged intention of giving impunity to crimes against humanity and crimes of war. The bill was later modified somewhat to include politically correct notions such as truth, justice, and reparations, but in essence it conveys the same original idea of impunity. On the other hand, the attitudes and the language of the paramilitary leaders who are negotiating reflect, not peace and reconciliation, but rather arrogance and the desire to impose their demands—particularly those related to impunity and conservation of land and property illegally obtained—on the nation and the international community. There is no consideration of their victims. In these circumstances, it is quite unlikely that Colombia will enjoy peace and security as a result of these negotiations. It is more likely that there will be, sooner or later, a popular reaction against this wrong-headed approach that does not attack the root causes of human rights violations in the country.[51]

Colombia is in no way destined to suffer fatalistically through a national security regime as a result of the current human rights crisis. But to arrive at a suitable solution to this crisis, the prevailing theory of the Colombian state as victim must be abandoned. The state's acknowledgment of its responsibility in this crisis is a decisive factor necessary for overcoming these difficulties. Only this type of recognition can provide the solid basis for a process of reducing and eliminating this country's chronic disrespect for human rights once and for all.

How to Overcome the Human Rights Crisis in Colombia

War and Human Rights Violations: A Vicious Cycle

The serious human rights situation that exists in Colombia, which has been explored in the first two sections of this chapter, is normally interpreted by expert analysts and common people alike as an inevitable consequence of the armed conflict that has plagued this country for over thirty years. There seems to be some evidence to support this belief. In effect, the magnitude of the violations would not be so high if there were no guerrilla warfare, nor would paramilitary organizations have flourished in another context.

Nevertheless, not all human rights violations derive directly from the armed conflict. The basis for most of the politically motivated human rights violations in Colombia is a different type of social conflict, especially labor, peasant, and ethnic strife. Of course, the context of war does aggravate such violations because the authorities tend to view social protest as part of the wartime confrontation, and hence their response to it tends to be military. Yet even if the armed conflict in Colombia were to come to an end, there would be no guarantee that the murders of indigenous people and peasants would automatically cease, since it is a method that has been used for many years to resolve conflicts over land. Nor is it certain that there would no longer be numerous trade unionists killed in confrontations between workers and employers. Even less certain is the overnight elimination of illegal aggression against indigent individuals, which currently causes the death of one person per day because they are considered common criminals. This type of violation seems to be grounded in a deep-rooted discriminatory mentality characteristic of Colombian society, a mind-set that is not about to disappear as if by magic whenever there is a definitive cease-fire (Comisión de Superación de la Violencia 1992: 144–50).

Furthermore, the eventual and much desired end to the armed conflict in Colombia will not necessarily and automatically put an end to common violence and the ensuing human rights violations. As indicated before, murders committed for political or ideological reasons, though numerous, represent only 15 percent of violent deaths per year in Colombia.[52] To significantly reduce the number of murders committed or tolerated by state agents from among the remaining 85 percent of cases will require much more than a simple signature on a peace agreement. The experience in El Salvador shows how the demobilization of the guerrillas has unfortunately not cut the high level of violent deaths. In fact, the Salvadoran state has been unable to stop or even adequately sanction this phenomenon.

The reality, though it is often forgotten, is that war is not the only cause of human rights violations. War may actually be the result of such violations, as seems to be the case in Colombia. One of the main reasons that the armed insurgency arose in the 1960s was the strong policy of political exclusion established in the 1957 constitutional reform, which left a wider playing field only for the Liberal and Conservative parties. The "National Front," a pact between these two to share the power exclusively with one another, was approved by plebiscite. The two forces continue to be the dominant players, despite the deep cracks that have appeared in their armor. The 1991 Constitution, however, removed most of the legal privileges held by those two parties and was truly oriented toward promoting mechanisms for a pluralistic and participatory democracy. Under these conditions, though social injustice continues to be as notorious as it was in the past, it might no longer be a sufficient reason to justify the continued existence of Colombian guerrilla groups involved in armed struggle if it were not for ongoing human rights violations. After the fall of the Berlin Wall and the elimination of the "National Front," forced disappearances and political murders are conclusive proof of the exclusion on which the goals of guerrilla movements feed. The long-standing, albeit illegal, existence of these groups cannot be explained away as a simple matter of their having gotten used to the funds generated by kidnapping and extortion. On the contrary, their self-definition and existence owe more to their indignation regarding the deaths of the past and the need for protection in the future.

It is impossible to view the relationship between war and human rights violations as going in one direction only; it is definitely a two-way street. To be more exact, it is a vicious cycle that tends to become a spiral and that can be adequately faced only by attacking both ends at once, as is the case with any vicious cycle.

A partial examination of the evidence seems to point to the conclusion that human rights violations are the inevitable consequence of war. This view, though tempting, is somewhat misleading. It is not unlike the widely held notion from days past that the sun revolved around the earth, a conviction that was justified simply because the sun appeared during the day and went away at night. But the danger of believing the first myth may be even greater than the pitfalls of accepting the second. An erroneous conclusion could lead—and in fact has led—to conforming to accepted attitudes about current violations, with the justification that "war is hell," and to knee-jerk reactions or passivity about overcoming such actions in the future, once the dream of having annihilated the enemy has become a reality. Following this path, it will be difficult to achieve peace, which will never be based on the solid terrain of respect for human rights.

Perhaps the surest route, though it is also the hardest and the one least followed, is the opposite one: avoid human rights violations as much as possible, even during the war, in the hope of preparing more fertile ground for peace. Instead of waiting for a serious human rights situation to get better on its own after signing a peace agreement or reaching a military victory, this position implies the simultaneous and tireless struggle for a cease-fire and for the creation of the prerequisites and postarmistice conditions that facilitate peace's viability and make it more solid.

Respect for Human Rights as a Path out of War

The multiple measures needed to lay solid groundwork for the respect of human rights in Colombia can be categorized in five overall topic areas: preventing future violations; punishing past violations; strengthening institutions, especially in the justice system; guaranteeing minimum levels of economic, social, and cultural rights; and overcoming the existing discriminatory mentality.

Preventing Future Violations

Preventing future violations means eliminating the factors that are known to cause violations now and controlling the factors that may lead to future violations. One known factor is policies or standards that favor arbitrary practices, or, more specifically, the state of exception. This is the means used to give the police and military forces exorbitant powers to arrest individuals, raid homes, and register property. It also involves excessive powers granted in the area of justice administration that limit procedural guarantees. These arbitrary powers often lead to more serious violations, such as torture, disappearance, and murder. For this reason, the United Nations and the IACHR have urged the Colombian government not to abuse the state of exception or emergency.[53] Unfortunately, the current government has moved in the opposite direction since it declared the state of exception on August 11, 2002, and authorized the armed forces to arrest people without a warrant, as was outlined in the previous section.[54] The government has also announced its intention of modifying the constitution in order to use the state of exception more freely. Specifically, the government proposes to eliminate the time limits of the state of exception (currently, a maximum of 270 days) and ban the Constitutional Court from reviewing a decree that declares a state of exception. As was mentioned above, the government amended the constitution in December 2003 in order to authorize the military forces to investigate civilians.

The government has in the past received recommendations to act regarding another factor known to lead to violations, the ongoing service of state agents previously involved in serious violations.[55] Without detriment to the corresponding investigations and legal sanctions, and with full respect for the legal guarantees, the government can and must make use of the variety of legal mechanisms in place to remove these individuals from active duty, just as is done with any high-ranking government official who does not share or duly execute state policy. As long as these notorious violators remain in state employ, they will continue to be a source of serious violations and will represent an obstacle to any investigations that are put forward. Their removal, on the other hand—provided it is accompanied by proper investigation and timely trial and sentencing, where applicable—will weaken paramilitary groups that rely on their power. This is one more way to decisively oppose these groups.

Control of factors contributing to future violations involves the guaranteed commitment of high-ranking military and police commanders to develop a policy that is scrupulously respectful of human rights. This must also be reinforced through the appropriate training of members of the armed forces, based on their understanding that their mission to guarantee security must include human rights as both the ends and the means of carrying out their duties. They must be made aware that, paradoxically, if they do not adopt this attitude, they themselves run the risk of becoming a severe threat to security. Some important efforts have already been made in the last fifteen years to discuss and make agreements with the armed forces concerning their behavior in this area, discussions that would have been unthinkable in prior years. Nevertheless, it is evident that much greater efforts must still be made.

These initiatives must be complemented with corrective mechanisms to guarantee that respecting human rights is the rule and violating them the exception. The Inspector General's Office (Procuraduría) should have to take on a more active and effective role than the one it has performed to date. The military criminal justice system will have to refrain from trying serious human rights or humanitarian law violations, allowing them to be judged impartially by the ordinary justice system, which must be duly strengthened. This is precisely what the civil sector recommended when the government formed a commission to design a new military criminal code in 1995 (Gallón 1995). In 1997, the Constitutional Court issued a definitive decision to the same effect,[56] a ruling that after many difficulties was finally adopted by the Consejo Superior de la Judicatura (Superior Council of the Judiciary) in 2000 and was also included to a certain extent in the new military criminal code adopted in 1999.

Punishing Past Violations

There are three major reasons why punishment of past violations is a condition needed to guarantee respect for human rights. In the first place, it is meant to satisfy the victims' and families' rights to truth, justice, and reparation. In the second place, it allows for the neutralization of violators and prevents them from acting again. In the third place, it is a necessary condition for building the minimum level of trust between members of society to enable civilized coexistence. A group of people who are certain that violations committed in the past will continue to have impunity have no security regarding the protection of their rights against eventual violations in the future. This is why, though the amnesty proposals (i.e., "turning over a new leaf") for serious violations of human rights and humanitarian law may seem reasonable to many, they offer no guarantee of a solid social foundation. On the contrary, what is needed in cases of mass violations are special mechanisms that allow for the clarification, punition, and reparation of the many atrocities committed. This trend is gaining acceptance worldwide, to the extent that progress has been made in the late 1990s in the development of universal jurisdiction regarding human rights violations; noteworthy are Pinochet's arrest in London followed by the revocation of his amnesty and arrest in Chile, the extradition and trial requests regarding Argentinean generals, and the creation of the International Criminal Court.

In Colombia, it has been proposed many times that a special investigation commission be created to this end. Such a commission would be made up of high-ranking government officials and members of national and international NGOs. Their duties would be, not to try cases, but rather to promote and oversee legal processes through the collection and contribution of evidence using existing trial mechanisms, without modification and without restricting guarantees. A UN expert formally made this proposal to the Colombian government in 1989 as part of the advisory services that the Colombian authorities had requested from Geneva at that time.[57] The government did not even bother to reply to the suggestion or to disclose it. Nor have subsequent administrations responded to similar proposals made repeatedly at the beginning of the 1990s by different Colombian and international NGOs, as well as by the Commission for Overcoming Violence. That commission was created by the government in 1991 to receive recommendations on peace and human rights for a six-month period after the peace agreement reached with the former guerrilla group Popular Liberation Army (EPL) (Amnistía Internacional 1994: 89–91; Comisión de la Superación de la Violencia 1992: 167–77). Important national and international human rights organizations, along with the human rights bodies of the United Nations and the Inter-American system, have also repeatedly insisted on the need to guarantee the rights to truth, justice, and reparation, as well as the search for the means to achieve those rights (see, for instance, IACHR 1999).

Such a proposal is even more important today, when the government has openly promoted granting amnesty for crimes against humanity and crimes of war while simultaneously negotiating with paramilitary groups, as described earlier. The secretary general of the United Nations himself requested the Colombian authorities not to allow impunity for such kinds of crimes, in a statement released July 1, 2004, when the demilitarized zone for formalizing those negotiations was inaugurated.[58] It must be said that never before had such an explicit amnesty been proposed in Colombia. On the contrary, all amnesties granted in previous peace processes, since the mid-1980s, explicitly excluded heinous crimes. That is why several members of guerrilla groups who reached peace agreements with the government in the 1980s and the 1990s were sentenced to prison as a result of judicial procedures stipulated in those agreements.[59]

It is difficult to define the period of time that this special mechanism of truth, justice, and reparation should cover. According to some proposals, it should include crimes committed since 1965, when the government legalized the existence of paramilitary groups by authorizing the armed forces to give weapons of war to civilians.[60] In other proposals, the date of departure should be 1948, generally acknowledged as the benchmark for exacerbation of violence in Colombia after the murder of Liberal Party chief Jorge Eliécer Gaitán, who was widely supported by popular sectors. There are people who think that the period should be very short, no more than the last five or ten years, because they think that otherwise the task would be impossible. In any case, what is certain is the need to ensure as much justice as is possible through the judicial system, to disclose and to officially acknowledge the truth of what has happened, and to give reparation to the thousands of victims whose rights the state has not been able to protect so far.

This initiative has many opponents, including those who honestly believe that a negotiated solution for peace in Colombia requires total amnesty. It is true that pardon for combatants is a necessary component of the negotiated settlement of any armed conflict. Yet a true pardon must be based on the recognition of human rights violations and on the restoration of rights that were outraged. There are no valid reasons to eliminate the two aspects of truth and reparation from any peace process. As far as the third aspect—justice—is concerned, some crimes are so serious that they cannot be forgiven. The history of Colombia is a succession of accounts of total impunity for horrendous abuses against the population. What must be done to obtain a solid peace is exactly the opposite: to guarantee a reasonable but certain dose of justice, truth, and reparation for everybody.

Institutional Strengthening

Institutional strengthening, or in another way of putting it, the full applicability of the social rule of law, is of course another condition necessary to guarantee respect and enforcement of human rights. This obviously involves effective separation of powers and the existence of control mechanisms over those powers. It also implies the quick availability of resources for the protection and operation of the agencies that oversee the authorities and aid victims, such as the national Ombudsman's Office (Defensoría del Pueblo). Above all, it requires the actions of a reliable justice apparatus, one that is independent, impartial, and effective. Though stating this may sound like an empty platitude, in Colombia it is a heartfelt necessity.

The country shows a marked contrast between a high level of sophistication in the legal area, as reflected by the professionalism and training of many of its judges (Comisión Andina de Juristas 1988), and a low level of credibility of the judicial system and its results. This deficiency is relatively well known in the criminal area, where the rate of impunity is officially recognized as being very high. The debate has centered on whether the rate is actually 70, 90, or 97 percent, but all analysts agree that whatever the actual figure is, the rate is extremely high.[61] It is only natural that this generates feelings of vulnerability, which in turn lead to behaviors indicating a lack of solidarity with society, since everyone tends to feel that it is best to look out for his or her own interests, come what may.

This phenomenon is not limited to the criminal area. It also arises, though to a somewhat lesser extent, in civil, labor, and agricultural jurisdictions. These conflicts are normally considered minor by the authorities, though they may in fact have far-reaching consequences for the affected parties. Be that as it may, these are the most common types of conflict, and they are difficult to process through the legal system and before judges because costs tend to be higher than benefits. Breaches of small work contracts, transit accidents, and disputes over plots of land or illegal housing developments are part of the day-to-day life of many Colombians. The sad thing is that there are no real institutional channels for resolving these matters. Certain initiatives such as conciliation procedures have been promoted since the end of the 1980s in this area, yet their coverage remains fairly limited.

In the midst of this precarious situation, it is surprising that people's willingness to turn to the official justice apparatus has not been destroyed altogether. The possibility of a citizen's injunction called *tutela* in Colombian law (already mentioned in the previous section as a quick remedy, created in the 1991 Constitution, for the protection of fundamental rights) has been used more and more in a variety of conflicts, increasing from ten thousand in 1992 to close to two hundred thousand in 2002.[62] This shows that the generalized skepticism toward institutions can be overcome when the institutions prove to be capable of satisfying people's basic needs, one of which is the administration of justice (see CCJ 2003b).

Guaranteeing a Minimum Level of Economic, Social, and Cultural Rights

The other basic needs that must also be satisfied—or at the very least guaranteed at certain minimum levels—as a condition for ensuring a prevailing climate of respect for human rights, are economic, social, and cultural rights. The relationship existing between those rights and civil and political ones becomes more obvious with each passing day. Many violations of the right to life are brought about through violations of the right to land, for example. If membership in a society does not bring with it adequate food, housing, health care, education, and employment, it is only natural that harmful behaviors arise in the attempt to acquire such things. Furthermore, if many people lack these basic rights, the abusive use of power to repress these behaviors tends to become the rule rather than the exception.

With more than 60 percent of its population below the poverty line, Colombia must make a serious effort to redress economic distribution. It is evident that guaranteeing a minimum level of economic, social, and cultural rights is not something that can be achieved overnight, which is why the progressive nature of the process has been pointed out by the International Covenant on Economic, Social, and Cultural Rights. Yet the other side of this argument is that achieving these changes cannot be put off indefinitely. Setting goals and time frames in which these levels can become a reality must be the state's policy in compliance with its international obligations, which transcend the particular goals of each transitory administration.

Specifically, rural reform for redistributing land within the "agricultural frontier" is essential for reducing the current levels of social exclusion in Colombia. Land redistribution could also have the positive effect of lowering levels of poverty and ethnic marginalization. Further, it could encourage colonizers now established in the Amazon region to return to their places of origin, which would facilitate dealing with the illegal coca crop problem and the protection of the rain forest.

Land redistribution following rural reform may be one of the results of a peace process. However, initiating such a redistribution prior to a peace settlement would be even more positive, since it could facilitate the definition and implementation of a lasting peace process and also contribute substantially to the elimination of the reasons for the continuation of war, should it prove impossible to reach a negotiated solution to the conflict in the short term. However, neither former administrations nor the current Uribe government has thus far made any proposal for land redistribution in Colombia.

A successful approach to the problem of land reform implies guaranteed respect for civil and political rights. This approach is another reason to undertake both initiatives (i.e., agrarian reform and respect for human rights) as goals contributing to a future negotiated peace process. These goals must be approached independently—but in an interrelated manner—to allow the peace process to be successful. Any rural reform process will face resistance from traditional and newer large landowners. Some of the latter have gained access to land due to forced displacements caused by human rights violations or as a result of the monetary profits and violence of drug trafficking. Those landowners will most likely react with violence to any redistribution policies, a strategy that will in turn require confrontation by credible armed forces willing to protect the rights of those who have been forcibly expelled and uprooted from their lands.

Another requirement is a robust judicial system to deal with these reactions and the political will to clarify, repair, and punish serious past violations, many of which have resulted in abusive land occupation. Therefore, any recommendations made for dealing with social exclusion in Colombia, such as those expressed in 1995 and 2000 by the UN Committee on Economic, Social, and Cultural Rights, are crucial for achieving peace and truly improving human rights in the country. It is important to emphasize that, in addition to the recommendations in this area related to land distribution, there are others that relate directly to poverty levels, ethnic marginalization, and the situation of women (Defensoría del Pueblo and Comisión Colombiana de Juristas 1997: 143–49).[63]

Overcoming the Discriminatory Mentality

The absence of a serious plan to guarantee economic, social, and cultural rights may well be related to the fifth of the problems that must be faced to bring about a favorable environment and respect for human rights: the discriminatory mind-set. For years, Colombian society has been marked by an exclusionary attitude toward the least favored sectors of the population. The demands for land presented by peasants and indigenous peoples, as well as workers' labor claims and pleas for better living conditions, have often been denied as extending beyond the bounds of reasonable and moderate defense of the interests of the social sectors that would be affected by such claims (i.e., landowners, entrepreneurs, or political leaders). Going well beyond the level of understandable selfishness, the excessive zeal with which these interests are defended devalues the humanity of those who want their rights to be recognized.

Colombia made a fairly rapid transition into the twentieth century from a system of social relations based on inequality and servitude to one based on the postulate of equality and competition among social subjects and groups. The admission that all Colombians, without exception, have the same rights is something that almost no one dares to deny in theory. Yet putting this tenet into practice in day-to-day life has been traumatic and difficult in a context where there are differences of culture and physiognomy so pronounced that at times members of one group can find another group abhorrent.

This discriminatory mentality still present in Colombian society today also exists among some state agents responsible for ensuring the safety of the citizens. Imbued with the idea that they have an official right to bear arms, those agents have their discriminatory attitudes strengthened in their daily confrontations with people from the most destitute sectors of the population, who, statistics show, constitute the bulk of those captured committing crimes.

The armed conflict has accentuated this discriminatory mind-set. The view of the other as the enemy, which is a normal assumption in armed confrontations, has become commonplace as well in civil conflicts. For this reason, Colombian society needs to make greater efforts to reduce the discriminatory mentality that is predominant, perhaps even greater efforts than other populations with similar origins and discriminatory practices in principle. Educational campaigns are not enough, though they are undeniably important. The starting point must be to investigate where this exclusionary trend arises in real conditions in each region of the country. This type of blunt and honest examination may shed light on how specifically to counteract these attitudes in each different context.

It is also crucial to promote in-depth human rights education for Colombian society, as required under the constitution and the General Educational Law, as well as under the international human rights treaties that Colombia has ratified. Unfortunately, since the inauguration of Uribe's government in August 2002, the discriminatory mentality has tended to be strengthened instead of weakened, due to the government's evident disdain for the basic notions and principles of human rights, as mentioned before.

Factors Hindering and Favoring Democratic Coexistence

The story that has just been told is not a very heartening one. It is difficult to promote and expect significant results in the medium term regarding the five aspects described above: prevention, impunity, justice, socioeconomic rights, and discrimination. Progress in the short term is even less likely after the talks between the government and guerrillas failed in February 2002. That failure led to frequent and more clamorous demands from important sectors of the Colombian population for a hard line and all-out war, accompanied by already adopted restrictions on rights under the pretext of preparing a much stronger front against the guerrilla groups. The armed conflict thus tends to make the human rights situation even more precarious, and more and more people feel that the pursuit of peace through human rights is an unrealistic and utopian ideal.

After the ratification of the 1991 Constitution, constitutional counter-reforms have been proposed once and again. These are geared toward suppressing restrictions on the use of the state of exception in the hope that the military will be permitted to initiate legal investigations of civilians. As mentioned above, the current government definitely wants to promote these reforms and has already obtained the approval of some of them from Congress. Instead of combating paramilitary groups, multiple efforts in the 1990s concentrated on legalizing their activity through provisions to authorize the operations of "rural security cooperatives" and through a proposal to allow the constitutional formation of militias. Although the legalization of paramilitary groups through this means has been declared unconstitutional, there is nothing to prevent these initiatives or others like them to come back with a vengeance in the first decade of the new century.

Nor has significant progress been made in terms of countering impunity for human rights violations. The Prosecutor General's Office was making serious and significant efforts in this area until 2001 but was not sufficiently supported by the government, the police, and the armed forces, since all three have been reluctant to implement arrest warrants issued for paramilitary members. The authorities are also unwilling to transfer serious cases of human rights violations that are still under the military criminal justice system to the ordinary system. In 2000, overcoming much resistance, human rights advocates achieved an important victory: laws ordering that human rights violations must be investigated and processed by the ordinary justice system went into effect, when the Superior Council of the Judiciary finally complied with a ruling by the Constitutional Court that had so decreed in 1997. These are, without a doubt, great legislative and judicial advances. Nevertheless, there is still much doubt about whether these standards will be truly complied with, how long they will remain in effect, and what kind of decisions will be issued in the future. During the Pastrana and Uribe administrations, the Ministry of National Defense and other sectors have continued to push their proposals to strengthen military jurisdiction (instead of ordinary jurisdiction) to deal with allegations against members of the armed forces. This has clearly been an effort to prevent action on the part of the Prosecutor General's Office (Fiscalía) and the Inspector General's Office (Procuraduría).

Furthermore, the administration of justice is still a long way from including among its priorities the necessary attention to the everyday needs of the people, which have more to do with muggings and violence as a result of common crime and breach of smaller contracts than with rebellion or drug trafficking. The resources of the judicial system continue to represent a mere 3 percent of the national budget, while funding for security forces still exceeds 20 percent, as it has since the 1970s. It seems likely that the situation will get worse with the decision taken by the Uribe administration to strengthen the military budget.

Social spending cuts have been a constant during the last three administrations, a situation that was further aggravated by the 1998–2000 budget deficit. The discovery by the government inaugurated in August 2002 of a new deficit has led to announcements of more social spending cuts. No serious goals have been set for housing, employment, nutrition, health, or education in the last decade or at the start of the new century. As far as tolerance and fighting discrimination are concerned, some valuable efforts have been put forth around ethnic struggles and gender sensitivity, yet they have not been able to eradicate the military mentality that automatically sees the specter of the guerrilla behind every social conflict.

Colombia is going through a difficult time. The persistent and growing aggression against the population by guerrilla groups—as shown in the alarming number of kidnappings, the horrifying use of terrorism, and attacks on towns using weapons that wreak indiscriminate damage, such as gas tanks—have done nothing to put matters on a more positive course. Instead of complying with humanitarian law, the tactics of war have degraded, as seen in new methods used by paramilitary groups since the mid-1990s: the kidnapping or murder of family members of guerrillas and the increase in massacres of the general population. In the midst of this highly dangerous situation, proposals and measures aimed at militarizing the society tend to prevail. The undeniable gravity of the current situation does not eliminate the necessity to continue requiring and putting forward proposals for a suitable human rights policy. On the contrary, it makes it even more urgent.

For this demand for human rights to be viable, and if peace is to be reached by choosing the path of respect for human rights and humanitarian law, the collaboration of the international community will be decisive. Colombia is currently subject to international supervision in the area of human rights. The Permanent Office of the UN High Commissioner for Human Rights in Colombia, created by decision of the UN Human Rights

Commission in 1996 with the approval of the Colombian government, should be firmly backed by the international community in its effort to compel the Colombian government to implement its recommendations. Both the actions of this office and those of the UN Human Rights Commission itself may contribute to containing some of the authoritarian initiatives currently in vogue as well as to inhibiting new human rights violations. When looked at in the most positive light, if these efforts are performed in keeping with the principles of transparency, objectivity, and impartiality inherent to the United Nations, they may even contribute to promoting a true understanding of the importance of human rights in broad sectors of the population and undermining ideological preconceptions regarding this topic.

Numerous important international human rights organizations are awaiting the appropriate implementation of this mandate, as are a significant number of states that consider themselves to be Colombia's friends. Among them, the United States plays an important role, as does the European Union, whose parliament and Council of Ministers of Foreign Affairs have examined the human rights situation in the country with great care and concern and have continuously approved resolutions and statements, each successively more decisive and well documented, on Colombia's need to respect human rights and reach a negotiated peace settlement. At the same time, the IACHR has maintained sharp watchfulness over the Colombian situation in terms of the individual cases of human rights violations that have been submitted for its review, as well as in its evaluation of the whole series of events that have come up in this area.

International accompaniment is not enough on its own to prevent greater deterioration of the human rights situation, yet its insufficiency should not be grounds for discarding it altogether. This is a factor that did not exist before the mid-1990s, and it is likely that it will be more common in the future. It is also a factor that must be complemented with greater consolidation and strengthening of the Colombian social sectors that are in favor of peace based on respect for human rights. The key to success for these social sectors in terms of accompaniment by the international community must be measured in terms of the shift in the current prevailing mentality, which has been conditioned to the possibility of enjoying human rights only at the termination of the war.

When Colombia's military and political leadership stops treating human rights as another card to play at the negotiating table, one that must be saved to trump the guerrillas in the event of a future peace agreement, the first step will have been taken not only toward achieving consistent protection of human rights but also toward the construction of peace. Respect for human rights as an attitude determinedly assumed by the Colombian state and society is the surest path toward building democracy and neutralizing acts of war in this country.

Notes

1. *Sociopolitical violence* is understood to mean events that constitute attacks on life, physical integrity, and personal freedom (1) as a result of the abuse of authority by state agents; (2) arising due to political motivations; (3) stemming from discrimination against socially marginalized people; (4) or caused by the internal armed conflict.

2. Data cited in this chapter regarding human rights in Colombia correspond to information that has been processed by the Colombian Commission of Jurists based upon allegations that have been received directly, press follow-up, and the verification of several databases. These include those of the Popular Research and Education Center (CINEP), the Inter-Congregational Commission for Justice and Peace, the National Police Department, the Governmental Program for the Protection of Personal Liberties, the Free Country Foundation, and the Consulting Agency for Human Rights and Displacement (CODHES), among others. Regarding these figures, the following writings published by the Colombian Commission of Jurists can be consulted: CCJ 1996, 1997, 2000, 2001, 2002, 2003a, 2004, and 2005.

3. Participation of state agents in kidnappings is a frequent news story in Colombia. For instance, in November 1998, a police colonel who was then agency chief for the Anti-Kidnapping Unit (GAULA) was subpoenaed to testify before the Prosecutor General's Office (Fiscalía General de la Nación) about kidnappings allegedly attributed to him (*El Tiempo*, November 26, 1998, Legal Section). Similarly, in November 2002, an army colonel was sentenced to forty years in prison as a result of being found guilty of leading a kidnapping ring in Bogotá in 2000 when he was the chief intelligence officer in the 13th Brigade.

4. The exact figures are 76.3 percent, 5.6 percent, and 18.2 percent, respectively (CCJ 2005: table 3, pp. 48–51).

5. See, for instance, Colombian National Ministry of Defense, *Annual Human Rights and International Humanitarian Law Report, 2000* (Bogotá: Colombian National Ministry of Defense, January 2001).

6. *Prosecutor General's Office* is the name the U.S. State Department has given in English to the Fiscalía General de la Nación, which is the state agency that carries out criminal investigations. It belongs to the judicial branch. See U.S. State Department, *Country Reports on Human Rights Practices, 2000* (Washington, DC: U.S. State Department, 2001), 6, 18.

7. The Ministry of Defense reports that only 349 arrest warrants issued against paramilitary agents between 1998 and August 2000 have been served out of a total of 1,662 warrants issued by the Prosecutor General's Office. Colombian National Ministry of Defense, *Illegal Self-Defense Groups in Colombia* (Bogotá: Colombian National Ministry of Defense, 2000), 29.

8. U.S. State Department, *Country Report on Human Rights Practices, 1999* (Washington, DC: U.S. State Department, 1999), chapter on Colombia.

9. The year 1998 was particularly terrible for human rights defenders. Two prominent lawyers were slain in their offices in the first half of 1998: Jesús María Valle, chairman of the Antioquian Human Rights Committee, on February 27 in Medellín, and Eduardo Umaña-Mendoza, on April 18 in Bogotá. In yet another case, Jairo Ortega, human rights officer and vice president of Colombia's most important trade union, the Central Workers' Union (CUT), was murdered as he arrived home on October 20. The UN high commissioner for human rights, Mrs. Mary Robinson, who was in Bogotá that day, called a press conference to express her heartfelt concern about the situation of human rights defenders in Colombia. See "The High Commissioner for Human Rights Condemns the Murder of Trade Union Leader in Bogota: Mrs. Robinson Issues a Call for Full Protection of Human Rights Defenders," UN press release, Bogotá, October 21, 1998 (my translation). See also editorial in *El Tiempo,* Bogota, October 25, 1998, 4A; and "Guerra Sucia, ¿Quién está matando a los defensores de los derechos humanos en Colombia? ¿Por qué ahora?" in *Revue Semana,* Bogotá, April 27, 1998, 24–30.

10. The president of the republic himself decided to get involved in these accusations. In a speech before the military forces on September 8, 2003, he defined human rights defenders as supporters of terrorists and called them "human rights traffickers." Several organizations requested that the president withdraw these accusations or provide evidence for them, which the president formally declined to do in January 2004. The case was then taken to court by the petitioners, in March 2004.

11. Senate Bill 105, 2003.

12. UN document E/CN 4/2002/106/Add.2, which can be seen on the Web page of the UN high commissioner for human rights at www.unhchr.ch.

13. Some 315,000 people in 2000, according to the Consulting Agency for Human Rights and Displacement [CODHES] (2001). See also U.S. Committee for Refugees (1998) and figures for 2000–2003 at www.codhes.org.co.

14. Law 387, adopted on July 18, 1997.

15. Decree 2569, December 12, 2000.

16. Constitutional Court, Decision SU-1150, August 30, 2000.

17. "Reports of the Special Representative of the United Nations Secretary-General for Internal Displacement, Mr. Francis Deng," UN documents E/CN.4/1995/50/Add.1 and E/CN.4/2000/83/Add.1.

18. E1 Salvador's rate is even higher than Colombia's, at over 100 per 100,000. Following Colombia is Brazil, with a rate of fewer than 50 per 100,000. See Cruz, Trigueros, and González (1999). According to this report, after the peace agreements in El Salvador in January 1992, "more than 100 deaths per year from homicide for every 100,000 inhabitants experienced by this country in recent years" (4). And "homicide rates in the greater metropolitan area of San Salvador from 1993 to 1998 have been 85.4, 89.5, 89.8, 77.3, 72.6, 80.4 per 100,000 inhabitants" (20).

19. Colombian National Planning Department (DNP), *La paz: El desafió para el desarrollo* (Bogotá: Tercer Mundo Editores, 1998), 102, my translation. The essay on justice included in this book (99–122), prepared by Los Andes University's Center for Legal Research under the direction of Professor Mauricio García, is an excellent brief and authoritative diagnosis of the problem, including some important proposals for its solution. The justice data cited in this chapter come from this study unless otherwise indicated.

20. See reports presented on Colombia to the UN Human Rights Commission in 2002 by the special rapporteur on the independence of judges and lawyers (doc. E/CN.4/2002/72, para. 27–36); the special rapporteur on violence against women (doc. E/CN.4/2002/83/Add.3, para. 16–21); the special representative of the secretary general on human rights defenders (doc. E/CN.4/2002/106/Add.2, para.195–200); and the high commissioner for human rights (speech given on April 18, 2002). See also Human Rights Watch (2002).

21. An accurate analysis of the social and economic exclusion in Colombia can be seen in Garay and Ossa (2002). See also United Nations, *Observations and Recommendations Made in 2000 by the United Nations Committee on Social, Economic, and Cultural Rights to the Report Presented by the Government of Colombia*, 2000, Document E/C.12/1/Add.74.

22. More detailed information on this issue can be seen in Gallón (1997: 202–31 and 2002b: 237–82).

23. To facilitate an easy reading of the text, the five periods are expressed in terms of decades (using the distinctions *mid-*, *early*, and *late*). The first period (mid-1960s to mid-1980s) corresponds more precisely to years 1963 to 1982. On May 23, 1963, President Guillermo León Valencia declared a state of emergency to deal with a strike organized by oil workers in Barrancabermeja and three other neighboring towns. This decision inaugurated a long period in which governments dealt with social conflicts predominantly with a show of force, including bombing of peasant settlements. The predominant and almost exclusive use of force and of state-of-siege decrees in the face of social protest was the clear response until the end of the government of President Julio César Turbay (August 7, 1982), when arbitrary legislation known as the Anti-Terrorist Act was adopted.

The state of emergency was lifted on June 12, 1982. In general terms, no human rights violations were recognized by the government during this period.

24. Actually, from 1982 to 1994. In December 1982, Congress approved a bill proposed by the government to grant amnesty to guerrillas in order to launch negotiations with guerrilla groups. This was a period of political reform, including the adoption of the popular election of mayors (1986) and a new and more democratic constitution (1991). This was also a period of increasing violence in the country, which coincided with the administrations of Belisario Betancur (August 1982–August 1986), Virgilio Barco (1986–1990), and César Gaviria (1990–1994). In general terms, limited recognition of human rights violations was gradually made during this period.

25. The U.S. State Department uses the name *Attorney General's Office* for the Procuraduría General de la Nación, a state agency that "oversees the performance of all public sector employees." It belongs to the Public Ministry and, like the Prosecutor General's Office, is independent from the executive branch. See U.S. State Department, *Country Reports on Human Rights Practices, 2000*, 6, 18. This chapter stays away from that terminology and prefers the term *Inspector General's Office* because it corresponds better to the disciplinary functions of the Procuraduría in Colombia.

26. This standard authorized the armed forces to release weapons of war (which are restricted by law for the exclusive use of the armed forces) to groups of civilians (Decree 3398 of 1965, art. 33, par. 3, approved as a "temporary measure" under a state of exception, and later enacted as permanent legislation through Law 48 of 1968). In May 1989, one month after the suspension of the standard, achieved through Decree 815 of 1989, the Supreme Court took action against that standard and also annulled it as being unconstitutional.

27. Decree 814, April 1989.

28. In 1989, with M19; in 1991, with the Revolutionary Party of Workers (PRT), the indigenous group Quintín Lame Armed Movement, and an important faction of the Popular Liberation Army (EPL); and, in 1994, with the Socialist Renovation Stream, a group formerly belonging to the National Liberation Army (ELN).

29. This third period corresponds to the administration of Ernesto Samper (1994–98). There was more recognition of human rights violations in this period, as well as an increase in decisions taken, nationally and internationally, to deal with human rights in Colombia. Nevertheless, these decisions continued to be very limited in terms of their actual effects. Paramilitary groups and paramilitary action grew enormously in this period.

30. UN documents E/CN.4/1998/16, E/CN.4/1999/8, E/CN.4/2000/11, E/CN.4/2001/15, and E/CN.4/2002/17.

31. Bill 288 of 1996.

32. Constitutional Court, Sentence C-572, November 7, 1997.

33. Constitutional Court, Sentence C-295, July 5, 1996.

34. Constitutional Court, Sentence C-358, August 5, 1997.

35. This fourth period (late 1990s) corresponds to the administration of Andrés Pastrana (1998–2002). Political negotiations with guerrilla groups, such as the Revolutionary Armed Forces of Colombia (FARC) and the National Liberation Army (ELN), were on this administration's agenda until February 20, 2002, when President Pastrana decided to put an end to the process. The government tried to counterbalance UN involvement as monitors of the Colombian human rights crisis by increasing U.S. military and political support.

36. Intervention by the Colombian vice-president (he was also the minister of defense and the officer responsible for human rights and humanitarian law policy) before the 58th session of the UN Human Rights Commission, responding to the *Report of the High Commissioner for Human Rights on Colombia,* Geneva, April 18, 2002

37. Basic data on Plan Colombia can be seen in *Congressional Record,* June 29, 2000, 5527–530; document available at www.ciponline.org/colombia/confrep.pdf.

38. So far, it seems that the 1997 ruling of the Constitutional Court has generally been respected. Nevertheless, the uncertainty on this issue increases with the policies of the new government, which was inaugurated in August 2002.

39. The Constitutional Court found the trial before the military court invalid and ordered that the case be sent for a new trial in the ordinary (civilian) courts: Sentence SU-1884, 2001.

40. A more limited process was also started with the ELN and was broken off by the government in 2001.

41. For further details on this issue, see Gallón (2002a: 179–82); and also see CCJ (2005).

42. Law 684 of 2000.

43. Constitutional Court, Sentence C-251, April 11/02.

44. This fifth period (early 2000s) corresponds to the end of the administration of Andrés Pastrana (after the termination of peace talks with the FARC on February 20, 2002) and the beginning of the administration of Alvaro Uribe (August 7, 2002). The government implements security measures contrary to recommendations made over many years by the United Nations and the Inter-American system to the current administration and to previous governments.

45. Senate Bill 19 of 2003.

46. Decree 2002 of September 9, 2002, preambular par. no. 3.

47. See Procuraduría General de la Nación, *Estados de excepción* (Bogotá: Procuraduría General de la Nación, 2004), especially Part 2, relating to special reports about the implementation of the state of exception in two particular regions and in the whole territory of the country. On April 29, 2003, the Constitutional Court declared unconstitutional the prorogation of the state of exception ordered by the government through Decree 245 of February 5, 2003: Constitutional Court, Sentence C-327 of 2003, Judge Alfredo Beltrán.

48. Legislative Act 002 of 2003.

49. One of these commitments was made by the Colombian government before the UN Human Rights Commission, whose chairperson adopted a statement on Colombia on April 25, 2003. This statement, as well as all statements on Colombia made by the commission's chairperson every year since 1995, was previously negotiated with and accepted by the government of Colombia. Par. 13 says that the commission "takes note of the ruling of the Constitutional Court declaring unconstitutional part of the 2002 decree granting judicial powers to the armed forces and appeals to the Government not to seek to make these power permanent through law" (UN document OHCHR/STM/CHR/03/2). Afterwards, during the congressional debates on the reform of the constitution, the government eluded this commitment by arguing that it was only a decision taken by a minor officer in Geneva without consulting with high-ranking government officials. As this argument was unacceptable, the chairperson's statement on Colombia adopted one year later, on April 21, 2004, reacted by saying in par. 36 that "the Commission reminds the Government of Colombia of its commitment to take into account and implement recommendations contained in the statement by the Chairperson" (UN document E/CN.4/2004/future.5).

50. On August 30, 2004, after this chapter was finished, the Constitutional Court declared this bill, known as Legislative Act 02 of 2003, unconstitutional.

51. For more details, see Gallón and Díaz (2004a, 2004b).

52. Fifteen percent is the average of the past three decades. More recently, since 2000, it has increased until it is near 30 percent today (CCJ 2005).

53. United Nations, *Report of the United Nations Working Group on Forced or Involuntary Disappearances on Its Visit to Colombia in 1988*, 1989, Document E/CN.4/1989/Add.1, para. 132.

54. Legislative Decrees 1837 (August 11, 2002) and 2002 (September 9, 2002).

55. United Nations, *Report of the Special Rapporteur on Extrajudicial, Summary, or Arbitrary Executions Regarding His Visit to Colombia in October 1989*, 1990, Document E/CN.4/1990/22/Add.1, para. 67.

56. Sentence C-358, August 1997.

57. Report by Argentinean expert Raul Aragón, sent to the UN Center for Human Rights on August 18, 1990, entitled "La desaparición forzada e involuntaria en Colombia."

58. "The process should not permit blanket amnesties or de facto impunity. The Secretary-General reiterates his belief that the rights of truth, justice and reparations for victims must be fully respected." United Nations, press release SG/SM/9400, July 1, 2004.

59. Several members of the former guerrilla group M19 reminded President Uribe of precisely that in a public letter sent to answer his assertions on past amnesties. *El Tiempo*, Bogotá, September 28, 2003.

60. Decree 3398 of December 24, 1965, art. 33.3.

61. Comisión de Racionalización del Gasto y de las Finanzas Públicas, Ministerio de Hacienda, 1997. *El saneamiento fiscal, un compromiso de la sociedad: Informe final, tema V: Seguridad y orden público. Justicia y derechos civiles* (Bogotá: Ministerio de Hacienda, 1997), 71.

62. Corte Constitucional and Consejo Superior de la Judicatura, *Estadísticas sobre la acción de tutela* (Bogotá: Corte Constitucional and Consejo Superior de la Judicatura, 1999), 31, 39. The exact figures are as follows:10,732 from December 1991 to late December 1992; 20,181 in 1993; 26,715 in 1994; 29,950 in 1995; 31,248 in 1996; 33,663 in 1997; 38,248 in 1998; 33,401 from January to June 1999. According to unofficial sources from the Constitutional Court, by 2002 the weekly rate was 4,000. That would mean an approximate total of 200,000 actions in one year.

63. See also United Nations, *Recomendaciones de órganos internacionales de derechos humanos al estado colombiano, 1980–2000* (Bogotá: Alto Comisionado de las Naciones Unidas para los Derechos Humanos-Oficina en Colombia and Universidad Nacional de Colombia-Facultad de Derecho, Ciencias Políticas y Sociales, November 2002).

References

Amnistía Internacional. 1994. *Violencia política en Colombia: Mito y realidad.* Madrid: Amnistía Internacional.

CINEP (Popular Research and Education Center). 1995. "Human Rights Report." Mimeo. Bogotá, CINEP.

Colombian Commission of Jurists. 1996. *Colombia, derechos humanos y derecho humanitario: 1995.* Bogotá: CCJ.

————. 1997. *Colombia, derechos humanos y derecho humanitario: 1996.* Bogotá: CCJ.

————. 2000. *Panorama de derechos humanos y derecho humanitario en Colombia: Informe de avance sobre 2000.* Bogotá: CCJ.

————. 2001. *Panorama de derechos humanos y derecho humanitario en Colombia. Informe de avance: Abril a septiembre de 2000.* Bogotá: CCJ.

————. 2002. *Panorama de derechos humanos y derecho humanitario en Colombia. Informe de avance: Octubre de 2000 a marzo de 2001.* Bogotá: CCJ.

————. 2003a. *A Growing Absence of Guarantees: Situation of Human Rights and Humanitarian Law in Colombia, 1997–2003.* Bogotá: CCJ.

————. 2003b. *El papel de la Corte Constitucional y la tutela en la realización del estado social de derecho.* Bogotá: CCJ.

————. 2004. *Colombia: Twenty Reasons for Stating That the Human Rights and Humanitarian Law Situation Is Critical and Tending to Worsen.* Bogotá: CCJ.

————. 2005. *Colombia, derechos humanos y derecho humanitario: 1997–2001.* Vol. 1. Bogotá: CCJ.

Comisión Andina de Juristas. 1988. *Colombia: El derecho a la justicia*. Lima: CAJ.

Comisión de Superación de la Violencia. 1992. *Pacificar la paz*. Bogotá: Instituto de Estudios Políticos y Relaciones Internacionales de la Universidad Nacional, ClNEP, CECOIN, Comisión Andina de Juristas Seccional Colombiana (now CCJ).

Consulting Agency for Human Rights and Displacement. 2001. "Quarterly Monitoring 2000." Mimeo, January 19, CODHES-SISDES, Bogotá.

Cruz, José Miguel, Álvaro Trigueros, and Francisco González. 1999. "The Social and Economic Factors Associated with Violent Crime in El Salvador." In *Crime and Violence in Latin America*. Washington, DC: World Bank (November).

Defensoría del Pueblo and Comisión Colombiana de Juristas. 1997. *Contra viento y marea: Conclusiones y recomendaciones de la ONU y de la OEA para garantizar la vigencia de los derechos humanos en Colombia: 1980–1997*. Bogotá: Tercer Mundo Editores.

Gallón, Gustavo. 1995. *¿Ser o no ser? Justicia penal militar*. Bogotá: CCJ. Mimeo.

———. 1997. "Diplomacia y derechos humanos: Entre la inserción y el aislamiento." In *Colombia: Entre la inserción y el aislamiento. La política exterior colombiana en los años noventa*, ed. Socorro Ramírez and Luis Alberto Restrepo. Bogotá: Siglo del Hombre Editores and IEPRI (National University of Colombia).

———. 2002a. "Derechos humanos, la cuerda floja de la búsqueda de la paz en Colombia." In *Panorama de derechos humanos y derecho humanitario en Colombia: Informe de avance: Octubre de 2000 a marzo de 2001*, ed. Colombian Commission of Jurists, 179–82. Bogotá: CCJ.

———. 2002b. "Diplomacia y derechos humanos en Colombia: Más de una década de ambigüedad." In *Prioridades y desafíos de la política exterior colombiana*, ed. Martha Ardila, Diego Cardona, and Arlene B. Tickner. Bogotá: Friedrich Ebert Stiftung for Colombia and Hanns Seidel Stiftung.

———. 2005. "Derechos humanos en la Constitución de 1991." In *Historia del derecho colombiano en la segunda mitad del siglo XX*. Vol. 6. *Derechos de última generación*, ed. Pedro Pablo Morcillo. Bogotá: Ediciones Jurídicas Gustavo Ibáñez.

Gallón, Gustavo, and Catalina Díaz. 2004a. "Justicia simulada: Una propuesta indecente." Mimeo, February, Colombian Commission of Jurists, Bogotá.

———. 2004b. "Ni verdad ni reparación, ni paz: Negociaciones para la impunidad de los paramilitares en Colombia." Mimeo, June, Colombian Commission of Jurists, Bogotá.

Garay, Luis Jorge, and Carlos Ossa, eds. 2002. *Colombia: Entre la exclusión y el desarrollo. Propuestas para la transición al estado social de derecho*. Bogotá: Contraloría General de la República and Alfaomega Colombiana S.A. (July).

Giraldo, Javier. 1988. "Los Modelos de la Represión." *Revista Solidaridad* (Bogotà), no. 100, November.

Human Rights Watch. *A Wrong Turn: The Record of the Colombian Attorney General's Office*. Vol. 14:2(B). New York: Human Rights Watch, 2002.

Inter-American Commission on Human Rights. 1999. "Final Considerations: Human Rights, Justice, and Peace in Colombia." In *Third Report on the Human Rights Situation in Colombia,* Organization of American States, ser. L/V/II.102, doc. 9, rev. 1. Washington, DC: Inter-American Commission on Human Rights.

Londoño Hoyos, Fernando. 2001. "La economía en la Constitución de 1991." *Revista Javeriana* 137 (September).

Torres, Jaime, et al. 1982. *Colombia: Represión, 1970–1981*. Bogotá: CINEP.

U.S. Committee for Refugees. 1998. *Colombia's Silent Crisis: One Million Displaced by Violence*. Washington, DC: U.S. Committee for Refugees.

Conclusion

chapter eleven

This War Cannot Be Won with Bullets

Gustavo Gallón

Gustavo Gallón begins by detailing the vast toll the current conflict has taken on Colombian society. Against this backdrop, he sharply criticizes the current government's apparent inclination to solve that conflict by escalating it—justice, respect for rights, and democracy, not more bullets, will win this war, he says. He argues that Uribe's electoral success should not be taken as an indicator of majoritarian support for his government's current approach to the conflict and then exposes the dark underside of that approach: the commissioning of thousands or millions of civilians into proto-security forces that he fears will only lead to more paramilitary activity, the curtailing of judicial oversight over investigations of alleged guerrilla collaborators, and the exemption of counterinsurgency activity from international and domestic judicial competence. He describes attempts to weaken institutions of accountability and legal protection, including ombudsman organizations such as the Personerías Municipales, the Defensoría del Pueblo, and legal avenues like the acción de tutela and the Constitutional Court. The government's bullet-based security policy, he argues, fails to confront paramilitarism and misses the opportunity for a truly democratic security policy that makes respect for human rights its strategy as well as its goal.

"War is won with bullets," said a top Colombian official in August 2002 when Alvaro Uribe assumed office as president. If this remark had been made by the commander of the armed forces or the defense minister, nobody would have paid much attention. Nor would this sentence have sounded odd coming from a guerrilla leader or a paramilitary chief. But the man who uttered it was no less than the person in charge of ensuring that those who do violence in Colombia are answerable to the law—the nation's prosecutor general.[1]

Given this way of thinking, it is not hard to understand why things are as they are in Colombia. Nor is it hard to imagine how things shall be in the years to come, for the mentality revealed by the nation's prosecutor general (whose job does not make him a government functionary, but who is marvelously in tune with the executive) seems to be the one inspiring the security and human rights policies of the new administration.

Endless Gunfire

Guns and bullets, that has been the story of our country. Thus by 1980 there were one hundred politically motivated deaths a year, a significantly high figure denoting a very grave situation. Today, the number of people dead or disappeared for sociopolitical reasons is close to seven thousand a year. That means approximately twenty people are dying or being "disappeared" in Colombia every day. Eight of these (or 40 percent) are killed in combat, and this includes combatants as well as civilians caught in cross-fire. The twelve remaining (60 percent) do not die in combat: they are murdered on the street, at home, or at work.[2]

In instances where there is a known perpetrator, 75 percent of the victims have reportedly been killed by agents of the government or by paramilitary groups. Public servants are directly responsible for 3 percent of the deaths and play a role in the other 72 percent, either through omission or through collaboration in offenses reportedly committed by paramilitary groups. The remaining 25 percent of the victims are said to have been slain by guerrillas.

Forced displacement has also reached alarming proportions. In Colombia today, more than 3,000,000 people find themselves in that distressing situation. In 1996, 180,000 people were forcibly displaced. In 2001, the number of displaced persons was twice that—360,000. In 2003, there were 200,000 more new displaced people. The majority of these are women (often single mothers) and young children. And, of the total, more than half are Afro-Colombians, the black population, for whose rights the country has shown little respect. Slightly more than 60 percent of the instances of displacement are reportedly the result of actions by paramilitary groups and agents of the state. Around 40 percent are said to be the work of guerrillas.

The country has also seen a considerable increase in kidnappings. At present there are about six kidnappings a day, for a total of around 2,000 kidnappings annually. In 2001 the number reached 3,000; in 1997, there were approximately 1,500. About 60 percent of the abductions are said to be the work of guerrilla groups. Paramilitary groups are also involved in kidnappings, and they are reportedly responsible for about 10 percent of the incidents. The slightly more than 30 percent remaining are ordinary crimes; it appears that state agents (on active duty or retired) are frequently involved, as are, on occasion, even officials in charge of preventing and prosecuting the crime of kidnapping.

Civilian property and entire villages are destroyed almost daily during armed conflict and in open violation of humanitarian law. Common violence has also grown worse in the last several decades. From 1980 to 1990, the country's homicide rate (including both political and common murders) increased from ten thousand to twenty thousand murders a year. The annual homicide rate now stands at around thirty thousand.

Now, If We Just Use More Ammunition

So it is obvious that the formula of using bullets to win this war is nothing new. Certainly, it has not brought victory but only succeeded in turning Colombia into a vast, overcrowded graveyard, since violence leads to more violence. In spite of its obvious failure, this old, worn-out formula is in fashion once more, with the election of a presidential candidate who made security the watchword of his campaign and the focus of his administration.

That is not to say Uribe managed to garner a huge number of votes. Actually, he obtained fewer than Andrés Pastrana.[3] However, it cannot be denied that he did win the election, receiving 53 percent of the votes cast. Voters perhaps endorsed the idea of putting security at the top of the list of problems the new government would have to confront. But they were not necessarily expressing a preference for the bullets formula divulged by the prosecutor general. Of course, there are some who favor it and other measures as well, and there are even those who would like to see American troops invade Colombia and put things right in this country as they supposedly did in Afghanistan. But they are not the majority. Most of the people voting for the new president did so because they saw in him the antithesis of Pastrana and his frustrating process of peace talks, which went on for three and a half years with no results, against the background of an exorbitant increase in violence and the brazen misuse of the "demilitarized zone" by the Revolutionary Armed Forces of Colombia (FARC).

The failure of this peace effort was predictable from the start. The government did not bolster the process with a responsible human rights policy that would have led to resolutely confronting both paramilitarism and impunity and would have required from the FARC a minimum of respect for humanitarian law in exchange for conceding the demilitarized zone.[4] This was not the type of peace ten million voters had endorsed four years earlier, in 1998. Accordingly, in 2002, more than five million electors reacted against this mockery of the desire for peace, justifiably demanding that the state protect their rights. And some did not even vote with that in mind but mainly to cast a ballot against the official Liberal Party candidate, Horacio Serpa, who had earned the intense dislike of a large segment of the electorate.[5]

Nevertheless, the new government seems to have interpreted its first-round electoral victory of 53 percent as a blank check for promoting a policy of security at any cost: in other words, a mandate for using more bullets, as the prosecutor general would put it, and for doing away with institutions that stand in the way of more shooting, institutions that punish those who use violence in an abuse of their official duties, and institutions designed to see that the state gives the Colombian people rights rather than gunfire.

The New "Rambos": Civilian Informants and Peasant-Soldiers

This security policy's star program, announced during the election campaign, was the creation of a national network of informants. Once the new administration was in power, it added another element—that dangerous figure, the peasant-soldier. Not much is known about the makeup of the network or the number of informants. According to some government spokespersons, there could be a hundred thousand. Others say a million. And there are those who claim that the idea is to have forty-four million Colombians join the network—in other words, the entire population. Initially it was announced that the informants would be armed; later there was an incredible statement to the effect that their only weapon would be the telephone. Oddly enough, the same was said about the *convivir* groups in 1994 when they were still in the planning stages. Their members ended up armed to the teeth, as the superintendent for vigilante and private security groups had to admit before the Constitutional Court in 1997. That official, responsible for supervising the *convivir,* also had to admit on the spot that his office was not, nor had it ever been, capable of keeping the movement's bands under control. Accordingly, the court declared unconstitutional the obscurely worded regulation allowing the groups access to weapons designed for the exclusive use of the armed forces.[6] The informants' network could end up similarly armed.

And it could happen with the peasant-soldiers too. Various government officials have made a mess of trying to explain what these half-time soldiers would do with their weapons for the rest of the day, during the hours they toil in the fields. Some of the bureaucrats said the guns would be taken home; others, that they would be left in the barracks; still others even babbled about how the peasants would be carrying machetes, not firearms,[7] as if the public were simple-minded enough to swallow such stories—and as if there had not been enough experience, both inside and outside Colombia, to demonstrate that uniting civilians with the forces of public order to carry out military activities (whether you want to call them intelligence, information gathering, or combat) inexorably leads to paramilitarism. That is why, on April 18, 2002, Mary Robinson, UN high commissioner for human rights, presenting her report on Colombia to the Commission in Geneva, warned: "Even more worrying is the fact that an important segment of society now views paramilitarism as a legitimate option and certain political candidates appear to condone paramilitary activities as demonstrated by the proposal presented by one of the main candidates, to arm one million civilians. The international community must repudiate any attempt to draw the civilian population into the conflict or any other expression of support for violence."[8]

And, to cite an obvious example, by the end of August 2002 there was already a flagrant demonstration of the insecurity engendered by this type of clever arrangement, supposedly intended to bring citizens greater security. Twenty-one people were arbitrarily deprived of liberty by military forces in Ovejas (Sucre Department) during an operation in which the soldiers went around, without the constitutionally required warrants, arresting everyone pointed out by a masked woman, said to be a guerrilla deserter.[9] The soldiers were acting as judicial investigators without warrants, contrary to what was clearly set out in the constitution. But such constitutional hindrances are not going to stand in the way of the army's doing all over the country what it did so shamelessly in Ovejas.

First and Foremost, Attack . . . the Civilian Population

The "state of internal unrest" or state of emergency declared on August 11, 2002, justifies, among other things, the arrest of great numbers of people, with no warrant required.[10] Moreover, the government has made no secret of its intention to amend the constitution to revive the old "state of siege" regulations so that those arrested without warrants can be interrogated by the army in military establishments and so that the state of siege may go on indefinitely, with no supervision by the Constitutional Court[11]—in other words, so people can be shot without anyone interfering.

The odd thing is that the bullets the government wants to fire are aimed primarily at the civilian population, and this explains why the authorities feel an obsessive need to make civilian arrests without warrants. In contrast, although there are warrants out for combatants, combatants are not being taken into custody. Moreover, it appears that there are some fighters the state does not want to get its hands on. There is no other explanation of why rewards are offered for information on the whereabouts of guerrilla leaders, while the same offer was not made for paramilitary leaders before the inauguration of their demilitarized zone in July 2004. This Manichean reward system was established by the former government and has been kept intact by the new one.[12]

National and International Impunity for Thugs

The reality is that the new government is the natural continuation of the previous one, as is demonstrated by facts gradually being made public. One of the most telling revelations is that, upon the ratification of the Rome Statute on August 5, 2002, the incoming and outgoing administrations jointly agreed to invoke Article 124 of the treaty to ensure that war crimes committed in Colombia could not be investigated or tried by the International Criminal Court. Both governments kept the agreement secret for nearly a month, never discussing it with the Colombian people or with Congress. They simply decided, behind closed doors, that it was "a generous gesture of goodwill on the part of the incoming and outgoing administrations" to leave a "window open" for a possible peace process, as the presidential high commissioner on peace later disclosed.[13] A tenderhearted explanation, no doubt. The truth is, however, that this decision amounted to letting war crimes go on being committed with impunity for seven more years.

In actuality, there is only a remote possibility of such crimes or human rights violations in general coming to trial in Colombia. In spite of valiant efforts in the past by the Office of the Prosecutor General, there is almost 100 percent impunity for human rights violations. This impunity has accumulated over several decades and has of course increased as the number of violations has risen.

The magnitude of the impunity can be gauged more clearly by looking at forced displacement. In spite of its now being classified as a crime (according to Article 284 of the 2001 penal code), which in the abstract represents progress in the fight against impunity, in practice forced displacement has only once been the subject of an investigation by the Prosecutor General's Office.[14]

Many judicial investigators, prosecutors, and judges have been murdered by human rights and humanitarian law violators or have been threatened and forced to leave the country. The Human Rights Unit, created in the mid-1990s to strengthen action around human rights, is now less able to carry out its specific functions, owing to some singular changes introduced in 2001. That is why High Commissioner Mary Robinson, in the April 18, 2002, Colombia report mentioned above, called attention to this particular subject: "The report reiterates concerns that I have expressed before over the administration of justice and impunity. This most serious problem is exemplified by the recent change of institutional policy in the Fiscalía General de la Nación (General Prosecutor's Office), which has resulted in the undermining of the independence of its investigators when they have pursued cases that involve alleged human rights violations committed by State agents."[15]

There is some consolation in knowing that the root cause of this impunity is not a lack of resources or inefficiency and incompetence within the institutions, although these factors do play a role. Basically, this impunity is a result of prioritizing to win the war with bullets. By the same token, it was no surprise that the Colombian government accepted the U.S. government's unseemly proposal to conclude an agreement that will keep Americans who commit crimes in Colombia from being sent to the International Criminal Court.[16]

The agreement in question is a distortion of Article 98 of the Rome Statute, which allows state parties to make agreements among themselves to return those committing crimes on foreign soil to their home countries for trial prior to the International Criminal Court's exercising its jurisdiction. The article is an outgrowth of the principle of complementarity that informs the Rome Statute—that is, the International Criminal Court is the complement and not the rival of national jurisdictions.

Thus Article 98 is aimed at strengthening the commitment of the state parties to render justice in cases involving war crimes, genocide, and crimes against humanity. In contrast, the agreement with the United States, which is not a signatory to the Rome Statute, is aimed at guaranteeing impunity. In other words, the government's agreement to such a proposal gave Americans permission to commit such crimes in Colombia.

Eliminating the Protection of Rights, to Make It Easier to Kill

Besides maintaining or increasing impunity, the government suggested abolishing the institution of the municipal *personero* or local ombudsperson, which would make it far less likely for victims of human rights violations or displaced persons to have access to justice or assistance. The institution of the *personero* plays an important role in providing access to justice when citizens think their basic rights have been violated.[17] In addition, local *personero* offices are the key to granting assistance to displaced persons: they are a component of the Central Internal Displaced People (CID) Registry and are thereby authorized to receive declarations from the displaced,[18] especially as to their right of possession.[19] The *personero* offices also serve as local points of information[20] and are participants in the Group for Assistance to Those Displaced by Violence.[21]

The government has also announced its intention to abolish the National Ombudsperson's Office (Defensoría del Pueblo) or merge it with the Inspector General's Office (Procuraduría).[22] The Defensoría del Pueblo was created by the Constitution of 1991 as the state institution in charge of promoting human rights. Since its goal is the true exercise of these rights by the entire population, the Defensoría is largely concerned with protection, basic to which is preventing conditions that pose a threat to rights. In connection with forced displacement, the Defensoría also has duties that involve the dissemination and promotion of humanitarian law, such as those assigned by Law 387;[23] and its regional representatives, the *defensores,* are responsible for participating in efforts to prevent displacement.[24]

The *acción de tutela,* a kind of writ of injunction,[25] is also endangered, following an announcement by the minister of the interior that he wanted to amend it so as to exclude the protection of economic and social rights.[26] This violates the principle that violations of these rights are actionable. Such a change would be especially serious for the displaced population, which, already faced with the government's failure to enforce a large body of existing laws and regulations, has had to employ the *acción de tutela* as a last resort to require the state to fulfill its obligations. Significant Constitutional Court decisions on matters of *tutela* have recognized the rights of displaced persons, especially their economic, social, and cultural rights.[27]

The decisive action of the Constitutional Court in protecting the forcibly displaced is only one of many examples of the essential role played by the court in recognizing human rights. That is why another cause for concern is the announced intention of members of the government to limit the jurisdiction of the institution or turn it into a subordinate section of the Supreme Court of Justice.[28]

Besides all the above, it is possible to mention other initiatives the new administration has been gradually making public, all of which boil down to the idea of setting things to rights with bullets. On the list are concepts such as ostensibly abolishing mandatory military service but actually extending it to women through a new program of mandatory social service with military training;[29] a security law to replace the one declared unconstitutional in April 2002, and an antiterrorism statute to accompany it;[30] a bill threatening freedom of the press;[31] and another bill designed to control NGOs under the pretext of regulating international cooperation.[32]

A Security Policy Instead of a Human Rights Policy

All these measures and many others like them constituting, actively or passively, the current security policy are understood by the government as its human rights policy. The obsession with using bullets is such that it has led to the audacity of imagining that the security police can in itself take care of ensuring human rights. A well-conceived security policy is of course closely tied up with human rights. Furthermore, democratic security has to be based on human rights as both means and end. In other words, its objective must be the protection of the rights of all persons; it cannot benefit some to the detriment of others. And it ought to be carried out by methods respectful of human rights. Otherwise, instead of security being provided, more insecurity is generated (Friedrich Ebert Stiftung for Colombia [FESCOL] 2002).

The elements of the government's policy commented on here are a long way from meeting those requirements. The state's measures are not designed to confront all the insecurity factors, which include, besides the guerrillas, state agents who violate human rights, paramilitary groups, and common criminals. Thus they are not aimed at protecting the rights of all persons. On the contrary, they endanger the rights of many people by encouraging violence by civilians and the military, by eliminating guarantees, and by limiting resources and weakening institutions that enforce guarantees. But even if the security policy did not have serious flaws and could justifiably be characterized as a democratic security policy, it is not correct for human rights policy to disappear into it.

A Difficult Challenge: A Comprehensive Human Rights Policy

Instead of restricting or eliminating the constitutional and legal mechanisms for achieving rights, a human rights policy should be aimed at strengthening them. It should also involve a resolute struggle against impunity and paramilitarism, along with a serious commitment to follow the past recommendations of concerned international bodies (see Colombian Commission of Jurists [CCJ] and Defensoría del Pueblo 1997; Office of the UN High Commissioner for Human Rights [UNHCHR] and Universidad Nacional 2000). And it must be comprehensive: that is, besides protecting civil and political rights, it should establish programs to guarantee, at the very least, enjoyment of the most basic economic, social, and cultural rights.

In Colombia, the unequal distribution of wealth continues to be one of the great obstacles to the enjoyment of human rights. Fifty-two percent of income is concentrated in 20 percent of the nation's households, while

60 percent of the population remains below the poverty line.[33] The proportion of the population that is indigent has increased from 20 to 23 percent in the 1990s.[34]

Within the "extreme inequity and social injustice prevailing in Colombia" described in 2001 by the UN Committee on Economic, Social, and Cultural Rights,[35] the plight of the peasant population is alarming. Approximately eight million country dwellers (or 69 percent) are below the poverty line, with more than four million of them indigent (Colombian Institute of Agrarian Reform [INCORA] 2002).[36] Land is concentrated in so few hands that approximately 2 percent of the nation's property owners hold 53 percent of the land.[37]

Especially affected by inequity and injustice are those sectors of the population historically the victims of discrimination. Women, for example, make up nearly 51 percent of the total population of the country and represent 54 percent of the poor population.[38] The fact that 80 percent of Colombia's population of African descent live in extreme poverty[39] is a grievous indication of racial segregation and of the marginal status of the nation's ethnic minorities.

For a large segment of Colombia's population, the possibility of real and enduring enjoyment of economic, social, and cultural rights has grown increasingly remote. The unemployment rate, 11 percent ten years ago, has today reached 15.3 percent,[40] an official figure that is far too low if underemployment and disguised employment are taken into account. In 2000, only 52.6 percent of the total population had health care coverage, a drop of 4.5 percentage points since 1997.[41] The Defensoría del Pueblo has reported that nearly three million minors of school age are outside the education system—that is, 21.5 percent of the nation's children (Defensoría del Pueblo 2000: 187).

The state's obligations with regard to forced displacement include prevention, protection, and assistance that offers lasting solutions to the victims of displacement. These obligations were established by the Guiding Principles on Internal Displacement, which the Constitutional Court has ruled constitutional, and which have the same weight as Colombian legislation.[42] They have also been recognized by Law 387 of 1997.[43]

Accordingly, the continuing statements of members of the government who restrict the phenomenon of forced displacement to a problem of law and order, refusing to recognize it as a multiple, massive, and constant violation of the basic rights of Colombians, are very disturbing.[44] The authorities and the public should see displaced persons as what they really are, the victims of an extremely grave human rights violation, and not as a security problem. It is essential to look at the humanitarian crisis represented by this increase in displacement and to be aware of the tragic situation in which this segment of the population finds itself. It is necessary to set in motion, without further delay, an emergency program using practiced and effective methods to confront head on the root causes of displacement. Such comprehensive actions depend on the state's having the genuine political will to carry them out and also on the allocation of adequate resources. However, "there are not sufficient resources to attend to the problem," since priorities are focused on the security policy and on the consequent strengthening of the forces of public order, according to statements by the vice president of the republic.[45]

A government response to forced displacement cannot be subordinated to managing the armed conflict, with or without peace negotiations. The current military strategy, developed with the end of "conquering by arms," cannot justify forcibly displacing populations. The spraying programs that are a component of Plan Colombia and form part of the war strategy have become one more element contributing to forced displacement. The intensification of the spraying program[46] gave rise to fears that there would be greater displacement of peasants, who have been turned into enemies although quite often they have no viable alternative to growing illegal crops.

The Colombian government must take effective action as soon as possible to prevent displacement and to guarantee protection and comprehensive assistance to displaced persons. It is obliged to do so, in accordance with the Guiding Principles on Internal Displacement drawn up by the UN Secretary General's representative on internally displaced persons. And while the conflict continues, the state must take measures to protect displaced populations and those at risk for displacement, specifically in connection with land possession for all and for the indigenous and Afro-Colombian communities in particular.

To Achieve Peace, Justice, and Rights Instead of Bullets

Besides dealing with immense challenges in matters of economic, social, and political rights, especially the question of displacement, a human rights policy should be tied in with a policy of seeking a negotiated peace. While the need to use force in dealing with the internal armed conflict cannot be ignored, the idea of concluding humanitarian accords with armed insurgent groups as a way of reducing the rigors of war, especially for the civilian population, should never be abandoned, just as the possibility of achieving peace through negotiation should never be discarded. Nothing indicates that humanitarian accords or negotiation are components of the current government agenda.

What is needed to win the war, then, is not more bullets but justice and the achievement of rights. With such a strategy, combined of necessity with acts of force that scrupulously respect the civilian population, the war will come to an end because its root causes have been removed. Under the strategy we now pursue, more fuel is being added to the fire, greater motives for confrontation are being engendered, and more thugs are getting involved in the savagery. Over the last ten years, the Colombian people and the international community have learned how grave and complex the Colombian situation really is. They have become convinced of the decisive importance of ensuring rights and strengthening democracy in order to confront this acute crisis. Both Colombians and the international community now face the challenge of persevering in this worthy conviction, overcoming the doubts and uncertainties that currently obstruct the path to coexistence and inclusion with an obsession with military solutions. This war is not won with bullets. It is won by dispensing justice, guaranteeing rights, and building democracy.

Notes

1. *El Espectador*, August 25, 2002, 4A.

2. The facts and figures cited here and on the following page come from information that has been processed by the Colombian Commission of Jurists based upon allegations that have been received directly, press follow-up, and the verification of several databases. These include those of the Center of Popular Research and Education (CINEP), the Inter-Congregational Commission for Justice and Peace, the National Police Department, the Governmental Program for the Protection of Personal Liberties, the Free Country Foundation, and the Consulting Agency for Human Rights and Displacement (CODHES). Regarding these figures, the following works published by the Colombian Commission of Jurists can be consulted: CCJ 1996, 1997, 2000, 2001, 2002, 2003, 2004, 2005.

3. In 2002 Alvaro Uribe Vélez received 5,862,655 votes, compared with the 6,086,507 cast for Andrés Pastrana in 1998, according to figures from the National Civil Status Registry. It should be noted that this figure does not represent even 25 percent of the country's potential electorate: 24,208,311 persons (Web site at www.registraduria. gov.co).

4. On this question, see Gallón (2002: 179–82).

5. Serpa was the principal minister of Ernesto Samper, president from 1994 to 1998. Samper's election campaign was the subject of a sensational judicial investigation because it had accepted drug-trafficking funds.

6. The *convivir* groups or "Cooperativas de Vigilancia y Seguridad Rural" (rural watch cooperatives) were authorized by the government to bear arms meant for the exclusive use of the armed forces (in other words, weapons of war), a privilege declared unconstitutional by the Constitutional Court in Decision C–572 of 1997. See CCJ (1997: 16 and 101–7).

7. See "Campesinos armados," *Semana* 1060 (August 26–September 2, 2002): 26–32; *El Tiempo*, August 22, 2002, 1–11; "Presidente Uribe lanza red de informantes viales," noticias CNE, August 8, 2002, retrieved from www. presidencia.gov.co.

8. On September 3, 2002, the high commissioner reiterated this warning to the new government, once the candidate referred to above had assumed the presidency of Colombia and began to turn into reality his campaign pronouncements about establishing an informers' network, an idea now embellished with the new initiative on half-time peasant soldiers. *El Tiempo*, September 5, 2002, 1–11

9. *El Tiempo*, September 2, 2002, 1–14. At least 2,140 persons were arbitrarily detained in 2003 (CCJ 2004: 20).

10. This article was originally finished on September 4, 2002. A week later, on September 10, the government issued the Decree of State of Emergency of 2002, which authorized making arrests, intercepting communications, and searching homes and offices, all without a warrant. It also set up areas euphemistically labeled "zones of rehabilitation and consolidation," with military commanders in charge. The third paragraph of the decree advises that these measures are directed at confronting the civilian population, since (according to the same decree) one of the main problems in defeating criminal groups is that they "camouflage themselves amongst the civilian population."

11. "Será congreso admirable," *El Espectador*, August 11, 2002, 4A. Part of this intention was implemented by the constitutional reform approved through Legislative Act 2 of 2003 that authorized military forces to carry out judicial police functions on civilians.

12. "Se buscan," *Semana*, July 1, 2002, 1–14; "Se busca," *Cambio*, July 1, 2002.

13. "Salvedad se mantiene: Gobierno," *El Tiempo*, September 4, 2002, 1–11.

14. ACNUR and Red de Solidaridad Social, *Balance de la política de atención al desplazamiento forzado en Colombia, 1999–2002* (Bogotá: ACNUR and Red de Solidaridad Social, 2002), 19.

15. In their own reports, three rapporteurs echo Ms. Robinson's concern about the present management of the Prosecutor General's Office: the special rapporteur on violence against women (doc. E/CN.4/2002/83, Add. 3, par. 16–21); the special rapporteur on the independence of judges and lawyers (doc. E/CN.4/2002/72, par. 27–36); and the secretary general's special representative on human rights defenders (doc. E/CN.4/2002/106/Add. 2, par. 195–200).

16. *El Tiempo,* September 4, 2002, 1–11. The agreement was finally signed on September 17, 2003.

17. Municipal *personeros,* chosen by the town council in each city, represent society and are supposed to defend its rights. They are an institution created back in colonial days. With the incentive of a UN program of technical assistance and additional financial support from the Netherlands and Canada, their function as protectors of human rights in every city in the country was clarified and strengthened by Law 3 of 1990, which assigned them the duty of "receiving the complaints and claims that any individual or institution brings before them having to do with the violation by officials of the state or by agents outside the government of civil or political rights and social guarantees" (art. 4). See Manrique-Reyes (1990). The government included the proposal of eliminating this institution in a referendum held on October 2003 that was defeated as well as another thirteen among fifteen proposals.

18. Law 387 of July 18, 1997, art. 32.

19. Law 387 of July 18, 1997, art. 27: "*On the disturbance of possession.* The disturbance of possession or the abandonment of real or personal property, owing to a situation of violence that necessitates the forced displacement of the possessor, shall not interrupt the term of his positive prescription. The possessor interrupted in the exercise of his right shall report his displacement to the municipal *personero,* the Defensoría del Pueblo, the Agrarian Legal Office, or any entity of the Public Ministry."

20. Law 387 of July 18, 1997, art. 12.

21. Through the Defensoría del Pueblo's Resolution 113 of February 6, 1998.

22. "Preparan un revolcón en la justicia," *El Espectador,* July 14, 2002, 6A.

23. Law 387, arts. 14 and 19.

24. Resolution 113/98, "establishing the group of assistance to those forcibly displaced and assigning its duties," art. 5; "Special duties of the *defensores* . . . in compliance with the objectives listed in law 387/97 and in the present resolution are as follows: . . . : 2. Participation in efforts to prevent the phenomenon of forced displacement due to violence."

25. Art. 86 of the 1991 Constitution: "Every person has the right to file a writ of protection before a judge, at any time or place, through a preferential and summary proceeding, for himself or by whomever acts in his name, for the immediate protection of his basic constitutional rights when he fears they may be violated or threatened by the action or omission of any public authority."

26. *El Tiempo,* August 24, 2002.

27. Constitutional Court, Decision T-227/97 concerning various persons displaced to Cundinamarca from Hacienda Bellacruz in Pelaya (Cesar Department), where they resided, a property awarded by the National Agrarian Reform Institute (INCORA). In Cundinamarca, the governor declared she would not accept displaced persons in her department and launched a campaign to prevent their resettlement. The *tutela* was decided in favor of the persons displaced through an infringement of their basic rights. Decision T-1635/00 concerned the *acción de tutela* initiated by the Bogotá regional representative of the Defensoría del Pueblo against the Social Solidarity Network. In this case, the Constitutional Court reminded the state of its responsibility in the overall protection of the displaced population as outlined by the International Committee of the Red Cross and of its responsibility for attention to the food, clothing, and health needs of the displaced, as well as to the education of their children. Decision SU-1150/00 concerned various displaced persons who had petitioned not to be expelled from the place where they had resettled. The Constitutional Court declared that displacement was detrimental to their social, economic, and cultural rights, already affected by the mere fact of their having to leave their dwellings. Moreover, the violation of these rights was an implied infringement of several international treaties. In this case the *tutela* was denied because the property occupied by the displaced persons was uninhabitable, but the court reiterated the government's obligation to guarantee said rights to the displaced. Decision T-1346/01 concerned Resolution 127 of October 31, 2001, which ordered the eviction of a squatter from the property La Reliquia without resolving the woman's housing difficulties. In this case the High Court reiterated the obligation of the government to guarantee displaced persons a right to housing since their dilemma is not subject to a speedy resolution, and it ordered that those living on said property be relocated and guaranteed a fixed dwelling place. Decision T-025/04 concerned 109 *tutela* actions related to the lack of protection of 1,150 displaced families from various regions of Colombia. The Constitutional Court declared that forced displacement was an "unconstitutional state of affairs," due to the massive, generalized, and systematic disregard of the constitutional rights of the victims and due to the structural flaws of the state response. The court ordered the government to carry out measures to fulfill state commitments and to make available the necessary resources to achieve the effective enjoyment by displaced persons of their rights within the deadline set by the court.

28. "Preparan un revolcón," 6A.

29. Senate Bill 47 of 2002, "calling for a referendum to submit proposed constitutional reforms for the consideration of the people," question 15. Senate Bill 19 of 2003.

30. This initiative was approved by a constitutional reform adopted through Legislative Act 02 of 2003 and regulated by a law approved in June 2004 that must be reviewed by the Constitutional Court.

31. House Bill 246 of 2002/Senate Bill 278 of 2002, "which expands Article 73 of the Political Constitution of Colombia on guaranteeing the exercise of journalism and dictates other provisions."

32. House Bill 246 of 2002: "which creates the National System of International Cooperation, restructures the Colombian Agency of International Cooperation, and dictates other provisions." Senate Bill 105 of 2003.

33. The Gini coefficient of concentration of income went from .53 in 1978 to .57 in 1999, above the Latin American average. DNP, *Bases Plan Nacional de Desarrollo, 2002–2006* (Bogotá: National Planning Department, 2003), 25.

34. Office of the Comptroller General of the Republic, www.contraloríagen.gov.co.

35. UN Committee on Economic, Social, and Cultural Rights, E/C.12/1/Add. 74, November 30, 2001, pars. 8 and 29.

36. The INCORA has been closed down, but its Web page is still on line.

37. Office of the Comptroller General of the Republic, www.contraloríagen.gov.co.

38. National Planning Department (DNP) and UN Development Programme, Social Mission, *Informe de desarrollo humano para Colombia 2000* (Bogotá: Alfaomega, 2001), 167–69.

39. Office of the Vice President of Colombia, Presidential Human Rights Program, *Observatorio de los derechos humanos en Colombia*, Boletin no. 22 (May 2002), 7.

40. Departamento Administrativo Nacional de Estadística (DANE), "Documentos técnicos sobre mercado laboral," 2004, 2, retrieved from www.dane.gov.co/inf_est.htm.

41. DNP and UN Development Programme, Social Mission, *Informe de desarrollo humano para Colombia, versión preliminar,* mimeo, May 2002, 135.

42. In accordance with Constitutional Court Decision T-327/01 of March 26, 2001.

43. "It is the responsibility of the Colombian state to formulate policy and adopt measures for the prevention of forced displacement and for the providing of assistance, protection, and socioeconomic consolidation and stabilization to those internally displaced by force" (art. 3).

44. Constitutional Court Decision Su-1150/00, August 30, 2000.

45. *El Colombiano,* August 18, 2002, 16A.

46. "Gobierno de Álvaro Uribe inicia pruebas de fumigación con glifosato fortalecido," *El Tiempo,* August 26, 2000.

References

Colombian Commission of Jurists. 1996. *Colombia, derechos humanos y derecho humanitario: 1995.* Bogotá: CCJ.
———. 1997. *Colombia, derechos humanos y derecho humanitario: 1996.* Bogotá: CCJ.
———. 2000. *Panorama de derechos humanos y derecho humanitario en Colombia: Informe de avance sobre 2000.* Bogotá: CCJ.

———. 2001. *Panorama de derechos humanos y derecho humanitario en Colombia. Informe de avance: Abril a septiembre de 2000.* Bogotá: CCJ.

———. 2002. *Panorama de derechos humanos y derecho humanitario en Colombia. Informe de avance: Octubre de 2000 a marzo de 2001.* Bogotá: CCJ.

———. 2003. *A Growing Absence of Guarantees: Situation of Human Rights and Humanitarian Law in Colombia, 1997–2003.* Bogotá: CCJ.

———. 2004. *Colombia: Twenty Reasons for Stating That the Human Rights and Humanitarian Law Situation Is Critical and Tending to Worsen.* Bogotá: CCJ.

———. 2005. *Colombia, derechos humanos y derecho humanitario: 1997–2001.* Vol. 1. Bogotá: CCJ.

Colombian Commission of Jurists and Defensoría del Pueblo. 1997. *Contra viento y marea.* Bogotá: Tercer Mundo Editores.

Colombian Institute of Agrarian Reform (INCORA). 2002. "Dimensión de la problemática." Chap. 1 in *Plan cuatrienal.* Retrieved February 2, 2006, from www.incora.gov.co/plancuatrienal.htm.

Defensoría del Pueblo. 2000. *Bitácora informativa, 1999–2000.* (May).

Friedrich Ebert Stiftung for Colombia (FESCOL). 2002. "Sobre una estrategia de seguridad y defensa: La seguridad democrática y el estado social de derecho." Paper presented at the Taller sobre Seguridad Ciudadana, Bogotá. Mimeo.

Gallón, Gustavo. 2002. "Derechos humanos, la cuerda floja de la búsqueda de la paz en Colombia." In Colombian Commission of Jurists, *Panorama de derechos humanos y derecho humanitario en Colombia. Informe de avance: Octubre de 2000 a marzo de 2001,* 179–82. Bogotá: CCJ.

Manrique-Reyes, Alfredo. 1990. *El defensor del pueblo y de los derechos humanos (el personero municipal).* Bogotá: Consejería Presidencial para la Defensa, Protección y Promoción de los Derechos Humanos.

Office of the UN High Commissioner for Human Rights and Universidad Nacional. 2000. *Recomendaciones de órganos internacionales de derechos humanos al estado colombiano, 1980–2000.* Bogotá: UNHCHR and Universidad Nacional.

Contributors

Cynthia I. Arnson is deputy director of the Latin American Program of the Woodrow Wilson International Center for Scholars. As director of the Project on Comparative Peace Processes in Latin America, she has focused intensively over the last decade on Colombia, and has written and lectured frequently on issues related to the peace process and U.S. policy. She is editor of *Comparative Peace Processes in Latin America* (1999), co-editor (with I. William Zartman) of *The Economics of War: The Intersection of Need, Creed, and Greed* (2005), and author of *Crossroads: Congress, the President, and Central America, 1976–1993* (2d ed., 1993).

Arnson serves on the editorial advisory board of *Foreign Affairs en Español* and the advisory board of Human Rights Watch/Americas. Immediately prior to joining the Wilson Center, Arnson was associate director of Human Rights Watch/Americas. She holds an M.A. and Ph.D. from The Johns Hopkins University School of Advanced International Studies.

Ana María Bejarano is assistant professor of political science at the University of Toronto. She holds a Ph.D. in political science from Columbia University and was a Guest Scholar at the Kellogg Institute of International Affairs at the University of Notre Dame (2000–2001). She previously was professor of political science at the Universidad de Los Andes in Bogotá, where she also served as director of its Center for Social and Legal Research (CIJUS). She co-edited the book *Elecciones y Democracia en Colombia, 1997–1998* (1998) and co-authored a chapter on Colombia in *Advances and Setbacks in the Third Wave of Democratization in Latin America*, ed. Frances Hagopian and Scott Mainwaring (forthcoming). Recent publications include articles in *Constellations* and the *Canadian Journal of Latin American* *and Caribbean Studies.* She is finishing a book on the historical origins and divergent trajectories of democracy in Colombia and Venezuela. Her current research deals with regime change, institution building, and constitution-making in the Andes.

Herbert Tico Braun is a professor of history at the University of Virginia. He is the author of two books on twentieth-century Colombia: *The Assassination of Gaitán: Public Life and Urban Violence in Colombia,* and *Our Guerrillas, Our Sidewalks: A Journey into the Violence of Colombia,* a family memoir of a kidnapping. Both have been published in Spanish by Editorial Norma in Bogotá. The themes of peace and reconciliation in Colombia appear in "Honor, Amnesia, Maldad, y Reconciliación en Colombia" and in a paper presented to the XI Congreso Colombiano de Historia, in Bogotá, August 24, 2000, as "Una tradición inventada: La conversación política como medio de convivencia en el siglo veinte colombiano." Currently, he is working on a project on the history of Colombia between 1946 and 1964. Braun holds a Ph.D in history from the University of Wisconsin.

Álvaro Camacho Guizado is currently director of the Center for Social and International Studies (CESO) at the Universidad de los Andes in Bogotá. He was a Visiting Fellow at the Helen Kellogg Center for International Studies at the University of Notre Dame in 2000. Previously, he was director of the Institute for the Study of Politics and International Relations at the Universidad Nacional de Colombia. Camacho has written about war, violence, and survival. His most recent work, coauthored with Nora Segura, focuses on democracy and social exclusion in Colombia. He holds a Ph.D. in sociology from the University of Wisconsin.

Luis Eduardo Fajardo holds a B.A. from Princeton University, a master's degree in international relations from the University of California, San Diego, and an M.Sc. in economic history from the London School of Economics. He is currently a lecturer and researcher in the Department of Economics at the Universidad del Rosario, Bogotá. His research interests are in economic history, political economy, and New Institutional Economics.

Gustavo Gallón, a Visiting Fellow at the Kellogg Institute (1998–1999), has been director of the Colombian Commission of Jurists in Bogotá since its founding in 1988. A lawyer specializing in public law, he graduated from the

Universidad Externado de Colombia in Bogotá in 1974. In his distinguished career in law and government, he has been a representative of the UN Commission on Human Rights for Equatorial Guinea (1999–2002) and twice a member of Colombian governmental commissions, proposing recommendations for peace and a new military criminal code. He studied toward a doctorate in political sociology at the School of High Studies in Social Sciences of Paris and received his master's degree in political science from the University of Paris. Having published many works on human rights and democracy and received a number of awards, he has been a researcher, a professor, and the founder of the quarterly review *Cien Dias vistos por Cinep*. Since 2003 he has been a member of the Council of the National Program for Social and Human Sciences of the Colombian Institute for Science and Technology (COLCIENCIAS).

Daniel García-Peña Jaramillo is currently a professor of political science at the National University of Colombia in Bogotá and directs *Planeta Paz*, a national project dedicated to building effective grass-roots participation in the peace process. From August 1995 to August 1998 he served as Acting High Commissioner for Peace in Colombia. Since then, he has been a Public Policy Scholar at the Woodrow Wilson Center in Washington, DC, a consultant to the Inter-American Development Bank, and a Scholar in Residence at the School of International Service at American University. In 2002 he ran the presidential campaign of Lucho Garzón and, in 2003, Garzón's successful run for mayor of Bogotá and then his transition team. He writes frequently on the issues of war and peace in major newspapers and news magazines in Colombia.

Francisco Gutiérrez Sanín is an anthropologist with an M.A. and Ph.D. in political science. A researcher at the Instituto de Estudios Políticos of the Universidad Nacional de Colombia, Gutíerrez has studied political systems and political parties, democratic transitions in East and Central Europe, and in Latin America, war and organized crime. He coordinated the IEPRI project "War, Democracy and Globalization," sponsored by the Crisis States Programme (CSP) of the London School of Economics and COLCIENCIAS. Presently, he is finishing a CSP project on politics and criminality. His article "Criminal Rebels? A Discussion of Civil War and Criminality from the Colombian Experience" recently appeared in *Politics and Society* (2004).

Andrés López Restrepo is a professor in the Instituto de Estudios Políticos y Relaciones Internacionales (IEPRI), at the Universidad Nacional de Colombia, in Bogotá. He is interested in political theory, especially liberty and its limits, with an emphasis on prohibitions on drugs and the consequent effect on drug trafficking.

Erika Moreno is an assistant professor of political science at the University of Iowa. She conducts research on Latin American political institutions, with an emphasis on the effects of electoral rules on representation. Currently, her research and publications focus on small parties in Colombia and Venezuela. She holds a Ph.D. in political science from the University of Arizona.

Eduardo Pizarro Leongómez is a political sociologist who is an associate professor at the Institute of Political Studies and International Relations at the Universidad Nacional de Colombia. He is also a respected journalist and writes weekly for the Colombian newspaper *El Tiempo*. His area of specialization is political violence; his most recent publication is on the Colombian armed conflict and the prospects for a peaceful resolution. He has taught as a visiting professor at the University of Tübingen in Germany, the University of Paris, FLACSO Ecuador, and the Academia Diplomática de México. More recently, he has been the Edward Larocque Tinker Visiting Professor at Columbia University, a Visiting Fellow at the Kellogg Institute at the University of Notre Dame, and a Visiting Fellow in the Program in Latin American Studies (PLAS) at Princeton University.

Matthew Søberg Shugart is professor of political science at the Graduate School of International Relations and Pacific Studies, University of California, San Diego. He is a specialist on comparative electoral systems and constitutional design, including in Latin America. Since the early 1990s, he has worked on Colombian politics; he is the author of numerous publications, including four refereed journal articles and a book chapter on aspects of Colombian electoral politics. Shugart served as a member of a team of consultants to the Colombian Ministry of the Interior on electoral reform, and a portion of President Andrés Pastrana's referendum proposal justifying the electoral reform is drawn from Shugart's appendix to the consultancy report. He holds a Ph.D. in political science from University of California, Irvine.

Arlene B. Tickner obtained her M.A. in Latin American Studies at Georgetown University and her Ph.D. in international relations at the University of Miami. She is currently a full professor in the Political Science Department of the Universidad de los Andes, where she has worked since 1991, as well as an associate professor of the Universidad Nacional de Colombia, where she teaches courses on international relations.

Tickner has conducted research and written extensively on democracy in Latin America, U.S.-Colombian relations, Colombian foreign policy, security in the Andean region, and international relations theory. Recently, Tickner authored "Colombia: U.S. Subordinate, Autonomous Actor, or Something in-Between," in *Latin American and Caribbean Foreign Policy*, ed. Frank O. Mora and Jeanne A. K. Hey, and "Hearing Latin American Voices in International Relations Studies," in *International Studies Perspectives*.

Christopher Welna is excutive director of the Kellogg Institute for International Studies at the University of Notre Dame. He taught previously in the Sanford Institute for Public Policy at Duke University, and served as program officer with the Ford Foundation in the Mexico City and Rio de Janeiro offices. His volume co-edited with Scott Mainwaring, *Democratic Accountability in Latin America*, was published by Oxford University Press in 2003, and his article co-authored with George Lopez, "Breaking the Deadlock: European 'New Leadership' in a Colombian Peace Process," was published by the Centro de Investigación para la Paz (Madrid) in 2004. He holds an M.A. in Public and International Affairs, as well as in Urban and Regional Planning, from Princeton University, and earned his Ph.D. in political science at Duke University.

Index

439